Literary
Transvaluation

Literary Transvaluation

From Vergilian Epic to Shakespearean
Tragicomedy

Barbara J. Bono

UNIVERSITY OF CALIFORNIA PRESS

BERKELEY • LOS ANGELES • LONDON

University of California Press
Berkeley and Los Angeles, California

University of California Press, Ltd.
London, England

Library of Congress Cataloging in Publication Data

Bono, Barbara J.
    Literary transvaluation: from Vergilian epic to
Shakespearean tragicomedy.

    Bibliography: p.
    Includes index.
    1. Virgil—Influence. 2. Virgil—Influence—
Shakespeare. 3. Shakespeare, William, 1564–1616—Crit-
icism and interpretation. I. Title.
PA6825.B66   1984   873'.01   83–1069
ISBN 0-520-04743-5

Printed in the United States of America
1 2 3 4 5 6 7 8 9

To Jim

"Amore e 'l cor gentil sono una cosa."

(DANTE, *La vita nuova*)

Contents

Acknowledgments   ix

A Note on Sources   xi

Introduction   1

I. *Vergil's Dido and Aeneas: Tensions and Transformations*   7

Interpretative Problems   7
The Dido Episode   11
Interpretative Legacy   38

II. *From Vergilian Epic to Romantic Epic: Three Transvaluations*   41

Augustine   45
Dante   51
Spenser   61
From Renunciation to Accommodation   79

III. *Renaissance Dramatic Transvaluations*   83

Alessandro Pazzi de' Medici, Lodovico Dolce,
    Cesare de' Cesari, Celso Pistorelli   87
Giovambattista Giraldi Cinthio   90
Étienne Jodelle   103
Robert Garnier, Samuel Daniel   116
Christopher Marlowe   127
Epic into Tragedy, Romantic Epic into Tragicomedy   137

IV. *The Shakespearean Synthesis:* Antony and
     Cleopatra   140

     Prologue   140
     History: Tragedy and the Herculean Hero   151
     Philosophy: "What Venus did with Mars,"
        or the Debate of Love and Strife   167
     Fiction as Myth: Of Isis and Osiris, or the Myth of Egypt   191
     Summary: From Vergilian Epic
        to Shakespearean Tragicomedy   213
     Epilogue   220

Bibliography   225

Index   243

Acknowledgments

I cannot but be grateful to my masters and my authors. Many are cited in the course of my argument, but some of the most sweet are reserved for here. For several years now I have been sustained by the strong confluence of professional and personal lives. This study began at Brown University through the illumination of the late Rosalie Colie. It was first drafted and revised under the loyal and intelligent direction of Barbara Kiefer Lewalski. Its meaning for me grew and clarified in exchange with fine students at the University of Michigan, Ann Arbor; Theresa Krier and Janis Butler Holm stand for dozens of others. My colleagues there helped in many ways: I remember especially the practical aid of Ejner Jensen and Jay Robinson, and the detailed, long-standing intellectual support of C. A. Patrides and Ralph Williams. A fellowship grant from the Horace Rackham School of Graduate Studies of the University of Michigan allowed me to continue revisions rapidly. I completed editing and proofreading during the glorious *otium* of a year as junior fellow at the Cornell Society for the Humanities. Karen Reeds encouraged submission of the manuscript to the University of California Press, and Doris Kretschmer has ably directed its progress there. I am grateful to the careful readers for the Press; although I have not always been able to follow their recommendations completely, they have much improved this book. In particular, Amy Einsohn was a most attentive and intelligent editor of the whole. I owe a special debt of friendship to Steve Lavine and to Michael and Marie-Pierre Ellmann.

My husband's parents, Jean and the late Joseph Bono, and my own, Jane and John Nowik, were patient and understanding through many years of work that often kept us from them. I have, I hope, come to understand more closely the meaning of family, in both its genetic and extended senses, during the last several years, when I have so often had to trust my child to other true "care"-takers. My thanks to them all, especially to the Nobilette family. My husband, James Bono, is a talented historian who has helped me more than I can say, in every phase of this project, and yet never forgotten to warm the everyday. To Jim, then, and to our Joey, the most gentle thanks.

A Note on Sources

Unless otherwise noted, all editions cited are those listed alphabetically in the Bibliography under "Sources" or "Studies." In quotations I have retained old spelling and punctuation, but have expanded contractions. For ancient texts I have supplied quotations in the original language where relevant for close analysis, and either Renaissance or readily available modern English translations as seems most appropriate in context. For example, when analyzing Vergil, whom most Renaissance authors would have known well in the original Latin, I quote the Latin and English of the Loeb edition for the convenience of the modern reader; whereas in discussing Shakespeare I quote Plutarch and Apuleius in the form he would have known, the English translations of Sir Thomas North, Philemon Holland, and William Adlington. Quotations from Shakespeare's plays are from the new Arden editions, general editors Harold F. Brooks and Harold Jenkins.

Introduction

We need a more precise lexicon of literary imitation and influence, one that can mediate between narrowly defined source studies and sweeping claims about the patterns and directions of culture, one that can mediate between the conscious theoretical statements of a period and an actual literary practice that may respond to unrecognized forces.[1] This study hardly fills this need, although it does appropriate a term—*transvaluation*—to describe generally my observations of a single highly significant chain of influence from Vergil to Shakespeare.

What began long ago as an investigation of the sources of Shakespeare's *Antony and Cleopatra* soon broadened to include a recognition of that play's conscious reversal of the values of Vergil's *Aeneid* and an inquiry into the literary and cultural means of that inversion. Investigation of those means led me into that large creative middle ground where literary imitation is neither uncritical copying nor willful misprision, but rather what I call transvaluation, an artistic act of historical self-consciousness that at once acknowledges the perceived values of the antecedent text and transforms them to serve the uses of the present. Implicitly recognizing the complexities of the antecedent text and its destabilization through interpretation, the authors of such transvaluations seek to re-create it within history, sustaining a tradition through change. They supply the materials for a subtle literary history and, in the case of transvaluation of the *Aeneid*, for an important strand of cultural history as well, since especially in that text self-consciousness coincides with cultural consciousness.

---

[1] The most subtle general work I know on Renaissance literary imitation is Thomas Greene's *The Light in Troy*.

This book studies Vergil's *Aeneid* as itself the unstable source of a series of literary transvaluations within the western European narrative and dramatic tradition up to Shakespeare's *Antony and Cleopatra*. Throughout the Latin Middle Ages and the Renaissance Vergil's poem was our greatest literary classic, the subject of countless imitations. However, it is not this monumental heritage, but rather Vergil's own struggles with the problem of change, that make the *Aeneid* so fertile a ground for transvaluation. Vergil's artistic model is the Homeric epic, his cultural context the assimilation of the Hellenistic world into Roman rule. He contracts this model and this context into his poem's opening movement, the story of Aeneas and Dido. At Dido's banquet Aeneas narrates the fall of Troy, and with it the fall of the active Homeric hero. Modeled after Greek tragic heroines and Apollonius's Medea—regal, but also passionately violent and tinged with decadence—Dido sympathetically recapitulates Troy's catastrophe. Her tragedy, proleptically tied to the defeat of Cleopatra, defines Aeneas's epic mission and a more general myth of the Roman mind: in the face of rapid cultural change and the demands of world governance, individual will must be subordinated to the common good.

The care with which Vergil makes this argument—and the difficulty—is the matter of my first chapter, a detailed analysis of the story of Aeneas and Dido, set within the painful uncertainties of the poem as a whole. Later authors who are aware of Vergil's achievement and its cost unerringly focus on the story of Dido; as she was for Vergil the means of articulating his indebtedness to, yet distance from, Homeric epic, so she became for them the means of defining their poetic and historical identity. In the second chapter I focus on reminiscences of Dido in three major narrative transvaluations of Vergil's *Aeneid*: Augustine's *Confessions*, Dante's *Divine Comedy*, and Spenser's *The Faerie Queene*.

These are three texts—others might be argued—whose rich and precise transvaluations centrally illustrate a major movement from the cultural constraints experienced by Vergil to the expressive freedom of the Renaissance. Augustine, who later explicitly appropriates the language and values of the *Aeneid* to Christian eschatology in *The City of God*, unconsciously assimilates the thwarted love of Dido in the *Confessions* and uses it to fuel his intensely personal quest for a transcendent subject of desire. Dante in turn appropriates Augustine's Christian autobiography in *The Divine Comedy*.

Through the intimacy of his fictionalized relationship with Vergil, he specifies the difference between the Roman social hero and the Christian confessional hero. Using the language of Dido, he implies that Vergil's own resonant longing can take him and his poetic father to the very threshold of salvation:

> Adgnosco veteris vestigia flammae.
>
> (*Aen.* 4.23)
>
> Conosco i segni dell'antica fiamma.
>
> (*Purg.* 30.48)
>
> (I know the marks of the ancient flame).

Yet this longing must be radically redefined for Dante to cross that threshold. Spenser, writing within the context of Christian neo-Platonic syncretism in *The Faerie Queene*, tolerantly includes the *Aeneid* in his redefinition. The unresolved tensions in the *Aeneid* can be harmonized in the feminine epic quest of Britomart, who seeks to merge that poem's tragic incommensurability between eros and civilization in a reciprocal dynastic marriage. In her highest expressions she is a figure for the Renaissance ideal of the artist as co-creator with God, triumphantly assimilating classical epic in romance.

A comparable movement occurs in Renaissance classical drama that takes the *Aeneid* as its generic source—a heroic drama descended from epic—and its moral matrix. The third chapter surveys Renaissance vernacular dramas of the story of Aeneas and Dido and the typologically related history of Antony and Cleopatra. It does so to illuminate, from the perspective of drama, Shakespeare's long preoccupation with the poem, most thoroughly displayed in *Antony and Cleopatra*. Some of these plays, although they contain lengthy passages imitating Vergil's poem, do little to transvalue it, to re-create the poem within a contemporary context. However interesting they may be for other reasons, they are characterized only briefly here. Others, although in no way direct sources for Shakespeare's practice, illustrate a growing crisis in interpretation analogous to his own. Giovambattista Giraldi Cinthio uncomfortably imposes imperial and providential order on developing romantic expressiveness. Étienne Jodelle, writing within a context of an aspiring French Holy Roman Empire, develops a philosophical and religious defense of

Dido's love as an implied corrective to oppressive Roman tyranny. Yet other dramatic texts are arguably sources for Shakespeare, contributing widely varying specific features: Robert Garnier's development of Plutarch's Herculean Antony, Samuel Daniel's language of transcendent release, Christopher Marlowe's ironies toward his own hyperboles. Almost all these Renaissance plays interpret the *Aeneid*'s central tension as debate: individual versus community, love versus duty, will versus reason, eros versus civilization, nature versus power. In several instances the depth and intensity of the woman's appeal presses heroic tragedy toward a resolution romantic in theme, tragicomic in structure.

Shakespeare combines a Renaissance transvaluation of the interpretative crisis in the *Aeneid* with the limitations and potentials of dramatic form. In *Richard II*, examining his own country's history, he depicts a fall from a former heroic ideal, from traditional authority, and from Adamic meaning. However, his path back to that ideal is increasingly not through abnegation of the personal and passional, but through creative collaboration of both characters and audience. Imitating the *Aeneid*, in the second tetralogy he implies the strain, as well as the creative pleasure, of forging one's own myth of deity, of making theodicy. Transvaluing the *Aeneid*, he emphasizes the potential of the human creator. In the dramatic absence of an assured theological framework for his action, he encourages us, as audience, to collaborate in mortal attempts to "make defect perfection." Such immanence leads him to emphasize responsible emotional engagement and human sexuality, not only as social fact but also as metaphor for creative potential. From the appeal to skepticism of the great tragedies and the intricate marriage dance of the mature comedies comes the powerful *discordia concors* of *Antony and Cleopatra*. There the orthodox interpretation of the *Aeneid*, the powerful historical literalisms of the "common liar" at Rome, become the means of testing the romantic hyperbole of the lovers and elevating them, through our assent, above their tragic defeat. The play contextualizes the *Aeneid*, implying through its depiction of an Egyptian regeneration myth of transcendence achieved through immanence that its literal tragic action is a metaphor for tragicomic re-creation. In this way it prepares for Shakespeare's late tragicomic romances.

The detailed analysis of *Antony and Cleopatra* in the fourth chapter proceeds through a mythological and generic analysis of this *discordia concors*. The Roman tragedy of a Herculean Antony yields to the progressive reinterpretations of "What Venus did with Mars." The variety of Renaissance interpretations of Venereal energy here define the crisis of the *Aeneid* as a debate between love and strife. The pressure of Roman reality causes the lovers to understand their former romantic hyperbole as playful rehearsal for a serious transforming endeavor. At the *peripetia* of the play Shakespeare transvalues the *Aeneid* as Antony's motives for suicide change from Stoic resignation to transcendent erotic embrace, imagining the story of Aeneas and Dido as eternal romantic union, turning tragedy into tragicomedy. In its second climax, Cleopatra seeks to confirm this transvaluation as myth by evoking a neo-Platonic interpretation of the Egyptian regeneration myth of Isis and Osiris as the reunion of the Many of this world with the originative One. Through its constant emphasis on the humanity of the lovers and the staged literalism of their action, the play seeks to elicit our collaboration in the fulfillment of its skeptical late-Renaissance evocation of the powerful re-creative artist.

The impelling past here epitomized by the influence of the *Aeneid* was also a tremendous burden to sustain. *The Faerie Queene* and *Antony and Cleopatra* are among the great late-Renaissance recapitulations of culture. What in them is still a powerfully molded record of "fact" becomes for the next generations of artists a metaphor for the creative process, which they can appropriate with little or no reference to its historical details. This study closes with a brief analysis of Shakespeare's *The Tempest*, where ancient Carthage, modern Tunis, and Bermuda voyages are already rapidly conflated in a myth of creative power. The *Aeneid* is subtly remembered there, but the audience can understand the main outlines of the play's powerful psychological conflict without reference to its sources outside and within Shakespeare's art. Much of the depth and specificity of the *Aeneid*'s power as a re-creative source declines as universal Latin culture fades, and with it a particular ideal of the historically responsible artist. Milton summarizes history at the end of *Paradise Lost* precisely in order to illuminate the "paradise within"; Pope dismisses the fable from *The Essay on Man*; and Wordsworth assimilates culture to the self in *The Prelude*.

Today, in another age of rapid change, literary critics must constantly rethink the degree of historical responsibility they wish to exercise in deconstructing a text or a canon. This book in many ways remains a traditional influence study; nonetheless, it broaches questions of authorial intention, textual openness, and interpretative freedom at a historical distance from the workings of literary change that allows us a tentative description of what has occurred. It argues for that historical period a rich re-creative relationship with its past. If it does so with some sense of the intricacy, pluralism, and hope of that process, then it may in its own turn be useful for other studies.

I.

Vergil's Dido and Aeneas:

Tensions and Transformations

"Sunt lacrimae rerum et mentem mortalia tangunt."

(VERGIL, *Aeneid*)

Interpretative Problems

One's final judgment of Vergil's *Aeneid* is likely to depend on whether the unity in and among the various levels of the poem—moral, historical, metaphysical—seems achieved through a process of necessary sublimation or one of harsh repression. Does Vergil depict a problem difficult enough to warrant the extreme solutions the poem presents? And how adequate are these solutions? Historically, the chief interpretative focus of this discussion has been the first third of the poem, the story of Aeneas and Dido. Vergil's extraordinary negative capability in this section, his ability to characterize with utter precision and great resonance the course of Dido's passion and (what has been less frequently recognized) through it the sufferings of Aeneas and his culture, creates an irreducible tragic core in the work. What is sharply at debate is the nature and effect of that tragedy. For many readers it forever disrupts the epic purpose of the poem. The following analysis, in contrast, argues that the poem's tragedy is a strained and deliberately tentative and indirect means to defining its epic purpose, a shocked and pitying exploration of loss that paradoxically functions as an impetus to faith in what may yet be achieved. The analysis also provides the basis for my succeeding selective examination of how this episode was interpreted, imitated, and transvalued from its own

7

day through the Renaissance. The thwarted abilities of these characters instantiate Vergil's sharply bridled creative energies that
then make the *Aeneid* a fertile ground for reinterpretation. Vergil's
dialectical poem, often polemically simplified, fuels both sides of a
variously shaded debate between the virtues of immediacy and control, between emotion and rule, love and empire. Finally, for those
later authors who experience through the *Aeneid* Vergil's struggles
with change, the poem becomes an index to their own distance from
the past.

Modern studies of the *Aeneid* have emphasized imagery, both
verbal and situational; narrative techniques, studied within the
work and by comparison with its Homeric and Hellenistic models;
and the historical and philosophical significance and correlation of
the various levels of the poem. They have made us acutely aware
of the problem of gaining perspective *within* the work.[1] To this
end Brooks Otis carefully describes the coordination of extremes
of human intention and divine will in the poem.

> What is important for the understanding of Virgil is what
> he did with his subjective style. We can define this, in very
> general terms, as the erection of an inclusive frame of ref-
> erence that enabled him to correlate the principal elements of
> his epic material, as Homer and all objectively styled epic
> could not. Because he empathetically and sympathetically re-
> produces his divine and human characters' motives, they can
> be co-ordinated with one another.
> This principle holds for all levels of the plot. . . . Human
> and divine, natural and supernatural, physical and psychic

---

[1] On imagery, see especially the seminal work of Viktor Pöschl, *The Art
of Vergil: Image and Symbol in the "Aeneid,"* and Reuben Brower's illuminating study of influence, *Hero and Saint: Shakespeare and the Graeco-Roman
Heroic Tradition,* especially "Our Vergil," pp. 84–119. On narrative technique,
the pioneering work of such earlier scholars as Milman Parry, Albert Lord,
and C. M. Bowra informs the subtle distinctions by critics such as Thomas M.
Greene, *The Descent from Heaven: A Study in Epic Continuity;* W. R. Johnson,
Darkness Visible: A Study of Vergil's "Aeneid," especially Chapter 2, "Lessing,
Auerbach, Gombrich: The Norm of Reality and the Spectrum of Decorum," pp.
23–48; and Brooks Otis, *Virgil: A Study in Civilized Poetry,* and "The Originality of the *Aeneid.*" Regarding the correlation of the various levels of the
poem, Johnson, *Darkness Visible,* especially "The Worlds Vergil Lived In," pp.
135–154, provides a review.

are not arbitrarily mingled but logically connected so that a free human act, a plainly human motive or feeling, is at the same time an event on two or more divine levels and has also other repercussions.

("Originality," p. 49)

However, Otis does not stress the degree to which the coordination of the various levels of the poem is a retrospective or abstracting effort that is only hypothetically achieved. The characters in the *Aeneid* and the subjective narrator, in his wavering identification with them and his periodic immersion in the events he recounts, more often feel the poem's questioning movement as the fitful revelation of great distances, huge chambers in which the foreground action takes place and which only gradually take on a lambent clarity or an obscure, echoing claustrophobia. They are constantly amazed as the friezelike stability of their former mode of life dissolves, as they try to explore the psychological depths and philosophical extension opening within the old Homeric ethos, to comprehend their place in the ultimate cause and end of things.

What may finally become for the reader Otis's "fully contrived equilibrium" is at first experienced in the poem as a tremendous interpretative gap between feeling and form in which error and misapprehension abound and which we labor to fill, often in vain. W. R. Johnson declares:

> What Vergil has to imagine is, essentially, unknown and probably unknowable. This means that the Homeric norm and the forms it calls into being, though Vergil can and does make use of them frequently, must often be sacrificed in favor of both of the extreme modes that they mediate between: in favor of the exalted reifications of history and fate which Homer would not understand and which he would doubtless scorn if he could understand them; and in favor of a rich yet radically disordered complexity of impression, evocation, wild emotion, and incantation.
>
> (*Darkness Visible*, p. 47)

As Johnson and Otis both attest, on differing but complementary critical and historical grounds, the poem reflexively documents in its fiction and stylistic detail the shattering of the objective Homeric eternal present by the pressures of change.

The poem regains an intimation of that objectivity through what Otis describes as the furthest extension of its "subjective style," "the erection of an inclusive frame of reference"; in the poem's own language, "quietum . . . animum mentemque benignam" (1.303–4), the creation in its hero, its narrator, and its reader of a "gentle mind and gracious purpose" capable of organizing plastic, even cinematic, effects about a latent vanishing point and a postulated transcendent observer.[2] This process, scarcely serene, springs from the full experience of the tragic inadequacy of a loved past, and is rooted in a longing to re-create that past on a deeper and more secure plane. It is tentative, forwarded by the subordination—often seemingly suppression—of more partial points of view, points of view we are still aware of as the depths and shadowings of the picture. It remains finally subjective, a construct, because although Vergil at last coordinates his fiction—his gods confirm Aeneas's hard-won destiny—it is itself presented as a fiction, a mythic displacement of recent tragic Roman history that will possibly, but not necessarily, suggest the positive shape of the Roman future.

Thus the poem remains, as Johnson, following Erich Auerbach, suggests, profoundly questioning, incomplete,

> where mimesis does not illumine for us what we ourselves see in our daily lives, or shape or sharpen the focus of our vision or "bewitch us" or "make us forget our own reality for a few hours," but rather forces us to reexamine, indeed to criticize, "our own reality" which "it seeks to overcome."
>
> (*Darkness Visible*, p. 31)

At its heart Anchises' prophetic vision dissolves into mourning for the premature death of Augustus's successor Marcellus; the meaning of the entire *nekuia*, the descent to Hades, is cast into doubt by the ambiguous leave-taking through the ivory gate of "falsa . . . insomnia" ("false dreams" 6.896).[3] Even the next book, the long-

---

[2] All citations from the *Aeneid*, and their translations, are from *Virgil in Two Volumes*, trans. H. Rushton Fairclough, Loeb Classical Library, rev. ed., 2 vols.

[3] Michael Murrin, *The Allegorical Epic*, pp. 34–42, roots Vergil's persistent ambiguity in the epistemological skepticism of the New Academy, and suggests that the descent to the realm of the dead is actually an instance of sciomancy (a mystery-ritual summoning of the shades of the dead), which may be skeptically reduced to illusion.

awaited Hesperian landing, opens with this weary, skeptical aside
on the value of self-sacrifice:

> Tu quoque litoribus nostris, Aeneia nutrix,
> aeternam moriens famam, Caieta, dedisti;
> et nunc servat honos sedem tuus, ossaque nomen
> Hesperia in magna, *si qua est ea gloria,* signat.
>
> (7.1–4, emphasis mine)

> (Thou, too, Caieta, nurse of Aeneas, hast by thy death given
> deathless fame to our shores; and still thine honour guards
> thy resting-place, and in great Hesperia, *if such glory be aught,*
> thy name marks thy dust.)

Clearly the narrator, too, strains to build a work unflinching and
yet compassionate enough to support the continued quest for
theodicy, to still his own melancholy fears that in art he, like his
hero, feeds on an insubstantial picture, a false dream of suffering
pityingly righted as fame.

The Dido Episode

The following analysis of the Aeneas-Dido episode charts the
subtle dialectical process through which the narrator struggles to
gain for us that perspective, to create that equilibrium. After we are
given some broad indication of the tensions that inform the *Aeneid,*
the meeting of Aeneas and Dido at first seems to offer a resolution.
However, it is shadowed by a shared tragic past and the complex
responses that past elicits. Aeneas's groping account of the unspeak-
able horror of the fall of Troy conveys the dimensions of historical
change, of divine and human upheaval, that he must try to contain.
At the moment he can do so only through retrospective narrative;
enacting a solution must be deferred, in large part beyond his life-
time. His tale conveys both his sensitivity and his necessary detachment. Tragically, Dido responds only to the former, ignoring the
latter. The indirection of the sequence, its imagery and divine
machinery, depicts both the confluence and divergence of their
minds, their individual ways of responding to change and history.
The lovers are, to a point, complementary images, and it is only the
harsh extremism of the world Vergil envisions that tears them apart.
Later commentators and imitators who polarize them—sentimen-

talizing her, chilling and flattening him—distort the poet's truth. A complete resolution to the poem requires imagining another world.

The opening lines of the *Aeneid* hint at the great temporal, spatial, and spiritual distances to be explored and the form that may comprehend them. From Troy to Italy, over sea and land, from the first man through his dynasty, at the mercy of a high, mysterious wrath that is named but not fully explained as mythic Juno, both driven and drawn on by fate,[4] a man is racked until he becomes a symbolic architecture, a culture as well as a place, "altae moenia Romae," ("the walls of lofty Rome" 1.7). The questioning of that wrath and the description of its lashing storm map in swift, broad, largely discontinuous strokes the many layers of the poem the narrator must labor to unite. Juno's fury flashes forward and backward in time, ahead to the rivalry of Carthage and Rome, back to the sources of the Trojan War. Yet even these sweeping historical explanations are made to seem, in their primitive anthropomorphism, inadequate to the narrator's metaphysical probing, "tantaene animis caelestibus irae?" ("Can resentment so fierce dwell in heavenly breasts?" 1.11). Vergil exposes from the first the strain between his inherited Homeric-Olympian form and his sophisticated philosophical sensibility. The characterization of Juno here juxtaposes abruptly the petty and the monumental, her envy of Pallas with the evocative, portentous "Talia flammato secum dea corde volutans" ("Thus inwardly brooding with heart inflamed" 1.50), in a way that foreshadows the poem's later psychological synthesis of the detailed and the significant. The maneuverings of the gods are elaborated with a strangely literalizing human political language— the indication that Aeolus is a corrupt constitutional monarch (1.50–64), the interplay between the serene description of Neptune and the constricting simile of the noble orator (1.148–56)[5]—that at once reminds us of the contemporary, practical application of this

---

[4] Mario A. Di Cesare, *The Altar and the City*, p. 1, emphasizes the ambiguity.

[5] Di Cesare, *Altar and the City*, substantiates this first simile as a description of the type of hero capable of comprehending Vergil's "world"; see especially pp. 9 and 238. While I agree with much of Di Cesare's analysis, I view Aeneas's relationship with his past as more impacted than he does, as an aesthetic displacement rather than a radical break. Aeneas has, to the end, both more tentativeness and emotional power than Di Cesare's "high priest carrying out the ordained rite, sacrificing one man for the good of all" (p. 236).

work and forces that relationship. In short, the scope of the poem is arbitrarily, authoritatively laid down, outlined discursively, not yet created, not yet explained.

We then move to the human center on whom these events converge, and to his attempts to interpret them. At once we feel how crushingly this burden descends on him and the overwhelming nostalgia it evokes. In an instant the Trojans' clear purpose is disrupted; darkness and death rule; the ships are swept and battered from every direction. The line of resistance to these forces is the weakest anywhere in the poem, a supplicating figure whose words imply almost complete surrender. Aeneas's only detachment here is the knowledge that he did not die at Troy, which at this moment seems to have "saved" him for a meaningless death, alienated from native land, kin, and his own creative power. His first speech offers us immediate insight into his fragility. The events that follow and his second speech demonstrate how that weakness can be turned gradually into a source of strength.

Aeneas is upheld by a sense of responsibility to his past and the remnant of it he carries with him. As an individual he wishes he could die; as a leader he endures. As soon as the Trojan remnant lands communal activity starts: the men are "Aeneadae" ("sons of Aeneas" 1.157); his faithful friend Achates begins the rituals of civilization, and then accompanies his leader on a search for food and their lost comrades.[6] Aeneas's deeply moving address—"O socii" ("O comrades" 1.198–207)—is his first attempt to shape the past through memory in order to sustain the future. Alluding here briefly to the tragic history he will later "feast" on ("pascit" 1.464) at the Carthaginian temple wall and then "revive" ("renovare" 2.3) at Dido's banquet, he urges his men to try to sublimate these sufferings to re-creation:

> "revocate animos maestumque timorem
> mittite; forsan et haec olim meminisse iuvabit.
> per varios casus, per tot discrimina rerum
> tendimus in Latium, sedes ubi fata quietas
> ostendunt; illic fas regna resurgere Troiae.
> durate, et vosmet rebus servate secundis."
>
> (1.202–7)

---

[6] Johnson, *Darkness Visible*, pp. 32–36, provides an analysis of the symbolic aspects of this search.

("Recall your courage and put away sad fear. Perchance even this distress it will some day be a joy to recall. Through divers mishaps, through so many perilous chances, we fare towards Latium, where the fates point out a home of rest. There 'tis granted to Troy's realm to rise again; endure, and keep yourselves for days of happiness.")

His speech builds through the warm, mounting internal pressure of the murmuring and sibilant alliteration, the careful architecture of the building phrases and sustaining imperatives. However, the re-creation is not yet convincing to Aeneas; he feigns ("simulat" 1.209) hope. The narrative leaves the human plane with the Trojan remnant "spemque metumque inter *dubii*" ("between hope and fear *uncertain*" 1.218), with *uncertainty* obscuring both the preceding clause and the entire episode.

The poem then moves to Jupiter's great proleptic speech, which theoretically resolves the entire action ("iam finis erat"; "now all was ended" 1.223), as Jupiter looks forth from the most inclusive perspective ("aethere summo"; "from the sky's summit" 1.223). It is authoritative, but also premature and unconvincing. The central significance of the succeeding encounter with Dido is to show Aeneas's difficult attainment of an approximation of this Jovial perspective from within the experience of rending change, the human forging of that consciousness, as faith rather than certainty, and as need rather than divine dictate. Vergil does so by detailing the historical and psychological depth of the tragic past and Aeneas's aesthetic removal from it, set against a sympathetic portrait of Dido's loss of such critical distance. Books 1 through 4 prove Aeneas a man of feeling even while the narrative of Dido's fall elaborates why his is a sensitivity necessarily deferred. The episode implies, through the hero, and for the narrator and the prospective audience, a humane sensibility that attempts to compassionate the frequently grim work of history.

The remainder of Book 1 is couched as a gradual descent from Jove's perspective to an anatomy of human need. It opens the way for Aeneas's account of all he has lost. The apparent balance between Aeneas and Dido at their first meeting is subtly undermined by the strength of feeling they arouse in each other, a tension mounting throughout this book, climaxing in the wonderfully atmospheric hunt scene of Book 4. These early passages also offer a few hints of the momentous differences between Aeneas's and Dido's responses to that release of feeling, differences that lead to those stark misunderstandings in Books 4 and 6, to their divergent destinies: he will undergo catharsis as he gives way ("cessi" 2.804) and is stilled ("quievit" 3.718), while she will be wasted ("carpitur" 4.2), consumed.

The emotional undercurrent swells as Vergil moves us, first descriptively, then dramatically, first to Dido, then to Aeneas, toward the epiphanic encounter of the lovers. We start with the assurance that Dido, although "ignorant of fate" ("ne fati nescia" 1.299), has been favorably disposed toward the Trojans by Jove. But our first evidence of that gracious purpose, the commemorative temple frieze, is highly colored by emotion. We see the frieze through the eyes of Aeneas, who has not only experienced the horrors the panels depict but also has been slyly conditioned by his mother to see those panels as an expression of Dido's intimate sympathy. " 'O sola infandos Troiae miserata labores' " (" 'O thou that alone hast pitied Troy's unutterable woes' " 1.597), he exclaims.[7]

Nor does it seem that his interpretation is exaggerated, for Dido's first speech to him stresses their community in suffering and desire:

> "me quoque per multos similis fortuna labores
> iactatam hac demum voluit consistere terra.
> non ignara mali miseris succerrere disco."
>
> (1.628–30)

("Me, too, has a like fortune driven through many toils, and willed that at last I should find rest in this land. Not ignorant of ill do I learn to befriend the unhappy.")

Although Dido here maintains the Jovial balance, we sense within her a vulnerability on which Venus will play. In these first scenes longing continually threatens to burst through propriety. When Dido hears Ilioneus, she is "voltum demissa" ("with downcast face" 1.561)—is it because of royal shame at his accusation of barbarism, or because of an unexpected yearning toward the heroic Aeneas he describes? When Aeneas's heart "rises"—"surgit" 1.582, the verb that also describes rising city walls—is it with vague hope, or a more definite ambition toward this queen, this city?

---

[7] Otis, "Originality," p. 35, reminds us that "the *lacrimae rerum* are really Dido's tears; the temple and frieze were obviously her own doing."

Indeed, these unsuspected springs of feeling, human in expression yet cosmic in origin and scope, that well up under the surface of this regal encounter are complemented by the prominence of Venus, working in Book 1 independently of Jove. At the same time the differences between Aeneas's and Dido's experience of and reaction to Venus's intervention foreshadow the divergent action to come.

Despite Jove's firm assurance that " 'manent immota tuorum / fata tibi' " (" 'thy children's fates abide unmoved' " 1.257–58), Venus cannot resist covertly tightening the ties that bind Aeneas and Dido, adding to social bonds emotional and physical ones. As Aeneas approaches Carthage, Venus abruptly appears to him, disguised as a maiden huntress, seemingly chaste, but in fact an agent of desire.[8] She asks him if he has seen one of her sisters, a question designed to make him look for another like her; and so Dido will first appear, Diana-like, at the temple:

> qualis in Eurotae ripis aut per iuga Cynthi
> exercet Diana choros, quam mille secutae
> hinc atque hinc glomerantur Oreades; illa pharetram
> fert umero gradiensque deas supereminet omnis;
> Latonae tacitum pertemptant gaudia pectus:
> talis erat Dido, talem se laeta ferebat
> per medios, instans operi regnisque futuris.
>
> (1.498–504)

(Even as on Eurotas' banks or along the heights of Cynthus Diana guides her dancing bands, in whose train a thousand Oreads troop to right and left; she bears a quiver on her shoulder, and as she treads overtops all the goddesses; joys thrill Latona's silent breast—such was Dido, so moved she joyously through their midst, pressing on the work of her rising kingdom.)

Venus seems to prepare Aeneas to enter a realm of self-contained Amazonian women, but she also insinuates a more complex and

---

[8] Renaissance writers correctly fasten on this episode as a masterpiece of ambivalence, and employ it centrally in their reevaluations of desire. See, for example, Edmund Spenser's "Aprill" eclogue in *The Shepheardes Calender* and his introduction of Belphoebe, *Faerie Queene* 2.3, which I discuss in chapter 2. See also Edgar Wind, *Pagan Mysteries in the Renaissance*, pp. 74–78, and his comments on Venus, passim.

sympathetic portrait of Dido as a woman of tragic experience, like his own, now turned to triumphant achievement.[9] In Book 1 Venus's affecting description of Dido's trials is a cue sufficient to elicit from Aeneas a complaining summary of his troubles; later, at Dido's urgings, he will give a full account that involves her totally in his pain. Venus has modulated Aeneas's nascent feelings for Dido from respect toward desire.

Here Aeneas is moved, unbalanced, but not completely deceived. Although Venus appears to him in human guise, he is her son ("Veneris" 1.325), attentive to the depths of feeling she sets in motion, wary, in short, of the numinous. He senses she is a goddess, although he does not know which one until, as she leaves him, she glancingly reveals herself. Immediately, the effect of their meeting is to heighten for Aeneas the attractiveness of Dido's present achievement in comparison with the elusiveness of his own desire. " 'O fortunati, quorum iam moenia surgunt!' " (" 'Happy they whose walls already rise!' " 1.437), he exclaims as he looks over Carthage. The intensity of his desire is revealed by his lament:

> ille ubi matrem
> adgnovit, tali fugientem est voce secutus:
> "quid natum totiens, crudelis tu quoque, falsis
> ludis imaginibus? cur dextrae iungere dextram
> non datur ac veras audire et reddere voces?"
> talibus incusat gressumque ad moenia tendit.
>
> (1.405–10)

(He knew her as his mother, and as she fled pursued her with these words: "Thou also cruel! Why mockest thou thy son so often with vain phantoms? Why am I not allowed to clasp hand in hand and hear and utter words unfeigned?" Thus he reproaches her and bends his steps towards the city.)

---

[9] Besides the broad similarities of sacrilegious betrayal and enforced exile, Venus's account of Dido's trials contains many precise parallels of incident and language with Aeneas's later account of the sack of Troy. For example, compare the description of Pygmalion's murder of Sychaeus (1.346–50) with Aeneas's description of the degenerate Neoptolemus slaying Priam on the sacred altar in the deepest recesses of the Trojan palace (see especially 2.499–505, 547–53), and the ghost of Sychaeus (1.353–55) with the ghost of Hector (1.274–75). Dido explicitly acknowledges this similarity of experience (1.628–29).

The full significance of the imagery of this lament becomes clearer as the poem unfolds and we see Aeneas's vain attempts to grasp two other phantoms, Creusa and Anchises.[10] Aeneas yearns for his mother, his father, and his Trojan past more than for Dido. Once he recognizes them through tragic memory as irrevocably lost he will derive from that knowledge the desperate strength to revive them in appropriate forms; " 'hoc opus, hic labor est' " (" 'This is the task, this the toil!' " 6.129), cries the Sibyl of this strenuous resurrection, this ascent from the dead. The sympathetic respite offered by Dido allows him to move toward this recognition, as he gratefully acknowledges to the end (4.331–36). But insofar as she identifies with his past, he must finally leave her behind as well, just as he has left Troy; nostalgia, will, and pleasure must yield to his responsibility to re-create his people (4.340–61). Adam Parry has remarked in another context on the "sense of pregnant greatness in every detail of experience . . . impressed on us by the rhetorical exaggeration which pervades the *Aeneid*. . . . The potentialities of ages and empires . . . alive in the smallest details."[11] So it is with the great longing revealed in Aeneas at this moment.

Ominously, Dido has no comparable recognition of how she is being affected by Venus. At the end of Book 1 the goddess again works through a disguise, this time substituting her son Cupid for Aeneas's son, Ascanius. The picture of Dido unknowingly fondling the great god on her lap and bosom fuses the intimate sexual and maternal longings the handsome, heroic, and pious Aeneas has aroused in her. Ascanius is not only a surrogate son, but the image of his father.

> aut gremio Ascanium, genitoris imagine capta,
> detinet, infandum si fallere possit amorem.
>
> (4.84–85)

10

> "ter conatus ibi collo dare bracchia circum;
> ter frustra comprensa manus effugit imago."
>
> (2.792–93)

("Thrice there I strove to throw my arms about her neck; thrice the form, vainly clasped, fled from my hands.")

Here the formula is used for Creusa; at 6.700–2 it is repeated for the shade of Anchises.

[11] Parry, "The Two Voices of Virgil's *Aeneid*," p. 74.

(Captivated by his father's look, she holds Ascanius on her
lap, if so she may beguile a passion beyond all utterance.)

Dido's tragedy in large part results from the surprising strength
of these two strains of feeling curtailing the continued growth of a
comparable piety in her; she falls from the initial "gentle mind and
gracious purpose" ("animum mentemque benignam" 1.304) implanted in her by Jove to be victimized by the erotic and dynastic
maneuverings of Venus and Juno. She indicates a limited human
consciousness of this surrender in Book 4 in her persistent qualms
about unfaithfulness to Sychaeus and her disastrous clouding of
the precise status of her relationship to Aeneas. However, the language in which this access of love for Aeneas is described in Book
1 indicates that it comes upon her as a surprise, deceitfully, from
an act of friendship which she suddenly cannot dissociate from her
very identity.[12] Dido's own description of this development, at the
beginning of Book 4, relates her fall to the just-recounted fall of
Troy.

Dido's tragedy forms the generic link between Homeric epic
and the world Vergil depicts. She thinks she can welcome Aeneas
according to the archaic code of guest-friendship, remaining faithful to Sychaeus while forwarding her own masculine heroic endeavor. Yet Venus harbors a great disingenuousness in her admiring
exclamation, " 'dux femina facti' " (" 'the leader of the work a woman' " 1.364), for Dido is not only female but the embodiment of
an archetypal "femaleness" (in which Aeneas also participates)
that in its emotional capacity and vulnerability indicates the need
for something other than the Homeric active *virtú*. Dido is not another Odysseus, single-handedly capable of restoring the past, although she has struggled "manfully" to fill the part. Venus exposes

---

[12] For Dido's relationship to Sychaeus, see 4.15–30, 54–59, 321–23, 460–61,
550–52. For her relationship to Aeneas, see 4.160–72, 316–24, 337–39, 431–34.
Venus schemes (1.657, 658) to outwit Dido with guile (1.673–75). Particularly
menacing and distasteful is Venus's method, using Dido's joyful love of a seemingly innocent boy; see 1.685–88, 717–22.

In these passages both imagery and insinuating sound patterns anticipate
the master images of serpent and flame in Book 2, linking this seduction with
the archetypal fall depicted there. See Di Cesare, *Altar and the City*, p.
17, and Bernard Knox, "The Serpent and the Flame: The Imagery of the Second
Book of the *Aeneid*."

her need, which Dido mistakenly looks to a heroic Aeneas to fulfill. We see the seeds of her misapprehension perhaps as early as the description of the temple frieze, which, although it portrays the sufferings of all the Trojans, depicts Aeneas in vigorous battle, "se quoque principibus permixtum adgnovit Achivis" ("Himself too, in close combat with the Achaean chiefs, he recognized" 1.488). Certainly Venus's miraculous introduction of the hero, not a bedraggled shipwreck, but "claraque in luce refulsit, / os umerosque deo similis" ("gleaming in the clear light, godlike in face and shoulders" 1.588–89), fuels Dido's need, which then ignites at the banquet. Aeneas's account of the fall of Troy should reveal clearly that he too is a tragic victim whose heroism must consist in suffering as well as action. However, the distance between his weary detachment and Dido's passionate engagement with the past implicitly widens throughout his narration, until in Book 4 she is as a figure from Euripidean tragedy, overthrown by irrational forces surging beneath the fragile forms of civilization.

Dido is "fired" by Aeneas's account into a precipitate action that entails the destruction of herself and, eventually, her city. (See 1.659–60, 688, 713; 4.1–2, 23, 54, 65–69, 300, 360, 364, 669–71, and 697 for the metaphor of passion as flame, a metaphor whose climax appears in the comparison of her suicide and the conflagration of the city.) Believing she can reinstate the Homeric world of active heroism, she actually recapitulates its demise. She does not perceive the distance between the rending force of the events Aeneas has endured—events that have deprived him of the powers of action—and the tentative meaning he gives them in his narration. She is alive to his tale of tragic horror as if it were epic deed. Blind desire causes her to idealize his former heroism even while absorbing his shattered emotional condition. Taking on his fears, she now becomes fearful, transformed from the assured lawgiver to the doubt-torn listener of these lines, feasting her soul uncritically on another's "unsubstantial picture" that evokes their common memory of loss and travail:

> incipit effari, mediaque in voce resistit;
> nunc eadem labente die convivia quaerit,
> Iliacosque iterum demens audire labores
> exposcit pendetque iterum narrantis ab ore.
>
> (4.76–79)

(She essays to speak and stops with the word half-spoken. Now, as day wanes, she seeks that same banquet, again madly craves to hear the sorrows of Ilium and again hangs on the speaker's lips.)

Dido's revelations to Anna at the beginning of Book 4 offer the first direct testimony to her inner state; her words shock us in their similarity to Aeneas's account of the fall of Troy.

> "Anna soror, *quae me suspensam insomnia terrent!*
> *quis novus hic nostris successit sedibus hospes,*
> quem sese ore ferens, quam forti pectore et armis!
> credo equidem, nec vana fides, genus esse deorum.
> degeneres animos timor arguit. heu! quibus ille
> iactatus fatis! quae bella exhausta canebat!
> si mihi non animo fixum immotumque sederet,
> ne cui me vinclo vellem sociare iugali,
> postquam primus amor deceptam morte fefellit:
> si non pertaesum thalami taedaeque fuisset,
> huic uni forsan potui succumbere culpae.
> Anna, fatebor enim, miseri post fata Sychaei
> coniugis et sparsos fraterna caede Penatis
> *solus hic inflexit sensus animumque labantem*
> *impulit. adgnosco veteris vestigia flammae."*
>
> (4.9–23, emphasis mine)

("Anna, my sister, *what dreams thrill me with fears? Who is this stranger guest that hath entered our home?* How noble his mien! how brave in heart and feats of arms! I believe it well—nor is assurance vain—that he is sprung from gods. 'Tis fear that proves souls base-born. Alas! by what fates is he vexed! What wars, long endured, did he recount! Were the purpose not planted in my mind, fixed and immovable, to ally myself with none in bond of wedlock, since my first love, turning traitor, cheated me by death; were I not utterly weary of the bridal bed and torch, to this one weakness, perchance, I might have yielded! Anna—for I will own it—since the death of my hapless lord Sychaeus, and the shattering of our home by a brother's murder, *he alone has swayed my will and overthrown my tottering soul. I recognize the traces of the olden flame.*")

The dreams that thrill her with fears recall Aeneas's alarm at the dream vision of Hector; her language echoes Aeneas's uncertainty at the moment of exile, " 'nunc omnes terrent aurae, sonus excitat omnis / suspensum et pariter comitique onerique timentem' " (" 'I now am affrighted by every breeze and startled by every sound, tremulous as I am and fearing alike for my companion and my burden' " 2.728–29). The "stranger guest" who has entered her home ominously suggests the treachery of Sinon, the encroaching wooden horse, and Pyrrhus threatening at the palace gates. Dido's reluctance to violate the cherished image of her first husband, Sychaeus, recalls the total devastation Pyrrhus wreaks. Her picture of her will swayed, her tottering soul overthrown, is like the Trojans' desperate toppling of the citadel, " 'adgressi ferro circum, qua summa labantis / iuncturas tabulata dabant, convellimus altis / sedibus impulimusque' " (" 'Assailing this with iron round about, where the topmost stories offered weak joints, we wrenched it from its lofty place and thrust it forth' " 2.463–65). She becomes the last in a line of tragic figures whose self-sufficiency is shattered by the great fall into time and experience the Trojan War represents. In a heart-rending irony, "pius" Aeneas, its latest victim, becomes her unwitting Pyrrhus.

Most sadly, her fall is finally depicted as something she could not resist, as an imprisonment in a more primitive cast of mind.[13] She loses the aesthetic detachment represented by the temple frieze and celebrated by Aeneas there, to enter that tragic picture,

> Penthesilea furens mediisque in milibus ardet,
> aurea subnectens exsertae cingula mammae,
> bellatrix, audetque viris concurrere virgo.
>
> (1.491–93)

(Penthesilea in fury leads the crescent-shielded ranks of the Amazons and rages amid her thousands; a golden belt binds her naked breast, while she, a warrior queen, dares battle, a maid clashing with men.)

To Dido's unconscious overthrow by Venus is added her uncritical allegiance to Juno, which creates a level of tragic self-deceit in her

---

[13] Di Cesare's comments on the primitive, chthonic nature of Dido's passion, *Altar and the City*, especially pp. 19–30, enable us to evolve precise generic categories for what Otis succinctly describes as "the tremendous innovation of introducing a Euripidean *amoureuse* into an Homeric epic" ("Originality," p. 34).

liaison with Aeneas and turns it from friendship to bitter enmity. Driven by passion, but genuinely concerned lest she do something shameful and covert, she tries to legitimate the transfer of her affections from the dead Sychaeus to Aeneas by appealing to the gods, and particularly to Juno, "vincla iugalia curae" ("guardian of wedlock bonds" 4.59). Yet the "answer" she receives is not a prompting to confront him openly and resolve the ambiguities of the situation. Instead, she loses the rational powers of speech—"nunc media Aenean secum per moenia ducit / Sidoniasque ostentat opes urbemque paratam; / incipit effari, mediaque in voce resistit" ("Now through the city's midst she leads with her Aeneas, and displays her Sidonian wealth and the city built; she essays to speak and stops with the word half-spoken" 4.74–76, emphasis mine). The action then moves to the plane of the deities, where we witness the colloquy of Venus and Juno.

For her part, Juno promises to confirm a valid marriage for the pair with Jupiter, but then does not, because she knows he would forbid it. Still trying to circumvent the decrees of Fate, she presides at a charged, intimate, "inevitable" meeting that Dido can, although not without misgivings, interpret as a marriage (4.166–72), or at least as one begun (4.316, 431), while Aeneas remains innocent of these meanings (4.337–39).[14] Juno's willfulness ensures that of

---

[14] Dido did indeed begin the marriage when she offered sacrifice (4.56–59). Too, Juno pursued the woman's initiative in the ceremony by serving as "pronuba" at the cave (4.166), in accordance with Roman tradition:

> In the house of the bride, which was decked with garlands . . . were assembled the relations, friends, and clients as an *officium*. . . . Then the omens were taken and announced by the *auspices* . . . with the sacrifice of a sheep. . . . After these preliminaries, the omens being favourable, the marriage ceremonies began . . . a married woman, who must have been married only once, acting as *pronuba*, led the bride up to the bridegroom and joined their right hands . . . a prayer was recited by the Flamen to Iuno as the goddess of marriage, and the deities of the country and its fruits —Tellus, Picumnus, and Pilumnus.
>
> (*Harper's Dictionary of Classical Literature and Antiquities*, s.v. "matrimonium")

However, there is no mention of Aeneas or Jupiter having been consulted, and Aeneas later denies having fulfilled the marriage contract: " 'nec coniugis umquam / praetendi taedas aut haec in foedera veni' " (" 'I never held out the

Dido, who allows herself to be swept along by events rather than choosing them, shaping them. She shows a pathetic, partial awareness that she is losing self-control, but that lack of control results from the crude maneuverings of the powerful primitive gods she worships. She is stage-managed by them, until she is like a Bacchante (4.68–69, 300–3), or a tragic figure hounded by the chthonic gods:

> Eumenidum veluti demens videt agmina Pentheus
> et solem geminum et duplices se ostendere Thebas,
> aut Agamemnonius scaenis agitatus Orestes
> armatam facibus matrem et serpentibus atris
> cum fugit, ultricesque sedent in limine Dirae.
>
> (4.469–73)

> (Even as raving Pentheus sees the Furies' band, a double sun and two-fold Thebes rise to view; or as when Agamemnon's son, Orestes, driven over the stage, flees from his mother, who is armed with brands and black serpents, while at the doorway crouch the avenging Fiends.)

These two similes, by referring to classical Greek tragedy, specify exactly Dido's situation. They place her in that tragic moment of history and consciousness that succeeded the era of the Homeric epics, and that it is the task of Vergilian epic to overcome. Her bitter confrontation with the departing Aeneas reveals stark differences between their individual conceptions of the gods. She taunts him for his providential beliefs while appealing more and more ominously to the chthonic aspect of the gods who have betrayed her, to "Erebumque Chaosque / tergeminamque Hecaten, tria virginis ora Dianae" ("Erebus and Chaos, and threefold Hecate, triple-faced maiden Diana" 4.510–11); to " 'Sol, qui terrarum flammis opera omnia lustras, / tuque harum interpres curarum et conscia Iuno, / nocturnisque Hecate triviis ululata per urbes / et Dirae ultrices et di morientis Elissae' " (" 'O Sun, who with thy beams surveyest

---

bridegroom's torch nor entered such a compact' " 4.338–39), a reference to the conclusion of the marriage ceremony:

> At the entrance [to the bridegroom's house] the wife repeated the formula *ubi tu Gaius, ego Gaia;* and the husband met her bearing fire and water, to signify that he admitted her to a share in the family hearth and the family lustral rites.
>
> (Ibid.)

all the works of earth, and thou, Juno, mediatress and witness of these my sorrows, and Hecate, whose name is shrieked by night at the cross-roads of cities, ye avenging Furies, and ye gods of dying Elissa' " 4.607–10); and even to " 'sacra Iove *Stygio*' " ("the rites of *Stygian* Jove' " 4.638, emphasis mine). Finally, she immerses herself in a form of sympathetic black magic that draws her to suicide.[15] It is Juno who has become "omnipotens" (4.693) in her life and who at last offers her a pitying release from it.

Dido may imagine that she could have remained faithful to the values of her old world; her final speech celebrates her heroic identity before Aeneas's advent:

> "vixi et, quem dederat cursum Fortuna, peregi,
> et nunc magna mei sub terras ibit imago.
> urbem praeclaram statui, mea moenia vidi,
> ulta virum poenas inimico a fratre recepi,
> felix, heu! nimium felix, si litora tantum
> numquam Dardaniae tetigissent nostra carinae!"
>
> (4.653–58)

> ("I have lived, I have finished the course that Fortune gave; and now in majesty my shade shall pass beneath the earth. A noble city I have built; my own walls I have seen; avenging my husband, I have exacted punishment from my brother and foe—happy, ah! too happy, had but the Dardan keels never touched our shores!")

In the underworld, where " 'quisque suos patimur Manis' " (" 'Each of us suffers his own spirit' " 6.743), she is allowed to revert to this former shadowy ideal, denying Aeneas's vision. But in fact he did touch her shores, bringing with him a wider historical perspective on human action. Unable to distance her sympathy from immediate gratification, she is swept away with Aeneas's old world, " 'non ignara mali' " (" 'not ignorant of ill' " 1.630), yet "ne fati nescia" ("ignorant of fate" 1.299). In the values of her own archaic heroic

---

[15] See the notes of R. G. Austin, *P. Vergili Maronis Aeneidos: Liber Qvartvs*, pp. 140–57 on the persistent ambiguity of the sacrifice described in 4.474–521: is it meant to exorcise Aeneas's influence or to immolate Dido? Or does it begin as the former and end as the latter, as she becomes trapped in a primitive world from which he escapes?

code she is blameworthy, but he is "perfide" ("false" 4.305, 366), "improbe" ("shameless" 4.386), "hostem" ("foe" 4.424). Yet in the code of values developed in the *Aeneid* he would be blameworthy if he stayed, and is "pius" (4.393) in going, while she is "infelix" ("unhappy" 1.712, 749; 4.68, 450), "inscia" ("unknowing" 1.718), "misera ante diem subitoque accensa furore" ("hapless before her day, and fired by sudden madness" 4.697), the victim of "casu . . . iniquo" ("unjust doom" 6.475).[16]

Thus the meeting of Dido and Aeneas illustrates Vergil's vision of a former heroic ideal set against a tragic world of experience, and the resulting gulf of mutual misinterpretation. In Book 1, at the temple, Aeneas and Dido seem to meet as the lucid, assured controllers of destiny, two demigods; covertly they are drawn together in the shadowy, nervous dependence of fate's victims. Each will clutch at a premature, false security in the other, to awake with shock to the elemental feelings they expose. In Book 4 we are moved by the immense creative potential of their union. In a setting aglow with morning light, replete with the bursting yet purposive energy of the hunt, the Queen comes forth.

---

[16] Otis, "Originality," pp. 40–41, 57–58 notes how much Dido suggests the Homeric past, stressing in particular the parallelism between Odysseus's encounter with Ajax, himself the representative of an older heroic code, and Aeneas's with Dido in the underworld.

> Unlike Apollonius [Vergil] "reproduced" Homer. Dido could not therefore be a Medea—that is, a woman whose eroticism would detract from or cancel the dignity of his hero or his epic. So we have also Dido the queen. But the important thing, of course, is not her rank but her heroic and thus tragic quality. Her tragedy is that of shamed *arete*: in this sense her suicide is Sophoclean; she is, from this point of view, an Ajax. . . . she violates her self-respect, her heroic identity. That, therefore, she becomes the counterpart of the Homeric Ajax, when Aeneas sees her in the underworld, is marvelously apposite. And we can . . . see in the Dido-Ajax "transference" a tragic as well as an Homeric reminiscence. Ajax's pride insists on its tragic validation and cannot endure the pity or explanation that would quickly dissipate this: neither can Dido's.
>
> (pp. 57–58)

Unlike Otis, I argue that Vergil means to complicate the heroic with the erotic. However, his principal point stands: Dido belongs to an archaic world, one which Vergil's poetry respects.

tandem progreditur magna stipante caterva,
Sidoniam picto chlamydem circumdata limbo.
cui pharetra ex auro, crines nodantur in aurum,
aurea purpuream subnectit fibula vestem.
nec non et Phyrgii comites et laetus Iulus
incedunt; ipse ante alios pulcherrimus omnis
infert se socium Aeneas atque agmina iungit.
qualis ubi hibernam Lyciam Xanthique fluenta
deserit ac Delum maternam invisit Apollo
instauratque choros, mixtique altaria circum
Cretesque Dryopesque fremunt pictique Agathyrsi;
ipse iugis Cynthi graditur mollique fluentem
fronde premit crinem fingens atque implicat auro
tela sonant umeris: haud illo segnior ibat
Aeneas, tantum egregio decus enitet ore.

(4.136–50)

(At last she comes forth, attended by a mighty throng, and
clad in a Sidonian robe with embroidered border. Her quiver
is of gold, her tresses are knotted into gold, golden is the
buckle to clasp her purple cloak. With her pace a Phrygian
train and joyous Iülus. Aeneas himself, goodly beyond all
others, advances to join her and unites his band with hers.
As when Apollo quits Lycia, his winter home, and the streams
of Xanthus, to visit his mother's Delos, and renews the dance,
while mingling about his altars Cretans and Dryopes and
painted Agathyrsians raise their voices—he himself treads
the Cynthian ridges, and with soft leafage shapes and binds
his flowing locks, braiding it with golden diadem; the shafts
rattle on his shoulders: so no less lightly than he went Aeneas,
such beauty shines forth from his noble face!)

The chief impression conveyed by this emphatically celebratory,
luminous description is masterful control of tremendous energy.
The swelling simile comparing Aeneas to Apollo arches back to
draw in the earlier magnificent comparison of Dido to Diana (1.498–
506). And again, the sheer vividness and amplitude of the picture
presses the simile temporarily into a statement of fact; for a moment we actually believe we are in the presence of the twin deities.[17]

---

[17] Austin, *Liber Qvartvs*, pp. 60–67, especially the comment about 4.147.
For a moment this description does indeed "bewitch us"; its dissolution is
another sign of the problematic, "fallen" Vergilian world.

Besides glorifying the radiant appearance of the lovers, this image of Aeneas and Dido suggests they are like brother and sister, the sun-god and the virginal huntress, and thus seems to deny the sexual nature of their attraction.

But ominous foreshadowings hint that this appearance of sexual aloofness masks volatile sexual longing. Dido first lingers in her bedroom ("thalamo" 4.133), and Venus earlier appeared to Aeneas in Diana-like disguise to plant surreptitiously the seeds of love. Earlier images of hunting have modulated toward sympathy for the victim. In Book 1 Aeneas the leader felled a troop of deer (1.184–93), and Dido is like a maiden huntress (1.314–417 and 498–506). Now Dido in love has become an unwary hind wounded by an unknowing shepherd (4.68–73).[18] The vaunting lovers who commence this hunt will soon, like animals, be driven to ground in the "nuptial" cave (4.160–72). Similarly ambiguous are the rich gold and purple accoutrements that adorn the tresses of Dido and of Aeneas-as-Apollo. At first these diadems seem images of control, but in the larger symbolism of the poem, the Asiatic richness of Dido's kingdom is portrayed as a temptation to lawless indulgence.[19]

On the surface, then, this passage intensifies and joins the two previous ideal images that the lovers had of each other, and allows us to see the possibilities of their union as triumphant spectacle: the energies and accomplishments of the two peoples flow together,

---

[18] Di Cesare, *Altar and the City*, pp. 14–15 analyzes this transformation, including the foreshadowing of Diana in her chthonic aspect as Hecate, and remarks on its ominous echo of Euripides' *Hippolytus*. See also Johnson, *Darkness Visible*, pp. 78–82.

[19] Carthage revels in a gorgeous, potentially decadent and effeminating luxury that the duty-pressed Trojans must repudiate: see the description of the banquet (1.631–34), Mercury's jibe at Aeneas's embellished dress (4.259–67), and Iülus's sensitivity to Numanus's taunt (9.614–16). Vergil represents the Trojans as having to graft the remnants of their high culture onto a more vigorous primitive stock; hence Aeneas's welcome into the healthy rusticity of Evander's simple hut (8.362–65). The opposition between eastern skill in the arts and the uniquely Roman virtues of peace, law, and justice, which are the products of hardship, suffering, and conquest in war (6. 847–53) reflects the nascent Roman Empire's relationship to the Hellenistic Empire, and Vergil's aesthetic relationship to the highly sophisticated, precious, Hellenistic literature that he grafts onto the indigenous tradition of comparatively crude Latin historical and martial poetry. See Otis, *Virgil*, and *Ovid as an Epic Poet*, chap. 1.

civilization crowns striving, and the succession from the united races seems favorably determined by Dido's loving acceptance of the Trojan heir, Iülus-Ascanius. But the crosscurrents are stronger, pointing to Vergil's fears of the causes that act in history. Juno's storm breaks, scattering the company and plunging the lovers into an obscure union from which Dido never emerges, from which Aeneas must absolve himself. To Vergil's tragic sense of history, providential shaping powers are not accessible to individuals. They are only available indirectly through them to communities and institutions. Unlike the neo-Platonic Egyptian triumphal union envisioned by the lovers in Shakespeare's *Antony and Cleopatra*, in the *Aeneid* the differences between the reasons and powers of the gods and those of men are too marked to be bridged by a ladder of gradual ascent in understanding. Any imaginative ideal is severely tested by the material conditions that encourage or inhibit its possible fulfillment. In Shakespeare's Egypt these conditions—geography, flora and fauna, and human culture—support Antony and Cleopatra's imaginative ideal of eternal erotic union. Conversely, Aeneas's providential mission subordinates the material reality of Dido and Carthage to the projected reality of Rome; indeed, Aeneas experiences this material reality as a powerful drag on his ideal. Thus material conditions, which in Shakespeare's play can serve as metaphors for the divine, immanent signs of transcendence, are in Vergil's world temptations to be refined through renunciation into more extensive ideals.

Book 2 is the crucible of the *Aeneid*, the great trial from which the painful solutions of the poem are forged.[20] In it Aeneas, speaking "ab alto" (2.2) "revives" the fall of Troy, articulating fully the experience of loss already epitomized at 1.92–101 and

---

[20] See Knox, "The Serpent and the Flame." Otis remarks that "the function of the 'Fall of Troy' (*Aeneid* II) has often been missed or curiously underestimated. . . . Without it the *Aeneid* simply could not stand. We have to comprehend what Aeneas originally was if his subsequent story is to make any sense at all" ("Originality," pp. 35–36). "The problem was thus to retain the evocative or poetical power of the Homeric motifs while wholly changing their literal meaning or application. [Vergil] made it into the story of an Homeric hero's abandonment of his Homeric milieu and acceptance of a Roman milieu, and more specifically . . . into a motivational story—the story of the conversion of an Homeric into a Roman psyche" (pp. 59–60).

1.446–93. We witness his descent into a realm of shifting experience, of history, and its meaning for him. As a hallowed old world dies and a new world struggles to be born, events and language used to describe them darken from realistic to symbolic, from formulaic architecture to Vergilian mannerism.[21] Aeneas becomes a new kind of hero, or even an antihero, deprived of the ability to impose his own ordering on the world through the exercise of *arête*. He is now enduring Aeneas, the patient *sufferer*, the *medium* of Roman destiny. Vergil explicitly shows, through the change wrought in Aeneas on the night of Troy's fall, the transition from Homeric to Vergilian hero.

Aeneas remembers Troy on the night of its fall as a shadowy labyrinth of terrifying apparitions and irreversible events that constrained action and heightened emotion. He feels himself pressed inward both physically and psychologically as first he realizes that the walls of the city have been breached by deceit, then that the palace is under attack, then that even this last stronghold is pierced to its very heart. Early in the horrible night Aeneas leaps to battle like a Homeric hero, " 'furor iraque mentem / praecipitant, pulchrumque mori succurrit in armis' " (" 'Rage and wrath drive my soul headlong and I think how glorious it is to die in arms' " 2.316–17). Soon he is deprived of such certainties, as he first follows the counsel of Coroebus by adopting Greek deceit, wearing their arms (2.370–401), only to have the ruse turn on his company when they are counterattacked by the Trojans. The inevitability of Troy's fall is focused in the picture of the frantic defenders themselves tearing down their city,

> "Dardanidae contra turris ac tecta domorum
> culmina convellunt; his se, quando ultima cernunt,
> extrema iam in morte parant defendere telis;
> auratasque trabes, veterum decora illa parentum,
> devolvunt."
>
> (2.445–49)

("The Trojans in turn tear down the towers and roof-covering of the palace; with these as missiles—for they see the end near—even at the point of death they prepare to defend them-

---

[21] See Johnson, *Darkness Visible*, pp. 23–48, for an excellent theoretical formulation of the shift.

selves; and roll down gilded rafters, the splendours of their
fathers of old.")

The destruction is complete when, from the roof of the palace,
Aeneas must helplessly watch the sacrilegious murder of Priam by
Achilles' son Pyrrhus. Pyrrhus has reached the source of the city,
the shrine of the gods, fountain of vitality for old Priam and his
many children who, in the " 'famous fifty chambers,' " had formerly fulfilled the " 'rich promise of offspring' " (" 'quinquaginta illi
thalami, spes tanta nepotum' " 2.503). The seeds of Troy, instead
of being honored in the city's deep recesses as fire on the altars
of the gods and as the spark of generating life in the bodies of Troy's
people, are now released and scattered by Pyrrhus's desecrating act.

   This intensely personal and yet symbolic account concludes
with a shocking monumental image: Priam " 'once lord of so many
tribes and lands, the monarch of Asia,' " now " 'lies a huge trunk
upon the shore, a head severed from the shoulders, a nameless
corpse!' " (" 'tot quondam populis terrisque superbum / regnato-
rem Asiae. iacet ingens litore truncus, / avolsumque umeris caput
et sine nomine corpus' " 2.556–58). The death of the carefully characterized king, frail yet also kindly, paternal, noble, and sacral, symbolizes the fall of his city and his civilization. The narrative dis-
continuity—a moment earlier he was described as thrust through
the side, not decapitated—only serves to heighten the significance
of the final image of an edifice demolished, a huge tree cut down.
The image of the fallen tree is fully expanded in the apocalyptic
vision of 2.626–31, only to be reversed at the climactic moment of
Book 4.

   Although Aeneas is made to suffer with his city, he survives
its destruction. While moving inward, he also moves upward, gaining perspective and a shocked, raw understanding in proportion
to his helplessness to act. His experience of the death throes of
Troy gives an immediate, human meaning to Hector's original
warning to flee; the spectacle of Priam dead prompts memory of
his father, wife, and child:

> "At me tum primum saevus circumstetit horror.
> obstipui; subiit cari genitoris imago,
> ut regem aequaevum crudeli volnere vidi
> vitam exhalantem; subiit deserta Creusa
> et direpta domus et parvi casus Iuli."
>
> (2.559–63)

("Then first an awful horror encompassed me. I stood aghast, and there rose before me the form of my dear father, as I looked upon the king, of like age, gasping away his life under a cruel wound. There rose forlorn Creüsa, the pillaged house, and the fate of little Iülus.")

He recalls them tenderly: his father "cari," his wife "deserta," his son "parvi." For Aeneas his love of a particular place, of particular people, must animate those prophecies that he receives, but whose precise shape he only dimly understands. At the same time, the awesome events of that night make familiar things mysteriously significant, a part of a much larger action. Venus appears, appealing to this intimate love and yet making clear the apocalyptic upheaval it must bridge: it is the gods themselves—only they are powerful enough—who bring down Troy (2.588–633). The counteraction, the founding of an adequate "new Troy," must be similarly portentous, similarly numinous, as the events at Anchises's house illustrate.

From that moment Aeneas begins to live for tomorrow and to rely on his family as a chain linking the sanctity of the past and the promise of the future. He feels himself fallen: as he flees he bears the descending symbolic structure of three earlier ages: the golden-age images of the gods themselves; his father, silver-age lover of Venus, representative of that blissful time when men spoke with gods as "friend with friend"; and his own bronze-age heroic image, tarnished, turned to iron, by the events of the night. Gradually, over the course of the entire poem, he will acquire hope in the mysteriously illuminated son he leads, and in the vague prophecies of another city that sharpen, even as they expand in significance to include both Greek and Trojan worlds, both Europe and Asia, both mythic past and glorious future.[22] Now he is only at the beginning

---

[22] The poem seeks to describe a greater circle of permanence than its Odyssean model. Odysseus contains the disruption of the Trojan War by return to his homeland, where he barely restores an old order on the verge of dissolution. But his is a single man's heroic effort to save a primitive insular society. Vergil, capable of writing from "the point of view of the defeated," aware of much greater historical and geographical distances, circumscribes the mythic fall of Troy by having Aeneas subdue Italy only through the aid of a Greek, Arcadian Evander, and by suggesting that the glorious Trojan civilization was itself but a phase in a self-conscious, sophisticated return to the primitive, golden-age origins of the Dardanians in Italy. For Vergil the future of Rome was to be a glorious re-creation of its past, a paradox especially prominent in Book 8.

of that new phase of historical consciousness, " 'suspensum et pariter comitique onerique timentem' " (" 'tremulous . . . and fearing alike for my companion and burden' " 2.729).

The extent of what Aeneas has lost and the intensity of his feelings of loss reveal, then, not only the nature of his attraction to Dido but also the deeper impulses that prompt him to leave her. Deprived of the advice of his father, welcomed to Dido's realm— an event not mentioned in any of the prophecies[23]—which combines veneration for the past with vigorous new energy, it is no wonder he lapses into quiescence at the end of his narration. Yet through recounting the fall of Troy he has obtained an initial perspective ("ab alto") on it, and from now on he is never as engaged with Dido as she is with him. He does not initiate action; while he shares in the fault of cohabiting with her, he does not deceive himself and others by terming it a marriage.[24] He has portrayed his deepest love for the fallen Troy, and the remembered image reverberates, its pressure mounting subliminally, even as he thinks himself happy in Carthage. It surfaces in Book 4, in both divine and human form, as the peremptory commands of Mercury, the hauntings by his father's ghost, his guilt toward Ascanius, and the imperative to create a new Troy (4.351–61). The movement of his reply to Dido reveals how the sympathy she offered, the elegiac images she conjured in the temple frieze and the repeatedly evoked narration of the fall of Troy function to define his mission of self-sacrifice.

> "me si fata meis paterentur ducere vitam
> auspiciis et sponte mea componere curas,
> urbem Troianam primum dulcisque meorum
> reliquias colerem, Priami tecta alta manerent,
> et recidiva manu posuissem Pergama victis.

---

[23] Aeneas receives six prophecies, none of which mentions Carthage. These prophecies are delivered by Hector's ghost (2.268–97), Creüsa (2.771–89), the Apollonian oracle (3.94–98), the Penates (3.154–71), Celano (3.247–57), and Helenus (3.374–462).

[24] See n. 14 above for the legalistic line Aeneas draws. The narrator's reticence about Aeneas's feelings, compared with his exposure of Dido's, captures the hero's characteristic reserve. Aeneas has sincere recourse to the legalism; he has never allowed his incipient love full expression, even to himself.

sed nunc Italiam magnam Gryneus Apollo,
Italiam Lyciae iussere capessere sortes;
hic amor, haec patria est. si te Karthaginis arces
Phoenissam Libycaeque aspectus detinet urbis,
quae tandem Ausonia Teucros considere terra
invidia est? et nos fas extera quaerere regna."

(4.340–50)

("Did the Fates suffer me to shape my life after my own
pleasure and order my sorrows at my own will, my first care
should be the city of Troy and the sweet relics of my kin.
Priam's high house would still abide and my own hand should
have set up a revived Pergamus for the vanquished. But now
of great Italy has Grynean Apollo bidden me lay hold, of
Italy the Lycian oracles. There is my love, there my country!
If the towers of Carthage and the sight of the Libyan city charm
thee, a Phoenician, why, pray, grudge the Trojans their settling
on Ausonian land? We, too, may well seek a foreign realm.")

Even now he lingers over the sweet memory of Troy before assuming the disciplined lockstep, " 'nunc Italiam . . . Italiam . . . hic . . .
haec . . . est.' "

What seems insensitivity on his part is, on more careful examination, not the absence of feeling, but a suppression that obliquely shows us how much Dido's tragedy is rooted in his, even
as her tragedy propels him beyond tragedy. The catastrophe he has
experienced has forced him to enlarge indefinitely the distance
between emotion and action, between what he can acknowledge in
his words and in his deeds:

Tandem pauca refert: "ego te, *quae plurima fando
enumerare vales,* numquam, regina, negabo
promeritam, *nec me meminisse pigebit Elissae,*
dum memor ipse mei, dum spiritus hos regit artus.
pro re pauca loquar.

(4.333–37, emphasis mine)

(At last he briefly replies: "I will never deny, O Queen, that
thou hast deserved of me *the utmost thou canst set forth in
speech, nor shall my memory of Elissa be bitter,* while I have
memory of myself, and while breath still sways these limbs.
For *my course* few words will I say.")

It is their *mutual* tragedy that he cannot cherish, except in memory, what Dido so touchingly describes as what they had begun (4.314–19) and what might have been (4.327–29). His words here are a bleak attempt to reinstate the warmly sympathetic yet decorous initial relationship he earlier celebrated (1.595–610), before passion tipped that delicate balance toward impulsive action.

His sense of the sorrow of this leave-taking is actually *more* acute than hers, for his departure echoes the violence done him at the destruction of Troy. Now he must constrain her heroic identity to an object of memory, as he has already done with his own: " 'nor shall my memory of Elissa be bitter, while I have memory of myself.' " Her sympathy for the suffering at Troy, " 'sunt lacrimae rerum et mentem mortalia tangunt' " (" 'here, too, there are tears for misfortune and mortal sorrows touch the heart' " 1.462), has become participation, and he mourns the compound tragedy even as he struggles to see these fated events as Jove does.

> Talibus orabat, talisque miserrima fletus
> fertque refertque soror. sed nullis ille movetur
> fletibus, aut voces ullas tractabilis audit;
> fata obstant, placidasque viri deus obstruit auris.
> ac velut annoso validam cum robore quercum
> Alpini Boreae nunc hinc nunc flatibus illinc
> eruere inter se certant; it stridor, et altae
> consternunt terram concusso stipite frondes;
> ipsa haeret scopulis et, quantum vertice ad auras
> aetherias, tantum radice in Tartara tendit:
> haud secus adsiduis hinc atque hinc vocibus heros
> tunditur, et magno persentit pectore curas;
> mens immota manet, lacrimae volvuntur inanes.
>
> (4.437–49)

(Such was her prayer and such the tearful pleas the unhappy sister bears again and again. But by no tearful pleas is he moved, nor in yielding mood pays he heed to any words. Fate withstands and heaven seals his kindly, mortal ears. Even as when northern Alpine winds, blowing now hence, now thence, emulously strive to uproot an oak strong with the strength of years, there comes a roar, the stem quivers and the high leafage thickly strews the ground, but the oak clings to the crag, and as far as it lifts its top to the airs of heaven, so far it strikes its roots down towards hell—even so

with ceaseless appeals, from this side and from that, the hero
is buffeted, and in his mighty heart feels the thrill of grief:
steadfast stands his will; the tears fall in vain.)

Although Dido and Aeneas are apart, her tears and his tears flow
together in a powerful strain of pity for mortal things that gives an
elegiac cast to the entire poem, in which no single human life is
large enough to encompass the upheavals depicted.[25] At the same
time, the simile of the oak tree—which is deliberately "rather too
large for its setting"[26] recalls the horrible visions of Priam fallen
(1.512–14, 558–59) and Troy overthrown by the gods (1.626–29),
and anticipates the *nekuia* and the introduction to Latium (7.59–67).
The simile describes Aeneas as the organic medium through which
the past will finally be resurrected in a more universal form. He is a
life tree, uniting an archetypal primitive past with a more sophisticated, comprehensive culture.[27] At this terrible moment the man
and his mission are presented serially (his kindly mortal ears are
made deaf by Fate, tears cannot conquer his will), but the simile
of the great tree reminds us that his is a sacrifice made for human
community. Aeneas has not destroyed his humanity, although he
has had to drive it deeply underground, whence it emerges only

---

[25] Austin, *Liber Qvartvs*, calling 4.449 another of Vergil's universals, asks:
"Whose are the tears? Virgil is purposely ambiguous, and why may he not
remain so? . . . Formally it must be argued that *mens* and *lacrimae* are not
likely to refer to different persons. . . . These tears could not be denied to
Aeneas: but in the changing moods that repeated reading of Virgil always
brings, few could withhold them forever from Dido" (p. 135). Nor are they
withheld from the narrator, who thus directs our attention to the absolute
pathos of the episode.

[26] Robert A. Brooks, "Discolor Aura: Reflections on the Golden Bough,"
p. 277. Brooks uses the monumental image of the oak tree and the ambiguous
"golden bough" to discuss the impossible demands placed on Aeneas: "Aeneas
is continually arriving at a kind of order, a limited state of grace, and . . .
continually finding that this is not the whole condition of his destiny. Always
he must go on to more knowledge and suffering. The actual excludes consummation" (pp. 278–79).

[27] Homer concludes his epic with a sacred hearth tree, the great olive
around which Odysseus built his bed, and with which Penelope tests her re-
turning husband (*Odyssey* 23). However, whereas this concrete, particular
tree firmly concludes the *nostoi*, the metaphoric suggestiveness of the simili-
tude in the *Aeneid* medially adumbrates the superhuman scope of the work—
another example of Homeric "realism" and Vergilian "symbolism."

fitfully in the troubled remaining course of the poem. Its proper expression remains his ideal, and the first third of the *Aeneid*, while illustrating the lovers' tragic disjunction, implies a future when leadership and fellow-feeling will not exert opposing claims, when historical responsibility will not require emotional sacrifice:

> "Romane, memento
> (hae tibi erunt artes) pacique imponere morem,
> parcere subiectis et debellare superbos."
>
> (6.851–53)

("Remember thou, O Roman, to rule the nations with thy sway—these shall be thine arts—to crown Peace with Law, to spare the humbled, and to tame in war the proud!")

In short, the opening third of the poem attempts to effect a catharsis, to create a state of mind that can transcend tragedy instead of being condemned to reenact it, that can transmute the primitive and chthonic into the cultured and philosophic. The tragedy is conceived as the failure of the Homeric world of self-contained, active heroism in the face of overwhelming historical and emotional change. Dido's fall is the psychological correlative of the fall of Troy, indeed of ancient civilization in general. At the moment of Dido's suicide it was "quam si immissis ruat hostibus omnis / Karthago aut *antiqua Tyros*, flammaeque furentes / culmina perque hominum volvantur perque deorum" ("even as though all Carthage or *ancient Tyre* were falling before the inrushing foe, and fierce flames were rolling on over the roofs of men, over the roofs of gods" 4.669–71, emphasis mine).[28] Adopting much of the symbolic language of Euripidean tragedy, Vergil shows Dido as a conduit for irrational forces that swelled up outside and within the norms of Greek culture. For Vergil this tragic experience is inevitable, and those caught in it must attempt to constructively channel it through consciousness and over time. This is Aeneas's mission; his seeming detachment does not so much deny his feelings for Dido and his lost past as contain them, in his memory, in his retrospective art, until they can find positive expression in a more ample and secure future. He knowingly sacrifices his self, which otherwise would be destroyed by passion and time, to an as yet indefinite col-

---

[28] See Di Cesare, *Altar and the City*, chap. 1, especially pp. 29–30.

lective destiny, and thus he turns personal tragedy into an act of faith in his race. The poem as a whole attempts to prompt this complex (many readers have said impossible) response in its audience; we are to simultaneously acknowledge the pity and terror of these ancient events and their effect as a means to a greater good.

Interpretative Legacy

The oppositions in the *Aeneid*, then, are not essentially posed as alternatives, but rather as stages in a process whose evolution may surpass the suggested solutions of the poem. The basic problem Vergil confronts is that of historical change, of conflict in and enlargement of one's world beyond expectations, and seemingly beyond the capacity of traditional forms to contain or explain it. Vergil's Rome was undergoing just such a change, and Vergil himself was involved in it—Actium was still a recent event to counterweight centuries of the traumas of expansionism and decades of civil war, and there was the persistent worry that the Augustan peace might not outlast Octavius himself. Thus Vergil is as much concerned to present a method or attitude for encountering traumatic change as a definitive statement of its end. The latter must and does remain hypothetical or remote in the poem, a fact ignored by centuries of readers anxious to harden its fiction into orthodox meaning. Instead, Vergil proceeds dialectically: clear, painful, experiential knowledge of the inadequacies of the past is used to generate patient expectation; to deepen, strengthen, and expand the original ground of one's being, to enable it to support growth. Exile will be but the mode of a more triumphant return.

However, once this process is understood—in this poem there is no *direct* return to Troy, no possible unshadowed embrace with Dido—one must still confront squarely the immense cost for individual human beings. Dido, Turnus, and the other "primitive" figures in the poem simply cannot see their historical situation clearly enough to modify their desires accordingly. They live with a somewhat less than full consciousness of moral responsibility for their dilemmas; they feel this, and find themselves in a nightmare world of unspecified connections. They are offered a pale underworld consonant with this sense of constraint; can it compensate for their thwarted potential? As for Aeneas, whose way is only relatively more clear, can the glorious future prophesied for his descendents compensate for his self-sacrifice? One might respond that he will be rewarded with the bliss of the joyous fields or the gradual purifications of the cycle of reincarnation, but Aeneas's own question, " 'quae lucis miseris tam dira cupido?' " (" 'What means, alas! this their mad longing for the light?' " 6.721), resounds much more powerfully in the poem than Anchises' detached philosophical sermon.

In one sense, such objections are anachronistic and even sentimental. The type of individual freedom, the expressive will, we might want to champion for these characters is, for the most part, dispraised in the poem as the outmoded, destructive Homeric *arête*. The major argument of the *Aeneid* is the necessary subordination of that individuality to the community, the state. The great images of the work—the tree, the hearth, the terrifying labyrinth domesticated as the productive beehive—figure it forth. Although these values may seem to us impersonal, monolithic, totalitarian, or fascistic, Vergil so roots them in familiar Roman life as to lend warmth to every detail of the *Aeneid*. Ancient man was not man without place and society.[29] A deep reverence for traditional Roman landscape, ways, and values—the materials of the *Georgics* and Book 8 of the *Aeneid*—suffuses the entire epic and provides the positive complement to the more dramatic, sweeping, historical and generic tragedy that impels the poem. Indeed, one major strain of the interpretative tradition reduces the *Aeneid* to a glorification of things Roman.

As many of the best recent critics argue, Vergil consciously, painstakingly writes his poem in opposition to the world of Homeric heroism. For our purposes, however, we must also point to the world he intimates but cannot yet bespeak. If the poem looks backward to the ancient world, it also looks forward to Christian eschatology.

---

[29] Parry, "Two Voices," pp. 66–69. Aristotle begins the *Politics* by declaring:

> In the order of time, the state is later than the family or the individual, but in the order of nature, prior to them; for the whole is prior to the part. . . . when separated from his fellows, man is no longer man; he is either a god or a beast.
>
> (Jowett translation)

Peter Brown, *The Making of Late Antiquity*, stresses this point by contrast with the rise of the individual, which he argues is the most revolutionary feature of late antiquity.

The *Aeneid* exposes an intensity of longing more dynamic and creative than nostalgia, one in which Troy, Carthage, and even Rome itself function less as places, as a set of material conditions, and more as metaphors for the ideal. And here we find ourselves, following Johnson and Auerbach, in an area of perpetually re-creative fictions, not unlike those of the Bible, where the repeated displacements, the "pendulations" of the text, the interpretive gaps it opens, oblige us to enter into completing them.[30] This is where the *Aeneid* itself had to falter, and where a more personal creed like Christianity could enter and appropriate its rhythms. The "world" of the *Aeneid* did ultimately depend on the "conversion" of one man, Octavius Augustus Caesar, yet he could not sustain it alone. The mystery, interiority, subjectivity of the text had to become explicit; the text recreated in every mind. The drama of consciousness had to become central; the epic, autobiography. The allegorical impulse inherent in the text (unlike the Homeric epics, for which the frequent allegorizations were largely imposed), its negative suggestion of "another world," could combine powerfully with Judaeo-Christian and neo-Platonic myths of exile and purified striving. Then further layers of meaning could be added to the text; then the world of the *Aeneid*, the Roman world, could itself be used, without violation of the basic structure of the text, as the basis for more spiritual values. Although, as we shall see, later authors could slight the dialectical process of the text in favor of a single-minded defense of one of its components, it is this process, Vergil's use of a tragic sensibility to define epic purpose, that is the most poignant index to the uncertainties of his times and his most complex legacy to the ages.

---

[30] See Auerbach's discussion of the Abraham and Isaac narrative, *Mimesis*, chap. 1, adapted to discussion of the *Aeneid* by Johnson, *Darkness Visible*, chap. 2.

II.

From Vergilian Epic to Romantic Epic:
Three Transvaluations

"Tu se' lo mio maestro e 'l mio autore."
(DANTE, *Inferno*)

"Tosto che nella vista mi percosse
l'alta virtù che già m'avea trafitto
prima ch' io fuor di puerizia fosse,
volsimi alla sinistra col rispitto
col quale il fantolin corre alla mamma
quando ha paura o quando elli è afflitto,
per dicere a Virgilio: 'Men che dramma
di sangue m'è rimaso che non tremi:
conosco i segni dell'antica fiamma';
ma Virgilio n'avea lasciati scemi
di sè, Virgilio dolcissimo patre,
Virgilio a cui per mia salute die'mi;
nè quantunque perdeo l'antica matre
valse alle guance nette di rugiada,
che, lacrimando, non tornasser atre."

(DANTE, *Purgatorio*)

The *Aeneid* is, like all great works of literature, generative of commentary and imitation; but more than most, it self-consciously embodies its own critique and thus invites radical remaking. This self-critical quality accounts, in part, for the poem's antithetical interpretative traditions.

On the one hand, Ovid virtually defines himself by opposition to Vergil. Ironic and subversive, Ovid emphasizes the incommensurable and irresistible drive of eros, which impels both men and the gods. He embraces force, energy, and with it, change. His greatest work, the *Metamorphoses*, is a kind of anti-*Aeneid* that ironically recounts the erotic descents of the gods and the hubristic aspirations of men, and ultimately conflates them all in a vast cosmic naturalistic cycle.[1] In a minor work, the *Heroides*, he has various abandoned heroines of myth plead their sides of their stories in language that is alternately sentimental, sophistic, and moving. In the seventh letter of the *Heroides*, Dido, writing to Aeneas, stresses in particular the cruel paradox that the son of Venus, goddess of love and fruitful nature, should abandon her.[2] Ovid's subversive reading, with its emphasis on the sheer force of love and its sympathetic treatment of women, becomes an important element in the medieval and early Renaissance merging of the ideals of courtly love and the revived classical epic.[3] In Chaucer's *The Legend of Good Women*, for example, Dido appears with Cleopatra and eight other Ovidian martyrs for love. There Chaucer sharpens Ovid's antiheroic irony by setting the betrayal of Dido against the backdrop of the treachery that brought down Troy, by reducing Mercury's admonition to Aeneas to a self-serving rationalization, and by pointedly refusing to justify Aeneas's conduct by developing any of the epic context of his voyage.[4] Similarly, in early Renaissance France, Joachim Du Bellay translates Book 4 of the *Aeneid* in conjunction with Dido's complaint from the *Heroides* and some other classical

---

[1] See Otis, *Ovid as an Epic Poet*, for a persuasive argument for the epic structural units in the poem; my reading rests on the further overarching irony of Ovid's irreverent view of the gods.

[2] For an analysis of the *Heroides* and a comparison of Letter 7 with the *Aeneid*, see Howard Jacobson, *Ovid's "Heroides,"* especially pp. 77–82.

[3] For two ambitious attempts, which focus on the story of Aeneas and Dido, to assess this problem in broad cultural and literary contexts, see Raymond J. Cormier, *One Heart, One Mind*, and Eberhard Leube, *Fortuna in Karthago*.

[4] *The Works of Geoffrey Chaucer*, ed. F. N. Robinson, pp. 500–4. Robert Worth Frank, Jr., *Chaucer and "The Legend of Good Women,"* pp. 57–58, acknowledges Ovid as one of Chaucer's sources, but dwells chiefly on Chaucer's sentimental adaptation of Vergil in "The Legend of Dido." John M. Fyler, *Chaucer and Ovid*, pp. 30–41, 111–13, analyzes Chaucer's deliberate confrontation of Vergil's and Ovid's accounts of Dido. Both critics imply Chaucer's greater debt to Ovid than to Vergil, an argument which excludes the medieval writer from detailed discussion in my study of major transvaluations of Vergil's story.

materials that emphasize her pitiful "douceur."[5] By itself and through such intermediary sources Ovid's influence is pervasive, as we shall see, in Renaissance dramas about Dido.

On the other hand, Vergil's poem, saved by Varius from destruction by its overly scrupulous author, and published at the request of Augustus Caesar himself, swiftly became enshrined as the epitome of Roman values. It was the foundation of every schoolboy's education, the standard for the Latin language. It was extensively analyzed and cited by the grammarians; its fragments, from which we could, if necessary, reassemble virtually the entire poem, were collected as *centos* illustrating certain beloved themes. It received exhaustive scholarly commentary, and was increasingly viewed as a text of encyclopedic wisdom, even to the practice of the *sortes Vergilianae*, random, "prophetic" consultations of the text.[6]

In Europe, where the ideal of the Roman Empire remained strong during the Middle Ages, the language and values of the epic survived in various allegorical forms, often Christian eschatological ones, to be reinfused with secular significance as the new nationalisms of the Renaissance vied with one another to assume the imperial mantle. The transposition of the *Aeneid* to Christian eschatology was aided by early neo-Platonic and Stoic allegorizations of the text that were further adapted by the early Church Fathers. Fulgentius (ca. A.D. 467–532), a North African Christian whose interpretation of the *Aeneid* became tremendously influential in the Middle Ages, "uncovered" in the poem a continuous moral allegory of man's lifelong journey toward Ausonia, "increase of good." One twelfth-century commentator, Bernard, declares that the poem de-

---

[5] *Le quatriesme livre de l'Énéide de Vergile, traduict en vers Françoys. La Complaincte de Didon à Énée, prinse d' Ovide.* For the French Renaissance reception of Vergil, see Alice Hulubei, "Virgile en France au XVIe siècle."

[6] On the preservation of the *Aeneid*, see Suetonius, *The Lives of Illustrious Men*, "Vergil," 2:39–41. On the use of the *Aeneid* in education see, for example, Quintilian, *Institutio Oratoria*, 4.10.85ff. For its transmission see Domenico Comparetti, *Vergil in the Middle Ages*, especially pt. 1, chaps. 1–5. For the tradition of commentary, see especially the late fourth-century commentary of Servius, *Servii Grammatici*, which incorporates the earlier work of Aelius Donatus and the roughly contemporaneous *Saturnalia* of Macrobius, where Vergil is confidently declared "an authority in every branch of learning" (1.16.12). For the practice of the *sortes*, see Comparetti, *Vergil*, pp. 47–49.

scribes "in integumento . . . quid agat vel quid paciatur humanus spiritus in humano corpore temporaliter positus" ("under a veil . . . what the human spirit does and undergoes when it is for a time placed in a body"); while another, John of Salisbury, repeats the now commonplace etymology that *Aeneas = ennaios*, the indwelling of soul in the human body.[7]

This allegorical interpretation of the poem persists throughout the Renaissance, even as it is supplemented by renewed secular meanings. Thus Petrarch, although he seeks to appreciate the poetic texture of the *Aeneid* and to recapture its Roman values, sees veiled in the poem a Fulgentian allegory of human life. Boccaccio, in his influential *Genealogy of the Pagan Gods*, declares that Vergil's second purpose, "concealed within the poetic veil," in writing the *Aeneid*, "was to show with what passions human frailty is infested, and the strength with which a steady man subdues them." Christoforo Landino, writing in the latter part of the fifteenth century, devotes the second half of his *Disputationes Camaldulenses* to a Christian neo-Platonic allegorical exegesis of the poem. The Renaissance humanists Pier Candido Decembrio and Mapheus Vegius write neo-Vergilian thirteenth books for the *Aeneid*, in which Aeneas's marriage to Lavinia and the pious end of his life foreshadow the Christian marriage supper of the Lamb and eternal heavenly reward. At the same time the poem was the focus of literary imitation for the revived ambitions of the Holy Roman Empire and its European rivals.[8] Such orthodox and neo-orthodox readings tend to emphasize the poem's aesthetics of renunciation and its his-

---

[7] For late classical and patristic interpretation, see the work of Pierre Courcelle, especially "Interprétations neo-platonisantes du livre VI de l'Énéide." On Fulgentius, see the edition of his works, *Fulgentius the Mythographer.* For Bernard, see *The Commentary on the First Six Books of the "Aeneid" of Vergil*, p. 3, and see also *Fulgentius the Mythographer*, p. 113.

[8] On Petrarch, see Pierre de Nolhac, "Virgile chez Pétrarque." On Boccaccio, see *Boccaccio on Poetry*, trans. Charles G. Osgood, p. 68. On Landino, see Michael Murrin, *The Allegorical Epic*, chap. 2, pp. 27–50, and appendix, pp. 197–202. On Vegius and other Renaissance "completers" of the *Aeneid*, see *Mapheus Vegius and His Thirteenth Book of the "Aeneid,"* ed. Anna Cox Brinton. On neo-Vergilian imitation in general, see Thomas Greene, *The Descent from Heaven*, and Frances Yates, *Astraea*, for specific comments on the imperial programs of Holy Roman Emperor Charles V, England's Elizabeth I, and France's Charles IX.

torical or otherworldly goal at the expense of Vergil's thwarted energies and painful uncertainties.

However, comparatively few commentators and imitators grasped the re-creative depths of Vergil's impelling tragic sensibility within the epic frame: " 'sunt lacrimae rerum et mentem mortalia tangunt' " (" 'here, too, there are tears for misfortune and mortal sorrows touch the heart,' " *Aen.* 1.462). Among those who did are some who used Vergil as he himself used Homer, as the authoritative spokesman of a tragically shadowed, outmoded, way of life. They focus their transvaluations powerfully on reworking Vergil's story of Dido. Recognizing the sublimated erotic energy that fuels the poem, they harness it to their purposes. In this chapter, I briefly consider three authors who lead us toward Shakespeare's inversion, in *Antony and Cleopatra,* of the values of empire by the possibilities of imagination. Augustine in the *Confessions* substitutes the loving, creative interchange of the individual soul and a transcendent subject, God, for the potentially depersonalizing architecture of Rome; Dante in the *Comedy,* guided by Vergil, figures the subject of affection, thus a means to God, as Beatrice; and Spenser, in the context of celebrating female rule in *The Faerie Queene,* presents the neo-Vergilian love quest of his chief heroine, Britomart, to portray the development of a properly disciplined imagination. Extending the standard interpretations of these works, I concentrate on their powerful moments of reminiscence of Vergil's Dido and the creative implications of those moments.

Augustine

The passionate spirituality of Augustine should not blind us to the late imperial backdrop of beleaguered social and political values against which it took shape, and which lend it such concreteness and definition.[9] He was trained as a classical rhetorician; his first ambition was to teach and speak for the governing classes at Rome or the Imperial Court at Milan. The *Aeneid* formed an early and central part of his training: in *Confessions* 1.13 and 17 we glimpse—alive in the young African boy—the grammatical,

---

[9] See Peter Brown, *Augustine of Hippo,* especially chaps. 3, 7, and 26.

cultural, and emotional authority attributed to the epic in Macrobius's early fifth-century *Saturnalia*. The story shaped his early
imaginings: he competed in an oratorical contest based on Juno's
great speech (*Aen.* 1.37–49), and he sympathized with the fate of
Dido "et fornicanti sonabat undique: 'euge, euge' " ("while in the
mean time every one applauded me with Well done, well done!").[10]

Later, at Rome, Augustine came under the direct patronage of
Quintus Aurelius Symmachus, the elder statesman who in Macrobius's *Saturnalia* defends Vergil's mastery of rhetoric. For a time,
Augustine was imbued with the values of the late pagan revival.[11]
Many of the major image patterns in the *Confessions* (the sea voyage, the labyrinth) and even the structure and coloring of incidents
—especially the description of Carthage as a "sartago flagitiosorum
amorum" ("a whole frying-pan full of abominable loves") and the
multiple ironies of his Aeneas-like flight from Monica—mark the
rhetorician-turned-saint's transposition of the *Aeneid* into an eschatological key.[12] It is a thesis he later argues discursively when he
shows *Roma aeterna* superseded by the City of God.[13]

---

[10] Compare *Conf.* 1.13 and 17 with *Saturnalia* 1.24.8 for the reverence in
which Vergil was held, and 5.17.4–6 for the appeal of the story of Dido and
its dramatization. I cite *Confessions*, trans. William Watts, and *City of God*,
trans. George McCracken, throughout.

[11] Brown, *Augustine*, pp. 66–72, 300ff., discusses Augustine and the late
pagan revival. For the pagan revival of the fourth century and the circle of
Symmachus, see also Herbert Bloch, "The Pagan Revival in the West at the
End of the Fourth Century."

[12] *Conf.* 3.1. Could Augustine have known of a pre-Fulgentian allegory
of Aeneas's sojourn in Carthage as a temptation to adolescent lust? Compare
Aen. 4.296ff. with *Conf.* 5.8, when the young Augustine departs for Rome.
Monica is both a Dido figure, bewailing and lamenting Augustine's departure, and a daughter of Eve; too, she is finally the faithful, pious mother to
whom Augustine will return as the personal embodiment of *Mater Ecclesia*.

[13] Brown remarks:

> [the *City of God* ranks] in Roman literature as a work of "Chris-
> tian nationalism." Like most nationalisms, the form in which it is
> expressed is borrowed from its rulers. . . . *"Your"* Vergil is now de-
> liberately juxtaposed, at every turn, with *"Our"* Scriptures.
>
> Juxtaposition, indeed, is the basic literary device that deter-
> mines the structure of every book of the *City of God*. Augustine
> deliberately uses it to contrive a "stereoscopic" effect. The solu-
> tions of the new, Christian literature must "stand out the more

For Augustine this transposition introduced affective, personal, responses into history; a personal God would right tragedies through grace, rather than a Roman order imposing itself upon them. The broad cultural ambition of the *Aeneid* ramifies into the longing language of the Psalms, a need Augustine's sympathetic nature expressed in his youth when he identified so closely with the suffering Dido:

> et plorare Didonem mortuam, quia se occidit ab amore, cum interea me ipsum in his a te morientem, deus, vita mea, siccis oculis ferrem miserrimus.
>
> *(Conf.* 1.13)
>
> (to bewail dead Dido, because she killed herself for love; when in the mean time (wretch that I was) I with dry eyes endured myself dying towards thee, O God my Life!)

This passage forms an index to his appreciation of her tragedy, read as the tragedy of one who yearned after an inadequate earthly object of love, even while it sets forth its emendation of Aeneas's goal in the earthly city with his in the heavenly.

Augustine absorbs the tenor of the *Aeneid* as he rejects its explicit values. He gradually transmutes his own material drives and cultural displacement, which caused him to pass through the varieties of late antique philosophy and religion as so many way stations in an epic of the soul, into an embrace of bewildering personal and social change as a process of refinement toward God. He concludes Book 2 of *The City of God* with an exhortation to the Romans, couched in the language of the *Aeneid*, to see the Christian religion as the proper extension of their drive for glory:

> Ad quam patriam te invitamus et exhortamur ut eius adiciaris numero civium, cuius quodam modo asylum est vera remissio peccatorum. Non audias degeneres tuos Christo Christianisve detrahentes et accusantes velut tempora mala, cum quaerant

---

clearly" by always being imposed upon an elaborately constructed background of pagan answers to the same question. It is a method calculated to give a sense of richness and dramatic tension. . . .

(Augustine, p. 306)

tempora quibus non sit quieta vita, sed potius secura nequitia. Haec tibi numquam nec pro terrena patria placuerunt. Nunc iam caelestem arripe, pro qua minimum laborabis, et in ea veraciter semperque regnabis. Illic enim tibi non Vestalis focus, non lapis Capitolinus, sed Deus unus et verus

      nec metas rerum nec tempora ponit,
      Imperium sine finit dabit.

(2.29)

(To this fatherland we invite you and urge you to join the roster of the citizens of the city that offers its own asylum, so to speak, in a genuine remission of sins. Do not hearken to your degenerate sons who asperse Christ and Christians, and denounce their era as if the times were bad, since the times they require are not a time of peaceful living, but of carefree frivolity. You never approved such a goal even for your earthly fatherland. Lay hold without delay on the heavenly fatherland, which will cost you but the slightest toil and will enable you to reign in the true sense and forever. There thou shalt have no fire of Vesta, no Capitoline stone, but the one true God

      No times, no bounds will set to action
      But grant an empire without end. [*Aen.* 1.278–79])

In the *Confessions* Augustine transforms the *Aeneid*'s quest for a proper object of desire, sought amid the ruins of collective memory, the partial answers of a decaying culture, into an encounter with a loving transcendental subject of desire. This central discovery redefines Augustine's powerful erotic drive from arid possession to shared creativity, from proud cupidity to humble *caritas*:

Sed tunc, lectis Platonicorum illis libris, posteaquam inde admonitus quaerere incorpoream veritatem, invisibilia tua per ea quae facta sunt intellecta conspexi. . . . non habent illae paginae vultum pietatis illius, lacrimas confessionis, sacrificium tuum, spiritum contribulatum, cor contritum et humiliatum, populi salutem, sponsam civitatem, arram spiritus sancti, poculum pretii nostri. nemo ibi, cantat: Nonne deo subdita erit anima mea? ab ipso enim salutare meum: etenim ipse deus meus et salutaris meus, susceptor meus: non movebor amplius. nemo ibi audit vocantem: Venite ad me, qui laboratis. dedignantur ab eo discere, quoniam mitis est et humilis corde.

abscondisti enim haec a sapientibus et prudentibus et revelasti
ea parvulis.

(7.20–21)

(But having read as then these books of the Platonists, having
once gotten the hint from them, and falling upon the search
of incorporeal truth; I came to get a sight of these invisible
things of thine, which are understood by those things which
are made. . . . Those leaves can show nothing of this face of
pity, those tears of confession, that sacrifice of thine, a troubled
spirit, a broken and a contrite heart, the salvation of thy people, the Spouse, the city, the earnest of the Holy Ghost, the
Cup of our Redemption. No man sings there, Shall not my soul
wait upon God, seeing from him cometh my salvation? For he
is my God, and my Salvation, my Defense; I shall be no more
moved. No man in those books hears him calling: Come unto
me all ye that labour; Yea, they scorn to learn of him because
he is meek and lowly in heart. For these things hast thou hid
from the wise and prudent, and has revealed them unto babes.)

Augustine's final movement from neo-Platonic philosophy to Pauline Christianity is itself figured as an appropriation of the *sortes
Vergilianae* to the Bible, as he rushes into the garden and opens
the Epistles (8.12).

Augustine's legitimization of eros as *agape* also allows him to
develop a limited positive presentation of women that offsets the
more conventional view of them as temptresses. His loyal and affectionate concubine (a thoroughly sanctioned relationship for aspiring
young men of the time), the mother of his son, provides a temporary
repository for his overwhelming, underdifferentiated need to love,
but is eventually cast off as he turns to the Church.[14] With that he
returns to his abandoned mother, the powerful figure who united
primitive African custom with a visionary ability that allowed him

---

[14] When the young Augustine arrived at Carthage he declared: "nondum
amabam, et amare amabam, et secretiore indigentia oderam me minus in-
digentem. quaerebam quid amarem, amans amare" ("I was not in love as yet,
yet I loved to be in love, and with a more secret kind of want, I hated myself
having little want. I sought about for something to love, loving still to be in
love" *Conf.* 3.1). The remainder of the *Confessions* chronicles his dissatis-
faction with various love objects and his discovery of a satisfactory transcendental subject of desire.

to share with her a mystical experience of Wisdom itself: "et dum loquimur et inhiamus illi, attingimus eam modice toto ictu cordis" ("And while we were thus discoursing and panting after it [wisdom], we arrived to a little touch of it with the whole effort of our heart" 9.10). Contemporary social conventions supported this return to the mother, a regression that was also a diffusion into a sustaining, if tempestuous, ecclesiastical life:

> The imagination of African Christians of the time of Augustine had become riveted on the idea of the Church. This Church was the "*strong woman.*" "It would not be decent for us," Augustine said, "to speak of any other woman." In a land which, to judge from Monica, had a fair share of formidable mothers, the *Catholica*, the Catholic Church, was The Mother: "One Mother, prolific with offspring: of her are we born, by her milk we are nourished, by her spirit we are made alive."
>
> (Brown, *Augustine*, p. 212)

In his long pastoral and controversial career Augustine was to find a varied and permissible outlet for his tremendous emotional energies.

Augustine's conversion releases the form of the classical epic from the constraints of space and time to an apprehension of every thing and event, properly understood, as a trace of the divine, a footstep of God. It completes the *Aeneid*'s transposition of event to consciousness, making linear history fully symbolic, only meaningful *sub specie aeternitatis*. Augustine is quite fittingly both the time-bound, historical hero and the prophetic, retrospective and prospective, narrator of a spiritual autobiography that concludes in a paean to a larger story, God's creativity in the beginning: a commentary on Genesis. Augustine's transvaluation of the epic cultural quest of the *Aeneid* into the erotic autobiographical quest of the *Confessions* is thus a necessary precursor of Dante's Christian symbolic epic.[15]

---

[15] Augustine's formal contribution rests in presenting a narrator and chief character who exist explicitly as different historical moments of a single human consciousness symbolic of human consciousness in general, moving through a landscape symbolic of eternal things. This dual narrative perspective informs much of medieval lyric, dream vision, drama, and Dante's powerfully distilled opening lines of the *Comedy*: "Nel mezzo del cammin di nostra vita / mi ritrovai per una selva oscura / che la diritta via era smarrita."

Dante

The intertwined secular and religious strands of the conventions of "courtly love" and the theological values supporting what Auerbach terms "figural realism" combine in Dante's *Divine Comedy* to produce imitations of Vergil's Dido episode that work yet more forcefully to illustrate the proper exercise of desire.[16] Dante understood Vergil in many ways. Christian commentators from Fulgentius in the sixth century to Bernard and John of Salisbury in the twelfth had allegorized the *Aeneid* as the epic of the human soul in search of salvation, and this allegorization provides the broadest justification for Dante's dramatic development of Vergil as his guide through the first two realms of the afterlife in the *Comedy*.[17] In *Purgatorio* 21–22 Dante has Statius celebrate Vergil also for his "Messianic" fourth eclogue, in which he unwittingly prophesied the coming of Christ and which was the means of Statius's conversion: " 'Per te poeta fui, per te cristiano.' " In addition to these typically medieval readings of Vergil's importance, Dante, against Augustine, regards Vergil as the preeminent poet of providential empire, of the *pax romana* that was the cradle of universal Christianity. Viewed this way, the *Aeneid* became the model of imitation for a series of Renaissance "court" poets—Petrarch, Ronsard, Camoëns, Spenser—who sought to translate some of the ideals, powers, and compound secular and religious authority of this Holy Roman Empire to contemporary settings.[18]

---

[16] For an introductory discussion of the interpenetration of sacred and secular motives in medieval love lyric, see Peter Dronke, *The Medieval Lyric*. For a theoretical study, based on the ambiguous figure of the mirror, see Frederick Goldin, *The Mirror of Narcissus in the Courtly Love Lyric*. On figural realism, see Auerbach, *Mimesis*, chap. 8, "Farinata and Cavalcanti"; and *Scenes from the Drama of European Literature*, pp. 11–76.

[17] In *Conv.* 4.24.9 Dante, discussing the stages of the soul's voyage toward union with God, alludes to the Fulgentian "lo figurato che di questo diverso processo de l'etadi tiene Virgilio ne lo Eneida."

[18] Augustine's and Dante's views of the preeminent secular power and authority of Rome are similar. But Augustine emphasizes Rome as a negative instrument of God, checking and scourging man's sinful nature, while Dante emphasizes Rome's positive nature as the secular complement to the Church, providing the peace and order within which Christ's revelation can grow. For Dante's argument, see *De Monarchia*. For its extension throughout his

Most significantly for our study, Dante understood in a subtle and sympathetic way the Fulgentian commonplace reading of the Dido episode as an allegory of the temptation of youthful reason by passion or appetite. Already in the *Convivio* Dante resists an easy polarization of these two aspects of human nature, and he creates the possibility for a complex, constructive tension between them, rather than a mutually exclusive choice. A good Aristotelian, he argues for temperance, not abstinence—although "this appetite must be ridden by reason," the appetite or "natural impulse" is declared to be "of noble nature." In leaving Dido, Aeneas is not so much fleeing evil as exercising "self-restraint" in turning from "so much pleasure" to follow an "upright, fruitful, and praiseworthy path."[19] Dante's most direct imitation of the Dido episode, in *Inferno* 5, does indeed show the dead sinners of lust, who now exist *sub specie aeternitatis*, condemned forever to a "hellish storm": "a così fatto tormento / enno dannati i peccator carnali, / che la ragion sommettono al talento" (37–39).[20] But within the evolving consciousness

---

works, see Comparetti, *Vergil*, chaps. 14 and 15, and the work of J. H. Whitfield, especially *Dante and Virgil*. For the effect of this model on the Renaissance epic, see Greene, *Descent from Heaven*, especially pp. 3–4; and Yates, *Astraea*, especially pp. 8–12.

[19] Veramente questo appetito conviene essere cavalcato da la ragione; ché, sì come uno sciolto cavallo, quanto ch'ello sia di natura nobile, per sé, sanza lo buono cavalcatore, bene non si conduce, così questo appetito, che irascibile e concupiscibile si chiama, quanto ch'ello sia nobile, a la ragione obedire conviene, la quale guida quello con freno e con isproni, come buono cavaliere. Lo freno usa quando elli caccia, e chiamasi quello freno temperanza, la quale mostra lo termine infino al quale è da cacciare; lo sprone usa quando fugge, per lo tornare a lo loco onde fuggire vuole, e questo sprone si chiama fortezza, o vero magnanimitate, la quale vertute mostra lo loco dove è da fermarsi e da pugnare. E così infrenato mostra Virgilio, lo maggiore nostro poeta, che fosse Enea, ne la parte de lo Eneida ove questa etade [youth] si figura; la quale parte comprende lo quarto, lo quinto e lo sesto libro de lo Eneida. E quanto raffrenare fu quello, quando, avendo ricevuto da Dido tanto di piacere quanto di sotto nel settimo trattato si dicerà, e usando con essa tanto di dilettazione, elli si partio, per seguire onesta e laudabile via e fruttuosa, come nel quarto de l'Eneida scritto è. . . .

(*Conv.* 4.26.6–9)

[20] I cite the text of John D. Sinclair, *The Divine Comedy*, throughout.

of Dante the pilgrim, the encounter with his Dido figure presents itself as a tragedy of misplaced desire and a warning against improper poetry that functions subliminally as a spur to right loving and right making.

Francesca da Rimini is Dante's Dido. The manner in which she is introduced makes this clear even as it indicates some of the distance Dante feels between himself and his poetic master. In Dante's poem Vergil is at once majestic and lovingly intimate: " 'Tu se' lo mio maestro e 'l mio autore' " (*Inf.* 1.85), exclaims Dante the pilgrim on first meeting him; although he reveres him, he does not hesitate to use the familiar pronoun. Yet despite this intimacy, Dante knew that his Christian beliefs and his courtly aesthetic heritage both demanded an alteration in style from the Vergilian *gravitas* to a mixed *volgare*. Thus at first he tactfully alludes to Vergil's Dido, " 'colei che s'ancise amorosa, / e ruppe fede al cener di Sicheo' " (*Inf.* 5.61–62), gliding like a crane among the other great sinners of lust. He explicitly names Dido only at that point when he dramatizes his pilgrim's encounter with his Dido figure, the delicate, dovelike Francesca.[21] Like Vergil's Dido, Francesca, despite the intrinsic interest of her story, exists less as an object of condemnation than as a figure from an outmoded poetic world beyond which the hero is then impelled. Her story is important chiefly for our understanding of his. This evolution of epic consciousness is all the more tense and poignant in the *Comedy*, where the developing hero and the overseeing poet are but different moments of the same fused personality, the individual ethical center of the universal drama of salvation.

As Vergil's Dido is the representative of a dying Homeric heroism, so Dante's Francesca is the exemplar of an inadequate, "courtly" doctrine of love, one that is deracinated from the source of all being, God, and in which the hero is implicated as a former spokesman. From the beginning of the episode there are hints that *his* poetic education is the framework for *her* tragic experience. The

---

[21] Quali columbe, dal disio chiamate,
con l'ali alzate e ferme al dolce nido
vegnon per l'aere dal voler portate;
cotali uscir della schiera ov' è *Dido*,
a noi venendo per l'aere maligno,
sì forte fu l'affetüoso grido.

        (*Inf.* 5.82–87, emphasis mine)

"desire" to which these lovers subject reason is "talento" rather than "desiderio" or "voglia," a capacity *to make* rather than a mere undifferentiated will. And Dante the pilgrim is at first bewildered to learn that all the beloved heroes and heroines of romantic legend are here condemned to suffer for love: "le donne antiche e' cavalieri" (*Inf.* 5.71) he says, in a most courtly rendering of antiquity.

As Francesca's tale unfolds, he realizes with pity and pain that the doctrine of love she espouses is the echo of the poetry of the *dolce stil nuovo*. Unilluminated by the typological dimension that purifies it, such poetry cannot make the subtle but essential change, "Che libito fè licito" (*Inf.* 5.56). These are Venus's doves, not the dove of divine inspiration:

> "Amor, ch'al cor gentil ratto s'apprende,
>   prese costui della bella persona
>   che mi fu tolta; e 'l modo ancor m'offende.
> Amor, ch'a nullo amato amar perdona,
>   mi prese del costui piacer sì forte,
>   che, come vedi, ancor non m'abbandona.
> Amor condusse noi ad una morte."
>
>   (*Inf.* 5.100–106)

"*Amor* . . . ad un*a morte*"; love to one death. The "one point" of yielding recounted by the passive Francesca was a yielding of personality to pure sensation, to an uncritical role playing that culminates in a depersonalization of herself and her lover, now merely "this one." The literature she read—a French chivalric romance—both encouraged her to abandon responsibility for herself and to take as her model the euphemistically couched adultery between Lancelot and Guinevere. Although that chivalric tale, she says, played the go-between (a "Galeotto") in her affair, the pilgrim's gentle probing of the precise occasion of the lovers' fall suggests that he not only understands her desire (" 'Oh lasso, / quanti dolci pensier, quanto disio / menò costoro al doloroso passo!' " *Inf.* 5.112–13) but also fears that his early poetic aesthetic might have been such a pander.[22]

---

[22] Renato Poggioli in "Tragedy or Romance?" distinguishes the stages of poetic transmission and moral consciousness that separate Francesca from Dante the poet-narrator. However, Poggioli skirts the precise nature and extent of Dante the pilgrim's involvement in her sin and its reflections on his

The improper celebration of woman as an object of love: this is the characteristic sin of youth for Dante as man and poet. Of course, he witnesses and often implicates himself in many other failings in his journey through the other world. However, since for Dante, " 'comprender puoi ch'esser convene / amor sementa in voi d'ogni virtute / e d'ogne operazion che merta pene' " (*Purg.* 17.103–105), women in his work often function symbolically as more general indices of proper or improper love, as well as specific figures of sensual love. In the former sense the sin of Francesca and Dante's involvement in it become especially relevant to the entire poem. From the window lady of philosophy in *La vita nuova* to the metamorphic dream figure of the Siren in *Purgatorio* 19, the greatest danger for Dante is that love turn inward upon itself to become self-love or pride.

Francesca's self-involvement, her quiet narcissism that deprives both her and her lover of real identity and makes them seem victims of an all-powerful "Love," and the "fanciful" romance that prompts it, presage for Dante the more serious self-involvements of a philosophy untied to religious ends or an art that is pure aestheticism:

> mi venne in sogno una femmina balba,
>   nelli occhi guercia, e sovra i piè distorta,
>   con le man monche, e di colore scialba.
> Io la mirava; e come 'l sol conforta
>   le fredde membra che la notte aggrava,
>   così lo sguardo mio le facea scorta
> la lingua, e poscia tutta la drizzava
>   in poco d'ora, e lo smarrito volto,
>   com'amor vuol, così le colorava.
>
> .   .   .   .
>
>   quand'una donna apparve santa e presta
>   lunghesso me per far colei confusa.
> "O Virgilio, o Virgilio, chi è questa?"
>   fieramente dicea; ed el venìa
>   con li occhi fitti pur in quella onesta.

___

own aesthetic and moral development. René Girard's compressed comments on this episode, "*To double business bound*," pp. 1–8, likewise require completion with a discussion of a desire that is not ultimately autoerotic and destructive, one that can be successfully displaced through an "other" into the realm of creativity.

L'altra prendea, e dinanzi l'aprìa
fendendo i drappi, e mostravami'l ventre:
quel mi svegliò col puzzo che n'uscìa.

(*Purg.* 19.7–15, 26–33)

In his dream of the Siren Dante thus describes these lurid and fleeting pleasures, ugliness willfully colored "as love desires."

That the Siren of the *Odyssey* occasions these deceits points explicitly to Dante's redefinition of the epic tradition and his place within it.[23] In Homer's *Odyssey* she embodies the central danger of epic poetry, that one will substitute the song for the deeds it celebrates, will live in indulgent memories rather than forge the present day. She feeds that self-aggrandizing pride that in *Inferno* 26 has made Dante's medieval, allegorized Ulysses so dangerously persuasive a counsellor to a presumptuous assault on the unknown:

"Quando
mi diparti' da Circe, che sottrasse
me più d'un anno là presso a Gaeta,
prima che sì Enea la nomasse,
nè dolcezza di figlio, nè la pièta
del vecchio padre, nè 'l debito amore
lo qual dovea Penelopè far lieta,
vincer poter dentro da me l'ardore
ch'i'ebbi a divenir del mondo esperto,
e delli vizi umani e del valore."

(*Inf.* 26.90–99)

Vergil, as the preeminent spokesman for all these communal values that Ulysses rejects—love of son, father, wife, tradition—must serve as moral, as well as linguistic, translator for the ancient Homeric epic ideal.

In the historical drama of *Inferno* 26, the measured Vergil at

---

[23] The Siren says, " 'Io volsi *Ulisse* del suo cammin vago / al canto mio; e qual meco si ausa / rado sen parte, sì tutto l'appago' " (*Purg.* 19.22–24). My colleague Ralph Williams alerted me to the central importance of the Siren in Dante's poetic quest, with her implicit reference to Dante's earlier confrontation with the Homeric epic ideal (*Inf.* 26) and through it to his own initial epic dilemma "al piè d'un colle" in "il primo canto" (see the pun at *Inf.* 26.138).

once respectfully acknowledges the cultural aspiration of the Greeks, yet shields the overeager Dante from uncritical contact with their values. This episode in turn recalls Dante's own "mad flight" (*Inf.* 26.125; 1.25–27) in the first canto, when he, like Ulysses, tried to approach a blessed mountain without aid of the divine.[24] As in canto 1, Vergil again rescues Dante from himself, from that autoeroticism alternately figured in the *Comedy* as unaided philosophic speculation, cultural ambition, and aesthetic indulgence.

For at the beginning of the poem Vergil uses his own pervasively Roman expressions to intimate the new epic quest:

> "Ond' io per lo tuo me' penso e discerno
> che tu mi segui, e io sarò tua guida
> e trarrotti di qui per luogo etterno,
> ove udirai le disperate strida,
> vedrai li antichi spiriti dolenti,
> che la seconda morte ciascun grida;
> e vederai color che son contenti
> nel foco, perchè speran di venire
> quando che sia alle beate genti.
> Alle qua' poi se tu vorrai salire,
> anima fia a ciò piu di me degna;
> con lei ti lascerò nel mio partire:
> chè quello imperador che là su regna,
> perch' io fu' ribellante alla sua legge,
> non vuol che 'n sua città per me si vegna.
> In tutte parti impera e quivi regge;
> quivi è la sua città e l'alto seggio:
> oh felice colui cu' ivi elegge!"
>
> (*Inf.* 1.112–29)

---

[24] Dante the poet-narrator remarks at the beginning of the Ulysses episode that he must curb his powers "perchè non corra che virtù nol guidi" (*Inf.* 26.21–22); his virtue is still tempted to too uncritical an imitation of the Homeric *virtú.* Vergil carefully conjures Ulysses to tell the story most instructive to a Christian listener, that of his unsatisfied end. Here Vergil's redefined epic values are interposed between Ulysses, traditionally a figure representing the proud intellect, and Dante. Ulysses' lust for experience at the risk of his comrades' lives is defined against the values of family and community depicted in Aeneas's "O socii" speech. Dante is subtly directed away from his earlier mistaken philosophic assault on the delectable mountain of human happiness to "altro vïaggio" (*Inf.* 1.91) that acknowledges human sinfulness and builds Christian community for a heavenly city.

Here the diction—"Emperor," "His city," "His lofty seat"—historically defines Vergil, even while the transmutation of Aeneas's " 'O fortunati, quorum iam moenia surgunt!' " (" 'Happy they whose walls already rise!' " *Aen.* 1.437) to " 'oh felice colui cu' ivi elegge!' " captures quite exactly the change from the "architectural" Roman civic ideal to the essentially individual Christian salvational one.

This first encounter between Dante and his "autore" thus establishes the tension, which suffuses the first two realms of the *Comedy*, between what the very best of human wisdom, the height of antique civilization, can give to him, and its tragic absence of divine revelation. Dante's admiration for classical civilization causes him to press continually the conventional boundaries of the question of the salvation of the virtuous heathen, and he firmly establishes a fictional territory for continued debate. "Lacrimae rerum" well up for Vergil himself in his encounters with Sordello (*Purg.* 7.1–39) and Statius (*Purg.* 21.104–36), when he is revered as a poetic teacher but surpassed by the divine assurance of his Christian poetic successors. Vergil can enter the Earthly Paradise, and there be granted by Matilda "un corollario ancor per grazia" (*Purg.* 28.136)—the knowledge that poetic golden age visions shadow forth this real place; but he cannot see the actual telos of his own poem, the figuration of Christ that now appears to Dante in the uniquely personal form of Beatrice.[25]

Dante miraculously distills the essence of *Aeneid* 4 into his Christian epic's peripeteia at *Purgatorio* 30–31. In the *Aeneid*, the weight of remembered suffering rebounds as renewed desire. So Dante, having passed through the realms of sorrow, seeing Beatrice, seeks to convey his renewed vigor to Vergil using Dido's language: " 'I know the marks of the ancient flame' " (*Purg.* 30.48; *Aen.* 4.23). But Vergil is gone. Vergil's Dido felt ancient desire in herself only to arouse more sublime desire in Aeneas; Dante here, despite the immense Vergilian pathos of his address to his lost poetic father, no longer merely "autore" but threshold to salvation—"Virgilio *dolcis-*

---

[25] In *Purg.* 30, Beatrice, as Dante's personal figuration of Christ, is the fulfillment of both the biblical and Roman prophetic strains: she is both the type of Christ as he appears in Matt. 21:9, "Benedictus qui venis," and the successor to Vergil's disappointed imperial hope, Octavius's adopted son Marcellus, "Manibus o date lilia plenis" (*Aen.* 6.883).

simo patre, / Virgilio a cui per mia salute die'mi" (*Purg.* 30.50–51, emphasis mine)—must use this loss to define his new epic task, the acknowledgment of his own individual moral responsibility and dependence on God's grace. Dante is warned, like the youthful Augustine bewailing Dido, to weep, not for Vergil's loss, but for the threatened loss of his own soul (*Purg.* 30.55–57). In the *Aeneid*, shaken by Dido's pleas, Aeneas stood as firm as the ancient oak that symbolized his higher commitments to his race; at this crucial moment in the *Comedy*, when Dante raises his chin to accept Beatrice's rebuke, the supreme difficulty of this acceptance of his epic task, the care of his own eternal life, is described in language which specifically surpasses that of the *Aeneid*, uprooting its epic tree:

> Con men di resistenza si dibarba
>   robusto cerro, o vero al nostral vento
>   o vero a quel della terra di Iarba,
> ch' io non levai al suo comando il mento;
>   e quando per la barba il viso chiese,
>   ben conobbi il velen dell'argomento.
>
> (*Purg.* 31.70–75)[26]

"Hoc opus, hic labor est"; Dante is converted.

Dante's constant poetic recourse to the figure of Beatrice marks his attempt to substantiate the conventions of courtly love as an individual who could infold the creation and thus, standing in the place of Christ, manifest God to him. When she appears to him in the Earthly Paradise she is at once insistently real—a loving but corrective "Beatrice" to an accountable "Dante"—and pervasively symbolic; in short, a completely achieved "figure" or "type." She is the proper subject for a poetry that strives as nearly as possible to participate in God's intentions, to continue his *allegoria res*. We are meant to contrast the sharply individuated moral responsibility that she here presses upon Dante with the Siren's earlier temptation to narcissistic self-indulgence (" 'Io son,' cantava, 'io son dolce serena' " *Purg.* 19.19):

---

[26] On the oak tree in the *Aeneid*, see my conclusion to chapter 1. The reference to the south wind as "of the country of Iarbas" again reminds us of Aeneas's resistance to Dido's passionate pleas, and of Dante's greater task in accepting Beatrice's stern rebuke.

> "Dante, perchè Virgilio se ne vada,
> non pianger anco, non piangere ancora;
> chè pianger ti conven per altra spada."
>
> .   .   .   .
>
> quando mi volsi *al suon del nome mio,*
> *che di necessità qui si registra,*
> vidi la donna . . .
>
> .   .   .   .
>
> continüò come colui che dice
> e 'l più caldo parlar dietro reserva:
> "Guardaci ben! *Ben son, ben son Beatrice.*
> Come degnasti d'accedere al monte?
> non sapei tu che qui è l'uom felice?"
>
> (*Purg.* 30.55–57; 62–64; 71–75, emphasis mine)

While the Siren seductively yields to the impositions of fantasy, Beatrice remains emphatically opaque, a radical individual forcing moral consciousness upon Dante.

As Dante says, his name is noted here by necessity, its only mention in the *Comedy*, because this is the moment of his personal confession. To emphasize yet again the contrast between Ulysses' alluring epic aspiration and his own Christian confessional task, Dante here has Beatrice describe his prideful fall, the subject of *La vita nuova* and the opening canto of the *Comedy*, as a temptation by the Sirens:

> "Tuttavia, perchè mo vergogna porte
> del tuo errore, e perchè altra volta,
> udendo le serene, sie più forte,
> pon giù il seme del piangere ed ascolta."
>
> (*Purg.* 31.43–46)[27]

Beatrice specifies the other-directed ideal of individual moral responsibility that separates saved Christian from heroic pagan.

At her advent in the Earthly Paradise, Beatrice arouses in Dante the feelings of a purified Dido, and with them a purified classical tradition assimilable to Christianity; this at the very moment

---

[27] See also *Purg.* 31.47–63. Compare, also, with Augustine, *Conf.* 7.21: "those tears of confession . . . that sacrifice of thine, a troubled spirit, a broken and contrite heart . . . the Spouse, the city, the earnest of the Holy Ghost, the Cup of our Redemption."

when Vergil, the highest spokesman of that tradition, can himself go no farther. For Dante, the undifferentiated power of love must be firmly objectified as the acknowledgment of the self's inadequacy in the face of the beloved's reality, so that the lover himself may be reborn on a higher plane. Then the lover may comprehend the entire creation, and through it, ascend to God: *la vita nuova*. Hence the confrontation of Dante and Beatrice, his confession, and the conversion that allows him to see Christ incarnate in her and feel himself truly happy. "Quanti dolci pensier, quanto disio" (*Inf.* 5.113): it is the desire for a fully significant "other" that embraces the universal through the particular, that re-creates—not obliterates—the self and "il dolce mondo" in a more permanent form. This desire, first strongly awakened by Francesca's tragedy, finds its fulfillment in the person of Beatrice.

Spenser

The work of Spenser, the English Vergil, takes us the final step within the tradition of epic toward that disciplined release of the *Aeneid*'s constrained erotic energy that is Shakespeare's *Antony and Cleopatra*. The epic poet of England's growing sense of imperial mission, Spenser was also the self-conscious heir to the great and multifaceted medieval genre of romance—to the French romances, to Chaucer, to Malory's *Morte d'Arthur*, and to the modern Italian strain of Ariosto. Too, he was the poet of a formidable female monarch, and praising and instructing her entailed especially delicate treatments of interrelated problems of hierarchy, literary genre and style, and love. His many imitations of the *Aeneid* ought not be examined in the strictest formal terms, but rather in the context of a pervasive stylistic and thematic loosening of the severity of the classical genre of epic to suit a more freely creative age.[28] His de-

---

[28] Josephine Waters Bennett, *The Evolution of "The Faerie Queene,"* remains a good guide to the English and Ariostan sources of the work; C. S. Lewis, *The Allegory of Love*, to its place within the broad tradition of the romantic epic. Merritt Y. Hughes, "Virgil and Spenser," both exhaustively documents Spenser's precise linguistic and stylistic imitations of Vergil and broadly acknowledges certain interpretative principles that would have guided Spenser's imitations. However, most of Hughes's comparisons are invidious to Spenser, and he does not therefore offer a coherent exposition of Spenser's transvaluations of the *Aeneid*.

fense of his artistic practice in *The Faerie Queene* is worth citing in
full as a prelude to a detailed discussion of his work:

> The rugged forhead that with graue foresight
>   Welds kingdomes causes, and affaires of state,
>   My looser rimes (I wote) doth sharply wite,
>   For praising loue, as I haue done of late,
>   And magnifying louers deare debate;
>   By which fraile youth is oft to follie led,
>   Through false allurement of that pleasing baite,
>   That better were in vertues discipled,
> Then with vaine poemes weeds to haue their fancies fed.
>
> Such ones ill iudge of loue, that cannot loue,
>   Ne in their frosen hearts feele kindly flame:
>   For thy they ought not thing vnknowne reproue,
>   Ne naturall affection faultlesse blame,
>   For fault of few that haue abusd the same.
>   For it of honor and all vertue is
>   The roote, and brings forth glorious flowres of fame,
>   That crowne true louers with immortall blis,
> The meed of them that loue, and do not liue amisse.
>
> Which who so list looke backe to former ages,
>   And call to count the things that then were donne,
>   Shall find, that all the workes of those wise sages,
>   And braue exploits which great Heroes wonne,
>   In loue were either ended or begunne:
>   Witnesse the father of Philosophie,
>   Which to his *Critias*, shaded oft from sunne,
>   Of loue full manie lessons did apply,
> The which these Stoicke censours cannot well deny.
>
> To such therefore I do not sing at all,
>   But to that sacred Saint my soueraigne Queene,
>   In whose chast breast all bountie naturall,
>   And treasures of true loue enlocked beene,
>   Boue all her sexe that euer yet was seene;
>   To her I sing of loue, that loueth best,
>   And best is lou'd of all aliue I weene:
>   To her this song most fitly is addrest,
> The Queene of loue, and Prince of peace from heauen blest.
>
> Which that she may the better deigne to heare,
>   Do thou dred infant, *Venus* dearling doue,
>   From her high spirit chase imperious feare,

> And vse of awfull Maiestie romoue:
> In sted thereof with drops of melting loue,
> Deawd with ambrosiall kisses, by thee gotten
> From thy sweete smyling mother from aboue,
> Sprinkle her heart, and haughtie courage soften,
> That she may hearke to loue, and read this lesson often.
>
> (FQ 4. proem 1–5)[29]

In the first stanza Spenser establishes the Stoic moralist's "choice" between virtue and vice, statecraft and amorous dalliance. Through it he suggests as well generic and stylistic distinctions between epic and those "looser rimes" (looser prosodically and morally) of love poetry, including pastoral. These should presumably be cast aside with age and maturity. But in the following stanzas he explodes this distinction, arguing instead the organic outgrowth of epic deeds from proper love, and citing, against his Stoic critics, the authority of Plato. He thus implicitly provides us with a viewpoint for studying his own very Vergilian poetic progression from eclogues to epic,[30] and for understanding his practice of embedding, at the metaphorical and structural centers of his epic poem, pastoral interludes and a thematic preoccupation with love as the source and end of epic activity.

In the final stanzas of the Proem he sings to Elizabeth herself as the typological repository of this constructive erotic energy. A "sacred Saint" who is both "Queene of loue, and Prince of peace from heauen blest," she is urged to see herself as the androgynous vehicle of both secular and religious grace to her people. The concluding stanza hints, in ways instructive for a comparison of Belphoebe and Britomart, that she is in danger of being frozen by the opinion of the Stoic critic and must be mollified by a sacred Venus.

---

[29] I cite *Spenser: Poetical Works*, ed. J. C. Smith and E. de Selincourt, throughout.

[30] E. K., the commentator on *The Shepheardes Calender*, applies the Renaissance commonplace to Spenser's developing poetic vocation, "Which moued him rather in Æglogues, then other wise to write, doubting perhaps his habilitie, which he little needed, or mynding to furnish our tongue with this kinde, wherein it faulteth, or following the example of the best and most auncient Poetes, which deuised this kind of wryting, being both so base for the matter, and homely for the manner, at the first to trye theyr habilities" ("Epistle . . . to Gabriel Harvey," *Spenser: Poetical Works*, p. 418).

The Proem thus establishes the central theme of Spenser's poem as the specification of the right kind of love to motivate epic deeds. The reader, though here specifically Elizabeth, is urged to form a right imagination to receive the poem's message and transmute it from aesthetic experience to virtuous action.[31]

Spenser concludes his "Aprill" eclogue in *The Shepheardes Calender* with a pair of emblems that seem to crown with Vergilian authority the poet Colin's celebration of "fayre *Eliza*, Queene of shepheardes all." Queries Thenot, "*O quam te memorem virgo?*" ("O what shall I call you, how shall I memorialize you, virgin?"), to which Hobbinol replies, "*O dea certe*" ("Certainly, a goddess"). This appropriation of a Vergilian text alludes to a problem that underlies the rejoicing, a problem Spenser develops throughout the *Calender*. For the lines originally form part of the shipwrecked Aeneas's wondering address to his disguised mother, Venus, whom he encounters dressed in Diana-like huntress' garb in the woods outside Carthage (*Aen.* 1.314–417). They capture in miniature the paradoxes that inform the subsequent relationship between Aeneas and Dido, and they epitomize the *Aeneid*'s epic argument for the firm control that one must exert over the irrational energies that fuel change. To Vergil and his iconographically conscious imitators, Diana did contain a Venus.[32] Beauty and the emotional movement it arouses cannot be held at a contemplative distance but must be loved, reached for, embraced in the world, though often at heavy cost.

In the *Aeneid* Venus eludes her son's grasp; her evanescence becomes a symbol for the pressure of mutability on mortals, which

---

[31] Both Thomas Roche, *The Kindly Flame*, and Harry Berger, Jr., *The Allegorical Temper*, implicitly recognize the central place of a properly defined erotic energy in *The Faerie Queene*, Roche by studying the central themes of Books 3 and 4; and Berger by analyzing the inadequacies of the classically temperate Guyon as a guide to our responses in Book 2, and the epiphanic recognition of Spenser's central erotic theme at the Bower of Bliss. Crucial, too, is the insistence of Paul Alpers, *The Poetry of "The Faerie Queene,"* that the reader is always involved in the creation of the meaning of the poem. This rhetorical approach is triumphantly developed by Isabel MacCaffrey in *Spenser's Allegory*; she proposes that *The Faerie Queene* is "at once a treatise upon, and a dazzling instance of, the central role that imagination plays in human life" (pp. 6–7).

[32] Edgar Wind, *Pagan Mysteries in the Renaissance*, especially chaps. 4 and 5.

there leads to the strictest channeling and sublimation of desire into collective destiny.[33] In contrast, Spenser was eager to embrace Venus, though in appropriately refined and chastened forms. The precise nature of his sublimation of eros is figured through the increasing prominence and positive value assigned to women in his poems, even to making them, in his centrally dramatized subject, Britomart, and his omnipresent object, Elizabeth, the ruling consciousness of his epic poem. This argument requires us to first examine aspects of *The Shepheardes Calender*.

Love of a woman, which creates the problem in the *Calender*, also implies a solution, which in turn suggests why and how pastoral is incorporated into the epic texture of *The Faerie Queene*. This pastoral functions as a most thoughtful poetic apprenticeship: indeed, it can be read as a caution against the premature writing of epic. At two obvious, roughly symmetrical points, the "Aprill" and the "October" eclogues, the poem strains toward epic statement, toward celebrating Elizabeth. Both eclogues, however, are firmly contained, seriously qualified, by the prior need of the principal shepherd poet, Colin, to control the seemingly destructive force of his particular unrequited love for Rosalind.

In the "Aprill" eclogue Hobbinol's performance of Colin's reverent, lovely, and dignified "laye / Of fayre *Eliza*, Queene of shepheardes all" is dramatically enclosed by his discussion with Thenot of the damage love has since wreaked on Colin's pastoral calling:

> Shepheards delights he dooth them all forsweare,
> Hys pleasaunt Pipe, whych made vs meriment,
> He wylfully hath broke, and doth forbeare
> His wonted songs, wherein he all outwent.
>
> ("Aprill," 13–16)

The celebratory moment is retrospective, shadowed by Colin's present situation. Similarly, when Piers in "October" urges Cuddie to assume Colin's abandoned high poetic vocation, and sing of "fayre *Elisa*" or "the worthy whome shee loueth best" (47), we are at first tempted to say that Colin has already performed the task. Tempted,

---

[33] The frustrated embrace also characterizes Aeneas's effort to clasp the apparition of Creusa (2.792–94) and the shade of his father (6.770–72).

that is, until we realize that love has made him repudiate and abandon the effort. Nor can Cuddie assume it. He imagines that he might succeed, if flown with the *furor* of wine, but this passion quickly passes, and the pervasive debate of the *Calender* resumes: can love do other than destroy?

> CUDDIE: For *Colin* fittes such famous flight to scanne:
> He, were he not with loue so ill bedight,
> Would mount as high, and sing as soote as Swanne.

> PIERS: Ah fon, for loue does teach him climbe so hie,
> And lyftes him vp out of the loathsome myre:
> Such immortall mirrhor, as he doth admire,
> Would rayse ones mynd aboue the starry skie.
> And cause a caytiue corage to aspire,
> For lofty loue doth loath a lowly eye.

> CUDDIE: All otherwise the state of Poet stands,
> For lordly loue is such a Tyranne fell:
> That where he rules, all power he doth expell.
> The vaunted verse a vacant head demaundes,
> Ne wont with crabbed care the Muses dwell.
> Vnwisely weaues, that takes two webbes in hand.
> ("October," 88–102)

Even these two epic moments in the *Calender* direct us to its pastoral elegiac frame, to the Colin we see in "Janvarye" and "December." Here the pastoral poet is so overcome by love that he neglects his sheep, his leader's social responsibility to the other shepherds, and his celebratory art, to become trapped in the downward spiral of the seasons: "Winter is come, that blowes the balefull breath, / And after Winter commeth timely death" ("December," 149–50).

The strength of the feeling aroused by love exposes the limits of the natural pastoral world at the same time that the transience of love's human subjects embeds them within nature. Love makes us conscious of death; it lifts us above the temporal only to sharpen the cutting edge: *et in Arcadia ego*.[34] By his critical positioning of the lay of Eliza within the *Calender* Spenser implicitly raises a question about this type of complimentary poetry: isn't its object too

---

[34] On the elegiac tradition of *et in Arcadia ego*, see Erwin Panofsky, *Meaning in the Visual Arts*, chap. 7.

coolly, virginally, removed from the central stresses of human life, the subject of too precise an act of poetic calculation? Rosalind destroys any such possible poetic complacency in Colin; at the same time, she poisons his world.

If Colin as a character within the *Calender* does not escape the tragic predicament of a supernatural aspiration tied to mortal means, his pastoral elegy to Dido in "November" does demonstrate a successful exercise of the transforming imagination upon the very materials of nature. It becomes a model for the embodiment of pastoral, rightly understood, as the root of epic activity in *The Faerie Queene*. Spenser's choice of the name of Vergil's tragic heroine not only deepens the pathos of the elegy but also indirectly echoes the Vergilian paradox embedded in the previously hymned Elisa of "Aprill."

Elisa-Eliza suggests a pastoral Queen Elizabeth, "Yclad in Scarlot like a mayden Queene" ("Aprill," 57). And Elissa is an alternate name for Dido in the *Aeneid*. The original Elissa was a legendary Phoenician queen, renowned for chaste widowhood; but Vergil, to the outrage of many classical, medieval, and Renaissance commentators of an historical or moralistic bent, appropriated her name for his passionate queen.[35] For Dido to embody fully the fall of a former ideal of civilization, she had to be a figure of the greatest probity, a Dido-Elissa, not merely Apollonius's or Euripides' Medea. The immense pathos of Dido's situation derives from the tension generated by the Venus-within-Diana, the intense human longings beneath the cool facade of a woman required to act like a man, drawn toward a sensitive man whose historical situation precludes him from acting like one.

When Colin hymned Elisa in the days before he met Rosalind, he praised her as the epitome of virginal ordering and restraint, the Belphoebe figure of the *Calender*:

> Ye shepheards daughters, that dwell on the greene,
>   hye you there apace:

---

[35] For the alternate tradition of "widow Dido," see D. C. Allen, "Marlowe's *Dido* and the Tradition." Paul E. McLane further documents the Elisa-Dido connection in *Spenser's "Shepheardes Calender,"* pp. 52–53. He also presses for identification of both Eliza and Dido with Queen Elizabeth, an argument that supports my thematic analysis of the *Calender* and later discussion of the ambivalence of Belphoebe.

> Let none come there, but that Virgins bene,
>> to adorne her grace.
> And when you come, whereas shee is in place,
> See, that your rudenesse doe not you disgrace:
>> Binde your fillets faste,
>> And gird in your waste,
> For more finesse, with a tawdrie lace.
>
> ("Aprill," 127–35)

The calm public admiration is disrupted by the immediacy of his tragic personal love for Rosalind. His elegy for "my deare" (58) Dido may be read as an attempt to fuse these two attitudes, and, in the process, to sublimate the energies of love into imagination so as to transmute pastoral into "something of great constancy." This heartfelt poem about the death of Dido, "the greate shepehearde his daughter sheene" (38), is also "about his own dashed hopes, about Rosalind, about the breaking of human desire and the futility of action in a world borne down upon by death, decay, and suffering."[36] It achieves its refrain's reversal—"O carefull verse" becomes "O ioyfull verse"—by confronting, rather than denying, these facts and the pain they cause.

    The poem dwells on the dead weight, the brute fact of Dido's body become the body of dead nature:

> For what might be in earthlie mould,
> That did her buried body hould,
>> O heauie herse.
> Yet saw I on the beare when it was brought
>> O carefull verse.
>
> (158–62)

The verse *in-corporates* this weight (it is "carefull," full of care, bearing in rhyme the "herse"); then, in its ordered, rhythmic, careful attention, transubstantiates it:

> But maugre death, and dreaded sisters deadly spight,
>> And gates of hel, and fyrie furies forse:
> She hath the bonds broke of eternall night,

---

[36] Theresa Krier, "The Lineaments of Desire," p. 13.

Her soule vnbodied of the burdenous corpse.
Why then weepes Lobbin so without remorse?
  O Lobb, thy losse no longer lament,
  Dido nis dead, but into heauen hent.
    O happy herse,
Cease now my Muse, now cease thy sorrowes sourse,
    O ioyful verse.

(163–72)

Dido is at once a human subject of love and death, and through them made immortal and the secure "sourse" of the poet's celebratory verse.

The "November" eclogue proves insufficient to transubstantiate the *Calender* as a whole, which ends on a note of frustrated desire for Rosalind that causes Colin to hang his pipe on a tree and mournfully face death. Yet Spenser does not follow the Stoic course and condemn love as essentially a distraction from epic deeds. Throughout *The Faerie Queene* he seeks to establish the positive value of the heart's desire, rooted in an intensely particular love, but translatable to the enlarged contexts of social responsibility and, finally, permanence in and through mutability.

In that central pastoral within the epic, Book 6 of *The Faerie Queene*, a revived Colin pipes alone to his dear love, whose significance he is nonetheless able to translate to Calidore and to us as the public poetry of mythology and compliment (6.10.1–31). His apology to Gloriana, while explaining that his personal vision is fixed on a "poore handmayd," also stresses the visual parallel between this "fairy ring" and the courtly circle of courtesy flowing from Elizabeth in the proem to Book 6:

Then pardon me, most dreaded Soueraine,
  That from your selfe I doe this vertue bring,
  And to your selfe doe it returne againe:
  So from the Ocean all riuers spring,
  And tribute backe repay as to their King.
  Right so from you all goodly vertues well
  Into the rest, which round about you ring,
  Faire Lords and Ladies, which about you dwell,
And doe adorne your Court, where courtesies excell.

(stanza 7)

We are thus reminded that the Queen is the public symbol who unites our various individual sources of inspiration. Within the neo-Platonic and Tudor Protestant context of *The Fairie Queene*, these linked moments are the equivalent in intensity and extension to Dante's encounter with Beatrice in the Earthly Paradise, where she is the focus of all figuralism in the poem, at once absolutely concrete, " 'Io sono, io sono Beatrice,' " and his vision of the incarnate Christ. Both poems require that we, in turn, place our own heart's desire at these centers, and extend them to their poetic peripheries, and if possible, beyond.

Yet if the end of *The Faerie Queene* is the formation of a supple, disciplined, and comprehensive imagination in us, akin to Sidney's "erected wit,"[37] that aim is focused, as the proem to Book 4 hints, in the formation of the imagination of the head of society, Elizabeth herself. In addition to her invoked presence, she is explicitly figured twice in the poem:

> Ne let his fairest *Cynthia* refuse,
> In mirrours more then one her selfe to see,
> But either *Gloriana* let her chuse,
> Or in *Belphœbe* fashioned to bee:
> In th'one her rule, in th'other her rare chastitee.
>
> (3.proem 5)[38]

As Gloriana she governs Cleopolis and is the object of Arthur's love quest, although in the unfinished poem she never appears directly. As Belphoebe, however, she is present in Books 2, 3, and 4 in ways that stress her Vergilian dignity yet also suggest the importance Spenser placed on enlarging the definition of chastity to include the kindly flame of love. Although Belphoebe clearly evokes the mythic archetype of Diana so dear to Elizabeth, even this alabaster figure is molded and warmed by a Venereal ener-

---

[37] MacCaffrey, *Spenser's Allegory*, pp. 13–22.

[38] See also Spenser's "Letter to Raleigh." Thomas H. Cain, *Praise in "The Faerie Queene,"* disagrees with my claim that Elizabeth, the source of praise in the poem, may also be the object of its education (p. 5). However, his analysis of Belphoebe differs at several points from mine, and he does not consider her problematic relationship with Timias.

gy that if denied will reemerge in dangerously distorted forms.

Belphoebe's first numinous appearance in the poem (2.3), an obvious imitation of two passages in the *Aeneid*, implies a susceptibility to love beneath her imperial exterior.[39] The whole incident is couched as another Spenserian imitation of Aeneas encountering Venus disguised as a Diana-like huntress. The reminiscence both exalts and eroticizes Belphoebe, hinting at the possibility of a Venus with this Diana-like exterior, even while the comic vulgarity of Braggadocchio's grasp highlights the problem of proper responses to this divinely attractive power. Within the incident, the simile of stanza 31 fuses Vergil's simile of the triumphant, Diana-like Dido with his description of the picture of the Amazon, Penthesilea, on the wall of the temple of Juno at Carthage:

> Such as *Diana* by the sandie shore
>   Of swift *Eurotas,* or on *Cynthus* greene,
>   Where all the Nymphes haue her vnwares forlore,
>   Wandreth alone with bow and arrowes keene,
>   To seeke her game: Or as that famous Queene
>   Of *Amazons,* whom *Pyrrhus* did destroy,
>   The day that first of *Priame* she was seene,
>   Did shew her selfe in great triumphant ioy,
> To succour the weake state of sad afflicted *Troy.*
>
> (2.3.31)

> qualis in Eurotae ripis aut per iuga Cynthi
> exercet Diana choros, quam mille secutae
> hinc atque hinc glomerantur Oreades; illa pharetram
> fert umero gradiensque deas supereminet omnis;
> Latonae tacitum pertemptant gaudia pectus.
>
> (*Aen.* 1.498–502)

(Even as on Eurotas' banks or along the heights of Cynthus Diana guides her dancing bands, in whose train a thousand Oreads troop to right and left; she bears a quiver on her shoulder, and as she treads overtops all the goddesses; joys thrill Latona's silent breast.)

---

[39] Compare my analysis with Berger, *Allegorical Temper,* chaps. 5–7; and Cain, *Praise,* pp. 86–91.

Penthesilea furens mediisque in milibus ardet,
aurea subnectens exsertae cingula mammae,
bellatrix, audetque viris concurrere virgo.

(*Aen.* 1.491–93)

(Penthesilea in fury leads the crescent-shielded ranks of the
Amazons and rages amid her thousands; a golden belt binds
her naked breast, while she, a warrior queen, dares battle, a
maid clashing with men.)

As Vergil suggests that Dido's bondage to love is a recapitulation of
the fall of Troy, Spenser first shows Belphoebe heroically impressive
and then tragically vulnerable.

Indeed, the effect of this entire description of her and her action is a confusing intermingling of awed detachment and sexual
attraction. Many of her features in the traditional blazon are deliberately heightened to the godly or the architectural proportions
appropriate to a description of a virgin queen: her cheeks breathe
healing odors; her eyes are filled with "dredd Maiestie, and awfull
ire"; her "iuorie forhead, full of bountie braue, / Like a broad table
did it selfe dispred"; her words were like "heauenly musicke"; her
face a "glorious mirrhour of celestiall grace"; her legs "Like two
faire marble pillours." At the same time, her broad forehead is
declared fit "For Loue his loftie triumphes to engraue," and we are
encouraged to let our eyes linger on her buskined legs, on the curious folds of her clothes near which, were her legs "pillours," gar-
lands would hang, and on "Her daintie paps; which like young fruit
in May / Now little gan to swell, and being tide, / Through her thin
weed their places only signifide" (22–30). Braggadocchio's response,
grabbing at her even while she is telling him about the dangers of
pleasure, is only an exaggerated version of our own.

The nature of Belphoebe in this first abrupt introduction is
presented, through Braggadocchio, chiefly as a matter of reader
response. Within the strategy of Book 2 it offers a special problem
of temperance, the need for a finely developed tact, an appropriately
warm and yet refined attitude of compliment toward majesty. In
Book 3, in which her encounter with Timias is set forth within the
context of Britomart's feminized epic quest, the focus of our attention shifts from the correct response to her, which the honorable
Timias so obviously offers, to the propriety of her attitudes toward
him. In Book 2, canto 3 we saw and heard her; in Book 3, canto 5.

we are privileged with her states of mind and feeling. Belphoebe is both a vehicle of healing energy, of divine grace,[40] and fully human, subject to change and development through the mysterious powers of love. We first find her in chase,

> Of some wild beast, which with her arrowes keene
> She wounded had, the same along did trace
> By tract of bloud, which she had freshly seene,
> To haue besprinkled all the grassy greene;
> By the great persue, which she there perceau'd,
> Well hoped she the beast engor'd had beene,
> And made more hast, the life to haue bereau'd.
>
> (3.5.28)

She glories in the hunt with a pure, Artemisian cruelty—"But ah, her expectation greatly was deceau'd," for the bloody trail leads her to the severely wounded Timias. Suddenly she is not like Diana, able to reduce her unwitting admirer Actaeon to a hunted beast. Instead she responds with human horror, and then, blushing, with something milder: "Full of soft passion and vnwonted smart: / The point of pitty perced through her tender hart" (3.5.30). She is wounded, too. The remaining intermittent accounts of the relationship of Belphoebe and Timias treat the yet more delicate problem of how a

---

[40] The narrator says of her advent:

> Prouidence heauenly passeth liuing thought,
> And doth for wretched mens reliefe make way;
> For loe great grace or fortune thither brought
> Comfort to him, that comfortlesse now lay.
>
> (3.5.27)

And Timias, seeing "The goodly Mayd full of diuinities, / And gifts of heauenly grace," exclaims:

> Mercy deare Lord (said he) what grace is this,
> That thou hast shewed to me sinfull wight,
> To send thine Angell from her bowre of blis,
> To comfort me in my distressed plight?
> Angell, or Goddesse do I call thee right?
> What seruice may I do vnto thee meete,
> That hast from darkenesse me returnd to light,
> And with thy heauenly salues and med'cines sweete,
> Hast drest my sinfull wounds? I kisse thy blessed feete.
>
> (3.5.35)

monarch is to respond to her subject's tenders of affection to herself and transfers of affection to other people, especially when she is the wellspring of that ability to love. Belphoebe discovers, as does the Faerie Queene Titania in Shakespeare's *A Midsummer Night's Dream*, that although she may be in some sense above the affairs of mortals, she is not above a concern and responsibility for them.

The point is made as well in the myths of Belphoebe's birth and upbringing. The very infrequency, aloofness, and allusive weight of her appearances in *The Faerie Queene* strengthen our sense of her as an archetype of virginal chastity, the most "pure" human state, and therefore a seemingly unconditional tribute to Elizabeth.[41] However, Belphoebe and her twin Amoret either represent complementary versions of human virtue or, in the seeming conflict of the one's virginity and the other's sexuality, image the eternal strife of these principles. The account of their mother's impregnation and their birth, adoption, and upbringing argues the possibility of an imaginative concord of such seeming opposites.[42]

The virginal conception and the birth are described in language that smoothly conflates natural and supernatural explanations, audaciously juxtaposing classical and Christian myths. Unlike the classical tale of Leda and the swan, on which this episode is largely based, Chrysogonee bears only one set of twins. Will they be like Helen and Clytemnestra, archetypes of social discord, or like Castor and Pollux, emblems of enduring friendship? Spenser thus establishes one mythological nexus for his eventual enlargement of the theme of chaste love and the individual (Book 3) to the theme of concordant nature and society (Book 4).[43] The implication is that

---

[41] But see Mark Rose, *Heroic Love*, who argues that for Protestant Elizabethans married love had largely supplanted virginity as the ideal human state.

[42] Roche, *Kindly Flame*, pp. 96–116.

[43] See Wind, *Pagan Mysteries*, pp. 167–69, on Leonardo's "Leda." Spenser further explores this dual potential for discord or concord in his versions of the myth of Troy; cf. the contrasts between Britomart's heroic conception of her ancestry and love quest and Paridell's comic debasement of the fall of Ilium (2.9–10), or between Cambina and Ate (4.3), or between the true and the false Florimell (4 passim). (See Roche, *Kindly Flame*, pp. 62–66, 23–30, and 152–67, on these episodes.) In each case, Spenser acknowledges the risks of exploitation and conflict but suggests the possibility of loyal and selfless marital and societal bonds.

the twins will, over time, be complementary, not conflicting, images. Venus and Diana themselves come to a rare concordance before each taking one child to rear (3.6.11–12). And Belphoebe retains her genetic bond with Amoret, the exemplar of chaste wifehood in the poem, and through her is linked to the realms of generated things and the circles of social intercourse that she, a virgin, seemingly renounces. Even her archetypal chaste virginity must imaginatively contain the other evolutionary stages in female identity: lover, wife, mother, matriarch. Subtly, Spenser aims this arrow at Elizabeth, too:

> Do thou dred infant, *Venus* dearling doue,
> From her high spirit chase imperious feare,
> And vse of awfull Maiestie romoue:
> In sted thereof with drops of melting loue,
> Deawd with ambrosiall kisses, by thee gotten
> From thy sweete smyling mother from aboue,
> Sprinckle her heart, and haughtie courage soften,
> That she may hearke to loue, and read this lesson often.
>
> (4.proem 5)[44]

Finally, however, the problem of the testing and transformation of love is most thoroughly and engagingly traced in Britomart. Here the central epideictic role played by Elizabeth in the epic impels Spenser to chart, as the consciousness of a woman, the unfolding of imagination itself as it strives to embrace larger and larger worlds of experience, to move from a defensive virginity to an affirmation of its synthesizing powers. With great delicacy Spenser depicts Britomart's scruples as she finds her virginal self-sufficiency broken, finds herself "buxome" and "prone" to love (3.2.23), yet questioning the worthiness of her love object and her own motives in seeking it.

Her dilemma is symbolized by the magic looking glass in which she first sees her love Arthegall, for it is actually a little world that tests the imaginative capacity of the beholder:

---

[44] Both Erwin Panofsky, *Studies in Iconology*, pp. 129–69 and Wind, *Pagan Mysteries*, pp. 113–51, discuss the two Venuses, two neo-Platonic forms of chastened love—*amore celeste* and *amore humano*—existing above the purely sensual *amore bestiale*. These two correspond well to the complementary ideals of Belphoebe and Amoret; Elizabeth, who in the proem to Book 4 is entreated to feel the *amore celeste* inspired by Venus Urania, may still, through this softening, engage in sympathetic converse with the votaries of *amore humano*.

It vertue had, to shew in perfect sight,
What euer thing was in the world contaynd,
Betwixt the lowest earth and heauens hight,
So that it to the looker appertaynd;

. . . .

For thy it round and hollow shaped was,
Like to the world it selfe, and seem'd a world of glas.
(3.2.19)

The key phrase here is "So that it to the looker appertaynd." The glass can function as a mirror, narcissistically reflecting a self-image, or it can, in the Pauline language Spenser employs in the proem to Book 6, be the glass through which we see darkly. It can contain a world of possibility, a complete making other of the beholder, provided she has the personal strength and endurance to comprehend it.[45]

When Britomart, musing in general on her future husband, first sees Arthegall within the looking glass, her imagination yearns toward him, but fearfully, leaving her prey to nightmares and phantasms (3.2.29,39). Her love seems a tragic passion, a crime that Glauce's superstitious pagan charms cannot cure. In another instance of the Venus-within-a-Diana paradox, Spenser combines the passionate Scylla and the chaste Britomartis from his source, the pseudo-Vergilian *Ciris*.[46] The well-meaning but shortsighted Glauce, whose character type derives ultimately from the nurse-confidant of Euripidean drama, of which Vergil's Anna is another example, cannot resolve this paradox for Britomart. Indeed Glauce's ineffective exorcism (3.2.49–52) recalls the rites of the Massylian priestess (*Aen.* 4.478–521) that precede Dido's desperate suicide. Spenser fully evokes classical love tragedy before channeling this erotic energy into his British and Christian providential epic quest.

However, Spenser figures this passion as a painful stage in a growth toward sweet fruition (3.2.17). Fusing the love *furor* of Dido, and the Euripidean women on whom she is modeled, with an appropriately lightened version of Aeneas's underworld vision, he has Merlin offer Britomart the first assurance that this wracking

---

[45] For a discussion of the ambivalent properties of the mirror, see Goldin, *Mirror*, pp. 1–19.

[46] Roche, *Kindly Flame*, pp. 53–55; Rose, *Heroic Love*, pp. 94–96.

sensation has as its end a glorious historical order, provided she
will make her imaginings real through continued, disciplined effort.
The imagery of the entire episode strongly suggests Sidney's distinction between phantastic and eikastic art in the "Apology for Poetry."[47] The test of the quality of Britomart's imaginings will be
the difficult *praxis* she accomplishes as she first comprehends her
severe male "other," Arthegall, and beyond him envelops, sub-
limates, personal happiness in the history of their race, to create a
world, the idealized world of the Tudor myth.[48] Assuring her that
this hard beginning is a sign of the worth of her enterprise, Merlin
enlarges the figure of growth to the epic simile of the great tree,
uniting earth and heaven, past and future, "antique Peres" of Troy
and Greece and the "famous Progenie" of Spenser's own day
(3.3.22).

Britomart's feminine epic quest differs pervasively in tone
from its Vergilian model. Most basically, the Christian and neo-
Platonic background of *The Faerie Queene* not only assures us of
an ultimate order but also reveals it as love, rather than imposing
it as authority.[49] One need only contrast the amusingly archaic
fairy-tale terrors that surround Merlin with the real horror of
Aeneas's descent; Spenser, tongue in cheek, warns "dare thou not,
I charge, in any cace, / To enter into that same balefull Bowre, /
For fear the cruell Feends should thee vnwares deuowre" (3.3.8).[50]
In the *Aeneid*, the Apollonian Sibyl is raped by the god, her distorted and constrained body a most powerful image of change as

---

[47] Compare Britomart's debate with Glauce, 3.2.30–45, especially 38 and
44, with Sidney, *An Apology for Poetry*, pp. 125–26, or with Sidney's ultimate
source, Plato's *Sophist*.

[48] For the Tudor myth, see Yates, *Astraea*, pp. 29–120.

[49] Greene, *Descent from Heaven*, examines the heavenly messengers' descents as a key to their value structures; in *FQ* 2.8.1–2 the question "And
is there care in heauen?" yields to faith ("There is") and to the recognition
that God's messengers come "to succour vs, that succour want"; and ends
on a note of reverent amazement: "And all for loue, and nothing for reward: /
O why should heauenly God to men haue such regard?"

[50] Spenser's tenderness and wry humor, often the product of self-conscious
archaism, have only recently again become appreciated. The effect here is
similar to that of *FQ* 1.1.37, when Archimago's menace is momentarily heightened and then undercut by comic overstatement, in a manner presaging his
later comic decline.

suffered violence; Merlin, in contrast, prefaces his serious prophecy with benevolent laughter (3.2.19). Finally, Britomart herself can do more than endure as the vehicle of history; she can imaginatively shape it. Fired by Paridell's listless account of Troy's "fatal" fall and Aeneas's "constrained" marriage, she hymns her own prophecy to heroic Troynovant, product of Brute's expansive mind, "So huge a mind could not in lesser rest, / Ne in small meares containe his glory great" (3.9.46).[51]

Nor is Britomart's sexuality constrained by her historic mission; rather, it is expressive of it, as she acts to transcend the restraining courtly conventions of Spenser's day—her self-indulgent lament by the seashore, Amoret's courtly frigidity, Arthegall's emasculating idolatry of women, her own embittering jealousy—to create a reciprocal marriage.[52] Her sensitivity to love is given historical depth and direction by Merlin's prophecy and Paridell's reminiscence, and she employs this combined tact and power to free Amoret and befriend both men and women. Talus's news of Arthegall's bondage to Radigund finds Britomart in "loue-sicke fancies" and provokes her to selfish rage (5.6.3–15), but her watchful victory over the vengeful Dolon (25, 27), recalling Christ's agony in the Garden of Gethsemane, conquers her own bitter spirit with resurgent love. At Isis Church an ascetic worship (5.7.9–10) yields to a potent and threatening dream as Britomart imagines the white-robed, moon-crowned image of the goddess transfigured to herself, red-robed and golden-crowned. She is threatened by the burning temple and a rapacious crocodile, which she subdues only to be impregnated by it, and to deliver a Lion of great might (5.7.12–17). However, the priests assure her that this erotic dream signifies her dynastic reenaction of the myth of Isis and Osiris.

Britomart then constructively employs her erotic energy as a chaste and faithful wife, rescuing her husband, tempering his justice with equity, securing their succession. Understanding this reciprocity through the dream vision enables her to free Arthegall, who is suffering under the masculine version of Busyrane's perverse

---

[51] Roche, *Kindly Flame*, pp. 62–66, aptly contrasts Paridell's degenerate account of Troy with Britomart's generative response.

[52] See Rose, *Heroic Love*, pp. 101–2 (Britomart at the seashore); 118–28 (the House of Busyrane); 103–9 (Arthegall's idolatry of women and capture by Radigund).

restraints. As Amoret was held captive by a courtly code that inhibits the consummation of her marriage, so Arthegall, who from his first encounter with Britomart (4.6.21,22) has been in danger of uncritically idolizing women, has fallen victim to an emasculating, pitifully perverted woman, Radigund.[53] He must be rescued by another woman, the fully-tested Britomart, whose understanding of love is not narcissistic, but joyous and procreative, self-sacrificing and socially responsible. Finally, then, Britomart's energies are directed toward fusing both parts of her nature as a *Venus armata* or a Venus-in-a-Diana, toward wedding feminine longing and masculine fulfillment, romance and epic, in an androgynous union.

From Renunciation to Accommodation

Augustine, Dante, and Spenser thus represent a series of interpretative attitudes toward the *Aeneid* and the classical past it epitomizes. From Augustine's rhythm of renunciation, to Dante's Vergilian pathos, to Spenser's syncretic accommodation, epic impelled by tragedy becomes epic contained by romance.

Augustine translates Dido's longing in the *Aeneid* into an autobiographical account of his undifferentiated need to love. But he faces the exhaustion, the devaluation, of those classically enshrined places and things in which to repose this love. Late classical culture itself, in its various seductive forms, becomes his Dido; he must make it spiritual. Neo-Platonism gives him the strength of mind to escape its powerful hold, but it cannot answer the passion of his will until it becomes incorporated, not as a place, but as a person, Christ. Augustine's recognition of the difficulty of sustaining and communi-

---

[53] Spenser may have derived the name *Radigund* from a French saint, one of whose "virtues" was her determined virginity within marriage; see Cain, *Praise*, pp. 153–54. Such a strained virginity (as opposed to chastity) within marriage to Spenser seemed the utmost perversity. His attitude is conveyed through the novellalike atmosphere of frustrated, warped desire that suffuses his account of Radigund. Rose, *Heroic Love*, p. 108, remarks "Allegorically, Radigund is Britomart herself in her role as Arthegall's mistress and lady," the cruel courtly lady who threatens to become the unnatural virgin within marriage. In Radigund, Britomart battles a potential version of herself; for her union with Arthegall to become truly reciprocal, they must transcend the sterile power politics of the courtly code.

cating metaphysical flight in turn modifies his ascetic renunciation of classical culture. Viewed critically, pagan culture still contains "liberal disciplines more suited to the uses of truth, and some most useful precepts concerning morals."[54] In *The City of God*, as we have seen, denunciations of the shortcomings of pagan culture mingle with exhortations to understand that cultural ideal in a better way.

Dante maintains a more delicate tragic equipoise in his treatment of Vergil. His allegiances to the Holy Roman Empire and the powers of human reason cause him to acknowledge the achievement of Roman culture, which he longs to accommodate to a spiritual dimension. The *Comedy* is everywhere fraught with those precise turnings of the human will that of "libito fe licito," and the poem's main theme is the education of his own will to an epic ideal that transcends the autonomy of the Homeric hero and the collective consciousness of the Vergilian hero through the confessional humility of the Christian hero. These discriminations lead to that excruciating moment in the Earthly Paradise when Dante is told not to weep for the departed Vergil, but "pianger . . . per altra spada" (*Purg.* 30.57); no *nostoi* must distract from the central issue of individual responsibility.

But Dante's concern for the pagan "gente di molto valore" (*Inf.* 4.44) who, through what appears to be historical or geographical accident, are suspended in Limbo, arises again in *Paradiso* 19 and 20. He is "answered" by the unfathomableness and inexpressibility of divine justice and the unexpected salvation of the Trojan Ripheus:

> *Regnum coelorum* vïolenza pate
> da caldo amore e da viva speranza,
> che vince la divina volontate;
> non a guisa che l'omo a l'om sobranza,
> ma vince lei perchè vuole esser vinta,
> e, vinta, vince con sua beninanza.
>
> (*Par.* 20.94–99)

---

[54] Augustine, *On Christian Doctrine*, 2.40. See Brown, *Augustine*, chaps. 11–16, on Augustine's initial resolve on a retired life of Christian *otium*, and his complex attitude toward his past and culture that led him to the difficult choice of an active pastoral career.

Dante, as he grew older, seems to have become even more concerned that "i'erri / anzi ad aprir ch'a tenerla serrata" (*Purg.* 9.127–28). Perhaps he yet hoped Vergil and many of his company might one day blaze their way to heaven with the ardor of their "antica fiamma."

Such loving appreciation for the aspirations of classical culture eventually yields those Renaissance arguments for a common tradition of *prisca theologia* underlying both classical and Christian traditions and explaining their many similarities.[55] This syncretic spirit informs every aspect of Spenser's *Faerie Queene*, from its radical mingling of fictive and historical worlds to the details of its richly encrusted allusions. As a result, Spenser's relationship to Vergil can be at once strongly imitative and fully free. His open aspiration to be the English Vergil must be understood as a pervasive adaptation to a Christian *imperium* of yet higher moral seriousness and more broadly tolerant historical consciousness. The alternating, often seemingly conflicting, tales of Troy's fall and its epic heritage incorporated into *The Faerie Queene* contribute to an evolving Christian English myth.

The shifting presentation of women perhaps supplies us with our closest index to the transvaluations of the *Aeneid* in these central works. Augustine seemingly leaves behind the Dido figures, the daughters of Eve; but they reappear in the exceedingly displaced forms of his sanctified mother and *Mater Ecclesia*. For Dante women can be the vehicles of salvation or damnation, depending on whether the poet's will is turned inward upon itself or outward to the creation. And Spenser's central figure of Britomart is androgynous, containing within herself a world waiting to be realized. Both male and female in impulse, Artemisian and Venereal, she makes this totality objective through her dynastic marriage to Arthegall. In the final movements of her quest to rescue him, she is both self-sacrificing Christ figure and human image of Isis, strenuously circumventing her husband's tragic *sparagmos*. She is a metaphor for the high Renaissance ideal of the artist as co-creator with God, and as such she triumphantly assimilates classical epic in romance. Her creativity toward her Trojan past and English future provides us with

---

[55] See Frances Yates, *Giordano Bruno and the Hermetic Tradition*, and see also D. P. Walker, *The Ancient Theology*.

the ideological, mythological, and generic background for Shakespeare's subsuming of classical tragedy in romantic tragicomedy, his *Antony and Cleopatra*. But before we document this achievement, we must trace the much more halting approach of Renaissance vernacular dramatists to the typologically linked stories of Aeneas and Dido, and Antony and Cleopatra.

III.

Renaissance Dramatic
Transvaluations

Things base and vile, holding no quantity,
Love can transpose to form and dignity.
(SHAKESPEARE, *A Midsummer Night's Dream*)

In this chapter we move from epic to heroic tragedy, arguing that certain Renaissance tragic dramas take epic poetry as their generic source and moral matrix. The principal epic in Renaissance tradition, Vergil's *Aeneid*, establishes subtle typological ties between its foreground tragedy, the story of Aeneas and Dido, and the historical event that occasioned its composition, the defeat of Antony and Cleopatra by Octavius Caesar at Actium. Our survey of Renaissance dramatic treatments of the story of Dido is intended to examine the degree to which vernacular authors evoke the complexity of Vergil's text. Furthermore, to what extent does Vergil's richly ambivalent story inform those Renaissance plays on Antony and Cleopatra whose immediate source was the Roman historiographical tradition, in particular the newly recovered *Lives* of Plutarch? Finally, in what ways are these imitations also thoughtful contemporary transvaluations of their classical matter?

Renaissance dramatists looked to the revered authority of Aristotle as sanction for the derivation of tragedy from epic. In the *Poetics* he declares, "in the serious style, Homer is pre-eminent among poets, for he alone combined dramatic form with excellence of imitation. . . . and the Epic poets were succeeded by Tragedians." Modern scholars are apt to construe such a statement as part of a more general argument for the mimetic supremacy of tragedy over epic.[1] However, Renaissance theorists often felt less obliged to speak consistently to Aristotle's meaning than to redefine his statements to serve their own aesthetic principles. In practice, Renaissance dramatists could simplify the conceptual and chronological difficulties of Aristotle's statement, arguing, as does Alessandro Pazzi de' Medici, that as the ancient tragedians took their subject matter predominantly from the Homeric epics, so the modern playwright should look to his appropriate heroic material as the source for tragedy. They debated extensively the choice of appropriate heroic subject matter and such attendant questions as the relative artistic possibility granted by a subject matter historical or fictive, near or distanced in time and sensibility.[2]

More subtly, the main lines of Renaissance critical theory and artistic practice ran athwart those of the *Poetics*. The concept of imitation was redefined in neo-Platonic terms so that the reality to be mimed was not Aristotle's biological and historical substance, but the realm of ideas, often with an overlay of Christian eschatology. This permitted an anti-Aristotelian tendency to praise epic, with its cultural amplitude framed by an explicit divine perspective, over tragedy. The resulting drama was largely ideological; the "soul" it inherited from its epic sources was not dramatic action, but the secondary Aristotelian "character," conveyed in rhetorical gestures.[3]

---

[1] Aristotle, *Poetics*, 48b34 (Butcher trans.). See Gerald F. Else, *Aristotle's Poetics*, pp. 142–49 for a modern interpretation of Aristotle's genetic and formal argument for the relationship of Homer's poems to emergent comedy and tragedy.

[2] See Pazzi, "Prefatione . . . nelle tragedie Dido in Carthagine et Iphigenia in Taurio," in *Le Tragedie Metriche*, pp. 46–47. Tasso is perhaps the central figure in this debate; see *Discorso dell'arte poetica* and *Discorsi del poema heroico*. See also Bernard Weinberg, *A History of Literary Criticism in the Italian Renaissance* 2:635–714, especially 646–53; and Baxter Hathaway, *The Age of Criticism*, especially pt. 2.

[3] Hathaway, *Age of Criticism* and *Marvels and Commonplaces*, substantiates these claims. More often than not, Renaissance critics reverse Aristotle's judgment (*Poetics* 26) that tragedy, with its tighter organic unity and advantages of music and spectacle, is a higher form of imitation than epic; they stress instead epic's amplitude and higher morality. See O. B. Hardison, Jr., *The Enduring Monument*, pp. 69–71; Marvin Herrick, "The Fusion of Horatian and Aristotelian Literary Criticism, 1531–1555," especially pp. 58–66. For the emphasis on rhetoric rather than action, see, for example, Giovambattista Giraldi Cinthio's central discussions of decorum, "sentenza," and "costume" in *Discorsi*, pp. 242–45, 259–76.

Stylized declamation and debate were used to import some of the epic tradition's breadth and explicit values into drama's narrowed formal focus.

As Homer's epics were to the Greeks, so the Bible and the *Aeneid* were to the culture of Christian Europe. But as a source of literary material the Bible presented unique problems to the Renaissance dramatist. The Scriptures were at once too sacred a text for fictional elaboration, yet also the subject of a popular drama from which the classicizing temperament of the age sought distance. Vergil's epic, in contrast, posed neither of these problems. The universally acknowledged literary classic of a vital Latin tradition, it addressed political, philosophical, and theological issues still central to the times. Through the tradition of the grammarians it was a model of style; through its formative influence on the Augustan myth and subsequent Roman historiography, a justification of empire; through the allegorizing commentaries of Servius and Macrobius an encyclopedic authority; through the Christian tradition of commentary, from Fulgentius to the twelfth-century Platonists to Christoforo Landino, a poem of the trials of the soul.[4] Nor were sensitive readers blind to its dialectical properties; several saw the text as a forum for debate between the rational and the passionate, a debate that had to be reproportioned, structured anew, to become accountable to the ideals of contemporary Christian culture.

The dialectical properties of the *Aeneid*, epitomized by the disturbing appeal of the story of Dido, eventually complicate the literary treatments of the history of Antony and Cleopatra as well. The two episodes are, of course, first typologically linked in the *Aeneid*, where the defeat of Antony and Cleopatra by Octavius occupies, in Book 8, the central position on Aeneas's prophetic shield. As Adam Parry observes:

> Aeneas' shield shows the future version of himself.
> But Aeneas is not just Augustus. There is also the possibility of his being Augustus' bitter enemy, Mark Antony. Such is the identification we are led to make when, in the fourth book, he has become the consort of Dido, queen of Carthage. Thus the contemptuous description of him by Iarbas, his rival for

---

[4] The theory and epic practice of Marco Girolamo Vida established the preeminent suitability of Vergilian epic to Christian contexts; see Di Cesare, *Vida's Christiad and Vergilian Epic*, and Vida, *De arte poetica*.

Dido's love, "that Paris with his effeminate retinue," closely matches the image of Antony and Cleopatra with their corrupt eastern armies which Augustus created for Roman morale.

And Dido is Cleopatra. When she is about to die, she is said to be *pale with imminent death, pallida morte futura*. Cleopatra, in her own person, is described on Aeneas' shield in Book 8 as *paling before imminent death, pallentem morte futura*.

("Two Voices," p. 73)

The effect of this typological relationship in the *Aeneid*, however, is less to foreshadow the climactic historical event than to diffuse it into broader areas of meaning. In the interval between the composition of *Georgics* Book 3 and the *Aeneid*, the significance Vergil places on having Augustus Caesar "in the midst" seems to have shifted from panegyric to allegory.[5] In *Aeneid* Book 8 Vergil implants the raw dichotomies of this recent past in the now subtly developed perspectival frame of his myth of the Roman mind. History does not set the terms for his art; he reverses the mimetic equation. It is not so much that Dido is Cleopatra, but rather that the history of Antony and Cleopatra can now be understood as the domestication of a rich, evocative, barbaric culture to Roman values, a process fully mythologized in the fiction of Aeneas, stylized in the sharply bridled orientalism of Vergil's epic art.[6]

Roman historiography largely collapses these perspectives, stereotyping the conflict to the point that "the true history of Antony and Cleopatra will probably never be known. It is buried too deeply beneath the version of the victors."[7] Renaissance artists gradually re-create some of the complexities of Vergil's analysis. The beginning of this reevaluation is marked by their jarring juxtaposition of the conventional view of Cleopatra as temptress and betrayer, with a portrait of her as analogous to Dido and the other Ovidian martyrs for love. These juxtapositions develop into a debate that is intensified by Renaissance neo-Platonic distinctions between the corruptions of a merely sensual love and the divine fury of purified

---

[5] Cf. *Georg.* 3.16–39 and *Aen.* 8.675–728.

[6] For Eastern influences on Vergil's art, see Johnson, *Darkness Visible*, pp. 135–54.

[7] W. W. Tarn, "The Battle of Actium," pp. 173.

love, and by attention to those parts of the historical record that suggest Cleopatra as a magnificent and capable queen and faithful wife and mother.[8] The figures of Antony and Cleopatra develop from easily evoked stereotypes of culpable passion toward powerful exemplars of another way of life.

By examining various Renaissance dramatic treatments of Aeneas and Dido, and Antony and Cleopatra, and by analyzing the stories' interpenetration, we also look toward Shakespeare's *Antony and Cleopatra*. With that play, which inverts the general categories of Vergil's epic, turning Dido's tragedy into Cleopatra's triumph, we come full circle. *Antony and Cleopatra* elicits the full cultural context of the *Aeneid* in order to transmute it to romantic apotheosis.

Alessandro Pazzi de' Medici, Lodovico Dolce, Cesare de' Cesari, Celso Pistorelli

In the revived classical drama of the Renaissance, the early adaptations of the stories of Aeneas and Dido, and Antony and Cleopatra tend to be rather rigid in their imitative forms; the later versions are increasingly more detailed and playfully self-conscious. The first treatments of these materials, among them the Dido plays of Alessandro Pazzi de' Medici (1527–28) and Lodovico Dolce (1547), the *Cleopatra* of Cesare de' Cesari (1551), and the *Marc'Antonio e Cleopatra* of Celso Pistorelli (1576), subordinate the unique values of these stories to superficially understood Greek or Senecan dramatic models. The playwrights value the two stories more as subjects that allow them to infuse medieval themes of romantic love

---

[8] Literary historical studies, for example, F. M. Dickey's *Not Wisely but Too Well* and, more recently, Beverly Taylor's "The Medieval Cleopatra" tend to emphasize the largely negative portrait of Cleopatra inherited by the Middle Ages and Renaissance from the powerfully biased Augustan myth. However, such studies slight the tensions and ambiguities present in some of these historical accounts. Too, artists are often as influenced by literary sources as by exact recourse to history. Horace's ode "Nunc est bibendum," for example, transmutes Cleopatra's debauchery into a proud triumph in death; see Steele Commager, *The Odes of Horace*, pp. 88–97. Plutarch's "Life" of Antony, a text rediscovered in the Renaissance that became an increasingly important source for dramatists, strongly hints at a genuinely tragic Antony, while its later portion, based on the memoirs of Cleopatra's physician Olympus, portrays her last days with respectful sympathy.

into the literature of classical antiquity, than as materials of historical significance and epic magnitude. Reductive in form, these earliest
plays are reductive in content as well; within their classical shell they
follow the medieval tendencies toward either moral condemnation
or Ovidian exaltation of the force of love, without reference to any
deeply evoked historical, political, or philosophical context. For
these authors, Dido and Cleopatra join Medea, Canace, other classical tragic queens, and a host of more contemporary heroines; the
playwrights freely interchange images, motifs, and even incidents
among these stories. When they do attempt to evoke the particular
significance of Dido or Cleopatra in self-conscious relation to the
present day, the result is an inorganic afterthought, as in Dolce's
encomium to Venice as the successor to the Roman imperium, or a
forced pedantic parallelism, as in Pistorelli's play.

The Alessandro Pazzi de' Medici, one of the first translators of
Aristotle's *Poetics* and an avowed imitator of ancient Greek drama,
augments Vergil's story by turning to its literary source, Apollonius
Rhodius's version of the story of Medea in the *Argonautica*.[9] This
"amplification" actually diminishes the epic function of the episode;
Dido is reduced to a psychological stereotype of a frenzied woman
whose principal motive is not love for Aeneas, but rather a Senecan
revenge for the murder of her husband Sychaeus. The play's vision
of Dido-as-Medea is devoid of the specific philosophical and historical content perceived in the story by some later Renaissance
dramatists.

The influential *Didone* of Lodovico Dolce, a prolific professional writer and translator for the Venetian Giolito press, awk-
wardly jostles elements of Senecan dramatic structure and motif,
Ovidian characterization, and Vergilian theme, in a display of learning heavily worn.[10] His genuinely pathetic Dido fits oddly within a

---

[9] For Pazzi and the *Poetics*, see Weinberg, *History of Literary Criticism*,
pt. 1, chap. 9, especially pp. 371–73. For the "Grecians" see Marvin Herrick,
Italian Tragedy in the Renaissance, pp. 43–71, and also Ferdinando Neri, *La
Tragedia Italiana del Cinquecento*, pp. 27–57. For biobibliography, see Pazzi,
Le Tragedie Metriche; Neri, *Tragedia*, pp. 56–58, summarizes the plot; Robert
Turner, *Didon dans la tragédie de la renaissance italienne et française*, pp.
12–29, discusses the sources of episodes and details.

[10] On Dolce's life and works, see Emmanuele Antonio Cicogna, "Memoria
intorno la vita e gli scritti di Messer Lodovico Dolce." I have used the 1547
Aldine *editio princeps* of the *Didone*; the play was subsequently included in

framework of Senecan love *furor*—a bloodthirsty and portentuous Cupid—and undercuts his attempt to exalt Aeneas's mission as a prefiguration of Venetian glory. The result is a play of groping, partial, unassimilated historical consciousness, much more ambitious but much less unified than Pazzi's simple revenge drama.

The early Italian tragedies of Antony and Cleopatra by Cesare de' Cesari and Celso Pistorelli follow Dolce in straining Senecan dramatic norms with other literary models and issues of contemporary relevance. However, where Dolce sought to suggest through Dido's tragedy Aeneas's imperial mission and its "continuation" in Venetian cultural supremacy, these dramatists take the opposite view of Roman history. They develop a medieval interpretation of Cleopatra as an additional Ovidian martyr for love, and use the ambiguities in the Roman historical tradition to craft oppositions between the values of love and force. In these plays the nascent Roman Empire prefigures the tyranny so feared in their day.[11]

Despite this growing interest in the possibility of transvaluing precisely recovered historical materials to address present concerns, the dramatists continue to import patterns foreign to the fullest development of these materials, and their applications continue to be simplistic and forced. Within its Senecan framework Cesari's *Cleopatra*, modeled after Sophocles' *Antigone*, is a static, ahistorical debate between force and nature, between an Octavius obsessed by fame and a maternal Cleopatra.[12] Pistorelli's pompous *Marc'An-*

---

the 1560 and 1566 printings of Dolce's collected tragedies. Neri, *Tragedia*, pp. 89–90, summarizes the plot; Turner, *Didon*, pp. 51–84, discusses sources but neglects Ovid's *Heroides* 7. The encomium to Venice occurs in 2.2.

[11] For the classical background to Italian debates over the respective values of republicanism or empire, see Hans Baron, *The Crisis of the Early Italian Renaissance*.

[12] Cesari's *Cleopatra* is a pastiche of historical, biographical, and legendary materials. Geoffrey Bullough, *Narrative and Dramatic Sources of Shakespeare* 5:224–27, says that Cesari based the play on the Italian life of Cleopatra by Count Guilio Landi (Venice, 1551), a text I have not been able to examine. Another direct or indirect source is Plutarch's "Life" of Antony, to which Cesari imports additions from Dio Cassius's *Roman History* (especially the descriptions of Cleopatra's conduct toward Julius Caesar and Octavius's messenger) and from Pliny's *Natural History* (the wonders of Egypt and of Cleopatra's court). Suetonius's influence is felt in Cesari's overall portrait of an efficient and harshly consistent Octavius, and in Cleopatra's lament that Octavius mercilessly forced Antony to suicide.

tonio e Cleopatra undramatically jumbles a Homeric epic context, which concentrates on an Iliadic siege of Alexandria, with antityrannical polemics against Ottaviano.[13] Constrained by the academic understanding of classical tragic drama, Cesari's more controlled treatment and Pistorelli's diffuse one both remain, finally, rhetorical juxtapositions of ideas, rather than an evocation of the conflict of two worlds of value in a true dramatic action.

Giovambattista Giraldi Cinthio

Giovambattista Giraldi Cinthio (1504–1573), one of the earliest major modern playwrights, dramatized both the story of Aeneas and Dido and the history of Antony and Cleopatra. Commissioned by Ercole II of Ferrara, these were Giraldi's only plays based on traditional materials rather than his own malleable fictions. However, if anyone perceived and valued the potential Vergilian-Augustan typological connection between these stories, it was the patron and not the artist himself. For Giraldi's rich treatment of the two stories does not involve a deliberate reflection of the one story in the other; rather the plays are the product of separate interpretative traditions. Both, however, evidence Giraldi's dramatic theory in their movement toward romantic tragicomedy, the "modern" dramatic form Giraldi pioneered in his later drama and defended in his criticism. And both plays strain the moral categories Giraldi perceived in the traditional materials toward the "higher" morality of a purified love. In this way, Giraldi anticipates Shakespeare's careful loosening of erotic and imaginative constraints in *Antony and Cleopatra*, which romanticizes historical content and aesthetic form. Giraldi, who championed romantic epic over classi-

---

[13] Pistorelli also relies on Dio's *Roman History* for his treatment of Antony's son Antillo and Cleopatra's son Cesarione. The death scenes of Antillo and Cesarione are badly garbled in the printed text: the speeches assigned to Antillo, addressed to the image of Julius Caesar, are obviously Cesarione's, while the curse on Ottaviano for his parents' death, assigned to Cesarione, is Antillo's speech. Pistorelli develops these characters, while minimizing Marc Antonio and Cleopatra (explicitly modeled after Dolce's Dido), in order to stress the monstrous tyranny of Ottaviano and the decay of Homeric heroic ideals of virtuous language and action (see his references to Homer, pp. 26r–29r and 44r–v).

cal epic, and tragicomic drama over classical tragedy, is perhaps the central critical figure in this historical literary development.

In his *Discorsi*, a critical treatise published in 1554, Giraldi proposes a strictly didactic, moralistic, and ideal standard for the function and ends of art.[14] His moral didacticism and idealist ontology are the sources of his superficial disagreements with Aristotle's analysis of tragic drama in the *Poetics*. From these principles flow Giraldi's central concern with decorum as the standard of verisimilitude; his use of seemingly digressive sententiousness as a legitimate means of signaling the moral status of character in action; and the episodic, loosely causal structure of his plays. They account also for his frequent use of fictive rather than historical sources for tragedy; for his discomfort with Aristotle's preferred complex tragedy of single issue, and his defense of the morally reassuring "double issue" of the tragedy "di lieto fine" (of happy ending); and for his consequent modification of Aristotle's theory of tragic affects, which, combined with his comments on audience psychology, reveal his dominant concern for the moral enlightenment of his viewers. Finally, these concerns explain his willingness to attempt to investigate the "final causes" motivating the action, even to the point of introducing gods on the stage.[15]

In the *Didone*, Giraldi's didacticism supports a drama of ideas and transcendence that draws on postclassical moralizations of Vergil's epic. Action is subordinated to the illumination of ideal types of character and to the imparting of moral lessons. Giraldi's

---

[14] On the relationship between Giraldi's dramatic practice and his critical theory, see Weinberg, *History of Literary Criticism* 1:432–52, an analysis of the *Discorsi* and Giraldi's quarrel with his former pupil, Giovambattista Pigna; and 2:912ff. on Giraldi's prefatory letter in defense of the *Didone* and his position in the controversy surrounding Sperone's *Canace*. See also P. R. Horne, *The Tragedies of Giambattista Cinthio Giraldi*, which includes a bibliographical guide to earlier scholarship. For my use of the term *tragicomedy*, see chapter 4, n. 11.

[15] On decorum, "sentenza," "costume," and verisimilitude, see *Discorsi*, pp. 242–45; 259–76; the letter to Duke Ercole II d'Este in defense of *Didone* (in Giraldi, *Le Tragedie*; hereafter cited as *Defense*), pp. 152–53; on "sentenza" and the roles of chorus and prologue, *Discorsi*, 229–34; *Defense*, 142–48; episodic structure, *Discorsi*, 250–52; fictive sources, *Discorsi*, 208–10; tragedy "di lieto fine," *Discorsi*, 214–15, 219–22, 224–27; tragic affects and audience psychology, *Discorsi*, 216–22, 225; "gods" on stage, *Discorsi*, 211–13; *Defense*, 135–41.

prologue explains his interpretative principles. The great epic poets of antiquity, he declares, wrote with a didactic end, presenting "vna ben vera imago / De la vita miglior" through their stories of the moral struggles of their heroes. Tragic poets do not alter this didactic aim, but adapt similar heroic tales to an even more effective teaching medium. Drama, in performance, possesses greater rhetorical power:

> E l'esposero in scena, à gli occhi altrui.
> Per purgar l'humane alme col terrore,
> E, con compassion de gli altrui casi,
> Da la vana ridurle à miglior vita.[16]

Giraldi proceeds to summarize the foreaction of his play, Book 1 of the *Aeneid*, emphasizing certain words and phrases that will acquire moral significance in the succeeding action: his hero's "piety" and earlier "wanderings," his having been driven to Carthage "against his will," and his mission in Italy, where he must achieve his "promised seat" with "wisdom and the sword."[17]

Giraldi then explicitly states the moral of the tragic action his audience will see:

> Quiui Enea, conformandosi col fato,
> La ragion, ch'occupata era dal senso,
> Ripiglierà per guida, e ad ubidire
> Si disporra al Signor, che regge il Cielo.
> Ma sospinta Didon dal uan disio,
> Da desperation fia interna uinta.
> Or piacciaui benigni Spettatori
> Vdir questo soccesso, che il Poeta
> Ad utile comun conduce in scena,
> Così mai sempre a ben'amar u'induca,
> Con ben felice fine, honesto Amore.

Giraldi's son Celso, in the dedicatory epistle to the posthumously published edition of the play, further simplifies the "meaning" of this tragic action by reducing it to a personification allegory, "Oue Enea ci rappresenta uno prudentissimo heroe, Gioue la parte supe-

---

[16] I cite the text of *Didone Tragedia* given in Giraldi, *Le Tragedie*.

[17] This account of heroic action is given an eschatological, Christian tone; see especially 2.2, 3.3, and the chorus that concludes act 3.

riore dell'anima humana, Mercurio la discorsiua & ragioneuole, & Didone la parte inferiore & sensuale" (pp. 4–5).

The difference between Celso's stark summation and his father's play lies in the older man's sense of the gradual realization of these moral states through the action; although the play's moral issues are constantly voiced in the debates and soliloquies, our understanding of them is not clarified until the play's resolution. Even then, a final tragic irony redounds in this "tragedy of unhappy ending," since Giraldi, despite his firm justification of Aeneas's actions, does not simplify Dido's character, but presents her as a subtle, complex blend of victim and culpable agent. Dido insistently raises the problem, vital in Giraldi's Counter-Reformation milieu, of man's free will but limited knowledge in potential conflict with God's Providence and foreknowledge.[18]

The first three acts of the play, leading up to the scene of recognition and reversal effected by Mercury's appearance, elaborate, through action and debate, the theme of the limits of man's knowledge. The characters make repeated allusions to man's imperfect perception and the consequent handicap imposed on the exercise of his reason and free will. Although Giraldi structures the first two acts in a manner reminiscent of medieval morality plays, with Anna and Achates acting as counselors for seemingly opposite courses of action, their arguments present no clear-cut choice between good and evil, but rather a scale of values or relative goods. These include the satisfaction of the senses, the procreation of children, the immediate welfare of one's people, and Achates' ringing exhortation to pursue destiny and eternal glory:

> Italia, Italia, alto Signor, che detta
> Terrestre paradiso, è da' più saggi,
> Sia il uero fin de le fatiche uostre,
> Et paiaui minor d'essa ogni regno.
>
> (2.2)

---

[18] On the religious controversy in Ferrara and Giraldi's part in defending Catholic orthodoxy, see P. R. Horne, "Reformation and Counter-Reformation at Ferrara." General theological debates over the nature and extent of free will are reflected in Giraldi's play through debates on the topic itself, through discussions of the merits of various forms of divination, and through paraphrases of Pico della Mirandola's "Oration on the Dignity of Man" and the second chorus of Sophocles' *Antigone*.

Achates' allusion to Italy as a "terrestrial paradise" implies the Christian moral allegorical interpretation of Aeneas's journey to Italy as the trial-filled journey of the good man to his heavenly reward. While Giraldi's play directs us toward eventual recognition of this higher destiny, the first three acts sympathetically illustrate how man is led away from his higher good. They demonstrate fallible man's need for a sure and gracious illumination or revelation that both confirms and exceeds the best tendencies in human nature.

The greater part of act 1 depicts the stages by which Dido is led to accept the false but persuasive view that her union with Aeneas is the greatest good, and to quell any misgiving that the "nova sede" he seeks may not be her city. A debate between Venus and Juno (1.2), adapted from the *Aeneid* 4.90–128, reveals the first causes of the tragedy—Juno's refusal to acknowledge the inevitable decree of Fate, and Venus's inflaming of Dido. Giraldi develops Juno's intervention from the *Aeneid* by having her work on Anna's susceptibilities in a dream. The queen's sister then interprets this dream to Dido as an incentive toward union with Aeneas (1.4). The swift deterioration of Dido's objections to her sister's urgings, from a responsible leader's hesitations to coyly personal remarks, clearly shows that her misdirected adherence to an object of immediate desire is leading her away from an apprehension of the greatest good. Dido expresses the heart of the matter in her succeeding soliloquy:

> Se il buono, e il reo de la mortali cose
> S'offerissero à noi nel proprio aspetto,
> E l'humano saper fosse capace
> Di veder, da se stesso, il peggio, e il meglio,
> Io non credo, che mai cosa sinistra
> Auenisse ad alcuno in questa vita.
> Ma questi nostri sensi, che le forme
> Offrono, son da l'apparenze false
> Spesso ingannati, e'n sì mentite larue,
> Occurrono le imagini à la mente,
> Ch'à conoscere il ver, siam proprio come
> Ciechi à i colori, ò come Talpe al Sole.
> E quindi auien, che l'intelletto humano
> S'appiglia al falso, perche il crede vero.
> E auenendoci poi qualche sinistro,
> La colpa diamo à la Fortuna, ò al Fato,
> E sol cagion n'è l'ignoranza nostra.

(1.5)

The chorus that concludes act 1 explicitly warns against allowing our desire to rest uncritically in "goods": "che il tempo, e sorte solue," "E uanno, e uengon, come in arbor foglia." This chorus represents the play's first full statement of its complex mingling of Stoic notions of self-sufficiency, neo-Platonic ladders of being, and Christian reliance on grace. Dido is urged to apply "Il don de l'intelletto" to discriminate between worldly, vain desires, which tie us to perishable things, and "alto disio" for the true good, which gives us a perfect and everlasting contentment.

Giraldi's Aeneas is subject to the same attraction to an immediate good that creates the very human tension between affection and scrupulousness in Dido's character. At the beginning of act 2, scene 2 he recapitulates his wanderings and growing desire for rest in ways that immediately recall Dido's metaphorical lament for her own love-induced confusion, "Stò, come naue, che da uari uenti / Combattuta è nel mare" (1.5). The ensuing debate between Achates and Aeneas pits against each other two aspects of Aeneas's character lauded by Renaissance commentators: his care for his people within the limited, ethical sphere of the earthly leader, and his role as Everyman in search of salvation. Achates' arguments for Stoic resolution and fearlessness shade into Christian eschatology; Aeneas's fame would be "gloria eterna" and he is urged to seek Italy as a "Terrestre paradiso."

Mercury's unequivocal divine revelation in act 3 firmly establishes the play's Christian neo-Platonic perspective: it is Providence, not Fate, that rules the heavens, and man's highest fulfillment consists in the free exercise of his will and the direction of his emotions and intellect toward their spiritual end in God. Aeneas then acknowledges his error and prays to God to resolve, for Dido and others, the disparity between his original innocent, well-meaning intentions and his seeming unfaithfulness in deserting her. His is a confession of a failing, not of a sin. The chorus at the end of act 3 philosophically justifies Aeneas's act of abandonment and the separate destinies of the lovers. In a paraphrase of Pico della Mirandola's "Oration on the Dignity of Man," the chorus describes the hierarchies of creation and man's uniquely adaptable position within them:

> Et in suo arbitrio pose
> A qual di queste cose [created things]
> Piacesse à lui poter uolgere il core,

E sì à qualunque d'esse assimigliarsi,
Che potesse mortale, ò diuin farsi.

The action of the play and the chorus's application of the "moral" affirm that Aeneas is one of those "di miglior'alma" who are now embarked on the flight back, "Al suo natio paese," to union with the highest good, God. Dido is left behind without benefit of a special divine revelation—the signs from the gods are ambiguous for her —and cannot redirect her love. The chorus now describes her as "insano," deceived "da disir uano."

None of the characters in Giraldi's play, including Aeneas, can have a full and correct understanding of God's action in history. Aeneas and Achates semiconsciously link themselves to that providential pattern; what they experience as a sense of Roman mission, the Christian audience, by virtue of the Christian language Giraldi uses, interpret as an allegory of salvation. Dido, who is not privileged to participate in even these prophetic glimmerings of the Christian providential order, experiences the gods and the universe as hostile, and suffers a tragedy of fate.

Ultimately, then, Giraldi's attempt to write a moralistic "tragedy of unhappy ending" produces a morally ambiguous play. It is easy enough to portray Aeneas's error, to show him manfully repenting, and send him off toward a happy ending. However, Giraldi does not then accede to the condemning assumptions about Dido's character. He cannot, in the end, make her suffering depend on the view of moral responsibility central to his art, so he makes her failing ignorance and her final downfall contingent upon the further weakness of her "feminine nature." He is the only Renaissance dramatist of the Dido story who attempts to exploit fully the rich tradition of Fulgentian moralization of the *Aeneid* and its emphasis on the radical distinction between masculine purposive nature and feminine emotional susceptibility. Yet he also attempts to give a full and balanced picture that highlights the injustice to Dido, providing an area for her defense. Her "sin" is love and a limited perception of the good—but these are Aeneas's failings as well—and despite the play's prominent exposition of the doctrine of free will, it also demonstrates that the will is only truly free when it operates in conjunction with God's revelation. Why, then, is Aeneas granted that hopeful sign, while Dido and her Carthaginians must fall back upon pagan "consolation" within a deterministic universe?

Giraldi's dramatic adaptation thus opens the Pandora's box of conflicting value systems and tragic tensions inherent in the Aeneas-Dido story. The issues are translated from the Vergilian idiom of revised Homeric heroism, of conflicting mythologies, East against West, chthonic against rational deities, to the contemporary problems of predestination against free will and pagan against Christian moral schemes. His play represents a very serious attempt to address the full range and potential of his epic source, and the play's structure and content are consistent with the aesthetic criteria he sets forth in the *Discorsi* and his epistolary defense of *Didone*. Yet, as with Vergil, Giraldi's decision to grant full pathetic force and nobility to Dido's characterization raises serious challenges to a heroic ethic. Thus Giraldi's implicit doubt about the Christian heroic ethic invites a countertreatment of his themes, one that provides a positive justification for a woman's demand for love.

When we turn to Giraldi's *Cleopatra*, we encounter in much heightened form the tension between romantic and didactic interests present in *Didone* and resolved in his later tragicomedies. Once again Giraldi feels compelled to draw a moral lesson from the spectacle of the tragedy, yet once again he shows a fascination with the exalting power of romantic love. As a result, his attitude toward Cleopatra, who stands at this intersection of passion and judgment, veers sharply from condemnation, to pity, to admiration. Giraldi makes sentimental details of both Plutarch's and Dio's portraits of her, so that she is at moments culpably weak, but then deviously strong, in her love for Antony; yet her actual appearances on the stage are too infrequent to contain these tensions. Although the prologue and the choruses to acts 1 and 3 seem to claim the play to be a didactic tragedy of shameful passion, the choruses to acts 2 and 5, and the conclusion suggest that Antony and Cleopatra's story is a tragedy of fate in which their love somehow emerges a transcendent virtue. Confusing, too, is the extraneous stress in the second half on Octavius and his curious reaction to the lovers, a perspective related only tenuously to the main preoccupations of the play. The result, like *Didone*, offers us glimpses of a powerful and moving tragic heroine; but the play is so muddled in its description of the nature of her tragedy that our attention is completely fragmented.

As in *Didone*, the prologue to *Cleopatra* presents the moral categories that are to govern our understanding of the play:

> Nondimeno hà uoluto hoggi il Poeta
> (Quanto meglio hà potuto) addurre in scena
> Ad utile comun, nuoua Tragedia.
> Che in se contiene il fin di Cleopatra,
> A cui sopposto fù tutto l'Egitto.
> Et parimente il fin di Marco Antonio,
> Che l'armi haueua contra Ottauio prese.
> Per sopporre al suo Imperio il Mondo tutto.
> Quindi vedrete, spettatori, quanto
> Poco giouin gli Imperii, & i Thesori,
> E le potenze, e l'altre doti humane
> Quando il piacere à la uirtù preuale.
> Piacer che tragga l'huom fuor di se stesso.
> E che guerra maggior fanno à gli Imperi
> Le delitie, e i diletti, che son fuori
> De l'ordine comun de la ragione,
> Che molte squadre de nemici armati.
> E che puote regnar sol lungamente
> Chi, preso il lume di ragion per guida,
> Sà comandare à se, regger se stesso.[19]

Simply put, pleasure, which wages war against the individual's rational self-possession, more fully destroys his ability to control his destiny than the attacks of enemy armies destroy a kingdom. This disjunctive analogy is then amply illustrated in the first act, in which the military war between Antony and Cleopatra and Octavius Caesar is but the backdrop to the psychological war between the lovers' irrational passions and their self-command.

Giraldi systematically resolves the ambiguities in his principal source, Plutarch's "Life" of Antony, to show that the lovers' emotional instability, rather than any clear military superiority of Octavius or explicit treachery of Cleopatra, brings about their defeat and suicide. His Cleopatra flees Actium from "feminil paura" (1.1) and is unjustly suspected by Antony of complicity with Octavius. She stages her "suicide" in order to test his love; the imprudent plan backfires when he, in an excess of grief, immediately attempts

---

[19] I cite the text of *Cleopatra Tragedia*, given in Giraldi, *Le Tragedie*.

suicide, and is brought to her only to die in her arms. She is panic-stricken, while he is irrationally dependent on her. The chorus concludes the act with an abstract meditation on the human soul's unique ability to behave in accord with reason, with "un sottile, / E prudente discorso," rather than following, as do Antony and Cleopatra, the unreflective promptings of desire.

However, the very economy with which Giraldi sketches the mutually destructive passion of Antony and Cleopatra in act 1 impedes the firm extension of his moral framework over the remainder of the drama. Having made Octavius's entrance an anticlimax as a military triumph, Giraldi must find a way to turn it into a moral victory. At the same time, the lovers' reunion for Antony's death scene and that encounter's intricate rhetorical romanticism assert values that oppose doctrines of rational control and self-sufficiency:

> EUNUCH: Egli sì tosto,
> Che da me intese, ch'erauate uiua,
> Alquanto ricourossi, e lieto disse:
> Esser più non mi puo graue la morte.
>
> CLEOPATRA: Ahi lassa, ben sia à me graue la uita,
> Se uita si puo dir c'habba colei,
> Che ir oda à morte chi era la sua vita.
>
> EUNUCH: Poi replicò, non mi è graue la morte,
> Poi che colei, per cui mi son trafisso,
> È viua, e posso anchor l'ultimo fiato
> Spirar ne le sue braccia.
>
> (2.1)

Giraldi also must here resolve a practical problem: how to extend a plot fast drawing to its conclusion to the customary four hours' performance time demanded by his audience.[20]

Giraldi's solution is to insert the famous debate between Maecenas and Agrippa from a later portion of Dio Cassius's *Roman History* (bk. 52). He changes the topic from Dio's debate over the respective virtues of republicanism or monarchy to Seneca's debate in *Octavia* over clemency and retributive justice.[21] This debate

---

[20] See Horne, *Tragedies*, pp. 41–42, 86.

[21] See Herrick, *Italian Tragedy*, pp. 97, 113, for the influence of Seneca's *Octavia* on Giraldi's debates.

in no way forwards the action of the play, for it focuses on whether Octavius should slay or pardon the defeated Antony, although Antony is already dead. A learned marshaling of arguments from beast lore, political theory, history, and theology, it seems an extradramatic excursus on a topic of independent interest to Giraldi's aristocratic audience. However, the debate does discredit the character of Octavius, who appears petulant and defensive in dismissing Maecenas's arguments for clemency. The ironies thus generated seem unintentional, a result of Giraldi's uncritical imitation of Seneca's *Octavia* and his attempt to remain faithful to Plutarch's intricate narrative of Octavius's manipulations of Cleopatra. Nevertheless Octavius now appears a clumsy and unintelligent Machiavellian, at best self-deceived about his own nobility.

.   .While Giraldi's awkward handling of Octavius unconsciously discredits his norm for the rational leader of men, the increasingly enthusiastic portrait of Cleopatra reinforces the unstated value of romantic love. Act 1 depicts her crumbling under disastrous events that resulted directly from her "feminil paura." But by act 2, her tragedy becomes a general tragedy of fortune, which reason and good discourse cannot circumvent. Such fate strikes exalted rulers with particular force, and may one day fell even the self-confident Octavius. Contradicting the rational optimism that informs the choral statements in act 1, the chorus in act 2 exclaims:

> Io creder più non uò, che il saper nostro
> Regga le cose humane.
> Perche chiaro mi è mostro,
> Che il muouere del Cielo, e de le stelle
> Sia quel, che il mondo aggiri,
> E le nostre uirtù faccia esser uane.
>
> . . . .
>
> Nè ui ual buon discorso,
> Perche si solue ogni consiglio in uento,
> Che quel celeste corso,
> A cui sapere human non pone morso,
> Fa uano, in un momento,
> Tutto quel ch'à suo bene altri hà discorso,
> Che se fusse possente Cleopatra.
> Antiueder prudente
> Di opporsi à stelle rie,
> In tante parti è corso,

Tentate hà tante uie
L' ingegno de la mia cara Reina
Che con la saggia mente
Haurebbe à se, e à l'Impero suo soccorso,
Et ischi fata hauria questa ruina.
Ma riuolto hà in niente
Il tutto il Ciel, che morte le destina,
E la uuol far rapina
De la Romana gente.
E sol perche destin tal'hebbe in fasce,
Per far chiaro, ed aperto,
Che in questo ermo diserto,
Sua uentura hà ciascun dal dì che nasce.

The speeches of the various attendants who survive Cleopatra reveal that this supposedly weak woman has been a superb ruler and guardian of her people. In her reaction to inevitable fate, Giraldi's Cleopatra ironically emerges as the true moral hero; whereas Octavius merely persists in trying to exalt himself by degrading her in the triumph.

The war of wits between the fame-conscious emperor and the loving queen is the dramatic center of the play's final acts. Compressing Plutarch's detailed narrative of Octavius's capture of Cleopatra, adding certain details from Dio, Giraldi explains her delay in committing suicide as necessitated by Octavius's close watch on her actions. Simplifying the ambiguities of his sources, Giraldi never deviates from his depiction of Cleopatra as loyal to Antony. She details her clear understanding of the political situation, her deep love for Antony, and her self-command in a fine last soliloquy:

Dvnqve tu pensi Ottauio ch'io sia priua
D'ingegno sì, sì de me stessa fuori,
Ch'io non habbia compreso, à che fin brami
Ch'io resti viua, e ch'io non vegga chiaro,
Che le promesse tue, le tue lusinghe
Son tanti lacci, che mi metti intorno,
Per menarmi legata al Campidoglio?

. . . .

Morir già Sophonisba in libertade
Volle piu tosto, ch'esser serua, e viua.
E così anch'io vò col suo essempio fare.

. . . .

Libera veggo pur (mal grado tuo)
Ouunque io mi uolgo, questo Cielo,
Sotto cui nacque, e vissi, e fui Reina,
Et anche questo Ciel Cleopatra vede
Non co i legami, e le catene intorno,
Ma in habito real. Questo Cielo anche
Coglierà l'alma mia libera e sciolta.
Bene con tutto il cor prego, e riprego
Le Deità d'Egitto (se non sono
Rimase vinte con il Regno mio)
Ch' oprino tanto, che il mio corpo vnito
Sia à quel di Marco Antonio.

. . . .

À Dio, cara mia Patria, A Dio ti lascio
Populo mio, ti lascio cara Corte,
In cui mi uissi già tanto felice.
Pregate tutti à la Reina uostra,
Quant'esser puote più, morte tranquilla,
Pregate, che i miei Figli, che Signori
Esser deuean di questo eccelso Regno,
Et hora ne le man sono di Ottauio,
Facciano miglior fin, c'hor non faccio io.

(5.2)

Our original expectations are completely reversed. Cleopatra, apparently trapped by her unchecked emotions and by Octavius's conquest, finally embraces all her responsibilities to her gods, her husband, her children, and her people in a loving farewell. She liberates herself through death from the delights that have become her chains, from that royalty which would bring her such humiliation as a captive at Rome. Proud, intelligent, passionate, with affections tinged with ferocity, she wins a moral victory equal to that of the famous Carthaginian heroine of the Punic Wars, Sophonisba. Her character, which earlier seemed problematic, now has heroic clarity; while Octavius's, which seemed the touchstone of our values, is blurred. Notes of a romantic theme, "all for love," swell up through the hollow closing praise for Octavius's "magnanimity." Once again, and even more obviously than in *Didone*, Giraldi's play overflows his moral categories, and tragedy approaches tragicomedy.

Étienne Jodelle

Of the tragedies of Étienne Jodelle, the earliest dramatist of the French Renaissance and member of the Pléiade, we have only *Cléopatre captive* (1552–53) and *Didon se sacrifiant* (between 1552 and 1562). They share a rich, if not fully conscious, typological relationship, and their political and philosophical resonance, their interpretation and development of sources significantly prefigure Shakespeare's reworking of the *Aeneid* and its interpretative contexts in *Antony and Cleopatra*. Whereas Ercole d'Este's choice of stories constrained Giraldi's aesthetic and moral norms, the ideal of the French monarchy as a Christian corrective to and amplification of Roman empire and ideology inspires Jodelle's treatments of these same materials. He moves beyond mere literary exercises or inorganic political debate toward a thoroughgoing transvaluation of his sources.

We see this process in its awkward first phases in the early *Cléopatre captive*, a play written to celebrate the defeat at Metz of the Holy Roman Emperor Charles V by the French forces of Henry II, commanded by the Duc de Guise. Under pressure of this purpose, the drama shifts from condemnation of the lovers' immorality to criticism of the pride and brutality of the first Roman emperor, Octave. The play's topical framework, an expansive praise of the pious and benevolent Henry II as an exemplar of a new political ideal, partially unifies what would otherwise be a fragmented and formulaic treatment of the suffering woman and the tyrant.

The opening lines of the prologue—in which Henry II is apostrophized as King of Kings, as Lord over earth, sea, and heaven —clearly allude to the recent victory over Charles. Charles's emblematic device was two columns emblazoned with the motto "Plus oultra." Now Henry engraves his name over it:

> Puis que la terre (ô Roy des Rois la crainte),
> Qui ne refuse estre à tes loix estrainte,
> De la grandeur de son sainct nom s'estonne,
> Qu'elle a gravé dans sa double colonne.
>
> (p. 93)[22]

---

[22] I cite the modern critical edition of Jodelle's works, *Œuvres complètes*, ed. Enea Balmas, 2 vols., henceforth cited as *OC*.

Henry thus proves himself superior to the most recent successor in the imperial line that began with this play's central character, Octave:

> Ici les desirs et les flammes
> Des deux amants: d'Octavian aussi
> L'orgueil, l'audace et le journel souci
> De son trophee emprains tu sonderas
> Et plus qu'à luy le tien egaleras;
> Veu qui'il faudra que ses successeurs mesmes
> Cedent pour toy aux volontez supremes
> Qui ja le monde à ta couronne voüent,
> Et le commis de tous les Dieux t'avoüent.

(p. 94)

The unchecked passion of Antoine and Cléopatre led to their easy conquest by Octave; however, Octave should learn from their fall that, as the chorus repeatedly intones, "Si l'inconstante fortune / Au matin est opportune / Elle est importune au soir" (p. 132). Instead, during the course of the play Octave becomes culpably proud, a tyrant eager to display Cléopatre in his triumph. His disappointment at her suicide foreshadows his hubristic successor's defeat by Henry II.

Act 1 paints, through a tightly Senecan summary of Plutarch's "Life" of Antony, a largely condemnatory picture of Antoine and Cléopatre and their love. In an opening soliloquy reminiscent of Seneca's *Agamemnon* and *Thyestes*, the ghost of Antoine bewails the eternal torments he now endures, and summons Cléopatre to death. He accuses himself of having blatantly neglected his duties for the sake of pleasure. Cléopatre enters and reveals that a dream of this bloody ghost has infused her, too, with guilt. At the conclusion of act 1 even the partisan chorus of Alexandrian women declare that love, luxury, and delight lead to vice.

The scene is thus set for a moral Octave, enforcer of universal peace, to proclaim the great virtue of his triumph over these disorderly lovers. At the opening of act 2 Octave balances judgment and pity for them. Soon, however, prompted by his harsh general, Agrippe, he surrenders himself totally to the role of the gods' avenger on the prideful Antoine and Cléopatre. He jarringly appropriates the language of the *Aeneid* to support his growing sense of imperial providential mission, calling Agrippe, "Fidelle Achate," while thrilling at the prospect of destroying all his enemies, "Baignons en sang les armes et les cœurs, / Et souhaitons à l'ennemi cent vies, / Que luy seroient plus durement ravies" (p. 114). Caesar and Agrippe exit, leaving another Roman officer, Proculee, who is less severe in condemning Cléopatre. His qualifying comments prepare us to apply the succeeding chorus's admonition against pride—illustrated by allusions to the Titans, Prometheus, Icarus, and others who aspired against the gods—to Octave's ambitions, as well as those of the Egyptian Queen, "Elle qui, orgueilleuse, / Le nom d'Isis portoit" (p. 118). Octave seems in danger of becoming involved in, rather than dissociated from, her fall.

In act 3 Jodelle reworks Dio Cassius's account of Cleopatra's use of the letters and portraits of Julius Caesar. These actions represent her sincere appeal to Octave's pity, but his response is severe, literal-minded, and prosecuting. Octave's sudden magnanimity at the end of the act, when he thinks he has secured the triumph he desired, contrasts unfavorably with his earlier refusal of pity. The conclusion of the act directs our shifting response: the servant Seleucus, once willing to betray his mistress for her deceptions, now admires her indomitable spirit in adversity.

Act 4 then emphasizes Cléopatre's nobility in death. She and her maids compose a powerful sacrificial picture with a series of solemn, measured, invocations to fate and death:

> CLÉOPATRE: La Parque, et non Cesar, aura sus moy le pris;
> La Parque, et non Cesar, soulage mes esprits;
> La Parque, et non Cesar, triomphera de moy;
> La Parque, et non Cesar, finira mon esmoy;
>
> .   .   .   .
>
> Courage donc, courage (ô compagnes fatales),
> Jadis serves à moy, mais en la mort égales,
> Vous avez recogneu Cleopatre princesse,
> Or ne recognoissez que la Parque maistresse.
>
> ERAS: Ha mort, ô douce mort, mort, seule guarison
> Des esprits oppressez d'une estrange prison,
> Pourquoi soffres-tu à tes droits faire tort?
> T'avons-nous fait offense, ô douce et douce mort?
> Pourquoy n'approches-tu, ô Parque trop tardive?
> Pourquoy veux-tu souffrir ceste bande captive,
> Qui n'aura pas plustost le don de liberté,
> Que cet esprit ne soit par ton dard écarté?

> Haste doncq, haste-toy: vanter tu te pourras
> Que mesme sus Cesar une despouille auras.
>
> (pp. 135–36)

Cléopatre's heroic acceptance of death, making of herself a worthy sacrifice, "L'honneur que je te fais, l'honneur dernier sera / Qu'à son Antoine mort Cleopatre fera" (p. 139), contrasts favorably with Octave's priggishness, which can, when thwarted, erupt into violence.

Like the Italian dramatists, Jodelle at times seems hopelessly torn between stock thematic treatments of Cléopatre, the woman suffering for love, and Octave, the prototyrant. Too, his characterization of Cléopatre veers from Senecan to Ovidian stereotypes. Having once condemned her love for Antoine as a torment, she finally commands that they be buried in the same tomb and proposes their romantic epitaph:

> Icy sont deux amans qui, heureux en leur vie,
> D'heur, d'honneur, de liesse, ont leur ame assouvie.
> Mais, en fin, tel malheur on les vit encourir,
> Que le bon heur des deux fust de bien tost mourir.
>
> (p. 139)

However, the topical allusion to Henry II implies Jodelle's broader theme: the tragic conflict between the lovers and the disappointed conqueror yields a new ideal of rule that is a synthesis of power and sympathy. Hence the shift in Cléopatre's character from the frenzied queen to the priestess of love; hence the pervasive sense that the arrogant Octave is overshadowed by a later king, Henry II, who has a more inspiriting and sustaining relationship to his kingdom and his people:

> Reçoy donc (Sire) et d'un visage humain
> Prens ce devoir de ceux qui, sous ta main
> Tant les esprits que les corps entretiennent,
> Et devant toy agenouïller se viennent;
> En attendant que mieux nous te chantions,
> Et qu'à tes yeux sainctement presentions
> Ce que ja chante à toy, le fils des Dieux,
> La terre toute, et la mer, et les Cieux.
>
> (prologue, p. 94)

Rather than implying a neo-Vergilian ideal, the single specific allusion in the play to Vergil's *Aeneid*, the harsh Agrippe as "Fidelle Achate," may be read as an ironic intimation of Jodelle's Ovidian anti-imperial defense of Dido in his later play.

Jodelle's other extant tragedy, *Didon se sacrifiant*, was composed between 1552 and 1562, that is, between the publication of Du Bellay's collection of French translations of materials about Dido, on which Jodelle's play in part depends, and the beginning of the civil wars in France.[23] Du Bellay's collection seems intended to emphasize Dido's sympathetic appeal in Vergil, and her "defense" in Ovid's *Heroides* and the alternate "historical" tradition.[24] Jodelle follows this characteristically French romantic exaltation of Dido's character, enriching it with a line of political and philosophical reasoning that stresses her allegiance to a natural religion of tolerance opposed to Aeneas's dogmatism and harsh Roman imperialism.

Jodelle perceived in the Vergilian story much the same breadth of issue and relevance to contemporary polemic as had Giraldi a decade earlier in Ferrara. However, the two playwrights' formulations of the dramatic conflict and its resolution differ completely. In contrast to Giraldi's providentialism, Jodelle suggests very strongly that the values usually discerned in the fourth book of the *Aeneid* are harshly intolerant. This idea is implicit in the unusual characterizations of secondary figures, the consistent polemic against Aeneas's "revealed" destiny and the future Roman Imperium, and the com-

---

[23] For Balmas's conjectural dating, see *OC* 2:453–56 and *Un Poeta de Rinascimento Francese, Étienne Jodelle*, pp. 345–46.

[24] *Le quatriesme livre de l'Énéide de Vergile, traduict en vers Françoys. La Complaincte de Didon à Énée, prinse d'Ovide.* . . . Du Bellay's collection also includes a poem by Ausonius on the "historical" Dido, who never met Aeneas and committed suicide to escape the advances of Jarbas. Through this alternate tradition Dido was praised as a model of chastity. Du Bellay, in the letter to Morel that prefaces his translation, says of his choice of subject matter:

> mais par la translation du quatriesme livre de l'Énéide, qu'il n'est besoing recommander d'advantage, puis que sur le front elle porte le nom de Vergile. Je diray seulement qu'oeuvre ne se trouve en quelque langue que ce soit ou les passions amoureuses soyent plus vivement depeinctes, qu'en la personne de Didon.

For a partial review of the extent of the influence of Du Bellay's translations on Jodelle's play, see René Godenne, "Étienne Jodelle, traducteur de Virgile."

plex portrayal of Aeneas as the doubt-torn pawn of false and dogmatic religious principles. Jodelle's revisionism is consistent with
the widespread French patriotic claims that their royal line was
purer than the Holy Roman Empire in its Trojan descent and
morally superior to the empire and its emperor Charles V. And
Jodelle's view is also allied with eirenic attempts to avoid religious
warfare in France and Europe.[25] In *Cléopatre captive* the result
is an implied contrast between the culpably proud Octave and the
benign Henry II; in *Didon se sacrifiant*, a thoroughgoing criticism
of Roman political and religious imperialism through an Ovidian
and Lucretian presentation of the materials of the *Aeneid*.

The first act of *Didon se sacrifiant* is a striking testimony to
the extent of Jodelle's understanding of the *Aeneid* and his qualification of its positive aims. Jodelle focuses exclusively on the reaction
of the Trojans to their imminent departure from Carthage, allowing us to see first through their eyes the effect their leave-taking will
have on the city and its queen. From the initial words of the play
any joy in their election, any hint of the proud superiority of a
conquering race, is constrained by the cost of their eventual triumphs:

> Quel jour sombre! quel trouble avec ce jour te roulent
> Tes destins, ô Carthage! et pourquoi ne se soullent
> Les grands Dieux, qui leur veuë et leurs oreilles sainctes
> Aveuglent en nos maux, essourdent en nos plaintes?
> Pourquoy donques, jaloux, ne se soullent de faire,
> Ce qui fait aux mortels leur puissance desplaire?
>
> . . . .
>
> Encor que nostre Enee au havre nous envoye
> Apprester au depart les restes de la Troye;
> Encor que nous suivions ses redoutez oracles,
> Ses songes ambigus, ses monstrueux miracles;
> Encor que, comme il dit, du grand Atlas la race,
> Mercure, soit venu se planter à sa face,
> Afin que hors d'Afrique en mer il nous remeine,
> Pour faire aussi tost fin à nos ans qu'à la peine,
> Ne jettez-vous point l'œil (las se pourroit-il faire
> Que telle pitié peust à quelqu'un ne deplaire?)

---

[25] For the Franco-Trojan myth, see Yates, *The French Academies of the
Sixteenth Century*, and *Astraea*, especially pp. 121ff.

> Jettez-vous point donc l'œil sur l'amante animee?
> Sur Didon, qui, d'amour et de dueil renflammee,
> (Ja desja je la voy forcener, ce me semble,)
> Perdra son sens, son heur et son Enee ensemble?
>
> (p. 151)

It is "fortes et fides" Achates, the traditional supporter of Aeneas's destiny, who recites this extremely narrow and conditional catalogue of possible Trojan gains, and juxtaposes to it a profound sympathy for the devastation awaiting Carthage.

Achates' speech, filled with pity, counters the conventional defenses of the Trojan action offered by Ascanius and Palinurus. Ascanius, type of the youthful hero, argues for restraint from immediate pleasures and redoubled effort to attain their final good, moralistically contrasting Carthage's seductive, effeminate "sweetness" with their "glorious" repose in Italy:

> Bien qu' une *douce amorce*
> Desrobe bien souvent au jeune cœur sa force,
> Si m'aveuglé-je au bien que j'avois, et au trouble
> D'une amante insensee. Il faut que l'on redouble
> L'ame pour vaincre un dueil. Donc ceste *Afrique douce*
> En la laissant nous charme? Où le destin nous pousse
> Suivon, suivon tousjours. Toute troupe est sujette
> Au travail; le travail enduré nous rachette
> *Un glorieux repos.*
>
> (p. 153, emphasis mine)

The pious Palinurus then argues that given a choice between two seeming evils, one does best by having faith and making one's will and "fresle cognoissance" submissive, as far as possible, to the gods.

Achates, while respecting these views, is more skeptical, pursuing his first misgivings that Aeneas may be following a less than certain and virtuous course of action: "ses *redoutez* oracles, / Ses songes *ambigus*, ses *monstrueux* miracles." He suggests that the visitor Aeneas assumed to be Mercury might in fact have been the Trojan archenemy, Juno, disguised. By sending the fleet to shipwreck in the fierce winter weather she would destroy "Une Troye desja redressee en Carthage" (p. 154). Although Achates reluctantly concludes that his duty lies in the prompt execution of his orders, through his objections Jodelle lays the groundwork for the Ovidian defense of Dido against the orthodox moralistic reading of the *Aeneid*.

Aeneas then recapitulates in soliloquy the story of Troy's fall and his succeeding adventures. In the *Aeneid* his recital, narrated at Dido's banquet, not only impels the love tragedy and defines its cultural and mythic scope but also suggests the epic's goals: Aeneas must renovate the lost Troy for present and future ages, not merely retain it in memory. Jodelle, however, uses this epic content to precisely opposite ends, reducing Aeneas's former heroic energy in war to background coloring for his submission to the yet greater force of love and Dido's pitiful "douceur." As in the previous scene, doubt is cast on the value of Aeneas's imperial destiny and our sympathy is directed toward Dido's plight. At the close of act 1, the chorus of Trojans tries to place the most positive interpretation on the Trojan departure, but fears that "Tout n'est qu'un songe, une risee, / Un fantosme, une fable, un rien, / Qui tient nostre vie amusee / En ce qu'on ne peut dire sien," a dream in which

> l'homme, au lieu d'une asseurance,
> Ne peult avoir que l'esperance
> De plus grande felicité;
> Pendant que chetif il espere
> (Chacun en sa condition),
> La Mort oste l'occasion
> D'esperer rien de plus prospere.
>
> (pp. 159–160)

In the face of such uncertainties they can only recommend a Stoic self-sufficiency: "L'homme sage, sans s'esmouvoir, / Reçoit ce qu'il faut recevoir, / Mocqueur de la vicissitude."

In act 2 Dido enters and begins a series of arguments and imprecations against Aeneas. Jodelle, following Du Bellay, expands and reinterprets Vergil's text (*Aen.* 4.296 ff.), by incorporating material from Ovid's *Heroides*, specifically Dido's accusation in *Heroides* 7.31–36 and 56–60: "nec tibi diva parens ... / perfide" ("False one! no goddess was thy mother"). Jodelle develops these accusations into his Dido's absolute faith in Venus, which is then elaborated in the language of Lucretius's *De rerum natura*. Her argument is thus both a skeptical attack on Aeneas's Roman religion of special revelation and dogma, and a defense of her own "natural" religion of cosmic love.

As most commentators have noted, many of Jodelle's characters are uneasy with a religion that dictates Aeneas's leave-taking.[26] Achates has reservations about Roman destiny; the chorus of Trojans feels oppressed by an impersonal Fate; and the chorus of Phoenicians bitterly accuses Aeneas of being a man of false religion, one who would even condone human sacrifice on the altar of blind obedience. Aeneas himself quails under these charges; when Achates argues "celuy fait bien qui fait à bonne fin," Aeneas cries out, "Pourquoy me gesne donc ma conscience encore?" (p. 191). Finally, the historic consequences of this subordination of human sympathy to abstract principle are foretold in Dido's vision of an inhuman and oppressive Roman Empire, built on a cornerstone of religious hypocrisy:

> Quant à sa race fière,
> Qui sera, je ne sçay (et la fureur derniere
> Prophetise souvent), ainsi que luy traistresse,
> Qui par dol se fera de ce monde maistresse,
> Qui de cent pietez, ainsi que fait Enee,
> Abusera la terre en ses loix obstinee,
> Et qui toujours feindra, pour croistre sa puissance,
> Avec les plus grands Dieux avoir fait alliance,
> S'en forgeant bien souvent de nouveaux et d'estranges,
> Pour croistre avec ses Dieux ses biens et ses louanges.
> Qu'on ne la voye au moins en aucun temps paisible,
> Et que, quand peuple aucun ne luy sera nuisible,
> Elle en vueille à soy-mesme, et que Rome, grevee
> De sa grandeur, souvent soit de son sang lavee;
> Que sans fin dans ses murs la sedition regne
> Qu'en mille et mille estats elle change son regne,
> Qu'elle face en la fin de ses mains sa ruine,

---

[26] Balmas, for example, remarks,

les invectives de Didon contre le "pieux" Enée qui abandonne la reine de Carthage pour obéir à un commandement divin deviennent facilement, dans sa réélaboration dramatique, de violentes attaques contre la superstition, les miracles, le rôle néfaste des prêtres, la religion en général; les souffrances des protagonistes ... lui offrent de faciles occasions pour des réflexions désabusées sur la condition humaine, où s'étale un pessimisme âpre et âcre, d'où jaillissent aussi des accents non douteux de révolte, qui frôlent parfois le blasphème.

(OC 2:454)

Et qu'à l'envi chacun dessus elle domine,
Se voyant coup sus coup saccagée, ravie
Et à mille estrangers tous ensemble asservie.

(pp. 210–11)

Less remarked by commentators is the persuasive fervor of Dido's belief in a naturalistic religion of love. The rational skepticism toward traditional religion so often cited as a topical feature of this play must be set within the broader contemporary context of beleaguered late Renaissance religious syncretism, evangelical piety, and eirenicism. Indeed, from Rabelais to Montaigne and beyond, such skepticism toward received religion often functions to impel a more liberal faith.[27]

Jodelle appropriates what is a mere rhetorical objection in Ovid's *Heroides:* How can Venus, as Aeneas's mother, allow him to leave his devoted lover? Will she not work within her element, the wintry seas, to stay him, or destroy him if he goes? He then develops this argument to compose his play's setting and religious sentiment. Against a mood of lowering destiny, powerfully evoked by the poet's descriptions of the threatening winter weather, Jodelle's Dido erects her last line of defense. Unlike Achates, who in act 1 reads the "jour sombre" as a portent of the greater emotional storm about to break over Carthage, Dido claims that she can enlist the forces of nature to retain Aeneas. These forces, she declares, respond to the outrage of an abandoned lover:

---

[27] For the knotty question of Jodelle's seemingly shifting religious beliefs, viewed within the controversies of the time, see Balmas, *Un poeta,* pp. 489–567; and G. Spillebout, "Jodelle l'Hétérodoxe." Neither of these biographical discussions satisfactorily resolves the problem; both assume a series of changes in Jodelle's personal religious conviction, rather than hypothesize that he may have been struggling to reconcile changing religious definitions and external pressures.

On the relationship of skepticism and fideism, see the seminal work of Lucien Febvre, *Le Problème de l'incroyance au seizième siècle;* Richard Popkin, *The History of Scepticism from Erasmus to Descartes;* and the work of Frances Yates, especially *French Academies.* Simone Fraisse, *L'Influence de Lucrèce en France au seizième Siècle,* assembles a fascinating array of materials on the sixteenth-century revival of Epicureanism, but focuses on tracing specific allusions to Lucretius, without fully developing their contexts; her limited historical argument is *prospective,* toward the "conquest of rationalism," not retrospective, to the aspirations of Renaissance syncretism.

> La terre maugré soy soustient un homme lasche,
> Et contre le mechant la mer mesme se fasche.
> Quand mesme ton dessein ce jour je n'eusse veu,
> Ny entendu des miens, le Ciel ne l'eust pas teu;
> Ma terre en eust tremblé, et jusques à Carthage
> La mer le fust venu sonner à mon rivage.
>
> (p. 163)

Ovid's Dido says that the sea " 'perfidiae poenas exigit ille locus' " (" 'is the place that exacts the penalty for faithlessness' " *Her.* 7.58). Jodelle has his Dido enumerate the gods of sea and air, and even the fish, who are obedient, "aux lois d'Amour," as a prelude to enlisting the support of Aeneas's mother and Cupid against his departure. Her pleas ring constant alluring changes on the theme of the "sweetness" of their life together; it is this affecting "sweetness" that Jodelle's fellow Pléiadist Ronsard emphasized when he commented on the supreme poetic power of Dido's laments.[28]

This appeal to the sympathetic powers in nature culminates in act 3 when Dido calls on Venus under the Lucretian guise of "mere / De tout estre vivant" (p. 186), the same multiform goddess of Paphos, Cythera, and Gnidus whom Spenser later celebrates in the Temple of Venus.[29] Dido's reverent prayer, far more rich and sure than Aeneas's earlier halting appeal to the gods to prove his innocence, far exceeds the rhetorical resources of Ovid's defense. Jodelle, like Spenser, has tapped that rich stream of late classical syncretic myth, developed and expanded throughout the Middle Ages and Renaissance, that makes woman the expressive vehicle for

---

[28] Ronsard, in a poem to the Cardinal of Lorraine, speaks of the affects produced by accompanied singing of poetry at the French court:

> Mon Dieu! que de douceur, que d'aise et de plaisir
> L'ame reçoit alors qu'elle se sent saisir
> Et du geste et du son, et de la voix ensemble
> Que ton Ferabosco sur trois lyres assemble,
> Quand les trois Apollons chantant diuinement,
> Et mariant la lyre à la voix doucement,
> Tout d'un coup de la voix et de la main agile
> Refont mourir Didon par les vers de Vergile
> Mourant presques eux-mesme. . . .
>
> (Cited by Yates, French Academies, p. 50)

[29] Cf. *Didon*, pp. 186–88, and *FQ* 4.10.39–47, and see also my discussion of Spenser in chapter 2.

all the manifold life of nature.[30] Dido, priestess of Venus, fears that the goddess may prove as cruel as the bloodthirsty Diana, demanding her life as a "martyr" to Love.

Thus the character of Jodelle's Dido derives a mythic resonance from her allegiance to Venus:

> Toy, le but de Nature, à qui ne sçauroit plaire
> De defaire aucun œuvre, ains tousjours de refaire,
> Et qui dessus la Mort gaignes sans fin le pris,
> Luy faisant rendre autant qu'elle en a tousjours pris,
> A fin que, depeuplant et repeuplant la salle
> De Pluton, l'entretien de ce mond s'egalle.

> > (p. 186)

For us, these lines inevitably summon the image of another Venus, Shakespeare's Cleopatra. In her, however, the variety of an all-encompassing female goddess, Apuleius's great Queen Isis, is even more deeply and subtly implied, entwining contrary states so that what they "undid did." Jodelle's Dido concentrates on the life-giving powers of Venus, and her speeches to Aeneas attempt to draw from her defensive, victimized position the creative counterargu-

---

[30] Fraisse, *L'Influence de Lucrèce*, chaps. 4–6, documents the remarkable surge of interest in the *De rerum natura* among the writers of the Pléiade and their circle. This selective revival marks the confluence of two traditions of transmission. The first comprises the classical and late classical poetry of Ovid and Claudian, the medieval nature poetry of Bernardus Silvestris and Alain de Lille, and the French "naturalism" of Jean de Meun and Rabelais. The other, a more purely philosophical revival of the praise of pleasure, is transmitted through Cicero and Diogenes Laertius to the Italian humanist Lorenzo Valla, and through him to Erasmus, Rabelais, Thomas More, and eventually Montaigne and Shakespeare.

This Lucretian revival has its place within the Renaissance tradition of syncretistic mythology and debates over the rapprochement of Christianity and certain ideas in classical natural and moral philosophy (the praise of pleasure, the immortality of the soul, the role of providence, etc.). To some extent this revival prefigures the full-scale scientific and philosophical revival of Lucretius in the seventeenth century. Recent studies seem to indicate that the sixteenth- and seventeenth-century Epicurean revival may have had far more to do with Renaissance evangelicalism and liberal Protestantism than with atheistic libertinism, as has been previously argued; see Febvre, *Problème de L'incroyance*; Yates, *French Academies*, Edward Surtz, *The Praise of Pleasure*; Walter Kaiser, *Praisers of Folly*; and, despite his rather different conclusions, William Elton, *King Lear and the Gods*.

ment that will reanimate their union and win her a triumph over imminent death.

These lines also epitomize the marvelous ebb and flow in Dido's speeches as she moves between pleas for love and fascination with death. The very first time we see her, she is already embarked upon the stormy way that joins the sweetness of satisfied love to the bitterness of consummated life:

> Il faut que la pitié l'arreste encor ici,
> Ou que ma seule mort arreste mon souci.
> La mort est un grand bien, la mort seule contente
> L'esprit, qui en mourant voit perdre toute attente
> De pouvoir vivre heureux.
>
> (pp. 162–63)

> L'espoir flatte la vie, et doucement la pousse,
> L'estranglant à la fin d'une corde moins douce.
> Nostre espoir est-il tel?
>
> (p. 166)

Unlike Shakespeare's Cleopatra, who seeks that thing "which shackles accidents and bolts up change," and finds it in a perfect wedding of death and love, Dido finally sees her earlier unifying view of love—that force which triumphs over death to renew nature —broken and denied:

> Soyez au sacrifice, ô vous, les Dieux supremes!
> Je vous veux appaiser du meurdre de moymesmes;
> Vostre enfer, Dieu d'enfer, pour mon bien je desire,
> Sçachant l'enfer d'Amour de tous enfers le pire.
>
> (p. 206)

This is no melting fusion, "as sweet as balm, as soft as air," but rather a tragic "frisson" made all the more exquisitely horrifying through the penetrating "douceur" of the heroine.

Achates' initial judgment proves correct; doom hangs over Carthage. Dido does not control the elements. In the cruelest of all twists on the pathetic fallacy, they rage through her, tearing her apart with their fury:

> Foible, palle, sans cœur, sans raison, sans haleine,
> Anne, mon cher support, maugré moy je me traine

De rechef çà et là, mal apprise à souffrir
Un repos qui me vient l'impatience offrir.
Tant que, quand tu verras sus la prochaine rive
La mer, qui se tenoit dedans ses bords captive,
Lorsqu'un Aquilon vient dessus ses flancs donner,
Bruire, bondir, courir, jusqu'au ciel bouilloner,
Et sans aucun arrest, pousser jusqu'aux campagnes
De ses flots depitez les suivantes montagnes,
Tu verras, tu verras l'estat où un trompeur
A fait estre le corps et l'ame de ta sœur.

(p. 181)

In Jodelle's play, the triumph of Dido's characterization lies in the moving appeal she makes to us for the doomed cause of love, an appeal frozen within the ordained pattern of the tragic plot. Only a reversal of the action itself—the lovers' allegiance rather than separation—will allow that defense to generate something more than deep-felt pity.

Robert Garnier, Samuel Daniel

The seven tragedies and one tragicomedy of Robert Garnier (1545–1590), famous French lawyer and counselor to the King, all reflect the background of religious civil war against which they were composed. His *Marc Antoine*, translated into English in 1590 by Mary Sidney, Countess of Pembroke, is the first of the plays we are discussing that Shakespeare is likely to have known directly.[31] It is a striking adaptation of Plutarch's potentially tragic Antony, a man wracked by a neo-Vergilian conflict between love and duty. In particular, Garnier anticipates Shakespeare in his use of Antony's rumored Herculean ancestry to lend mythic and moral resonance to his involvement with Cleopatra. He deliberately reverses the value structure of the *Aeneid* by having the dying Cleopatra paraphrase Dido's speeches only to declare she will rejoin her lover in death, a "revision" that may well be a direct source for Shakespeare's climactic transvaluation of the epic in *Antony and Cleopatra* 4.14.50–

---

[31] For the political-religious background, see Gillian Jondorf, *Robert Garnier and the Themes of Political Tragedy in the Sixteenth Century*. I cite Garnier, *Marc Antoine, Hippolyte*, ed. Raymond Lebègue.

54. However, Garnier's abrupt, unconvincing ending contrasts starkly with the great original achievement of Shakespeare's play, his fully dramatic portrait of Egypt's and Cleopatra's ability to transubstantiate tragic nature.

Garnier selectively uses the past in a way he hopes will shape the present; he reads history philosophically, seeking to uncover universal moral categories for political conduct. Plutarch's biographies, in which ethical concerns dominate the record of events, readily suit Garnier's purpose, and he effectively adapts Plutarch's moralistic portrait of a tragically tinged Antony, caught between private and public needs, between the inclinations of his own excessive nature and the rule of reason, between love and duty. To this Garnier adds a timely debate on the "virtue" of clemency or rigor in a ruler.

Garnier's Plutarchan approach to the tragedy of Antoine is evident in the hero's long opening soliloquy, which occupies the entire first act. Antoine articulates his tragedy by combining the conventional languages of the moralistic condemnation and romantic exaltation of love, which are then developed throughout the play. He is caught between Cléopatre's irresistible power, which radiates to him from her eyes, and the fear that beneath this "douce amorce" (p. 18) lies a sharp hook, "les poisons de ta belle sorciere" (p. 19). Following Plutarch closely, Garnier shows Antoine profoundly conscious of the duties he has abjured for Cléopatre: the several abortive Parthian expeditions; the desertion of his Roman wife, Octavie, and their children.[32] Yet Antoine still loves Cléopatre, and his greatest fear is that she has now betrayed that love by making political approaches to Octave. When Cléopatre appears in the middle of act 2, she confirms every detail of Antoine's evaluation except the conscious betrayal of him. Garnier limits a romantic reading of his play by the strong strain of self-reproach in both lovers, and by firm emphasis on social and political responsibility.

Does the play therefore condemn personal passion and exalt political control? It seems to pose a carefully balanced debate rather than an unequivocal answer. We cannot completely approve of

---

[32] Marie-Madeleine Mouflard, *Robert Garnier* 3: pp. 175–83, claims that Garnier drew from the complex historiographical tradition concerning Antony and Cleopatra, but I find only the influence of Plutarch's "Life" of Antony in the play.

Cléopatre's passion, for we are vividly presented with its negative consequences; yet we cannot endorse Octave's goal of one-man rule, for we see the bloodthirsty single-mindedness of means it inspires in him. Although the chorus at the end of act 2 reminds us that Rome will fall as Troy once did and Alexandria now does, Octave begins to imagine himself "Egal à Jupiter . . . sur Fortune seigneur" (p. 70). In the debate between clemency and rigor that follows, Agrippa defends mercy and tolerance, while Cesar argues for a necessary severity to root out any possible rebellion. Garnier develops both sides fully, but he seems to weight the conclusion in favor of tolerance, allowing Agrippa the long last argument that universal rule itself imposes a duty of peacekeeping.

Further, Garnier's characterization of Octave includes both a topical reflection on the need for monarchical stability and a frank confrontation with the problem that so troubled Vergil: violence is necessary for the attainment and perhaps even the maintenance of power, but pity and piety are necessary for civilization; can both qualities be the property of one man? Garnier depicts an Octave whose character is relatively complex and unresolved: Antoine describes Octave's cowardice in battle and duplicity in politics; Cléopatre fears how that tyrant will treat her children. Yet Garnier also reports Cesar's true affection for his sister and his comradely pity for the fallen Antoine. In general, just as Garnier shows Cléopatre subordinating her real concerns for children and country to her passion for Antoine, he shows Octave repressing his fraternal and comradely affections in the *idée fixe* of one-man rule.

Antoine is trapped between these neo-Vergilian extremes of love and rigorous duty, feeling the pull of each in his character. The most important aspects of this play for our argument are the ways in which Garnier employs Plutarch's "Life" of Antony to portray his hero's consciousness of this fact, ways suggestive for Shakespeare's later use of this source. Expanding on Plutarch, Garnier includes a long scene between Antoine and Lucilius, the former follower of the noble Brutus whom Antoine befriended after Philippi. The dialogue renders explicit some of the mythic parallels that contribute to the heroic pathos of Antoine's fall. Such mythic parallels are first announced in Antoine's opening soliloquy, when he describes his subjugation to Cupid in language that recalls the classical topos of Mars disarmed by Venus:

> Antoine, pauvre Antoine, helas! dés ce jour-là
> Ton ancien bon-heur de toy se recula
>
> . . . .
>
> Dés l'heure les Lauriers, à ton front si connus
> Mesprisez, firent place aux Myrtes de Venus
> La trompette aux hauts-bois, les piques et les lances,
> Les harnois esclatans aux festins et aux dances.
> Dés l'heure, miserable! au lieu que tu devois
> Faire guerre sanglante aux Arsacides Rois,
> Vengeant l'honneur Romain, que la route de Crasse
> Avoit desembelly, tu quittes la cuirasse,
> Et l'armet effroyant, pour d'un courage mol
> Courir à Cleopatre et te pendre à son col,
> Languir entre ses bras, t'en faire l'idolatre.
>
> (p. 19)

Now he and Lucilius mourn his surrender to "La douce volupté, delices de Cypris" (p. 63). Antoine's choice of Venus and *voluptas* is the obverse of Hercules' youthful choice of *virtú* over *voluptas*, a choice that launched his epic career as slayer of monsters, deeds later allegorized as the defeat of social and metaphysical evils.

Antoine, who in Plutarch claims descent from Hercules, in Garnier's play imitates the mature hero's downfall. In a passage that anticipates Shakespeare's extensive treatment of the topos, Lucilius parallels Hercules' emasculation by Omphale with Antoine's submission to Cléopatre, and describes the horrifying consequences for the world:

> Quoy? ce fameux Alcide, Alcide la merveille
> De la terre et du ciel, en force nompareille,
> Qui Geryon, Antee, et Lyce a combatu,
> Qui Cerbere attraina, monstre trois fois testu,
> Qui vainquit Achelois, qui l'Hydre rendit morte,
> Qui le ciel souleva de son espaule forte,
> Ne ploya sous le faix de cette volupté?
> De cette passion ne se veit pas domté?
> Quand d'Omphale captif, Meonienne Royne,
> Il bruisloit comme vous de Cleopatre, Antoine,
> Dormoit en son giron, luy baisottoit le sein,
> Achetoit son amour d'un servage vilain,
> Tirant à la quenouille e de sa main nerveuse

Retordant au fuzeau la filace chambreuse.
Sa masse domteresse aux solives pendoit,
Son arc comme jadis encordé ne tendoit,
Sur ses fleches filoit la mesnagere araigne,
Et son dur vestement estoit percé de teigne.
Les monstres, à plaisir, sans crainte cependant
S'alloyent multipliez par le monde espandant:
Les peuples tourmentoyent mesprisant sa mollesse
Et son cœur amoureux, esbat d'une maistresse.
                              (pp. 64–65, emphasis mine)

Garnier's Antoine, in his despair, fully agrees with this assessment, "En cela seulement semblable je luy suis, / En cela de sa race avoüer je me puis, / En cela je l'imite, et ses mœurs je rapporte, / Bref il est mon ancestre en ceste seule sorte" (p. 65).

But suddenly at the end of the play Garnier simplifies Antoine and Cléopatre, as a messenger reports that Antoine has revised his harsh judgment of her. He commits suicide not only because his worldly fame is gone but also because he longs to be reunited with her. Garnier has done nothing to explain Antoine's change of heart, and the sentimental conventional death scene is inevitably less convincing than the earlier condemning direct discourse. Cléopatre, too, is abruptly ennobled. In her last soliloquy she paraphrases several of Dido's speeches in the *Aeneid* and thereby reverses the epic's values. Instead of Dido's curse of eternal Carthaginian enmity and her frigid aloofness in the underworld, Cléopatre sheds her worldly accomplishments and declares, "Et ja fugitive Ombre avec toy je serois, / Errant sous les cyprés des rives escartees, / Au lamentable bruit des eaux Acherontees" (p. 97). But this impressive moment rings hollow in a play that has carefully stressed political responsibility and has done little to substantiate Cléopatre's value. The play's romantic conclusion seems a conventional rhetorical flourish unrelated to the political and psychological subtlety of the text.

However, Garnier's faithful rendition of Plutarch's complex and self-conscious Antony and the play's scrupulous regard for the political realities of civil war and imperial ambition focus our attention on a problem in the Plutarchan source, one which Shakespeare will address and solve: the need for detailed enrichment of Cleopatra's character if she is to stand out from the historical plot within which she is involved. The story of Antony and Cleopatra becomes in Garnier's hands something more than another example of the archetypal tragedy of suffering. Garnier is on the verge of vivifying what in previous plays had been a rhetorical debate between love and duty as a tragic action—a movement of consciousness in Antoine, and of culture in the play as a whole. The play fails when it attempts to be more than a tragedy, but in ways that underscore Shakespeare's later success. In the difficult period from Antoine's suicide attempt to Cléopatre's death, a period blurred by propaganda and inconsistent historical sources, Garnier encounters his greatest difficulties and resorts to arid conventional formulas such as the messenger's report of Antoine's death. It is this confused period that Shakespeare's Cleopatra will attempt to shape, poetically and mythologically.

In 1594 Samuel Daniel published the first of several versions of his gravely beautiful *Cleopatra*. He wrote it, he declares, at the urging of Mary Sidney, translator of Garnier's *Marc Antoine*, because "thy well graced *Antony*, / (Who all alone having remained long,) / Requir'd his Cleopatra's company."[33] Daniel revised the play several times; most notably, in the 1607 edition he shifted scenes and dramatized much of the previously narrated action. If this revision was prompted in part by the appearance of Shakespeare's *Antony and Cleopatra*, the substantive influence of Shakespeare's play upon Daniel's is nonetheless slight. Daniel, like other members of the Sidney circle, sought to merit Sir Philip Sidney's praise of drama, "full of stately speeches and well-sounding phrases climbing to the height of Seneca's style, and as full of notable morality"; his revisions were intended to balance further his play's structure and to alter its original declamatory "closet" form toward enacted drama.[34] He did not discover in Shakespeare's drama ways to unify the sharply paradoxical features of his own play, his wholehearted adaptation of Machiavellian ideas of cyclical history and his exaltation of Cleopatra's love triumph.

However, from the early version of Daniel's *Cleopatra* Shakespeare develops the antithesis of history and romance into a subtle

---

[33] From the dedication to the original 1594 edition, reprinted in A. M. Witherspoon, *The Influence of Robert Garnier on Elizabethan Drama*, pp. 99–100.

[34] Russell E. Leavenworth, *Daniel's Cleopatra*, pp. 16–18, offers a very clear discussion of the essentially formal nature of Daniel's revisions. See also Ernest Schanzer, "Daniel's Revision of His *Cleopatra*."

discordia concors of life-in-death that he then embodies in many imitated details of language in *Antony and Cleopatra*. In general, though, Daniel's cool formalism indicates by contrast Shakespeare's need for a full-bodied, playful "epic" language of love for which Christopher Marlowe's *Dido, Queene of Carthage* offers the most direct dramatic precedent.

Daniel thought of tragedy as set against a backdrop of universal political process, and his tendency to generalize beyond individual characters and particular events intensified over time. It is central to his critical treatise "The Defense of Ryme," his philosophical poem "Musophilus," his poetic *Civil Wars*, and his prose *Historie of England*. But *Cleopatra* marks his first full-scale attempt, imperfectly achieved, to depict the conjunction of character and fate as part of a large, patterned movement of history.[35] Yet within this deterministic historical framework, Daniel movingly develops the private love triumph of Cleopatra in ways influential for Shakespeare's portrayal of this heroine.

From her opening soliloquy Daniel's Cleopatra untangles Plutarch's ambiguities, clearly separating the political from the romantic, the judicious from the emotive, the public from the private. The public tragedy is the fall of Egypt, which she admits she has hastened with her luxury. Within it she only now discovers a true love for the noble Antony:

> And even affliction makes me truely love thee
> Which *Antony*, I must confesse my fault
> I never did sincerely untill now:
> Now I protest I do, now am I taught
> In death to love, in life that knew not how.[36]

Love is a private value she belatedly finds in their union.

For the first four acts Daniel emphasizes the public tragedy of Egypt in its universal political implications. As in Shakespeare's *Richard II*, setting and character complement each other as the symbolic representation of historic decline. Cleopatra discovers that her much-praised beauty has faded under time's assault. Looking at her-

---

[35] Cecil Seronsy, "The Doctrine of Cyclical Recurrence and Some Related Ideas in the Works of Samuel Daniel."

[36] Bullough, *Narrative and Dramatic Sources of Shakespeare* 5:411. I refer to this readily accessible reprint of the 1599 edition throughout.

self, she sees "Desolation" and feels that "my dissolution is become / The grave of Egypt" (p. 408). Looking about her, she finds that the magnificent architecture of the world which she, as Isis, inhabited and which Antony, as Atlas, sustained has now contracted into a tomb: "Of all, see what remaines, / This monument, two maides, and wretched I" (p. 409). A chorus of Alexandrian women at the end of act 1 completes the picture of ruin:

> For now is nothing hid,
> Of what feare did restraine.
> No secret closely done,
> But now is uttered.
> The text is made most plaine
> That flattry glos'd upon,
> The bed of sinne reveal'd
> And all the luxurie that shame would have conceal'd.
> The scene is broken downe,
> And all uncov'red lyes,
> The purple actors knowne
> Scarce men, whom men despise.
>
> (p. 413–14)

For readers of the play, this chorus provides a gloss; for theater-goers, the chorus now points, from their perspective at the fore-ground of the stage, to the revealed educative spectacle within.

At the end of act 1 the chorus blames all their misfortunes on Cleopatra. By the end of act 2 they imply that such decline is a more general problem, and by the end of act 3 they implicate themselves in Egypt's fall, "Ah no, the gods are ever just, / Our faults excuse their rigour must" (p. 427). To enlarge this philosophical message, in act 3 Daniel develops from Plutarch the minor character of the philosopher Arius. After recounting the swift moral decline of Egypt, Arius adds:

> O thou and I have heard, and read, and knowne
> Of like proude states, as wofully incombred,
> And fram'd by them, examples for our owne:
> Which now among examples must be numbred.
> For this decree a law from high is given,
> An ancient Canon, of eternall date,
> In Consistorie of the starres of heaven,
> Entred the Booke of unavoyded Fate;

> That no state can in height of happinesse,
> In th' exaltation of their glory stand:
> But thither once arriv'd, declining lesse,
> Ruine themselves, or fall by others hand.
> Thus doth the ever-changing course of things
> Runne a perpetuall circle, ever turning:
> And that same day that hiest glory brings,
> Brings us unto the poynt of backe-returning.
>
> (pp. 420–21)

This cyclical political movement is portrayed as inevitable, forged from men's unlimitable drive and bondage to material reality. At best, knowledge of it allows one to retard its speed; this is the tactic of Daniel's Octavius. At worst, it allows one to develop fortitude in one's fall; this is the tactic of Daniel's Cleopatra. In the world of politics, Daniel, like Machiavelli, opposes any providential or progressive reading of history: over time, in any civilization, "virtue produces peace, peace idleness, idleness disorder, disorder ruin."[37] The pattern is universal: Egypt could have read it in the history of previous civilizations; Rome should read it in the fall of Egypt; and Daniel's audience will find it still true. Both Daniel's Octavius and his Cleopatra see part of this pattern, and Cleopatra, as defeated prince, now readies herself to perform with honor the only appropriate action left her: suicide.

But here Daniel depicts Cleopatra in ways inconsistent with his political-historical theme. Earlier in the play Octavius affirmed the existence of a world of value apart from material constraint:

> Kingdoms I see we winne, we conquere Climates,
> Yet cannot vanquish hearts, nor force obedience,
>
> . . . .
>
> Free is the heart, *the temple of the minde*,
> The *Sanctuarie* sacred from above,
> Where nature keeps the *keies* that loose and bind.
> *No mortall hand force open can that doore,*
> So close shut up, and lockt to all mankind:
> I see mens bodies onely ours, no more,
> The rest, anothers right, that rules the minde.
>
> (p. 414, emphasis mine)

---

[37] Leavenworth, *Daniel's Cleopatra*, p. 60.

Cleopatra, in all other respects a politic queen, now, in her newly discovered love for Antony, seeks to burst through the ruined life that constrains her:

> I must my selfe force open wide a *dore*
> To let out life, and so *unhouse* my spirit.
> These hands must breake the *prison* of my soule
> To come to thee, there to enjoy like state,
> As doth the long-pent solitaire Foule,
> That hath escapt her *cage*, and found her mate.
>
> : (p. 435, emphasis mine)

Developing this idea of escape, she apostrophizes the asp as "of wonders wonder chiefe / That open canst with such an easie key / The doore of life" (p. 444).

However, Cleopatra's final detachment from the dominant political realism of the play declines from this splendid Stoic aloofness to Ovidian bathos. Daniel, who had imitated Ovid's *Heroides* in his "A Letter from Octavia to Marcus Antonius" (1599), sentimentalizes Plutarch's young Roman officer, Dolabella. This romantic Dolabella, himself in love with Cleopatra, seeks to spare her not the political humiliation of a Roman triumph, but the envy of the Roman ladies. In Daniel's play, unlike Shakespeare's, Cleopatra's growing enthusiasm for death, whether Stoic or romantic in origin, is in abrupt opposition to the values by which she, as a queen, had hitherto lived her life.

Nonetheless, Daniel's final scene is a poetic tour de force that nearly succeeds in pulling together the political and romantic movements in the play by tightly juxtaposing them as contending explanations of the reported action. According to the messenger, Cleopatra at once longs to defy Caesar and fly to Antony. As she alternates between royalty and submission, the audience alternates between awe and pity. One example of the scene-long tension is the messenger's report of the moment of her death:

> This said, she staies and makes a sodaine pause,
> As twere to feele whether the poyson wrought:
> Or rather else the working might be cause
> That made her stay, and intertain'd her thought.
> For in that instant I might well perceive
> The drowsie humor in her falling brow:

And how each powre, each part opprest did leave
Their former office, and did sencelesse grow.
Looke how a new pluckt branch against the Sunne,
Declines his fading leaves in feeble sort;
So her disjoyned joyntures as undone,
Let fall her weake dissolved limbes support.
Yet loe that face the wonder of her life,
Retains in death, a grace that graceth death,
Colour so lively, cheere so lovely rife,
That none would thinke such beauty could want breath.
And in that cheere th'impression of a smile,
Did seeme to shew she scorned Death and *Cæsar*,
As glorying that she could them both beguile,
And telling Death how much her death did please her.

                                             (p. 446)

This description, tremendously influential for Shakespeare's portrait of the queen, balances active and passive interpretations of her death.[38] Did she control her destiny, triumphing as queen, or did she yield to it in a quasi-sexual, quasi-religious ecstasy? Did she self-consciously chart the advance of the poison, or did she "drowsily" succumb to it? Did she fade and dissolve into death, or did she shine forth still more vital, defying Caesar? Reading this passage, we are continually aware of Shakespeare's echoes of its language and thought; of Antony contemplating suicide and seeing himself as the cloudy, ever mutable "rack [that] dislimns, and makes it indistinct / As water is in water" (4.14.10–11); of Cleopatra, whose death, which suggests to her maid a universal dissolution in nature, is at once regal and colloquially vibrant: "Give me my robe, put on my crown, I have / Immortal longings in me" (5.2.280); "Now boast thee, death, in thy possession lies / A lass unparallel'd" (5.2.315–16).

The antithetical effect for which Daniel strove is, I believe, his most pervasive influence upon *Antony and Cleopatra*. But whereas in Shakespeare's play the antitheses, the multiple, often contend-

---

[38] Of central importance to Shakespeare's play are Daniel's diction (*undone, dissolved, grace, beguile, please*) and use of transposed figures of thought ("her disjoyned joyntures as undone"); cf. Enobarbus's praise of Cleopatra making "defect perfection," and her cry to the asp, "Come, thou mortal wretch, / With thy sharp teeth this knot intrinsicate / Of life at once untie" (5.2.302–4).

ing, perspectives point to a numinous heart of Cleopatra's mystery —a capacity for fusing and transcending opposites—in Daniel's play the antitheses are didactically exposed as rhetorical debating points, temporarily left unreconciled in the final scene, and then harshly determined by the concluding chorus.

In that final chorus we are decisively left with political and historical explanations. Our shock at the reintroduction of the themes that dominated the play to the end of the fourth act is an indication of how far Daniel has imaginatively strayed into romanticism in the last act. Once again the chorus speculates that the Egyptians' indulgence of appetite and power had led to political disorder and their overthrow by Rome, while Rome itself is soon likely to follow the same pattern: "And now wilt yeelde thy streames / A prey to other Reames?" (p. 448). In this paradoxical pattern the only certainty is an ordered revolution of disorders, "Doth Order order so / Disorders overthrow?" (p. 449). Cleopatra is not mentioned in this highly abstract ending, from which we may conclude either that she has made the only dignified human response to this inhuman pattern or that an understanding of the cycle's pattern is the play's real lesson. In either case, after finding so many emotional and ideational virtues in the play, we are discomfited by Daniel's inability to balance them during the play and resolve them at its end.

Christopher Marlowe

Christopher Marlowe's *Dido, Queene of Carthage* is a play of multiple perspectives, a theater for many ironies, both verbal and visual. The interpreter's task lies less in locating specific instances of disjunctive meaning than in weighing their total effect. Marlowe's play does not imitate the constant pull of experience against idealism that creates the pervasive tragic undertow in Vergil's epic. Its irony is of another sort, less directly reflective, more prismatic, deflected from a single course by a medium of complex and contradictory properties.

This multivalent and frequently disconcerting quality results to a large extent from the particular traditions of stagecraft, acting, and audience expectation in the private theater company of boy actors for which Marlowe composed the play. He employed these defining characteristics self-consciously, in ways that give the play a quite different technical cast than his other works, written for the public stage.[39] However, this particular example of technical adaptation also points to a characteristic of Marlowe's corpus: an extremism that makes his plays problems in values rather than statements and explorations of values themselves.[40] Through this extremism, Marlowe's irony cuts both ways, destroying his overreachers but also undermining our faith in the boundaries that effect their falls.

Hence the perennial interpretative controversies between critics of ideological and skeptical bent, for Marlowe often makes the structures he evokes appear arbitrary, and undermines sure judgment. His works are profoundly subversive and problematic not only because of their protagonists' energetic heterodoxy but also because of their conclusions' empty orthodoxy. Like so much of Ovid and many witty and darkly humorous moderns, Marlowe's plays are devoid of satisfactory ending. *Dido, Queene of Carthage* is no exception.

Marlowe's amoral virtuosity seems especially pronounced in his reworking of the *Aeneid*, a source that supports a superficial moralistic interpretation but challenges us to a more complex one. Marlowe neither restores epic content to the story, as does Giraldi, nor tightens its tragic tension, as Pazzi, Dolce, and Jodelle, working from different perspectives, attempt. Instead, he responds to each of the emotional vectors suggested in the *Aeneid* and creates a few of his own. The result is a play of jostling moods, superficially unified by its theatrical playfulness, as the most helpful studies of the piece argue.[41]

---

[39] The title page of the only extant early edition of *Dido, Queene of Carthage*, the 1594 quarto, states that the play was "Played by the Children of her Maiesties Chappell," which H. J. Oliver explains as indicating that it "would presumably have been written especially for performance in a 'private' indoor theatre, such as the first Blackfriars, or at Court, and it seems to have been intended for the stage with fixed multiple set as distinct from the probably bare stage of public theatres, such as the Theatre and the Curtain" (Introduction to *Dido*, p. xxx).

[40] For a general evaluation of Marlowe's work that argues this thesis, and to which my analysis is much indebted, see Russell Fraser, "On Christopher Marlowe."

[41] See Jackson Cope, "Marlowe's *Dido* and the Titillating Children"; Clifford Leech, "Marlowe's Humor"; and Brian Gibbons, "Unstable Proteus."

Just before the play's decisive turning point in act 5, Marlowe inserts a scene of comic antitheses that reveals the imaginative limits of his poetic argument. Here, as he prepares to resume the main argument of his Vergilian theme, he abruptly focuses our attention on its relativism and, therefore, final nihilistic collapse. In a piece of stage action that bears amusing, uncomfortable, and pointed visual analogy to the earlier "courtship" scenes of Jove and Ganymede, Venus and Ascanius, and Dido and Aeneas, Dido's ancient nurse finds herself fatally wounded by little Cupid-Ascanius, caught in the embarrassing position of the seemingly powerful yet totally victimized wooer. The succeeding interchange presents with imaginative clarity the coincidence of opposites that Marlowe plays with throughout his drama, allowing us to question whether these jarring differences fuse into a *discordia concors* or provoke a tragic catharsis.

The old nurse, dandling Cupid in her arms, has just pulled herself up short from erotic musing about a former suitor:

> O what meane I to have such foolish thoughts!
> Foolish is love, a toy.—O sacred love,
> If there be any heaven in earth, tis love:
> Especially in women of our yeares.—
>
> (4.5.25–28)[42]

Within this marvelously realized scene we can assent to both sides of the proposition, the shamed repudiation of and the buoyant invocation to a power that even so momentarily could make the green shoots of anticipation spring from a withered stock. However, embedded in this antithesis are the critical conditional "if" and the sharp irony of time that destroys the fragile equilibrium, for, "A grave, and not a lover fits thy age. . . . Why doe I thinke of love now I should dye?" (4.5.30, 34). The scene verges on painful farce;

Press analysis too far, as does D. C. Allen in "Marlowe's *Dido* and the Tradition," and the play collapses under a too-heavy weight of reductive irony. Suspend disbelief altogether, and the play is inflated to an uncritical romance in which hyperbole is too easily accepted as fact—a misjudgment that weakens many comparative studies of *Dido* and *Antony and Cleopatra*.

[42] I cite the critical edition of Fredson Bowers, *The Complete Works of Christopher Marlowe.*

the very brevity with which Marlowe sketches it allows him to strike an exact and richly suggestive balance between the nurse's praise and the ironic qualifications she herself offers: love is sweet, but aging and death are likewise real. We feel a moment of genuine unforced pity, within this very artificial setting, for her lost pleasure with an unknown rejected beau.

The nurse's bemusement leads us to the heart of our evaluation of Marlowe's "tragedy" of Dido: can love transcend the play's destined tragic action? Time and death preclude any absolute "heaven in earth," leaving us with the painful and delicate task of accommodating experience and the ideal, or perhaps of projecting our yearnings onto a transcendent order. The nurse's iconic representation of love's power and limits causes us to review much more critically the love of Aeneas and Dido. But their love will not bear close scrutiny; Marlowe's depiction of it appears a shallow idealization when contrasted with his major source, Vergil's *Aeneid*, or with the imitations of his most famous follower, Shakespeare. This shallowness both obviates the unsentimental romanticism of the latter and invades the thoughtful epic context of the former. It corrupts the defining values that create in the *Aeneid* a love tragedy and there substitute for love a glorification of heroism.

The nurse's scene occurs just after Aeneas's attempted departure has prompted Dido to her most extravagant excesses in defense of beleaguered love. It precedes the play's reversal—Aeneas's departure—and swift denouement, in which Marlowe, despite his subversion of Vergil's story, tries unsuccessfully to rise, through strained imitation, to the full dignity of Dido's death scene. Dido's death explodes the nurse's conditional; there is no heaven on earth. But the shallowness of Dido's love finally undermines not only her hyperbole but also our sense of its tragic seriousness. Moreover, through verbal and visual parallels, the nurse's scene recalls the disturbing opening moments of the play, when "there is discovered *Jupiter* dandling *Ganimed* upon his knee." That opening leads us to doubt seriously if there is even a "heaven" in heaven, and therefore, a supernatural justification for the homiletic "tragedy" of Dido with which Marlowe rather cynically flirts throughout the play.

The special conditions of the boys' theater for which *Dido* was written also threaten to lend a particularly decadent aura to Aeneas's and Dido's love affair. Jackson Cope conjectures that the boy who played Aeneas was intermediate in stature between the little boys who played the parts of Cupid, Ascanius, and Ganymede, and the much bigger boys who carried them about the stage.[43] Aeneas's frequently emphasized boyish beauty (see, for example, 1.1.124, 155–56) and Dido's aggressive infatuation (she would have been played by an older boy) uncomfortably recall the homosexual suggestion of the Jove-Ganymede opening, inverting neo-Platonic allegory to base desire.

This very deliberate excess embarrasses or, as Cope suggests, titillates the audience when after Cupid's assault, Dido's dignified sympathy for a broken young warrior turns into the highly erotic seduction of an only vaguely comprehending boy. She courts Aeneas as though he were a maiden:

> O dull conceipted *Dido*, that till now
> Didst never thinke *Æneas* beautifull:
> But now for quittance of this oversight,
> Ile make me bracelets of his golden haire,
> His glistering eyes shall be my looking glasse,
> His lips an altar, where Ile offer up
> As many kisses as the Sea hath sands.
>
> (3.1.82–88)

She offers to repair his ships (for Achates to sail) in extravagant, impractical terms that show her now complete obliviousness to daily care and her obsession with sensual, especially tactile, imagery:

> Ile give thee tackling made of riveld gold,
> Wound on the barkes of odoriferous trees,
> Oares of massie Ivorie full of holes,
> Through which the water shall delight to play:
> Thy Anchors shall be hewed from Christall Rockes,
> Which if thou lose shall shine above the waves:

---

[43] Cope, "Titillating Children," pp. 321–23, makes special reference to 3.4, with such lines as "*Æneas* thoughts dare not ascend so high" and "If that your majestie can looke so lowe," which he reads as broad visual puns; Cope suggests an obvious disparity in the age and size of the "lovers" to account for Aeneas's incomprehension of and vague shrinking before Dido's authoritarianism and aggressive amorous advances.

The Masts whereon thy swelling sailes shall hang,
Hollow Pyramides of silver plate:
The sailes of foulded Lawne, where shall be wrought
The warres of *Troy*, but not *Troyes* overthrow:
For ballace, emptie *Didos* treasurie,
Take what ye will, but leave *Æneas* here.

(3.1.116–27) [44]

There are no Vergilian "tears for things" in these self-gratify-ing images, a catalogue of bribing gifts that echoes so exactly the pattern of extravagances Jove promises Ganymede, "if thou wilt be my love" (1.1.49). This movement has its climax in the scene played before the cave, when Dido finally elicits from the rather callow Aeneas a promise of love. The ominous parallel with the opening scene might have been further emphasized if the cave— which in the multiple staging of the early private theater would have been a detached construction, or "house"—were placed near center stage, in the wooded area separating the city of Carthage from the shore. There it would have been directly under—a ground floor, as it were—the second-story curtained construction that represented Olympus. [45]

If we need any further proof that this love is an arbitrary in-fatuation rather than a "marriage of true minds," we need only note how Marlowe alters Vergil even as he closely follows the *Aeneid*. In the woodland interview between Aeneas and his disguised mother Venus, Marlowe omits the entire account of Dido's history, which in so many ways resembles Aeneas's flight and exile. In the scene before Carthage's walls (based on *Aen.* 1.441ff., at the Temple of Juno) Marlowe dwells exclusively on Aeneas's indulgent sorrow, without dramatizing any melancholy affinity he might feel for the sympathetic queen who would erect such a memorial. Further, Mar-lowe dissipates the full emotional force of Aeneas's story of Troy's

---

[44] J. B. Steane, *Marlowe*, p. 36, comments on the thinly veiled eroticism of these lines.

[45] For a brief summary of the function of private-theater multiple staging in *Dido*, which differs at several points from my conjecture, see Oliver, Intro-duction to *Dido*, pp. xxx–xxxi. Peter Saccio, in *The Court Comedies of John Lyly*, chap. 1, summarizes much of the evidence we have about multiple staging and discusses its particular dramatic possibilities.

siege and capture on Dido's "tottering soul" *(Aen.* 4.22) by having her listen to his tale with judicial sympathy *before* Cupid strikes her breast. In all these innovations, Marlowe discards the psychological and emotional bonds with which Vergil ties his lovers' feelings to his epic's main action.

The same extremist view colors Marlowe's adaptation of the imperial theme that moves Aeneas's destiny and necessitates the tragedy of Dido. He grasps the "main heads" of the story, its obvious dramatic peaks, seemingly without any desire or skill to explore its motives and workings. Consider, for example, the characterization of Aeneas. Marlowe often stretches, with good effect, to grasp some particularly vaunting or pathetic moment, as when he infuses Aeneas's measured speech to his comrades ("O socii," *Aen.* 1.198–207) with a youthfully jaunty tone, or captures, with great fidelity and yet slight exaggeration, the telling details of Aeneas's encounter with the huntswoman Venus. But Marlowe's Aeneas never exhibits any of that reflective, conditioned personality that Vergil achieves for his hero through narrative commentary and his Aeneas's own care-filled words. His Aeneas does not by force of his character focus and weight the epic action; rather, his most consistent quality is an extreme malleability to the pressures of each dramatic situation. This quality provokes situations that verge on the amusing, especially when we realize that a youth is acting the role: he sees a statue of Priam, so he cries, he has a raptly attentive audience, so he (quite effectively) hams it up; he is seduced, and after a few moments of incomprehension, rises to the occasion; he is ordered to leave Carthage, and he goes.

The scene in which Aeneas's leave-taking is first broached represents Marlowe's most intense effort to draw together the contending demands of love and duty. Although rhetorically neat, it fails dramatically. This Aeneas voices neither any concern for the claims of justice nor any sympathy for Dido's feelings. Nor do Aeneas's men say much to validate the former concept, for they are willing enough to enter into the pleasures of Carthage and then hypocritical enough to heap abuse on the "ticing dame" who rules it. Thus the play does not provide sufficient support for the ideal of Aeneas's Roman destiny, and Dido is too obviously the victim of the gods to be moralistically condemned. The episodes that Fulgentius read as an example of the trials of adolescent lust have become more a warning against the perils of loving beautiful but immature boys.[46]

Dido and Aeneas's love in Marlowe's play, despite some marvelously engaging poetry, is not a true ideal, tested in the drama by time and experience, but a false idyll compact between a boy who lacks substance and a victimized woman who seeks to clothe this immaturity with beautiful words, rich garments, and spectacle. This artificial "heaven in earth," one of cloying, contrived "comfits"—"Sugar-almonds, sweete Conserves" (2.1.305)—is finally tested by the nurse's one great condition, devouring Time. The implicit irony that underlies Marlowe's sweet pastoral seduction lyric, "Come live with me, and be my love," becomes explicit, for gamesome love persists only "while time serves, and we are but decaying"; soon empire calls.[47]

Finally, Marlowe's play bears only the most tenuous relationship to either the emotional or rational content of love or heroism, which are but useful labels for his consuming concern with force, power, and energy. Marlowe's favorite rhetorical figure, hyperbole, also suggests a quality far greater than content; the object of comparison becomes the springboard for the force that exceeds it, just as the catalogues of objects that fill out the love rhetoric in *Dido* suggest an imaginative range much greater than a simple sum of parts.

The true enemy of this sort of poetic imagination is limitation itself, which to its extremist cast seems totally negative and arbi-

---

[46] Marlowe's Ganymede and adolescent Aeneas can be read as an elaborate mockery of Fulgentius's moral allegorical reading of the *Aeneid* as the journey of the soul to God. Marlowe's Ganymede, rather than representing the soul rapt in neo-Platonic contemplation, is merely Jupiter's petulant plaything, who "directs" the play's tragic action for his own amusement, and Aeneas's sojourn in Carthage represents the sexual trials of adolescence, but with comic, rather than homiletic, ends. D. C. Allen, "Marlowe's *Dido*," hints at Marlowe's conscious inversion of this allegorical tradition: "There is also a possible allegorical reading of their love affair, but I am inclined to believe that if there is allegory, as there certainly is in Giraldi Cinthio, it is laughingly metaphysical rather than solemnly moral" (p. 68). Erwin Panofsky, *Studies in Iconology*, pp. 213–18, cites some of the principal sources for neo-Platonic interpretations of the Ganymede story.

[47] John Cutts, "*Dido, Queen of Carthage*," comments skillfully on the play's dramatic juxtapositions as an ironic development of the implicit *carpe diem* theme of "The Passionate Shepherd to His Love."

trary. In Marlowe's fictions, the protagonists are finally made to acknowledge the containing structures of fate and death, but they do so unwillingly, straining all their resources to overcome or circumvent them. They do so quite correctly, by their own lights, for when these limits close in on a Marlovian character, they are final; there is no feel for immortality, unless one counts Faustus's immortality of pain.

Various technical effects, too, contribute to this negative valuation of the principle of limitation, which is employed as the destructive edge of irony rather than the constructive shape of decorum. In *Dido*, for example, Marlowe at times confines himself to a fairly strict imitation of Vergil's verse and episode (though not always, as noted, to tone and thematic content), chiefly in acts 1, 2, and 5; but this source of balance evaporates as soon as he launches on free invention. Among some of the more obvious instances of his characteristic excess are: the mournful verbal embroidery at Aeneas's viewing of Priam's statue; the heightening of the narration of Troy's destruction, including the report of the street fighting; the descriptions of the death of Priam and the final abandonment of the Trojan women; and Dido's love hyperbole, which continues past the Vergilian confrontation scene to the passage that begins "Ile frame me wings of waxe like *Icarus*" (5.1.243–61).

Some of these passages are just verbal and emotional indulgence; more often they contain their own verbal and situational ironies, as in Dido's Icarus speech, in which she is still appealing to a sympathetic world of love that is already riven by a traitorous act. Occasionally these passages carry the seeds of a more pervasive structural irony, as when Aeneas's martial impotence at Troy and his reluctant abandonment of Polyxena foreshadows his later abandonment of Dido; a parallelism explicit in the echoed "*Æneas*, stay . . ." (2.1.281; 5.1.228). Marlowe's greater tragic power in *Faustus* results from his much more exactly and consistently tuning the verbal and situational ironies to each new development; his control there is, in large part, the result of the well-developed traditional structural pattern of the morality play.[48]

But in *Dido*, a play unrestrained by a conventional structural pattern, even the tragic boundaries of fate and death begin to yield to Marlowe's poetic assaults. Dido's love rhetoric, which tries to

---

[48] See David Bevington, *From Mankind to Marlowe*, pp. 245–62.

create a new "heaven in earth" ("And heele make me immortall with a kisse" 4.4.123) is, taken by itself, rather grandly heroic, and in its immediate context, pathetically and fearfully tragic. Yet it is destroyed by one final Ovidian ironic twist: is the immortality, so fervidly sought, worthwhile? Recall that at the beginning of the play Jupiter offers to his boy lover Ganymede a release from limitation:

> Controule proud Fate, and cut the thred of time.
> Why, are not all the Gods at thy commaund,
> And heaven and earth the bounds of thy delight?
>
> (1.1.29–31)

The little boy can have unparalleled "poetic license"! With these powers Ganymede could rewrite the story of Aeneas and Dido in a purely romantic vein, complete with happy ending—improving on Jupiter in the *Aeneid*, who though compassionate, must follow Fate. The truth is, however, as the venality and pettishness of the boy and the silly infatuation of the great god reveal, that in Marlowe's play there is not even a heaven in heaven. In fact, the gods are much less noble and constructive than the mortals. Despite the uneven charm of much of Marlowe's verse for the boy players, a totally destructive "playfulness" haunts the concluding image of this scene. The boy Ganymede, who in neo-Platonic allegorizations represents the most exalted aspirations of the human soul, is granted power over Fate and Time; with it he effects not a poetic synthesis, but a titillating tale of immature heroism and delusive love. Jupiter's little love does make the world go round, but then, in this play love is a blind child, "Foolish is love, a toy" (4.5.26).

Even more significant, therefore, than Marlowe's hyperbolic language in *Dido* is the figure of thought it embodies, the allegorical straining that in this play, written for the children's theater, deliberately overreaches and collapses into reductive ironies. With developing Ovidian mock-heroic sensibility Marlowe counters his Aeneas's puerile "other world" of arms with the intense this-worldly *carpe diem* pleas of his heroine. Examined, these shallow ideals fade from passion, to wit, to pathos, to bathos. But such comic inadequacy can generate sublimity, such pervasive skepticism a graceful belief, if presided over by a genial intelligence and controlled imagination. Shakespeare consciously overcomes Marlowe's difficulties with the heroic. His heroes and heroines, from the governing figures in *A Midsummer Night's Dream*, to Hal in the second tetralogy, to Cleopatra, make of Marlowe's highlighted heroic defects, perfection.

Epic into Tragedy, Romantic Epic into Tragicomedy

Seneca's plays supplied the most accessible formal model for Renaissance classical drama. However, even the rigidly neo-Senecan *Didone* of Lodovico Dolce exhibits some understanding and adaptation of Vergilian cultural history in its encomium to Venice as the successor to the Roman *imperium*. Cesare de Cesari's *Cleopatra* and Celso Pistorelli's *Marc'Antonio e Cleopatra* take the opposite attitude toward the Vergilian political heritage, emphasizing Rome's tyranny. These plays also exemplify how the most academic dramas of the Renaissance enrich complex traditions of literary sources, even when they cannot unify them. Some of the playwrights unconsciously transmute the deep ambiguities in their sources as more superficial ambivalences and discontinuities; others explicitly develop them as debates. For example, Dolce's Dido is inconsistently sympathized with as Ovidian victim and condemned as guilty lover, while Cesare polemically and unconventionally contrasts Cleopatra as regal and maternal heroine with a brutal Octavius. For the more thoughtful and accomplished artist, such evidence of the dissolution of an earlier aesthetic synthesis—especially as it becomes more difficult to "save appearances"—provides impetus for a new synthesis.

We approach this interpretative crisis in the theory and practice of Giovambattista Giraldi Cinthio. In his *Didone* he is at once a subtle dramatist of the Fulgentian Christian moral allegorization of the *Aeneid* and a neo-Platonic opponent of its arid dichotomies. The contemporary issue of the relationship between Providence and free will morally engages him in the similar crux of the *Aeneid*. Fidelity to the outline of his source material does not allow him the freedom to radically rewrite it; however, in *Didone* and *Cleopatra* there are everywhere signs of his conscious critical disposition to turn tragedy into tragicomedy.

In the two tragedies of Étienne Jodelle the interpretative crisis is becoming fully conscious as part of a historical redefinition of Roman Empire as French Holy Roman Empire. Jodelle's *Cléopatre captive* is more an implied corrective of tyrannical Roman rule than a condemnation of the two lovers. His *Dido se sacrifiant,* in its consistent modifications of the *Aeneid* and additions from Ovid's *Heroides* and Lucretius's *De rerum natura,* comes as close as it can to rewriting the epic as romantic tragicomedy without altering the essentials of Vergil's plot. Dido's death becomes an indictment of oppressive Roman hypocrisy rather than Vergil's painful argument for Roman rule.

The French romanticizing of Vergil's epic, of which Jodelle's *Didon* forms a part, was paralleled in England by Spenser's *The Faerie Queene.* Meanwhile, in his second tetralogy of history plays Shakespeare began revising the Vergilian problem of the tenacity of the past and the cathartic violence deemed necessary for its reformulation. His later plays suggest more strongly that the ability to displace potential conflict into an area of imaginative play can make historical change gradual and evolutionary, and psychological growth possible. Spenser's imaginative allegorical displacements of historical event, especially in Britomart's romantic epic transvaluations of the *Aeneid,* provide Shakespeare with the most direct literary precedent, outside his own work, for the fictional freedom of his *Antony and Cleopatra,* in which Antony declares that they will join a reunited Dido and Aeneas in the afterlife.

In addition to such thoughtful romanticizing of Vergil's epic, Shakespeare had the very specific lessons of Robert Garnier's *Marc Antoine* and Samuel Daniel's *Cleopatra.* From Garnier he could discover the tragic potential and mythic resonance of Plutarch's Antony. Garnier's conflation of Dido's death speeches with Cleopatra's vision of reunion with Antony in the afterlife forms a direct precedent for Shakespeare's re-imagining of the significance of Dido's death for his Alexandrian lovers. From Daniel's thoroughgoing divorce of the political and personal significance of the story of Antony and Cleopatra, Shakespeare could have taken the necessity of wedding them in his own version, of anchoring Daniel's language of transcendent release to an immanent reality.

This method is also Marlowe's. However, for Marlowe an immanent reality serves, consciously or unconsciously, to undercut hyperbole, whereas Shakespeare consistently works to make his ironies support a chastened and purified imagination. He offers us "the worst of words" and of actions—precisely in order to test our own re-creative abilities. In *Antony and Cleopatra* Vergil's Roman tragic and epic action becomes, as it was for Augustine, Dante, and Spenser, the platform for an ascent to higher values. The play is all the more effective because it appeals to us to transcend in our minds the inadequacy of staged action to an ideal object of imitation that exists on another plane. Shakespeare's dramatic evolution may be read as the increasingly subtle study of the intimate embrace of eros and civilization, with romantic epic the potent source of his tragicomedic art.

IV.

The Shakespearean Synthesis:
Antony and Cleopatra

That she did make defect perfection,
And, breathless, power breathe forth.

(SHAKESPEARE: *Antony and Cleopatra*)

Prologue

Once we have achieved this [i.e., knowledge of moral philosophy] by the art of discourse or reasoning, then, inspired by the Cherubic spirit, using philosophy through the steps of the ladder, that is, of nature, and penetrating all things from center to center, we shall sometimes descend, with titanic force rending the unity like Osiris into many parts, and we shall sometimes ascend, with the force of Phoebus collecting all the parts like the limbs of Osiris into a unity, until, resting at last in the bosom of the Father who is above the ladder, we shall be made perfect with the felicity of theology.

(Pico della Mirandola, "Oration on the Dignity of Man")

Neither let it be deemed too saucy a comparison to balance the highest point of man's wit with the efficacy of Nature; but rather give right honour to the heavenly Maker of that maker, who having made man to His own likeness, set him beyond and over all the works of that second nature: which in nothing he showeth so much as in Poetry, when with the force of a divine breath he bringeth things forth far surpassing her doings, with

> no small argument to the incredulous of that first ac-
> cursed fall of Adam: since our erected wit maketh us
> know what perfection is, and yet our infected will keep-
> eth us from reaching unto it.
>
> (Sidney, *An Apology for Poetry*)

Both Pico della Mirandola and Philip Sidney define man centrally as "maker," a creator collaborating with the First Creator,
God. The definition implies a complex attitude toward nature, human nature, and history. On the one hand, it encourages reverence
for nature and respect for the past as the record of God's creative
activity, within which man exists. On the other hand, both Pico's
enthusiasm for man's God-given creative mission and Sidney's more
conservative, post-Reformation sense of man's obligation to restore
a "first nature" dimmed by original sin, impel men to take from the
world and the past not a record of fact but a map for renovation. Both
men believe there occurred a fall from originative unity that it is
man's responsibility to restore. To do so he must assiduously study
the testimony of the past and the traces of God in nature, but he
cannot rest with that broken account, that shattered corpse. These
inductive fragments must be unified by a compelling faith in their
single source. For Pico's *magus*, a syncretic account of men's beliefs
(moral philosophy) enables a fruitful study of nature that allows us
to ascend "through the steps of the ladder" to confirm God's revelation. For Sidney's poet, the imperfect testimony of the historian
must be corrected by the precept of the moral philosopher to form
that "erected wit," those eikastic fictions, which move us to repair
the damage of our fall. The end of such poetic activity for Sidney
is not aesthetic contemplation, which verges close to mere fanciful
indulgence, but vigorous, restorative moral action; with Spenser he
wishes "to fashion a gentleman or noble person in vertuous and
gentle discipline."

Shakespeare's mature career offers us a particularly rich late-
Renaissance version of this ideal of the historically conscious, morally responsible creator-artist. His practice, however, is so heavily
fraught with skepticism and self-consciousness toward this definition of the artist's endeavor as to presage clearly the ideal's decline
in the seventeenth and eighteenth centuries. Shakespeare articulates
his abilities and doubts against the constantly evoked background
of Vergil's *Aeneid*. His own "epic," the second tetralogy, not only

depicts a Biblical and Vergilian fall into the tragic world of history but also, as drama, elicits the conscious collaboration of the audience in its redemption. We can here only outline Shakespeare's recognition of Vergilian sacrifice and his own contrary decision to develop his audience's involvement in history into an exhortation to re-creative fiction, as prelude to an analysis of *Antony and Cleopatra*, which recapitulates the several stages in this process against the explicitly evoked backdrop of Vergil's Rome.[1]

Shakespeare's investigations of the history of his own country deepened from the overt providentialism of *Richard III* to a myth of fall and re-creation in the second tetralogy. His chief character there, Hal, figures forth the artist's own historical dilemma. Having witnessed the decline of the divinely anointed Richard II and the crisis of authority generated for his father, Hal vows to "imitate" the sun, restoring divine myth through an altogether human, even economic, calculus.[2] *1 Henry IV* is a largely exhilarating account of the success of this worldly-wise providential fiction, set against the background of the continuing tragedy of England's medieval order.

---

[1] E. M. W. Tillyard's orthodox readings in *Shakespeare's History Plays* are usefully supplemented by the detailed skeptical analyses of character and political realities offered by Robert Ornstein, *A Kingdom for a Stage*. For a more recent assessment of the influence of Renaissance historical and political theories on Shakespeare's history plays, see Moody Prior, *The Drama of Power*. My reading of the second tetralogy implies a resolution of the oppositions of political orthodoxy and skepticism in a multileveled interpretation that moves from naive patriotism, through the severe skepticism produced by close analysis of Richard's fall and the Lancastrian rise, to our critical assent to an immanent myth of divine authority. This reading complements studies of the metaphors of the stage and the application of speech-act theory; see James Calderwood, *Shakespearean Metadrama*. On the second tetralogy in particular, see Calderwood, *Metadrama in Shakespeare's Henriad*, and Joseph A. Porter, *The Drama of Speech Acts*.

[2] In his first soliloquy (*1H4* 1.2.190–212) Hal evinces an artist's consciousness that he merely "imitates" the divine myth of the sun-king that Richard had believed in as symbolic fact, and he implies through related image patterns that that myth has been debased to material, economic, calculation by Richard's irresponsibility ("sun" / "clouds" / "bright metal" / "sullen ground"). However, even this extraordinarily self-conscious and schematized speech, which ends with the same ominously powerful spondaic "I will" that closes the mock throne scene (2.4.475), is leavened by the re-creative motifs of holiday, play, and sport that later enliven his drama as improvisation, and engage us emotionally (1.2.199–202).

2 *Henry IV* explores the disturbing implications of Hal's mortal machinations, in large part through the Vergilian context of divine mission and doubt evoked by the "Induction" of Rumor. This figure, who in the *Aeneid* precipitated the tragedy of Aeneas and Dido (4.173–97), becomes the symbol for those contending human emotions that Hal must direct if he is to make teleological the flux of history. In an audacious reversal of morality-play patterns, Hal, the seemingly youthful everyman, actually "knows" everyone, and the major outlines of what is in fact his plot.[3] However, he discovers its cost gradually, in a series of moments improvised to evolving historical circumstance: cutting off Falstaff's moving self-justification, not only with his father's "I do," but with his own "I will" (*1H4* 2.4.475); longing for "small beer" (*2H4* 2.2.6); and continuing to distance himself from his father and enduring Henry's engrained mistrust (*2H4* 2.2.32–65; 4.5.88–137). Shakespeare's strategy in 2 *Henry IV* is Vergilian, immersing his hero in time, forcing upon him painful abnegation, having him plead "Let the end try the man" (2.2.45). Hal's rejection of Falstaff rings with the Pauline theological certainties he has intimated throughout his rise: "I know thee not, old man. Fall to thy prayers" (5.5.47–48).[4] But although he is now an anointed king, he is also a man, and his fear that he has "killed his heart" (*H5* 2.1.88), his doubts about whether his human efforts suffice, surface powerfully on the night before the battle of Agincourt (*H5* 4.1).

The rejection of Falstaff defines the epic context of the tetralogy as the abandonment of Dido defines that of the *Aeneid*. Her tragedy, which is also Aeneas's tragedy and the tragedy of the Homeric world view, involves us emotionally while at the same

---

[3] Richard Knowles, "Unquiet and the Double Plot of 2 *Henry IV*," p. 140, notes that Shakespeare may have derived his portrait of Rumor from intermediary Renaissance mythographical handbooks. Similarly, Northumberland's "strained passion" (*2H4* 1.1) seems a deliberately anachronistic echo of the English neo-Senecan plays such as that recalled by the Chief Player in *Ham.* 3.1., rather than a direct imitation of *Aen.* 2. However, the existence of such intermediary sources need not deny Shakespeare's evocation in *2H4* of a more general Vergilian ethos, grounded in a first-hand knowledge of the *Aeneid*; indeed two such independent reminiscences seem to argue strongly for it, as a striking secondary source may redirect an author's attention to the original work. See also Alan Dessen, "The Intemperate Knight and the Politic Prince."

[4] Cf. *1H4* 1.2.86–95, 203–12; 2.4.8–14.

time rarefying those emotions and projecting them outward toward the creation of some as-yet-unknown ideal. Although we may not concur with Vergil's dimly foreshadowed Roman goals, we sense the emotional pressure that impels Aeneas in the second, more "objective," Iliadic half of the epic, and are invited to collaborate in its fulfillment. Similarly, Hal's rejection of his orotund surrogate father is displaced into those rhetorical abilities that find their highest expression in *Henry V*. There he is able to hearten aristocrat and commoner alike in their epic adventure against the French. His rhetoric, ultimately poised yet showing subtle signs of strain, is the model for the chorus's broader exhortations to us to override the limitations of both historical action and the stage, and participate in creating an English nationalistic epic.

Yet even as we are swept up in this epic rhetoric, we realize that Hal's is a largely human imposition of order upon a much more complex dramatic "reality." We ask ourselves if Hal, having done his human best and been miraculously saved against overwhelming odds at Agincourt, ever explores fully the problem of having created his own divine myth. My argument, derived in part from analogy with the *Aeneid*, is that he goes some distance, and that these superhuman efforts take their toll on him as well. As with the *Aeneid*, the argument needs to be made by subtle inference, from those rare insights into consciousness that are so quickly glossed over by epic purpose: the hint that Aeneas, too, weeps at leaving Carthage (*Aen.* 4.449) or Hal's precisely weighted yet poignant aside over the body of the supposedly dead Falstaff, "Poor Jack, farewell! / I could have better spar'd a better man" (*1H4* 5.4.102–3).

However, if Hal does not fully plumb these depths, Shakespeare subsequently does. In the tetralogy Hal's efforts are in part sustained by preexisting theocratic myth; in *Julius Caesar* that myth must be created in the face of republican tradition and skeptical philosophical pluralism.[5] Julius Caesar is enigmatic, arguably be-

---

[5] For the divided interpretations of the character of Julius Caesar and of the Roman Empire, see Geoffrey Bullough, *Narrative and Dramatic Sources of Shakespeare* 5:4–57. Ernest Schanzer, *The Problem Plays of Shakespeare*, documents this divided tradition as the consciously implanted interpretative problem within *Julius Caesar* and thus potentially reconciles decades of partisan criticism of the play. Joseph Simmons, *Shakespeare's Pagan World*, pp. 65–108, implies that the characters' shortcomings and the tragic action are

cause he does not know himself thoroughly and thus cannot work out a properly inspiriting relationship between his humanity and the more-than-human demands of his role. He is also moving against established, if inadequate, republican tradition, and the play implies that perhaps no one man can consciously control such a change, although he may be its catalyst. Caesar's ambiguous narrated "fall" in act 1 is insufficient to define the action (1.2.212–84), but his assassination, played upon by Antony, is sufficient to establish autocracy; the full tragic sacrifice is required for catharsis, and the myth of the dead Caesar is far more powerful than the imperfect living man.

The other three major characters each delineate partial views of human nature and the body politic. Cassius, the skeptical Epicurean, begins by doubting the influence of the gods and the supremacy of any man. Brutus, the noble Stoic, represses emotion in the service of an unrealistic republican ideal. Antony, the actor and Asiatic orator, can arouse emotion but is limited in his ability to direct it; he clears the way for the implied ascendency of Octavius Caesar.

The play is a "problem play" not only because of its various sources but also because of its lack of a satisfying resolution. Cassius's metadramatic speech reminds us how little any of these characters comprehend the action taking place:

> How many ages hence
> Shall this our lofty scene be acted over,
> In states unborn, and accents yet unknown!
> . . . .
> So oft as that shall be,
> So often shall the knot of us be call'd
> The men that gave their country liberty.
> (3.1.111–13, 116–18)

We focus particularly on Brutus, whose repression of emotion would impose ideological statement upon tragic action. His attempted justification of the assassination of Caesar is as naive as Caesar's godlike posturing in its refusal to recognize his own human involvement in this "holy" deed. His impossible detachment pre-

---

generated by Shakespeare's historical awareness of the absence in Caesar's era of the Christian theocratic myth that informs the tetralogy.

pares us for Hamlet's imaginative embrace: "There are more things in heaven and earth, Horatio, / Than are dreamt of in your philosophy" (*Ham.* 1.5.174–75).[6]

Hamlet enters the crucible of the *Aeneid* and undergoes an even more severe trial. Aeneas recounts having witnessed from the palace roof the murder of Priam, a sacrilege that impelled him to gather his own family and flee. Hamlet's dilemma is more intricate, compacting the already dense ironies of the *Aeneid*. When he asks the players to recite Aeneas's tale, "especially when he speaks of Priam's slaughter," does he sympathize with "*Old grandsire Priam*" or identify with "*The rugged Pyrrhus, he whose sable arms, / Black as his purpose, did the night resemble*" (2.2.448–49)? When he requests *The Murder of Gonzago*, does he realize that the assassin, "one Lucianus, nephew to the King" (3.2.239) might as plausibly figure forth his own murderous intentions toward his uncle Claudius?

Hamlet's imaginative engagement, his Oedipal involvement, his ambiguous means of "feigned" madness and aesthetic response, his inability to determine the facts of the past (we overhear Claudius's confessions, but Hamlet does not), force him to recognize the extreme subjectivity of this plot and to simply be "ready" for its climax and unraveling. His invocation to Providence near the end of the play is that of the skeptical fideist (5.2.215–20), and at death he cannot tell his own story, although he desperately entrusts it to the rational Horatio. Hamlet wins our approval not through certainty, but through tenacity in confronting his own flawed human nature and his desire to make it mean something nonetheless.

Hamlet also psychologizes history, telescoping epic sweep into the more basic family drama. In the *Odyssey* Telemachus worries that no one knows his own father. Hamlet discovers this sexual instability of origins as he vividly imagines his mother's appetite, overidentifies with Claudius, and has great difficulty in properly "remembering" his father. It diseases his world and makes his envisioned end hallucinatory:

> To die, to sleep;
> To sleep, perchance to dream—ay, there's the rub:

---

[6] For a particularly subtle version of the commonplace argument for the pivotal position of *Julius Caesar* in Shakespeare's career and its relationship to the major tragedies, see Reuben Brower, *Hero and Saint*, pp. 204–38.

For in that sleep of death what dreams may come,
When we have shuffled off this mortal coil,
Must give us pause—

(3.1.64–68)

Each of Shakespeare's great tragedies is at heart a sexual crisis, a bitter confrontation with the alien other, and a failure of the capable imagination. The female world epitomizes that which cannot be perfectly controlled, and more supple and patient means of accommodation elude these plays' varied heroes. At the same time, Shakespeare in his mature comedies plays with both gender and genre, teasing us with the strong suggestion of tragedy: the plot of *Much Ado About Nothing* is a virtual comic rehearsal for *Othello*; *As You Like It* anticipates *King Lear* and *The Tempest*; and *Twelfth Night*'s sexual complications threaten a tragic catastrophe. Yet these comedies provide the imaginative resources of androgyny, disguises, and pastoral shifts of environment that permit comic resolution. In place of an ideal of historical truth, Shakespeare increasingly substitutes a mutually satisfying play.

Lear further exposes human frailty and the need to forge meaning through it. Lear's initial egotistical destructive act releases a monstrous world of unchecked appetite that pares man down to the unaccommodated animal.[7] Faced with such a spectacle, we make a primary choice:

O! reason not the need; our basest beggars
Are in the poorest thing superfluous:
Allow not nature more than nature needs,
Man's life is cheap as beast's.

(2.4.266–69)

The art of our necessities is strange,
And can make vile things precious.

(3.2.70–71)

Nature—human nature—demands we dress this barrenness, turning it from a universal blank to something with benign intention. We

---

[7] Maynard Mack, *King Lear in Our Time*, powerfully characterizes *Lear's* indebtedness to the moralities, its archetypal force, and the willful action that makes it an antigenesis of degenerative appetite.

are at the farthest remove from comforting providentialism here; to the blind, despairing Gloucester in this pre-Christian world, "As flies to wanton boys, are we to th' Gods; / They kill us for their sport" (4.1.36–37).[8]

Yet his son Edgar knowingly stages a drama of purgation and miraculous salvation to cure his father of despair. Edgar fails in his many attempts to give intellectually secure tragicomic shape to these apocalyptic events, concluding "The weight of this sad time we must obey; / Speak what we feel, not what we ought to say" (5.3.323–24). But feeling ties him to a more basic order, often expressed in tender gesture rather than words, that strives to create in this world and intimates such possibility for another. The intensity of Shakespeare's encounter with the ambivalent destructive and creative potential of human sexuality in *Hamlet* and the mature comedies climaxes in *Lear* in the opposed images of monstrous appetite ("Down from the waist they are Centaurs, / Though women all above" 4.6.126–27) and Nature, the great mother and nurse. The centrality of women here unites the strained dichotomies of power and suffering in the history plays, and ensures the major role of the female in the resolutions of the romances.[9]

In *King Lear* a subtle alliance with Nature is being wrought, one that offers the possibility of working through tragedy, if not in personal, then in generational, cultural, mythic, and perhaps even religious terms. Lear is a prototype for Leontes and Prospero, men who while looking frankly on that "thing of darkness" which

---

[8] For the thesis that *Lear* represents an attempt at a historical reproduction of various pagan attitudes toward the gods that would have complemented the incipient religious skepticism of the more thoughtful members of Shakespeare's audience, see Elton, *King Lear and the Gods*. Much of Elton's evidence and argument can be used to support a further conclusion: from the groping, obviously fictionalized faith of some of *Lear's* pagan characters, some members of Shakespeare's audience might deduce the need for both greater human compassion and more absolute, less dogmatic, faith in order to bridge contemporary religious skepticism.

[9] Madelon Gohlke, " 'I wooed thee with my sword,' " reading each of Shakespeare's mature tragedies as a sexual tragedy, suggestively unites Shakespeare's mature comedies and his tragedies through a "matriarchal substratum or subtext" which in the tragedies provides "a rationale for the manifold text of male dominance while constituting an avenue of continuity between these plays and the comedies in which women more obviously wield power" (pp. 161–62).

they must acknowledge theirs, can finally accept with equanimity the pleasant denouement of their own disappointed lives in the happiness of their children. Nature regenerates, even out of the slime of Nilus's mud or the long pastime of a winter's tale.

In addition, the aging characters of the romances do not struggle to resist this movement, but seek in known natural renewal the image of some greater supernatural renewal. Then they may indeed "find out new heaven, new earth," and discover in the "sleep of death" that present dreams of happy immortality are real. Such "imaginings" on their part desire not to debase nature, but to translate it from the world of becoming to its ideal end. Polixenes replies to the innocent Perdita:

> Yet nature is made better by no mean
> But nature makes that mean: so, over that art,
> Which you say adds to nature, is an art
> That nature makes. You see, sweet maid, we marry
> A gentler scion to the wildest stock,
> And make conceive a bark of baser kind
> By bud of nobler race. This is an art
> Which does mend nature—change it rather—but
> The art itself is nature.
>
> (WT 4.4.89–97)

The natural union of Florizel and Perdita will redeem the jealous fall of Leontes; the preservation of Hermione will intimate resurrection; Prospero's resignation will predispose cosmic forgiveness. Says G. Wilson Knight of *The Tempest*, "Here the poetry is preeminently in the events themselves, which are intrinsically poetic. . . . There is the less need for it in that the play itself is metaphor."[10]

Shakespeare's final plays are as much tragicomedies as romances.[11] Unlike Giraldi's counter-Reformation "tragedie de lieto fine," manipulated by an overt providentialism, their affirmation

---

[10] *The Crown of Life*, p. 224; see also Gayle Greene, " 'Excellent Dumb Discourse': Silence and Grace in Shakespeare's *Tempest*."

[11] The term *romance* summarizes a literary genealogy that ranges from Longus to medieval romance, and its members share certain broad thematic and structural features such as young lovers, pastoral interludes, and disguises and regenerations, based on an underlying delight in the marvelous. *Tragicomedy*, as I use it, is a more specific structural and generic term, implying that the premises of tragedy are fully present, and then deliberately reversed.

rises in the face of extreme doubt and questioning. As tragicomedies, they establish the full historical potential for tragedy and then reverse its norms; in a dialectical process evoking the neo-Platonic *discordia concors*—or, closer to Shakespeare, Montaigne's tested life —they must pass through Stoic denial to Epicurean acceptance and joy.[12] *Antony and Cleopatra* most fully articulates that turn as its lovers realize the potential of their earthly lives as metaphor for the next. They are prompted to this by the opposition of Rome, by its repression of creative energies to the service of a monumental state, by the Roman language of self-restraint and political mission. Antony invokes his creative freedom when, at the tragicomic turn of the play, he rewrites the tragedy of Dido and Aeneas as an ecstatic otherworldly reunion (4.14.50–54), and thus prepares the way for Cleopatra's complementary neo-Platonic interpretation of the myth of Isis and Osiris.

Antony and Cleopatra summarizes Shakespeare's preoccupation with Vergil's *Aeneid* as he transvalues Vergil's historical constraints into a tentative appeal for universal truth. The stages of this process can be described in categories that parallel Sidney's *discordia concors* of historian, philosopher, and poet in "An Apology for Poetry." History records the defeat of Antony; Shakespeare explores the mythic and psychological dimensions of this tragic action through the archetype of Hercules. Philosophy debates its meaning; Shakespeare dramatizes this debate as the conflicting cultural ideals of Rome and Egypt. Poetry exhorts us to test our imaginations against what is, in order to affirm the enduring value of what should be; Shakespeare dramatizes interpretative possibility when he has Cleopatra confront the version of "the common liar" and die staging herself as Isis.[13] Cleopatra's attempt to dramatize the central redemptive myth of Egypt also allies her with Pico's syncretic thought. Pico conflates the creation accounts of Moses, Plato, and the "Egyptian" Asclepius; for him the

---

[12] The relationship between Shakespeare's and Montaigne's dialectic of experience is implied throughout Walter Kaiser's *Praisers of Folly*. For Montagne's biographical passage from tragedy to tragicomedy, from Stoicism to Epicurean acceptance and joy, see Donald Frame, *Montaigne's Discovery of Man*.

[13] My argument parallels in many respects that of Janet Adelman, "*The Common Liar*." Although I read Richard Ide's *Possessed with Greatness* too late to incorporate it into my argument, I profited from his generic discussion of "the improbable heroics" of *Antony and Cleopatra*, pp. 102–31.

myth of the dismemberment and re-membering of Osiris is an account of the analytic and re-creative powers of the human mind, applied to the study of nature.

Shakespeare's play is, on one level, consummately literal and realistic, acknowledging specifically time- and culture-bound perceptions, including, implicitly, those we are likely to bring to it. Cleopatra, for most Romans, can be nothing more than a magnificent whore. Members of Shakespeare's audience might add a dimension of Christian connotation to this condemnation. But she characterizes such readings as reductive, and exhorts us to tolerant synthesis, in harmony with those late humanist, eirenic movements in Shakespeare's day that assumed a liberal, conciliatory attitude toward the remnants of the past, toward the discoveries of the present, and toward the areas of cultural conflict generated between them. Thus through the complex refracting prism of a "play" upon history, Shakespeare's Cleopatra captures exactly the change undergone by the Renaissance ideal of man as maker since Pico's confident oration: from an assertive myth of origins to a wry appeal to the intransigent material of human nature, of which our own willing or unwilling suspension of disbelief forms the core. Shakespeare ends by asking us, What meaning are we willing to make from this action?

History: Tragedy and the Herculean Hero

LEPIDUS: I must not think there are
Evils enow to darken all his goodness:
His faults, in him, seem as the spots of heaven,
More fiery by night's blackness; hereditary,
Rather than purchas'd; what he cannot change,
Than what he chooses.

(*Ant.* 1.4.10–15)[14]

Shakespeare grasped Plutarch's purpose and method in writing the *Lives* and turned them to the exposition of tragedy. Like those arresting portrait busts of late antiquity that move us into the recesses of mind, Plutarch's oblique emphasis on "a light occasion, a word, or some sporte" impels us toward a hidden truth of char-

---

[14] I cite the Arden edition of *Antony and Cleopatra*, ed. M. R. Ridley.

acter that might not find expression in the external world of deeds. Most of Plutarch's biographies are of universally admired and successful men; convinced that history was more than an impersonal movement that could make undifferentiated use of any human instrument, he sought to illuminate the hidden springs of, if not a purely individual, then at least a distinctly typical, greatness. Emphasizing ethical responsibility, he studied famous men for clues to an intention that might fail under certain circumstances but flourish under others. For him, therefore, it was as important to record the seemingly inconsequent smaller actions of life that are the tricks of a man's disposition as to chronicle his *res gestae*.

In his comparison of Demetrius and Marc Antony, Plutarch offers us a rare instance in the *Lives* of men who were generally held to have "increased their fame with infamy."[15] The resulting portrait of Antony is far more complex than a record of failure or a moralistic admonition against an evil man. Antony was clearly a "great" man; as Plutarch remarks in "The Comparison of Demetrius with Antonius," he elevated himself to world power from comparatively humble beginnings:

> borne of an honest man, who otherwise was no man of warre, and had not left him any meane to arise to such greatnes; durst take upon him to contend for the Empire with Cæsar, that had no right unto it by inheritaunce, but yet made him selfe successor of the power, the which the other by great paine and travell had obteyned, and by his owne industrie became so great, without the helpe of any other: that the Empire of the whole worlde being devided into two partes, he had the one halfe, and tooke that of the greatest countenaunce and power.[16]

Plutarch explores why such promise, and indeed such achievement, dissipated. From his position within the moderate tradition of Graeco-Roman ethical and political thinking he could not but dis-

---

[15] *The Lives of the Noble Grecians and Romanes, Compared*, trans. Thomas North, p. 941. The significance of these examples of infamy is discussed by Alan Wardman, *Plutarch's Lives*, pp. 27–37.

[16] Cited by Bullough, *Narrative and Dramatic Sources* 5:318; my citations from North's translation of "The Life of Marcus Antonius" refer to this text.

approve of Antony's tendency toward unchecked excess, an inclination that eventually led the triumvir to such passionate sympathy with the culture of the East and such uncritical complicity with Cleopatra. But Plutarch never lets us forget that those actions which he condemns were the product of a character as promising as it was subsequently corrupt; his focus on the irreducible qualities of Antony's nature bring the account of his fall close to tragedy.

Shakespeare responds to every nuance of this tragic potential and also develops from it other layers of interpretation of Antony's actions. Plutarch, who had access to subsequently lost Hellenistic accounts of Antony's Egyptian life, convincingly portrays its attractions for a man of his temperament. Even while condemning Cleopatra, his report of her retains traces of sources more sympathetic to her values. Shakespeare is sensitive to this suppressed level of meaning. Exploiting the multiple perspectives available in drama, he qualifies Plutarch's moralistic narratorial stance. While he retains a full sense of Antony's Roman tragedy, he allows two ways of life, the Roman and Egyptian, an enacted vividness that produces in the mind of an audience an ideological debate over their relative claims. My analysis begins by observing how Shakespeare follows and deepens Plutarch's account by developing a tragic archetype from history and internalizing a political action as psychological discovery: how Antony experiences himself as a Roman and a descendent of Hercules. It concludes with a transitional sketch of opposed interpretations of this discovery: Octavius's attempt to judge and fix it, and Cleopatra's to transmute it.

When we first see Octavius Caesar in *Antony and Cleopatra*, he flatly declares Antony to be "the abstract of all faults / That all men follow" (1.4.9–10). Then Lepidus interposes his magnanimous and more complex judgment: Antony's faults are but one sign of a great nature. Plutarch, in his "Life" of Antony, derives this ambivalent greatness from Antony's conception of himself as a Herculean man. Hercules, as Eugene Waith demonstrates, was a mythic figure of deep moral ambiguity and tragic potential, a potential developed by Sophocles, Euripides, and Seneca, and by Renaissance and neoclassical imitators.[17]

---

[17] *The Herculean Hero in Marlowe, Chapman, Shakespeare, and Dryden.* My exposition of the legend of Hercules is based largely on Waith's discussion in chaps. 1 and 2.

The myth of the twelve labors of Hercules codifies the primitive conception of the hero as a man of extraordinary deeds. However, even in the earliest written sources these stories began to be allegorized "as triumphs of man's higher nature over bestiality and evil," and later classical authors followed this tendency.[18] For example, Vergil has Evander narrate Hercules' defeat of the monster Cacus, a tale that captures impressively as myth the conflict between civilization and brutality that runs throughout the *Aeneid*.[19] Some surprising, almost paradoxical, developments occur in the tradition as the hero's moral virtue begins to outweigh his rough physical beginnings. In Prodicus's late story of the choice of Hercules, the young Hercules elects to follow the fair but modest Arête up the steep path of virtue, rather than the alluring Hedone in her primrosed landscape. The rhetoricians Isocrates and Lucian discuss a Gallic Hercules who is a model of eloquence.[20] In the Renaissance these morally edifying allegorical readings assume great prominence: Coluccio Salutati uses them as the fabric for his defense of an active civic-minded virtue in his influential *De Laboribus Herculis*, and the interpretations are collected and illustrated in such mythographical handbooks at Natale Conti's *Mythologiae* (1551) and Vincenzo Cartari's *Imagini de i Dei de gli Antichi* (1556).

At the same time, Hercules had a nature given to excess, an aspect of his character that even resolute Renaissance moral allegorizers observed. As Waith remarks of Renaissance treatments of the Hercules myth, "one sometimes has the impression that a somewhat subversive meaning asserts itself under cover of the respectable official interpretation." Of Herculean magnanimity he says: "Only in a very special sense is this virtue a mean. It is justifiable pride, and hence, from a Christian point of view, closely related to the most dangerous of all excesses. The meaning of Hercules in the Renaissance approaches a paradox when it includes both justifiable pride and reason subduing passion."[21] The paradox was already fully present in the antique sources. Euripides' *Heracles* and Seneca's re-

---

[18] Waith, *Herculean Hero*, p. 18.

[19] See Otis, *Virgil*, pp. 334–39.

[20] For Prodicus's story, see Xenophon, *Memorabilia and Oeconomicus* 2.1.21–22. For the Gallic Hercules, see Raymond Waddington, "The Iconography of Silence and Chapman's Hercules."

[21] Waith, *Herculean Hero*, p. 41.

working, the *Hercules Furens*, show Hercules maddened, murdering his wife Megara and their children. His youthful Stoic choice of Arête over Hedone, *virtú* over *voluptas*, contends with the many tales of his sexual indulgence. A prodigious lover, he coupled with the fifty daughters of Thespius in one night; was sexually humiliated by the Amazonian Omphale, who forced him to spin dressed in women's clothes; and was married, in addition to Megara, to Deianira, whose jealousy proved the unwitting cause of his death. Deianira was told by the centaur Nessus, whom Hercules fatally wounded for having attempted to steal her, to soak her robe in his blood and use it to lure back Hercules if he proved unfaithful. When Hercules took Iole as his mistress, Deianira sent her messenger Lichas with the robe, unaware that it would act as a corrosive poison. The tormented hero immolated himself on a huge funeral pyre, a death that can be read, as Waith remarks, "either to assert the limits beyond which even the greatest of men cannot go," or to prepare for his deification.[22]

These then, in brief, are the elements of the Herculean archetype. Plutarch summarizes the type in Lepidus's central paradox: traits that would be faults in another man demonstrate greatness in him. According to Plutarch, Antony, having based his resemblance to Hercules on genealogy, sought to reinforce it in every appearance and action:

> But besides all this, he had a noble presence, and shewed a countenaunce of one of a noble house: he had a goodly thicke beard, a broad forehead, crooke nosed, and there appeared such a manly looke in his countenaunce, as is commonly seene in Hercules pictures, stamped or graven in mettell. Now it had bene a speeche of old time, that the familie of the Antonii were discended from one Anton, the sonne of Hercules, whereof the familie tooke name. This opinion did Antonius seeke to confirme in all his doings: not onely resembling him in the likenes of his bodye, as we have sayd before, but also in the wearing of his garments. For when he would openly shewe him selfe abroad before many people, he would alwayes weare his cassocke gyrt downe lowe upon his hippes, with a great sword hanging by his side, and upon that, some ill favored cloke. Furthermore, things that seeme intollerable in other men, as to boast commonly, to jeast with one or other, to drinke like a

---

[22] *Herculean Hero*, p. 19.

> good fellow with every body, to sit with the souldiers when
> they dine, and to eate and drinke with them souldier-like: it is
> incredible what wonderfull love it wanne him amongest them.
> And furthermore, being given to love: that made him the more
> desired, and by that meanes he brought many to love him.
>
> (p. 257)

Plutarch's sketches of Antony's ancestors lend depth to these Her-
culean-Antonian traits: his grandfather was an orator; his father
was generous, indeed overgenerous. The anecdote of the father's
surreptitious gift of a silver basin to a needy friend suggests basic
liberality, the alternate insecurity and bravado typical of his son's
later public deeds, and a tendency to be cowed by women (p. 254).

Plutarch must square Antony's frequently devious political behavior with his reputation as a plain, blunt man. Against the background of the Herculean archetype of the eloquent strongman, he
stresses Antony's emotional, rhetorical, theatrical nature, one honed
to an expressive perfection in Greece by his youthful training in
Asiatic oratory, "which carried the best grace and estimation at
that time, and was much like to his manners and life: for it was
full of ostentation, foolishe braverie, and vaine ambition" (p. 255).
His Antony seldom consciously deceives; he merely responds to the
eddies of context. Thus he is a wonderful public speaker and master
of apt gesture; in addition to reporting his well-known funeral oration for Caesar, Plutarch also describes his remarkable persuasive
tactics with Lepidus, his attempted sallies with Cleopatra, who always outdid him at his own game, and his eloquence before his
troops. The account of his behavior toward his soldiers in Parthia,
even as the possibility of military success was fading for want of
long-range planning, is a veritable summary of Herculean virtues,
the virtues of an open, affectionate, unselfconscious man.

> Antonius nobility and ancient house, his eloquence, his plaine
> nature, his liberality and magnificence, and his familiarity to
> sport and to be mery in company: but specially the care he
> tooke at that time to help, visite, and lament those that were
> sicke and wounded, seing every man to have that which was
> meete for him: that was of such force and effect, as it made
> them that were sicke and wounded to love him better, and were
> more desirous to do him service, then those that were whole
> and sound.
>
> (pp. 286–87)

Almost as revealing in the oblique, anecdotal Plutarchan mode, is the amusing picture of Antony's "Herculean" response to a very private brand of adversity, his marriage to the "somewhat sower" Fulvia, who "was not contented to master her husband at home, but would also rule him in his office abroad, and commaund him, that commaunded legions and great armies" (p. 262). He plays a comic actor's trick, a rough practical joke, dressing like one of his men and bearing letters supposedly containing bad news to her. When this most serious and politic of women turns immediately to the letters, the disguised Antony "ramped of her necke, and kissed her." The verbs capture the essence; this shaggy man who affects the behavior and appearance of his mythic ancestor, slayer of the Nemean lion, now jestingly plays his role to the hilt in order to win an affectionate response from his crabby, preoccupied wife. His flair in battle, his emotive speech, his display in the East, his generous gifts to his friends, and even such ugly deeds as his grudge feud with Dolabella and his vicious revenge on Cicero—in every gesture Antony reveals himself, as Shakespeare noted, to be a great-hearted, spirited man.

How then, Plutarch asks, did so much potential for virtue go "awry"? Precisely because those same appetitive drives that when limited and constrained enabled Antony to heroically "o'erflow the measure," once indulged exceed any discernible shape or control. The pattern began early; already in his youth he was patronized by a man named Curio, "given over to all lust and insolencie, who to have Antonius the better at his commaundement, trayned him on into great follies, and vain expenses upon women, in rioting and banketing" (p. 255). To excesses of physical appetite were soon added the more subtle excesses of political drives: Antony narrowly escaped involvement with the demagogue Clodius. His early contacts with Eastern opulence seem to have sharpened his taste for spectacular display, and, as Julius Caesar's protégé at Rome, he had the power to indulge his desires, to the occasional detriment of his duties and the outrage of more austere Romans.

However, several incidents that Plutarch labels as excesses, such as Antony's honoring of actors and his actress-mistress Cytheride, or his love of exotic cooking and ostentatious "progresses," are more accurately understood as signs of orientalization that the less cosmopolitan Romans would fail to comprehend; his harnessing lions to draw his cart is another piece of Herculean theatricality that subsequently fed his Eastern reputation as a Bacchus. Cicero in the *Philippics* accuses him of drunkenness; Plutarch reports a particularly disgraceful hangover before a political assembly. In Plutarch's judgment Antony led a "naughty life" with his "banckets and dronken feasts he made at unseasonable times, and his extreme wastful expences upon vaine light huswives. . . . In his house they did nothing but feast, daunce, and maske: and him selfe passed away the time in hearing of foolish playes, or in marrying these plaiers, tomblers, jeasters, and such sort of people" (p. 261). Given political power, he similarly lost all sense of restraint. Plutarch, unlike several other ancient historians, does not blame Antony exclusively for the excesses of those post-assassination proscriptions that served all the triumvirs so well; nonetheless, he does report that Antony pursued Cicero, a particular object of revenge, with great cruelty.

After Antony's great personal triumph at Philippi, he returned to Greece as governor of the East. Indulgence became the order of the day, and he freely showed the loving side of his emotional disposition: "they call him Philellen (as much to say, a lover of the Græcians)." His subjects responded with offers of more and more extravagant pleasures. As he moved from Athens, where he still exercised some restraint as lawgiver, into Asia Minor, deeper into the East, "he easely fell againe to his old licentious life . . . such a rabble of minstrells and fit ministers for the pleasures of Asia, (who in finenes and flattery passed all the other plagues he brought with him out of Italie) all these flocked in his court, and bare the whole sway: and after that, all went awry" (p. 271). Plutarch's vocabulary of excess—*please, pleasure, exceed, merry, flatter, sway, awry, riot, delight, sweet, perfume, ease*—as well as his general evocation of this sinuous, undulating world will become central to Shakespeare's depiction of Antony in Egypt.

It was then that Cleopatra met him on her barge on the river Cydnus in Cilicia, and won him to her with a round of feasting and playfully wielded accomplishments that drew his appetites on with new urgency. Plutarch does her the justice of exhibiting the range of her attractions: not only could she awe the "gross and souldier like" Roman with the glories of her person and household, but she could prick Antony on with her wit, the grace of her conversation, and her mastery of Eastern languages. In their life together excess was espoused as a positive value, "they made an order betwene them, which they called Amimetobion (as much to say, no life comparable and matcheable with it) one feasting ech other by turnes, and in cost, exceeding all measure and reason" (p. 275). But she blatantly manipulates Antony; Plutarch characterizes her as the most skilled in the chain of flatterers who easily victimized this quite sincere man, using him to advance her political schemes for the resurgence of Alexander's empire, and later betraying him in their conflict with Octavius Caesar.

Her influence threatens to polarize and rend Antony's Herculean nature as a man of allied flaws and virtues. In the East he becomes like Bacchus, the wonderful androgyne of Euripides' play, "most lovely and most terrible to men"; "father of mirth, curteous, and gentle: and so was he unto some, but to the most parte of men, cruell, and extreame" (p. 272). The people conclude from their union, "that the goddesse Venus was come to play with the god Bacchus, for the generall good of all Asia" (p. 274). However, the god Bacchus brings destructive frenzy in the wake of his mirth, and Antony and Cleopatra's order of excess, Amimetobion, in time becomes "Synapothanumenon (signifying the order and agreement of those that will dye together)" (p. 305).

Antony, thrown on the defensive by Octavius Caesar and alienated from Cleopatra, is reduced in the last sections of Plutarch's account to the compass of a Stoic sage. He strips himself of most of his companions; retires, leaving his army without direction; reenters the Alexandrian revels in a spirit of deepest fatalism; asks Octavius to be allowed to live as a private man; and fights on only from desperation and a desire to die honorably. He dies with values much more limited than the Herculean ones by which he had lived, "a Romane by an other Romane" slain (p. 310). He has failed to redefine the Roman ideal and dies defeated by it. Despite this carefully nuanced portrait of Antony, Plutarch's final judgment of him, as compressed in "The Comparison of Demetrius and Antony," is harsh: he was lured into licentiousness, indulgence, cruelty, and tyranny by his appetites, and only narrowly escaped total disgrace through his clumsy suicide.

Shakespeare's Antony resembles Hercules not only in his martial bearing, complete with full beard and prominent sword, but also in his values and behavior.[23] Like his mythic ancestor, Antony

---

[23] Antony the soldier is repeatedly compared to "plated Mars." *Sword* occurs 23 times in the play; 14 instances are references to Antony's sword, often

is an unselfconscious, emotional, yet eloquent man, easily swayed by changing contexts; like Plutarch's Antony, he is "a plaine man, without suttletie" (p. 272). Yet his sophisticated rhetorical training enables him to play many roles, and he repeatedly contradicts himself, from scene to scene, or even within scenes.[24] In act 1, with magnificent Asiatic excess, he vows absolute allegiance to Cleopatra, then exclaims, "These strong Egyptian fetters I must break, / Or lose myself in dotage" (1.2.113–14). In act 2 he solemnly swears the most temperate and conventional behavior before Octavia and Caesar, then, within the same scene, turns to the Soothsayer and declares, "And though I make this marriage for my peace, / I' the east my pleasure lies" (2.3.38–39). After Actium his conduct becomes even more erratic: at one moment he reviles Cleopatra viciously, then claims he'll "return once more / To kiss these lips" (3.13.173–74); he wants to hearten his troops, but instead descends into maudlin self-pity (4.2). He is finally driven to recognize these inconsistencies, to see himself as actor without substantial reality, "here I am Antony, / Yet cannot hold this visible shape, my knave" (4.14.13–14).

Octavius Caesar powerfully evokes the Stoic ideal of Antony's former conduct at Modena: "Thou didst drink / The stale of horses, and the gilded puddle / Which beasts would cough at" (1.4.61–63). Early in the play Antony is presented with two women who suggest the story of Hercules' youthful choice between a Stoic *arêté*, or *virtú*, and an Epicurean *hedone*, or *voluptas*. Antony marries the "holy, cold, and still" Octavia, but quickly returns to his "Egyptian dish" (2.6.120, 123). He thus recapitulates his mythic ancestor's "fall" under female domination, with Cleopatra's jocular reminiscence of their exchange of clothes echoing Hercules' bondage to Omphale (2.5.18–23). His tragic dependence on her climaxes when, believing that she has betrayed him to Caesar, he cries out:

---

named as synecdoche for his total martial and sexual nature, as at 1.3.99; 2.5.23; 3.11.67; 3.13.175; 4.14.22–23. Antony's deprecating exclamations against the boyish "scarse-bearded Caesar" (1.1.21) indirectly allude to his own grizzled, rough, and full-bearded head.

[24] Rosalie Colie explores the significance of Antony's Asiatic style as expression of an aesthetic and a value system in *Shakespeare's Living Art*, pp. 168–207.

The shirt of Nessus is upon me, teach me,
Alcides, thou mine ancestor, thy rage.
Let me lodge Lichas on the horns o' the moon,
And with those hands that grasp'd the heaviest club,
Subdue my worthiest self.

(4.12.43–47)

This Herculean fury drives Cleopatra to the monument, where she feigns suicide, and it prepares for Antony's own death. As he readies for suicide, he identifies with the elusive configurations of the clouds, not with celestial limitation, but with spatial nullity: "The rack dislimns, and makes it indistinct / As water is in water" (4.14.10–11). Alone, he is not grandly and pathetically tragic, but self-canceling. The play's emphasis on Antony's emotional nature and his dependence on others for definition precludes his being a purely tragic figure. In this play of generic transformations, the audience moves quickly from experiencing Antony's recognition scene as tragedy to speculating upon its meaning.

Octavius and the Romans read his actions through the moral dichotomies implied by "choice," taking Prodicus's story as the paradigm. For them, Octavia and Cleopatra represent opposed and absolute values. Caesar's sister, the "studied" (2.2.138) match for Antony, is to Maecenas "a blessed lottery" of "beauty, wisdom, modesty"; to Antony, a "lady" and a "gem" to whom he would keep his square, and do all by the rule. Cleopatra, in contrast, is to Philo a "gypsy" and "strumpet"; to Pompey, a bewitching, sensual temptress; to Maecenas and Agrippa, a magnificent sex object and a "trull"; to Octavius, a "whore"; to Scarrus, "Yon ribaudred nag of Egypt"; and to Antony himself, when he fears she has betrayed him, a "kite," "boggler," "fragment," "foul Egyptian," "triple-turn'd whore," "false soul of Egypt," "right gypsy," and "spell." Cleopatra's world is an enticing way of excess: "Eight wild-boars roasted whole at a breakfast, and but twelve persons there; is this true?" (2.2.179–80); it threatens dissolution and decay, hatching harms, breeding weeds. Octavia symbolizes those virtues of the mean or measure that can reconcile the calculating Caesar and the passionate Antony, and "hoop," "knot," and "cement" them together in one world-conquering enterprise.[25]

---

[25] Sources of quotations, by speaker, are: Maecenas, 2.2.241–43; Antony, 2.3.6–7 and 3.13.105–9; Philo, 1.1.10, 13; Pompey, 2.1.20–27; Maecenas and

Roman moral absolutism arguably hastens Antony's alliance with Cleopatra, hardening inclination into irrevocable choice. Ambivalent, rather than consciously treacherous, in his relationship with the two women, and constrained by Caesar's power, Antony is as willing to bend in Cleopatra's direction as Octavius is to cut short Octavia's mediation and define Antony as the enemy. Although the Romans continue to mourn his fall from former greatness, their condemnation is unequivocal. They offer Antony no quarter, denying his request to live "A private man in Athens" (3.12.15), negotiating for his betrayal with Cleopatra, and ordering: "Plant those that have revolted in the vant, / That Antony may seem to spend his fury / Upon himself" (4.6.9–11). The ruthless single-mindedness of Caesar's command is contrasted with Antony's magnanimity in sending Enobarbus's treasure after him, a comparison that makes the wavering soldier repent his desertion.

The Romans, in their drive to make one world, seek to isolate Antony's fall from any wider implications, to treat it as a disease in the body politic that must be "launched" (5.1.36) to obtain health. Caesar histrionically muses that Antony's death "should make / A greater crack" (5.1.14–15), but he quickly halts such pathetic speculation to continue his "business."[26] The Romans distance themselves from any tragedy of Antony through moral judgment, proposing instead an orthodox Vergilian plot of purpose and power —"The time of universal peace is near: / Prove this a prosperous day, the three-nook'd world / Shall bear the olive freely" (4.6.5–7); this plot will receive its ceremonial expression in Octavius's triumph.

Cleopatra, in contrast, seeks to make Antony "become" his

Agrippa, 2.2.226–28 and 3.6.95; Octavius, 3.6.67; Scarrus, 3.10.10; Antony, 3.13.89, 110, 117 and 4.12.10, 13, 25, 28, 30. On harms and weeds, see 1.2.126–27, 190–192; on world-conquering enterprise, see 2.2.114–153; 3.2.23–33; 3.4.

[26] Robert Fitch's argument in " 'No Greater Crack?' " applies only to the Roman interpretation of the play's action. J. Leeds Barroll, "Antony and Pleasure," argues that Antony should be condemned for yielding to the sins of gluttony, lust, and sloth; in "Enobarbus' Description of Cleopatra" he reads the entire play in light of the exclusive moralistic motif of the choice. F. M. Dickey, Not Wisely but Too Well, makes an historical argument through sources for a moralistic reading of the play. All these studies support the Roman interpretation of the play's action without acknowledging alternate interpretative traditions.

Herculean nature: to live it fully and to adorn it. Those of her actions that to the Romans appear at best a teasing, often exasperating "play," and at worst conscious treacheries may, however, be read as a seriously espoused fictional transforming endeavor. From the first scenes of the play her tantalizing method of contrarieties and antitheses suggests a subliminal attempt to make Antony synthesize the tragic tendencies of his Herculean nature. She reflects back the ostentation of his Asiatic oratory, challenging him to find an adequate expression of love (1.1.14–17), paraphrasing his own extravagances. "Eternity was in our lips, and eyes, / Bliss in our brows' bent; none our parts so poor, / But was a race of heaven" (1.3.35–37). She would have him confirm their love in a higher language than mere fiction or hyperbolical lies.

Repeatedly, Cleopatra urges Antony to understand the seeming contradictions of his Herculean nature and to embrace them as indivisible truth of character, rather than a series of hypocritical roles. She taunts him about his love for Fulvia: "Excellent falsehood! / Why did he marry Fulvia, and not love her? / I'll seem the fool I am not; Antony / Will be himself" (1.1.40–43); but such taunts veil her serious concern about his ability to love: "O most false love! / Where be the sacred vials thou should'st fill / With sorrowful water? Now I see, I see, / In Fulvia's death, how mine receiv'd shall be" (1.3.62–65). She verbally robs him of his sword:

> CLEOPATRA: Good now, play one scene
> Of excellent dissembling, and let it look
> Like perfect honour.
>
> ANTONY: You'll heat my blood: no more.
> CLEOPATRA: You can do better yet; but this is meetly.
> ANTONY: Now, by my sword,—
>
> CLEOPATRA: And target. Still he mends.
> But this is not the best. Look, prithee, Charmian,
> How this Herculean Roman does become
> The carriage of his chafe.
>
> (1.3.78–85)

But these emasculating criticisms of his Herculean bombast disarm him to a recognition of the mutuality of their love, and their quarrels conclude with the rhythms of sexual union:

ANTONY: Let us go. Come;
Our separation so abides and flies,
That thou, residing here, goes yet with me;
And I, hence fleeting, here remain with thee.
Away!

                                        (1.3.101–5)

Their interdependence allows Antony to express his emotional Herculean nature and to transcend its needs through reliance on another.

Throughout, Cleopatra seeks to evoke a sophisticated synthesis
from Roman analytical distinctions: for their sense of sexual and
social differentiation, she would have androgyny and emotionally
charged intimacy; for moralistic "choice," syncretism; for their antitheses of work and play, fact and fiction, truth and lying, the possibility of re-creation. The Romans condemn Antony's attraction to
Cleopatra as emasculating;[27] she remembers the sexual exchange as
a rollicking shared pleasure:

                        That time? O times!
I laugh'd him out of patience; and that night
I laugh'd him into patience, and next morn,
Ere the ninth hour, I drunk him to his bed;
Then put my tires and mantles on him, whilst
I wore his sword Philippan.

                                        (2.5.18–23)

The incident of the salt-fish (2.5.10–18) ominously echoes "salt"
Cleopatra (2.1.21) as the emblem of baited vice; she recalls it as a
glorious game of one-upmanship, in which she triumphed over
Antony's male Roman earnestness, and she will reenact it with
transcendent levity at the monument (4.15.32–40).

Similarly, Caesar disapproves of their mingling with the commons, a "lightness" beside his moral gravity:

                        Let's grant it is not
Amiss to tumble on the bed of Ptolemy,
To give a kingdom for a mirth, to sit
And keep the turn of tippling with a slave,
To reel the streets at noon, and stand the buffet
With knaves that smells of sweat: say this becomes him,—

---

[27] For example, comments by Philo, 1.1.1–13; Caesar, 1.4.5–6; Canidius,
3.7.69–70; and Antony himself, 3.11.65–68 and 4:14.23–24.

As his composure must be rare indeed
Whom these things cannot blemish,—yet must Antony
No way excuse his foils, when we do bear
So great weight in his lightness.

(1.4.16–25).

Yet the Herculean Antony and the erotically attractive Cleopatra thrive on such dangerous intimacy: "all alone, / To-night we'll wander through the streets, and note / The qualities of people" (1.1.52–54).

Cleopatra herself is hardly tolerant of Octavia, as the scenes with the messenger from Rome comically illustrate (2.5; 3.3); there she is capable of petty power plays and self-deceiving lies.[28] Nonetheless, her more usual self-consciousness, wit, and intelligence toward the Roman "opposition" heightens the attractiveness of her way of life, elevating moralistic "choice" into an exhoration to synthesis. The Romans would reduce her to a sensual temptress whom they can condemn; she exhibits an awareness of their judgment and tries to circumscribe and translate it. While contemptuous of Antony's reductive Roman thoughts, she admires his magnanimous and valorous disposition, identifies with his martial and political ambitions, and seeks to include his Roman Stoicism in her death.[29] Her appeal to our emotions strengthens, in the course of the play, in direct proportion to her more complex encounter with Roman reality; what at the beginning of the play appears an excessive pastoral release in Egypt, is refined by the end into a metaphor for transcendent re-creation of a constrictive Roman world.[30]

---

[28] As recorded from Herodotus on, one aspect of Asiatic emotionalism is its tendency toward tyranny, which Cleopatra's extreme attitudes toward the commons illustrates.

[29] For her contempt, see 1.2.80; her admiration, 1.5.53–61; 3.13.167–94; 4.4.35–38; her identification, 3.7.1–19; her Stoic inclinations, 4.15.80–91; 5.2.1–8, 236–40.

[30] Shakespeare often used pastoral interludes to revivify his characters' sense of the everyday world. In *As You Like It* and *A Midsummer Night's Dream*, the action moves from the court to the country, site of re-creative release, and then returns to the court, but now with the country retained as a metaphor for the possibilities of psychological release. In contrast, in *Antony and Cleopatra* the re-creation subsumes the everyday, as the play moves from the Egyptian pastoral to Roman reality, and then returns to an Egypt that subsumes the Roman interpretation.

Cleopatra thus alters the Roman paradigm of the "choice" in ways analogous to other Renaissance syntheses of moral dyads. As Edgar Wind argues, Renaissance neo-Platonism derived from the dichotomies of Stoicism and Epicureanism, virtue and pleasure, the unifying concept of a passionate spiritual love for divine truth, assimilable in turn to Christian gospel exhortations to joy. He interprets Titian's allegorical painting "Sacred and Profane Love" as one such reworking of the iconographic convention of the "choice": instead of rejecting an alluring naked woman for her modestly clothed opposite, we "read" the picture from left to right, approving the sedate representative of human love, but also "inspired" by the stirring power of Cupid to identify with the hortatory nude figure of celestial love. Wind's analysis focuses on Botticelli's neo-Platonic complication of the conventional distinction between the two Venuses in his "Primavera" and "The Birth of Venus." He cautions us not to oversimplify the contrast between the *Venere vulgare*, or *Aphrodite Pandemos*, the Lucretian Venus of fruitful nature, and the *Venere celeste*, or *Aphrodite Urania*, born of the seed of Zeus and the ocean spume, and a symbol of divine inspiration. One should not assume "that the vulgar Venus is purely sensuous and does not share in the celestial glory. . . . While a purely sensuous instinct will incline to misplace the source of visual beauty in the body and seek the fruition of beauty in animal pleasures alone, the human lover will recognize that the Venus who appears clothed in an earthly garment is an 'image' of the celestial."[31] Cleopatra fears exactly such interpretative simplification by the "common liar" at Rome (see 1.1.1–62; 1.2.102–6; 5.2.207–21).

Placed beside such analogies, Antony's "choice" of Cleopatra may be read in a different light. The "still, cold" Octavia offers him the "getting of a lawful race" (3.13.107–8), and respectability in the eyes of history. Cleopatra, who can be reduced to a "whore," can, in her interpretative probing, also suggest a purified *amor voluptas*, a love of natural things irradiated by the eternal. She can draw Antony out beyond the tragic paradox of his own nature, infusing his death with the full transcendent thrust of the *Hercules Oetaeus*, and

---

[31] Wind, *Pagan Mysteries*, pp. 138–39. For Renaissance neo-Epicureanism, its meanings and proponents, see also Edward Surtz, *The Praise of Pleasure*, especially chap. 4; and Kaiser, *Praisers of Folly*, especially pp. 76–83.

turning it from love tragedy to love triumph.[32] She exhorts her Herculean hero to something beyond even self-consciousness. Understanding his own heroic nature should bring self-transcendence. Antony instinctively recognizes her "stirring" power in him. At the beginning of the play he comes close to apostrophizing her as Venus, the animator of all nature. When Cleopatra taunts, "Antony / Will be himself," he replies:

> But stirr'd by Cleopatra.
> Now for the love of Love, and her soft hours,
> Let's not confound the time with conference harsh:
> There's not a minute of our lives should stretch
> Without some pleasure now.
>
> (1.1.43–47)

We must now explore Cleopatra's generative force through her association with the goddess Venus, and the debate of values that ensues over her effect on the martial Antony.

Philosophy: "What Venus did with Mars," or the Debate of Love and Strife

> Now, though most men misliked this maner, yet the Alexandrians were commonly glad of this jolity, and liked it well, saying verie gallantly, and wisely: that Antonius shewed them a commicall face, to wit, a merie countenaunce: and the Romanes a tragicall face, to say, a grimme looke.
>
> (Plutarch, "Life," p. 276)

> Let him for ever go, let him not—Charmian,
> Though he be painted one way like a Gorgon,
> The other way's a Mars.
>
> (Ant. 2.5.116–18)

Shakespeare reflects the many Renaissance interpretations of Venus in his characters' responses to Cleopatra and to what she does

---

[32] Waith, Herculean Hero, pp. 35–38, 118–21, suggests interesting parallels between the movement of Seneca's Hercules Oetaeus and Shakespeare's Antony and Cleopatra.

with the martial Antony.[33] The eunuch Mardian, who has "fierce affections," but "can do nothing / But what indeed is honest to be done," refers to the Homeric story of "What Venus did with Mars" (1.5.15–18). In Book 8 of the *Odyssey* Demodocus sings of how the lame but clever Hephaistos (Vulcan) netted his wife Aphrodite (Venus) and her handsome lover Ares (Mars) in an adulterous act. Vulcan demands restitution, and all the other male gods gather to rejoice, as Chapman's translation reads, "that no impiety / Finds good success at th' end." However, even the moral Chapman must follow Homer's shifting tone: the scene of shameful exposure dissolves into laughter, and Hermes, in an aside to Apollo, admits appreciatively he'd willingly endure any censure "So golden *Venus* slumbred in mine Armes."[34] Similarly, in *Antony and Cleopatra* the most moralistic readings of Cleopatra as a bestial Venus (*amor bestiale* or *ferinus*) of sensual temptation, become, through recognition of her powerful attraction, representations of the *Venere vulgare* or *Aphrodite Pandemos* of fruitful nature. Through that Venus's ability to suggest a permanence underlying the cycles of change, she may even intimate the *Venere celeste* or *Aphrodite Urania*. Mardian, who literally cannot "perform" successfully, but who is one of the instruments of Antony's erotic transformation into the afterlife, will be our guide to these final interpretations of the action of Antony and Cleopatra.[35]

The Roman Philo attempts to fix our interpretation of the martial Antony's attraction to Cleopatra in the opening speech:

> Nay, but this dotage of our general's
> O'erflows the measure: those his goodly eyes,
> That o'er the files and musters of the war
> Have glow'd like plated Mars, now bend, now turn
> The office and devotion of their view

---

[33] My analysis concurs at many points with Raymond Waddington, "*Antony and Cleopatra*: 'What Venus did with Mars.'" However, Waddington argues that the Mars-Venus allusion pattern subsumes all others in the play, while I see it as a bridge between acts 4 and 5, and the final poetic-dramatic transformations effected by Cleopatra as Isis.

[34] *Homer's Odysses*, trans. George Chapman, p. 119.

[35] I am indebted to my colleague Marie-Pierre Ellmann for suggesting Mardian's importance.

Upon a tawny front: his captain's heart,
Which in the scuffles of great fights hath burst
The buckles on his breast, reneges all temper,
And is become the bellows and the fan
To cool a gipsy's lust. Look, where they come:
Take but good note, and you shall see in him
The triple pillar of the world transform'd
Into a strumpet's fool: behold and see.

(1.1.1–13)

Two strong spatial images inform his speech: Antony has declined
or bent and in the process has lost shape or definition. A glowing
martial colossus has turned his gaze from a battle front to Cleopatra's tarnished "tawny front" (face or forehead); an erect "triple
pillar" has become an effeminate "strumpet's fool." He dotes, rather
than loves; his dotage "o'erflows the measure"; his eyes "bend";
his heart, in a punning play on "temper," softens its martial ferocity
to a lover's submission, its expansive heat to an amorous flutter.
The speech approves Antony's heroic energy, but would harness it
to the service of Roman ideals of measure, public authority, and
world conquest. Philo fears the "motion" Cleopatra induces in Antony as a dissolution of his nature, which we link metaphorically to
more general Roman ambivalence toward the common people, toward idleness, revelry, and indulgence, and toward material nature.

Octavius Caesar exemplifies in its purest form this spirit of
Roman judicial distance from Cleopatra's attractions, condemning
Antony's "lascivious wassails" (1.4.56), frowning at the "Egyptian
bacchanals" aboard Pompey's galley (2.7.97–125), and single-
mindedly determined to possess Cleopatra for his triumph. Other
Romans show a repressed fascination with her and her dangerous
and fertile culture. Lepidus, drunk, presses Antony to describe the
Egyptian serpents and crocodiles "bred now of your mud by the
operation of your sun" (2.7.26–27). Caesar's closest associates,
Maecenas and Agrippa, privately draw Enobarbus aside to dilate
upon Egypt's wonders; his description of Cleopatra on her barge
causes Agrippa to exclaim in warm admiration:

Royal wench!
She made great Cæsar lay his sword to bed;
He plough'd her, and she cropp'd.

(2.2.226–28)

Like Hermes' comment on the naked Venus, Agrippa's words temporarily subvert the established moral order: for a moment, common and aristocratic diction mingle ("Royal wench"), masculine "submission" to a woman is productive, and Rome collaborates with Egypt. Agrippa's reaction to Enobarbus's description of her "triumph" verges on lewd parody of golden age and biblical pastoral ideals ("They shall beat their swords into ploughshares," Isaiah 2:4), but in its genuine admiration for her surprisingly resubstantiates them.

Enobarbus's report of Cleopatra dialectically transforms Philo's negative judgment, making Cleopatra's defects perfections. At once judicious and affectionate, Enobarbus attempts to mediate between the Roman and Egyptian worlds. In the first half of the play he is both ironic and appreciative; in the second half these responses polarize. His shifting loyalties there mirror our own complex responses; his death from a broken heart prepares us for the tested emotional values at the play's end.

His speech is derived directly from Plutarch's "Life":

Her barge in the river of Cydnus,	*The barge* she sat in, like a burnish'd throne
the poope whereof was of gold, the	Burn'd on the water: *the poop was beaten gold;*
sailes of purple, and the owers of	*Purple the sails,* and so perfumed that
silver, which kept stroke in row-	The winds were love-sick with them; *the oars were silver,*
ing after the sounde of the musicke	*Which to the tune of flutes kept stroke,* and made
of flutes. . . . And now for the	The water which they beat to follow faster,
person of her selfe: she was	As amorous of their strokes. *For her own person,*
layed under a pavillion of cloth	It beggar'd all description: *she did lie*
of gold of tissue, apparelled and	*In her pavilion—cloth of gold, of tissue—*
attired like the goddesse Venus,	O'er-*picturing that Venus* where we see
commonly drawn in picture: and	The fancy outwork nature. *On each side her,*

hard by her, on either hand of

her, pretie faire boyes apparelled

as painters doe set forth god

Cupide, with litle fannes in their

hands, with the which they fanned

wind upon her. Her Ladies and the

gentlewomen also, the fairest of

them were apparelled like the

nymphes Nereides (which are

the mermaides of the waters) . . .

some stearing . . . others tending

. . . the barge, out of the which

there came a wonderfull passing

sweete savor of perfumes, that

perfumed the wharfes side, pes-

tered with innumerable multitudes

of people. Some . . . followed . . .

others also ranne out of the citie.

. . . So that . . . Antonius was left

post alone in the market place,

in his Imperiall seate to geve

Stood pretty, dimpled *boys, like*
smiling *Cupids,*
With divers-color'd *fans, whose*
wind did seem
To glow the delicate cheeks which
they did cool,
And what they undid did.

. . . .

Her gentlewomen, like the Nere-
ides,
So many mermaids, tended her
i' the eyes,
And made their bends adornings.
At the helm
A seeming mermaid *steeres*: the
silken tackle
Swell with the touches of those
flower-soft hands,
That yarely frame the office. *From*
the barge
A strange invisible *perfume* hits
the sense
Of *the* adjacent *wharfs.* The city
cast
Her *people* out upon her; *and*
Antony,
Enthron'd i' the market-place, did
sit alone,
Whistling to the air; which, but for
vacancy,
Had gone to gaze on Cleopatra
too,
And made a gap in nature.

. . . .

Upon her landing, Antony sent
to her,
Invited her to supper: she replied,
It should be better he became
her guest,
Which she entreated: our cour-
teous Antony,

audience: and there went a rumor
in the peoples mouthes, that the
goddesse Venus was come to
play with the god Bacchus, for

the generall good of all Asia.
When Cleopatra landed, Antonius
sent to invite her to supper to him.
But she sent him word againe,

he should doe better rather to
come and suppe with her. Antonius
therefore to shew him selfe
curteous unto her at her arrivall,
was contented to obey her, and
went to supper to her.
                    (p. 274)

Whom ne'er the word of "No"
        woman heard speak,
Being barber'd ten times o'er, *goes*
        to the feast;
And for his ordinary, pays his
        heart,
For what his eyes eat only.

. . . .

                    I saw her once
Hop forty paces through the pub-
        lic street,
And having lost her breath, she
        spoke, and panted,
That she did make defect per-
        fection,
And, breathless, power breathe
        forth.

. . . .

Age cannot wither her, nor custom
        stale
Her infinite variety: other women
        cloy
The appetites they feed, but she
        makes hungry,
Where most she satisfies. For
        vilest things
Become themselves in her, that
        the holy priests
Bless her, when she is riggish.
(2.2.191–226, 229–33, 235–40;
        emphasis mine)

Apart from minor compressions for meter, the only significant omission in Enobarbus's account is the allusion to Antony as Bacchus, which Shakespeare reserves for later development from the Egyptian perspective. He here orders and amplifies Plutarch's gorgeous but static picture into an erotic masterpiece that draws all the levels of elemental reality toward an inexpressible new plane of desire. Earth, water, air, and fire all amorously follow Cleopatra; she arouses every sense with her rich clothing, music, and perfume; "bending" to her is now redefined as "adornings" (a near-pun on

adorings); her manifest defects are alluring interpretative gaps
that all nature rushes to fill.

The entire description builds to two climaxes: her effect on her
people is so physically described ("The city cast / Her people out
upon her") as to aptly precede Enobarbus's wry account of Antony's
seduction and Agrippa's appreciative interjection; from it Enobarbus generalizes her "infinite" drawing power, her capacity to make
all things, even "riggish" conduct, "become" her. Enobarbus thus
implies her ability to translate her identification with Venus from
purely sensual to anagogic ends: in her self-conscious staging here,
she is not Plato's derogatory imitation of an imitation, but a living
neo-Platonic intimation of a spiritual realm shining through and
beyond nature: "O'erpicturing that Venus where we see / The fancy
outwork nature."

From whence did Shakespeare derive this conception of Cleopatra's extraordinary creative and transcendent powers? Our answer
requires not only a source—Lucretius's *De rerum natura*—but
also a tradition for interpretation of that source.

As early as the twelfth century revival of Platonism, philosophical poets such as Bernardus Sylvestris in his *De mundi universitate* and Alain de Lille in his *De planctu natura* had attempted to
tie the visible, corruptible world of nature to the eternal providential
order of the Christian God.[36] Their endeavor and the later syncretic
Christian neo-Platonism of the Florentine Academy form the background for the selective revival of Epicureanism in the fifteenth and
sixteenth centuries. Lorenzo Valla (1407–1457), who had only indirect access to Epicureanism through the biographies of Diogenes
Laertius, dialectically links Epicurean joys in transient, worldly
things with eternal heavenly joy in his dialogue *De voluptate*, or
De vero falsoque bono. He subverts the medieval criticism of Epicureanism as soulless sensual indulgence by recovering some of the
ascetic spirit and beliefs of its founder, and wedding them to a
Platonic and Christian belief in the immortality of the soul: "the
Christian in his spiritual fervour and the Epicurean of sensuous fantasy and caprice find it possible to come to terms with each other,

---

[36] Marie-Dominique Chenu, *Nature, Man, and Society in the Twelfth
Century*, especially pp. 18–24.

whereas neither is able to tolerate the frigidity which the Stoic mistakes for virtue."[37] In late versions of the dialogue Valla makes Maphaeus Vegius, Renaissance author of a Christian providential "thirteenth book" of the *Aeneid*, the spokesman for this revised Epicureanism. He thus suggests how such providential reading also warms the Vergilian impersonal Stoic *Fatum*, turning harsh destiny into a parable of individual salvation.[38] Valla's follower Erasmus was called the Christian Epicurus; his dialectically structured *Praise of Folly* concludes with a sincere praise of the fool for Christ, the conscious practitioner of learned ignorance and recipient of the eternal joy of heaven.[39] His friend Thomas More depicts his Utopians as already neo-Epicurean praisers of pleasure who also believe in the immortality of the soul; they are ripe for Christian conversion.

Although Epicurus believed in the gods, his doctrine of *ataraxia*, their indifference toward human affairs, made religion a contemplative discipline: "this dogma, far from abolishing religion, should purify it; the truly pious man does not approach the gods to appease them or to obtain some favor from them, but to unite himself to them by contemplation, to rejoice in their joy, and so to taste for himself, in this mortal life, their unending happiness."[40] Such religious belief downplayed culturally conditioned forms of observance; for Epicurus and his Renaissance Christian followers, it implied religious toleration.

But Christian humanist tolerance was increasingly besieged during the sixteenth century by the rival dogmatisms of Reformation and conservative reaction. This was particularly true in France,

---

[37] Wind, *Pagan Mysteries*, p. 141. See D. C. Allen's pioneering "The Rehabilitation of Epicurus and His Theory of Pleasure in the Early Renaissance," although more recent studies disagree with his evaluations of many of the authors.

[38] William Bouwsma, "The Two Faces of Humanism," emphasizes the sharp Renaissance debate between Stoic rational ideas of fatalism and determinism, and alternate systems of thought that stress process, creativity, and grace. See also Lorenzo Valla, *"De Vero Falsoque Bono,"* especially pp. xlv–xlviii; Vegius, *Thirteenth Book of the Aeneid*, ed. Anna Cox Brinton, especially pp. 24–29; and Maristella de Panizza Lorch, " *'Voluptas, molle quoddam et non invidiosum nomen.'* "

[39] For the influence of Valla on Erasmus, and Christian Epicureanism in *The Praise of Folly*, see Kaiser, *Praisers of Folly*, pp. 78–82.

[40] A. J. Festugière, *Epicurus and His Gods*, p. 64.

where religious warfare repeatedly threatened to rend the country. Yet the poets of the Pléiade sought to maintain the humanist ideal of religious toleration, and in their works one finds the earliest dense cluster of adaptations of Lucretius's *De rerum natura*, a repository of Romanized Epicurean philosophy.[41] The text, which had been recovered in the early fifteenth century, was widely printed in the late fifteenth and sixteenth centuries. The poets of the Pléiade imitated chiefly the great opening invocation to *Venus genetrix*. Rather than confronting Lucretius's materialistic, atomistic philosophy—as writers of the seventeenth century later did—they selectively adapt the poem to praises of nature as the handmaiden of God, and to pleas for religious tolerance. As noted earlier, Jodelle used the invocation to strengthen Dido's defense of a religion of love against Aeneas's harsh Roman imperial ideology. Toward the end of the century, Montaigne, who repeatedly paraphrases Lucretius, turns the praise of pleasure and of nature toward a fideist's arguments for tolerance and natural religion.[42]

Lucretius's invocation of Venus is the source for Shakespeare's additions to Plutarch's description of Cleopatra at Cydnus. The *Venus genetrix* not only of the Roman race but of all things under heaven, she conceives the good and dispels evil. She, too, attracts each element, inciting its creatures to procreation:

> For as soon as the vernal face of day is made manifest, and the breeze of the teeming west wind blows fresh and free, first the fowls of the air proclaim you, divine one, and your advent, pierced to the heart by your might. Next wild creatures and farm animals dance over the rich pastures and swim across rapid rivers: so greedily does each one follow you, held captive by your charm, whither you go on to lead them. Then throughout seas and mountains and sweeping torrents and the leafy

---

[41] See Yates, *French Academies*. George Depue Hadzsits, *Lucretius and His Influence*, gives a brief account of the recovery and dissemination of the *De rerum natura* in the Renaissance; however, he ignores the context for the text's reception and its interpretations by Renaissance readers. Fraisse, *L'Influence de Lucrèce*, is brief but much more illuminating on Renaissance adaptations of Lucretius to "une théologie allégorique" (p. 74).

[42] Thomas Franklin Mayo, *Epicurus in England*, pp. xxi–xxii, notes Montaigne's adherence to Epicurus's refined conception of pleasure as man's end and reports that he quotes Lucretius some 135 times in the *Essays*.

dwellings of birds and verdant plains, striking alluring love
into the breasts of all creatures, you cause them greedily to
beget their generations after their kind.

$$(1.10-20)^{43}$$

Venus's creative activity overcomes the god of war; what "Venus
did with Mars" is not the subject of moralistic condemnation, but
rather a hopeful allegory of how love may conquer strife:

> Mars mighty in battle . . . who often casts himself upon your
> lap wholly vanquished by the ever-living wound of love, and
> thus looking upward, with shapely neck thrown back, feeds
> his eager eyes with love, gaping upon you, goddess, and as
> he lies back, his breath hangs upon your lips. There as he re-
> clines, goddess, upon your sacred body, do you, bending
> around him from above, pour from your lips sweet coaxings.
>
> $$(1.33-40)$$

This passage is one important source for those many Renaissance idyllic paintings of Venus's "victory" that implicitly re-
evaluate the icon of "the choice" and the condemning judgment of
what it might mean to be "unmanned" by a woman.[44] To Renaissance readers of neo-Platonic philosophical leanings and eirenic
religious hopes, the Venus genetrix might suggest Nature herself,
intimating eternity through change and providing a more liberal
guide to morality and religion than does manmade custom.

Shakespeare might have known Lucretius's text directly, or
he might have culled the description of the Venus genetrix from
a mythographical handbook such as Conti's or Cartari's.[45] His understanding of the myth could have been subtly conditioned by his
reading of Montaigne or his acquaintance, perhaps through the Sidney circle, with the writings of the Pléiade. However, The Faerie
Queene contained a version of the source closer to hand, one whose
Lucretian material was probably derived from Conti's handbook

---

[43] I cite W. H. D. Rouse's translation, as revised by Martin F. Smith.

[44] Wind, Pagan Mysteries, pp. 89–96.

[45] Natale Conti, Mythologiae, pp. 396–98; Vincenzo Cartari, Le imagini de
i Dei de gli Antichi, pp. 529ff.

and was then set within the syncretic framework of Renaissance neo-Platonism.[46]

In Book 4, Scudamour describes how he claimed his true love Amoret from the Temple of Venus. A rich garden that "In such luxurious plentie of all pleasure . . . seem'd a second paradise" surrounds the temple; a woman named Concord reconciles the opposed half-brothers, Love and Hate, who guard the porch. Once within, one beholds "the Goddesse selfe," who evokes a version of the Lucretian hymn from one of her worshippers:

> Great *Venus*, Queene of beautie and of grace,
>   The ioy of Gods and men, that vnder skie
>   Doest fayrest shine, and most adorne thy place,
>   That with thy smyling looke doest pacifie
>   The raging seas, and makst the stormes to flie;
>   Thee goddesse, thee the winds, the clouds doe feare,
>   And when thou spredst thy mantle forth on hie,
>   The waters play and pleasant lands appeare,
> And heauens laugh, and all the world shews ioyous cheare.
>
> Then doth the dædale earth throw forth to thee
>   Out of her fruitfull lap aboundant flowres,
>   And then all liuing wights, soone as they see
>   The spring breake forth out of his lusty bowres,
>   They all doe learne to play the Paramours;
>   First doe the merry birds, thy prety pages
>   Priuily pricked with thy lustfull powres,
>   Chirpe loud to thee out of their leauy cages,
> And thee their mother call to coole their kindly rages.
>
> Then doe the saluage beasts begin to play
>   Their pleasant friskes, and loath their wonted food;
>   The Lyons rore, the Tygres loudly bray,
>   The raging Buls rebellow through the wood,
>   And breaking forth, dare tempt the deepest flood,
>   To come where thou doest draw them with desire:
>   So all things else, that nourish vitall blood,
>   Soone as with fury thou doest them inspire,
> In generation seeke to quenche their inward fire.
>
> So all the world by thee at first was made,
>   And dayly yet thou doest the same repayre:

---

[46] See Edwin Greenlaw, "Spenser and Lucretius."

> Ne ought on earth that merry is and glad
> Ne ought on earth that louely is and fayre,
> But thou the same for pleasure didst prepayre.
> Thou art the root of all that ioyous is,
> Great God of men and women, queene of th'ayre,
> Mother of laughter, and welspring of blisse,
> O graunt that of my loue at last I may not misse.
>
> (4.10.44–47)

Both this hymn, which follows Lucretius's text closely, and its context, provide illuminating precedent for Shakespeare's adaptation of the allusion. Like Lucretius's Venus, Spenser's goddess draws the creatures of each element on to generation. However, Spenser is also at pains to purify this erotic power, to refine it from mere bestial lust toward the transcendent perfection of nature. Thus he adds to Lucretius's inclusive catalogue a summary stanza that, as with Montaigne's Mother Nature, comes daringly close to conflating her with the creator-God of Genesis: "So all the world by thee at first was made." In addition, her present activity is directed to restoring that former creative perfection: "And daily yet thou doest the same repayre." Hence the "Goddesse selfe" does not rest on any element, but rather on some quintessential substance "vneath to vnderstand" (4.10.39). She is attended by "litle loues," whose shapes "seem'd not like to terrestriall boyes, / But like to Angels playing heauenly toyes" (4.10.42), another conflation of the classical and Christian. Her appearance is deeply ambiguous: radiant, yet veiled; "twyned" with a circled serpent; rumored to be hermaphroditic, so that "she syre and mother is her selfe alone, / Begets and eke conceives, ne needeth other none" (4.10.40–41).

Most perplexing is the ontological status of the image: is it an idol or the laughing and smiling "Goddesse selfe"? All these seeming paradoxes may be resolved by Spenser's mistaken allusion to Phidias's statue of Venus:

> But it in shape and beautie did excell
> All other Idoles, which the heathen adore,
> Farre passing that, which by surpassing skill
> *Phidias* did make in *Paphos* Isle of yore,
> With which that wretched Greeke, that life forelore,
> Did fall in loue.
>
> (4.10.40)

The ultimate source of this story is Pliny's account of Praxiteles' marble statue of the nude Venus at Cnidus. This statue, "infinitely better" than his draped statue of Venus at Cos,

> was their chiefe credit, ennobled their cittie, and drew resort from all parts thither. This *Venus* was shrined in a little chapell by her selfe within a tabernacle; but of purpose so devised, that it might bee set open on all sides for to be seene and viewed all and whole on everie part: wherewith the goddesse her selfe (as men were verely persuaded) was well enough pleased, and shewed her contentment therein to all commers; for looke upon her as one would, amiable shee was and admirable everie way. It is reported, that a wretched fellow was enamoured of this *Venus*, and having lurked one night secretly within the chappell, behaved himselfe so and came so neare unto the image, that hee left behind him a marke of his leaud love and beastly lust; the spot of which pollution, appeared afterwards upon the bodie.[47]

By indicating that his representation surpasses that delusively lifelike statue, Spenser implies its real ideal (or, in Sidney's term, eikastic) function.[48] Rather than being an imperfect imitation of a fallen nature, this magically animated image is an intimation of a restored nature, to whose hortatory powers we may give ourselves with joy and bliss. The worshipper of the statue of Venus interpreted its attractions literally, and coupling with it, his "life forelore." The worshipper of Spenser's dynamic image should be inspired by its animation, transforming cupids into angels, serpents into symbols of eternity, sexual conflict into complementarity.

Scudamour here seeks from Venus approval of his lawful marriage to Amoret. Their tentative "courtly" union, which is given a particularly poetic and epic-romantic resonance by being compared to Orpheus's rescue of Euridyce from Hades, has already proleptically climaxed in ecstatic language that blends the pagan image of the hermaphrodite with the biblical-Edenic injunction that these two "shall be as one flesh" (*FQ* 3.12.46).

---

[47] Pliny, *The Historie of the World*, trans. Philemon Holland, 36.5.

[48] *Apology for Poetry*, p. 125. "For I will not deny but that man's wit may make Poesy, which should be *eikastike*, which some learned have defined 'figuring forth good things,' to be *phantastike*, which doth contrariwise infect the fancy with unworthy objects."

Properly understood, the Temple of Venus is no mere palace of art, but a nostalgic and prophetic image of paradise, enviable to the souls in Elysium (4.10.23), coalescing all that is best of pagan and Christian desire. As Christian neo-Platonic syncretist, Spenser has managed to suggest that all myths, including his own, are alluring veils to a single truth; rather than seeking to lustfully possess their appearance, we are urged to pursue their essence with an ever-living love.

Enobarbus's account of Cleopatra adds to Plutarch's description and to Lucretius's *Venus genetrix* exactly these elements of anagogic suggestion. His speech is not a precise picture, but a tissue of verbal implication: Cleopatra's "seemings"—her wrinkled age, her many roles, her riggish behavior, even the ludicrous picture of her decadent exhaustion—"become" her because they become her originative and restorative creativity. "Her own person" is never fully captured, since Enobarbus declares "It beggared all description." Instead, it lies at the center of an animated, beckoning frame that, with its amorous elements, Titianesque colorings and contours, and "adorning" attendants, is the opposite of Philo's definitive reductions. Here Shakespeare uses the exact figure of hyperbolic redefinition used by Spenser: "O'erpicturing that Venus where we see / The fancy outwork nature."

Shakespeare, who may have used Pliny's *Natural History* for Antony's description of "the flow o' the Nile" (2.7.17–23), then moves from Spenser's source, Pliny's account of Praxiteles' statue of Venus at Cnidus, to Pliny's account of Apelles' painting of *Aphrodite Anadyomene* ("Venus Rising from the Sea"). Apelles, an elegant Hellenistic painter whose art was famous for "a certaine lovely grace inimitable," lifelikeness, and brilliant and subtle color, used Campaspe, mistress of Alexander the Great, as his model for Venus; when he fell in love with her, Alexander presented her to him. Pliny continues:

> As for the painted table of *Venus,* arising out of the sea (which is commonly knowne by the name of *Anadyomene*) *Augustus Cæsar*, late Emperour of famous memorie, dedicated it in the temple of *Iulius Cæsar*, his father; which he enriched with an Epigram of certaine Greeke verses, in commendation as well of the picture, as the painter. And albeit the artificiall contriving of the said verses went beyond the worke, which they seemed to praise, yet they beautified and set out the

table not a little. The nether part of this picture had caught
some hurt by a mischance: but there never could bee found
that painter yet, who would take in hand to repaire the same
and make it up againe as it was at first: so as, this wrong &
harm done unto the worke, and continuing still upon the same,
turned to the glorie of the workeman.

(Historie, 35.10)

The results of Shakespeare's shift in sources are several. Instead of implicitly correcting an act of deluded love, we concentrate
on the inexpressibility topos and the surpassing of even the most
gorgeous fancy by a living ideal. Perhaps following the hint from
Pliny, "albeit the artificiall contriving of the said verses went beyond
the worke, which they seemed to praise," Shakespeare's description
is even less concrete, more verbally allusive than Spenser's ambiguous image. Finally, the allusion would seem to confirm that Cleopatra, in her triumphant staging of herself on the river Cydnus,
evokes not only the *Aphrodite Pandemos* of fruitful nature, but also
the *Aphrodite Urania*, born of the castration of Uranus, rising from
the sea, a neo-Platonic image of the Many in the One.[49]

The implication of these related icons of Venus for the structure of belief in Spenser's poem and Shakespeare's plays is far-
reaching and allied. Our critical imaginative assent to their poetry
becomes the means to an ascent toward the ideal they intimate. As
Spenser's poem unfolds, it falls away from the certain standards
of revealed truth in Book 1 into the increasingly complex problems
of the formation of the rectified imagination in the succeeding
books. Doubleness, or ambiguity, a perilous sign of fallen nature
in the first book, becomes the interpretative challenge. The repeated
icons of Venus in the later books cannot be univocally rejected;
instead, even the most limited of them functions comparatively to
suggest anagogic potential. Guyon's uncharacteristically immoder-
ate rage in destroying Acrasia's bower is not merely destructive;
it is caused by a dawning recognition of the Venereal ideal she
parodies.[50] The claustrophobic artifice of the tapestry of Venus
and Adonis (3.1.34–38) prepares us by contrast for the fruitful
naturalistic version of the myth in the Garden of Adonis (3.6.29–

---

[49] Wind, *Pagan Mysteries*, p. 132.
[50] Berger, *Allegorical Temper*, pp. 215–21.

52), and for the complex judgments we must make of the Venereal aspect of Amoret, Britomart, and even Belphoebe.

Venereal doubleness—whether we are to understand desire as a lustful fall into the world of matter, or an aspiration back toward divine unity—affects other mythic female figures as well: Britomart's dreaming animation of the statue of Isis into an ambivalent emblem of tyrannical power or just dynasty (5.7.12–24); Dame Nature, swayed by the claims of Mutability, but able to "dilate" them into a dynamic perfection which the Christian narrator then "rests" in the "God of Sabbaoth hight" (7.7.57–59; 8.1–2). The interpretative challenge radiates outward to the reader: whether he will, in Boccaccio's words, "find and gather, like fragments of a mighty wreck strewn on some vast shore, the relics of the Gentile gods," and, through a higher fiction, help redeem a fallen reality to its pristine unity.[51]

Shakespeare approaches the same problem through a dogged confrontation with the literalism of the stage and a complex appeal to expand its interpretative possibilities. In the second tetralogy he portrays a fall that entails a primary focus on human character as it creates its own destiny. At the same time he reasserts the transcendent as need, even while he accepts his dramatic medium's inability to confirm its ontological status. His later plays are at once psychologically verisimilar actions and pregnant with immortal longings. His characters express this desire to objectify and perfect this mortal world of incommensurable desire as "acting" or "staging" themselves on a higher plane: Hal "imitates" the sun and calls his own redemptive moment; Hamlet seeks to resolve doubt in play; Edgar "providentially" saves his father from suicide. They ask us, as audience, to dilate their reflexive action through our good will, approving it in our real world through applause and potentially collaborating to recreate it as a real ideal. Cleopatra's appearance as *Venus Anadyomene* or *Venus Urania* in Enobarbus's narration must, therefore, be substantiated through her actions and confirmed by our assent. This occurs through her and our gradual recognition that her former playful behavior may function as rehearsal for her later metaphorical displacements of meaning onto a transcendent plane. While remaining a fallible human character throughout, she

---

[51] *Boccaccio on Poetry*, p. 11.

—and to an even greater extent, we—discover that her "becomings" have allowed her a persuasive fictive escape from the reductions of the "common liar" at Rome.

At first creativity in Shakespeare's drama seems pure play, a sensual or fanciful desire to embroider the facts that often has a foolish or cruel dimension. In the opening scenes Cleopatra draws Antony out largely in jest, and he responds in untested hyperboles. Her maids idly speculate on the future, while she longs to sleep away the time of Antony's absence, and teases Mardian about his too-short stick. Antony contradicts himself, and she indulges in so many roles that we question her sincerity. When the messenger brings news of Antony's marriage to Octavia, she is altogether too willing that he "lie," or at least bend the truth, to salve her wounded ego. Comic pastoral release in Egypt threatens to become tyrannous emotional bondage.

Yet even here are hints that this playfulness, when pressured by the powerful literalism of Roman reality, can rise to an affecting and transforming seriousness. When Enobarbus hears from Antony that they are to leave Egypt, he is at first inclined to dismiss the women's stricken reaction curtly, "Under a compelling occasion let women die . . . between them and a great cause, they should be esteemed nothing" (1.2.134–37). He then jokes rather cynically about Cleopatra's theatrical moods and notorious promiscuity, "Cleopatra catching but the least noise of this, dies instantly. I have seen her die twenty times upon far poorer moment: I do think there is mettle in death, which commits some loving act upon her, she hath such a celerity in dying" (137–42). Yet, as with his description of her at Cydnus, when pressed by a skeptical auditor—in this case the disillusioned Antony, who wants to label these "becomings" of hers "cunning"—Enobarbus is suddenly moved to declare:

> Alack, sir, no, her passions are made of nothing but the finest part of pure love. We cannot call her winds and waters sighs and tears; they are greater storms and tempests than almanacs can report. This cannot be cunning in her; if it be, she makes a shower of rain as well as Jove.
>
> (144–49)

He here half-seriously suggests that her reality surpasses the usual fictive love hyperbole, the windy sighs, the watery tears.

Similarly, her teasing of Antony tests his love rhetoric, and, in the face of Fulvia's death and his departure, she seriously questions the authenticity of their love and taunts his sincerity:

> They are so still,
> Or thou, the greatest soldier of the world,
> Art turn'd the greatest liar.
>
> . . . .
>
> Good now, play one scene
> Of excellent dissembling, and let it look
> Like perfect honour.
>
> (1.3.37–39, 78–80)

Her actress's virtuosity wins from him a beautiful, if stylized, declaration of their mutual love. The scene establishes a dialectical *discordia concors* of fanciful excess, realistic criticism, and tested vision, one that is repeated many times in the play.

It must be repeated because Shakespeare is so tenacious in his presentation of the literal level: the acts of belief in the play are clearly defined in character- or culture-bound ways, as acts of human volition that we may either confirm or deny. Although the rhythm of the play draws us powerfully toward Cleopatra's final, more cohesive myth, we witness each stage in its evolution as fiction. Her multiplicity derives from a culture both immanent and transcendent. Antony's martial and Herculean character is forced into definition in response to it, and only his death and the closing off of worldly potential finally determines her to shape her metamorphic ability to transcendent ends.

Cleopatra, in her infinite variety suggesting *Aphrodite Pandemos,* seems to cling to her earthly power even while implying transcendent escape from its limits. Her motives are never completely clear, but those actions that so often seem to rise spontaneously, improvisationally, are quickly subject to a variety of interpretations, including her own most positive ones. The martial Antony is especially susceptible to two seemingly polar readings of her absolute ambiguity: earthly betrayal or transcendent loyalty. After Actium, when Caesar sends Thidias to persuade Cleopatra to betray Antony, she responds noncommittally, echoing Caesar's own terms. Antony flattens her subtle negotiation into out-and-out treachery;

she allows his rage its course, then quickly turns it to professions of affection by threatening to curse her fertility and that of her country (3.13).

In a series of scenes she then "heartens" him for a new battle, her erotic energy fueling his martial energy as he cries, "The next time I do fight / I'll make death love me; for I will contend / Even with his pestilent scythe" (3.13.192–94). The next morning he rises from their "gaudy night," calling for his armorer Eros and declaring of the impending fight, "To business that we love, we rise betime, / And go to't with delight" (4.4.20–21). He calls her the "armourer of my heart" (4.4.7), and her Venereal energy moves him to victory and a recasting of Philo's opening speech. There, in the mood of homiletic tragedy, a tawny strumpet "bent" a general "like plated Mars" into a fool, turning his great heart into a "bellows and the fan / To cool a gipsy's lust." Now, in the mood of romantic epic, a "great fairy," the "day o' the world," inspires his "gests" and an erotic triumph: "Chain mine arm'd neck, leap thou, attire and all, / Through proof of harness to my heart, and there / Ride on the pants triumphing!" (4.8.14–16). She explicitly rewrites the story of Vulcan's netting of Venus and Mars even as, with a final vehement verb, she bursts Philo's moralistic frame: "Lord of lords, / O infinite virtue, com'st thou smiling from / The world's great snare uncaught?" (4.8.16–18).

This refined worldly version of "What Venus did with Mars" undergoes ironic qualification even as it is articulated. Antony's military victory is desperate and short-lived. Cleopatra's sailors go over to Octavius; her role in the betrayal is unspecified. However, Antony's first reaction assumes her guilt, as with even greater fury he repeats Philo's condemnations, threatening to give her to Caesar's triumph or to kill her at once. His rage causes her to rush to the monument and send word of her feigned suicide.

Once again, her motives are potentially complex and impenetrable. She might be continuing a pattern of betrayal, provoking his suicide while maintaining her own freedom to negotiate with Octavius until his intentions are clear. She might be laying down the greatest test of Antony's hyperbolic love. Probably she is confused and improvising, continuing her teasing habits of opposition, dangerously maintaining some freedom for herself by playing on Antony's responses. And her desire that Mardian word the news

of her death "piteously" partially supports her messenger Diomedes' belated claim that she sought to purge Antony's rage, not
provoke his suicide (4.14.120–27).[52] We can, however, determine
what Antony makes of this ambivalent "matter": "how he takes my
death" (4.13.10). His succeeding interpretation constitutes the
great peripeteia in this play of fluctuating modes; through the mediation of the eunuch Mardian, he turns tragedy to tragicomedy.

Much earlier, when Cleopatra's hopes were still firmly centered on creativity in this world, she declared that she took "no
pleasure / In aught an eunuch has" (1.5.9–10). But later, knowing
of Mardian's "fierce affections" and thoughts of "What Venus
did with Mars," she tolerantly exclaims, "And when good will is
show'd, though't come too short, / The actor may plead pardon"
(2.5.8–9). This poor actor "in deed" becomes the ideal rhetorical
vehicle for Antony's "transmigration." Mardian's formally beautiful neo-Senecan report of Cleopatra's "death" transforms Antony's own motives for dying from Stoic despair to Epicurean joy.
From shapeless being, robbed of his sword, left only "Ourselves to
end ourselves" (4.14.22), Antony becomes transcendent erotic warrior:

---

[52] M. R. Ridley, editor of the Arden text, notes how stylized this type of
reported death-scene had become, even to the point of parody (p. 187). A
self-conscious artist like the mature Shakespeare could not but calculate
the precise degree of artifice in Mardian's speech, which falls short of parody,
but is designed by Cleopatra to carry a specific effect, the cathartic transformation of rage to love and pity:

> CLEOPATRA: To the monument!
> Mardian, go tell him I have slain myself:
> Say, that the last I spoke was "Antony,"
> And word it, prithee, piteously. Hence, Mardian,
> And bring me how he takes my death to the monument.
>   (4.13.6–10)
>
> MARDIAN: The last she spake
> Was "Antony! most noble Antony!"
> Then in the midst a tearing groan did break
> The name of Antony; it was divided
> Between her heart, and lips: she render'd life
> Thy name so buried in her.
>   (4.14.29–34)

Is it possible that she half intends the speech to be perceived as fiction?

Come then: for with a wound I must be cur'd.

. . . .

But I will be
A bridegroom in my death, and run into't
As to a lover's bed.

(4.14.78, 99–101)

Calling repeatedly on his armorer Eros, he "burst[s] / The buckles on his breast," not, as Philo would say, "disarmed," nor involved in the Herculean cloak, but *unarmed* to allow for the movement of his growing spirit to her:

Off, pluck off,
The seven-fold shield of Ajax cannot keep
The battery from my heart. O, cleave, my sides!
Heart, once be stronger than thy continent,
Crack thy frail case! Apace, Eros, apace!
No more a soldier: bruised pieces, go,
You have been nobly borne.

(4.14.37–43)

Antony thus decisively reverses Roman values, as Shakespeare rewrites Vergil's great fiction of erotic abnegation. In place of Dido's harsh rejection of Aeneas in the underworld (*Aen.* 6.440–76), Antony imagines Dido and Aeneas reunited, and even their reunion surpassed by his with Cleopatra:

Eros!—I come, my queen: —Eros!—Stay for me,
Where souls do couch on flowers, we'll hand in hand,
And with our sprightly port make the ghosts gaze:
Dido, and her Æneas, shall want troops,
And all the haunt be ours. Come, Eros, Eros!

(4.14.50–54)

For the tragedy of Dido that prefigures Octavius's triumph (*Aen.* 8.675–728), he substitutes this picture of their "sprightly" erotic progress.

Cleopatra then collaborates in this revision. Whatever her motives for feigning suicide, she now sends another messenger to proclaim the truth to the mortally wounded Antony. To Antony's "Where is she?" Diomedes replies:

> Lock'd in her monument; she had a prophesying fear
> Of what hath come to pass: for when she saw—
> Which never shall be found—you did suspect
> She had dispos'd with Cæsar, and that your rage
> Would not be purg'd, she sent you word she was dead;
> But fearing since how it might work, hath sent
> Me to proclaim the truth, and I am come,
> I dread, too late.
>
> (4.14.119–127)

Although she will continue to "play" with Caesar well after Antony's death, she here has Diomedes imply that her overwrought strategy was directed at the catharsis of her lover's rage. As the scene ends, Antony appears to accept this interpretation, welcoming his fate, bearing it lightly.

At the monument Cleopatra continues Antony's transcendent erotic transformations, turning their previous life into prophetic metaphors for their new life together. Drawing the dying Antony up to her, she recalls her previous "sport" with the "Tawny-finn'd fishes" (2.5.12) and Lucretius's description of Mars reclining in Venus's lap:

> Here's sport indeed! How heavy weighs my lord!
> Our strength is all gone into heaviness,
> That makes the weight. Had I great Juno's power,
> The strong-wing'd Mercury should fetch thee up,
> And set thee by Jove's side. Yet come a little,
> Wishers were ever fools. O, come, come, come.
> And welcome, welcome! Die when thou hast liv'd,
> Quicken with kissing: had my lips that power,
> Thus would I wear them out.
>
> (4.15.32–40)

Her previous "celerity in dying" (1.2.141)—in feigning death and using sex—is here optimistically transformed into an induction to the afterlife.

The ambiguity of Cleopatra's motives persists, and it is reflected in her critical tentativeness toward her own transcendent metaphors. The physical awkwardness of this elevation scene is matched by her verbal skepticism: "Had I great Juno's power,"

"Wishers were ever fools," "Had my lips that power." She refuses to come down to the dying Antony, "Lest I be taken" (23), and despite her immediate declaration that she will follow him in death, seems to delay suicide. It is Antony's ambiguous final directive to her—"Gentle, hear me, / None about Cæsar trust but Proculeius" (47–48)—that initiates her final movement toward transcendent definition, as if only his answer to her quicksilver changes, a "treachery," can impel her toward constancy, suicide, and union with him.

Betrayed by Proculeius into captivity, Cleopatra continues to test her this-worldly possibility even while preparing other-worldly escape. Her wary and masterful exchange with Dolabella secures his loyalty through a romantic apotheosis of Antony. Her picture of Antony gloriously matches Enobarbus's "o'erpicturing" description of her at Cydnus:

> But if there be, or ever were one such,
> It's past the size of dreaming: nature wants stuff
> To vie strange forms with fancy, yet to imagine
> An Antony were nature's piece, 'gainst fancy,
> Condemning shadows quite.
>
> (5.2.95–99)

However, she evokes this eikastic fiction only conditionally. Ironically, Dolabella, who attempts to deny it, is persuaded by it to tell Cleopatra that Caesar, no matter what he says, will lead her in triumph at Rome. Her anticipation of Caesar's reductive staging of her now provides the final impetus to her suicide.

Only when Dolabella reports Caesar's deceptive intentions does she wholeheartedly embrace an idealizing interpretation of her action with Antony. Her descriptions of how the conquering Romans will portray them summarize the dominant Roman reading of the play; they also achieve a particular force from the conventions of the Jacobean stage, in which a boy plays her role:

> Nay, 'tis most certain, Iras: saucy lictors
> Will catch at us like strumpets, and scald rhymers
> Ballad us out o' tune. The quick comedians
> Extemporally will stage us, and present
> Our Alexandrian revels: Antony
> Shall be brought drunken forth, and I shall see

> Some squeaking Cleopatra boy my greatness
> I' the posture of a whore.
>
> (5.2.213–20)

In place of this extemporaneous, parodic, lewd, transsexual performance, she would substitute a teleological, divinely comic, playful, and hermaphroditic interpretation.

Climaxing her and Antony's previous transcendent erotic
transformations, she again recalls Enobarbus's "o'erpicturing"
when she declares "I am again for Cydnus, / To meet Mark Antony"
(227–28). She further "quickens" that previous picture of immanent
sexuality to "immortal longings" (280). The languorous fullness of
the former description becomes aroused command as she abandons
"baser life" and rejoins her husband; what she cannot do "in deed"
becomes a metaphoric expression of transcendent union, "As sweet
as balm, as soft as air, as gentle. / O Antony!" (310–11).

Her punning exchanges with the clownish countryman confirm
her intention to make "good will . . . though't come too short . . .
plead pardon"; "What poor an instrument / May do a noble deed!"
she exclaims (235–36). The phallic serpent, bred of Nilus's slime,
which has made so many women "lie" (tell lies, have sex), becomes
the instrument of ecstatic transformation of her appearance at
Cydnus. For the snake's Edenic associations with the temptation
and fall of Eve, she substitutes the transcendent symbols of Egyptian
culture, the circled ouroboros and the serpent that sucks life from
the bosom of the great nature goddess Isis.[53] Her final revision of
her action with Antony subsumes Enobarbus's many-leveled, neo-
Platonic reading of "What Venus did with Mars" under the more
comprehensive regeneration myth of Isis.

---

[53] For Biblical allusion and values in the play, see Harold Fisch, "*Antony
and Cleopatra*: The Limits of Mythology"; Ethel Seaton, "*Antony and Cleopatra* and the *Book of Revelation*"; and, most thoroughly, Andrew Fichter,
"*Antony and Cleopatra*: 'The Time of Universal Peace.'" Shakespeare seems
intent on rounding his biblical irony through an Egyptian allegory of regeneration, an interplay of traditions that I discuss in the next section of this chapter.
On the ouroboros, see John Read, *Through Alchemy to Chemistry*, for the
ouroboros as the alchemical symbol of the "essential unity of all things" in
the pre-Cartesian great chain of being (p. 25), and as the symbol of re-
juvenation and eternity (pp. 46, 67); see also Michael Maier, *Atalanta Fugiens*,
pp. 132–35, on the historical Cleopatra's use of this sign to represent the idea
"The One Is the All."

Fiction as Myth: Of Isis and Osiris, or the Myth of Egypt

The Phrigiens call me the mother of the Goddes: The Athe-
nians, Minerue: the Cipriens, Venus: the Candians, Diana:
the Sicilians, Proserpina: the Eleusians, Ceres: some Juno,
other Bellona, other Hecate: and principally the Ethiopians
whiche dwell in the Orient, and the Egiptians whiche are
excellent in all kinde of auncient doctrine, & by their propre
ceremonies accustome to worshippe me, doe call me Queene
Isis.

(Apuleius, *The XI Bookes of the Golden Asse*)

The motives that impelled Renaissance Egyptology are quite
different from those that spur the modern archaeologist.[54] As a more
historically correct knowledge of classical culture was acquired
in the fifteenth and sixteenth centuries, it became increasingly difficult to achieve a detailed accommodation between these attractive
systems of ancient philosophical thought and religious belief and the
dominant Christian orthodoxy. No longer could the pagan gods be
easily explained as demons and their adherents as damned souls,
confined to hell. The salvation of the virtuous heathen is already a
crux in Dante's *Divine Comedy*;[55] the issue only became more acute
over time. Related problems were posed by the increasingly bitter
sectarian rivalries of the sixteenth century and the discovery of a
new class of "virtuous heathen," the indigenous peoples of the
Americas and the Far East.

Many ingenious arguments were offered by Europeans whose
consciences were troubled by these new races who had seemingly
lived and died without benefit of revelation. One explanation claimed
that these peoples were the descendents of the ten lost tribes of
Israel. Francis Bacon elaborates this theory in imagining the people
of his utopia, the New Atlantis, practicing the wisdom of Solomon
and receiving the New Testament, miraculously transported on an

---

[54] On Renaissance Egyptology, see Karl H. Dannenfeldt, "Egypt and
Egyptian Antiquities in the Renaissance"; and Eric Iversen, *The Myth of
Egypt and Its Hieroglyphs in European Tradition*.

[55] Consider *Inf.* 4; *Purg.* 1–2, 21–22, 27–30; *Par.* 29–30.

ark launched by the Apostle Bartholomew.[56] Other lines of argument would evolve into a defense of a natural religious impulse in all men. Thomas More's Utopians have the sound core of a natural religion that they practice with great piety; although some of its precepts require the refinement of Christianity, it is held up against the hypocrisies of European Christians and makes the Utopians highly receptive to true Christian teaching.[57] And Montaigne, repelled by the atrocities of the French wars of religion, sharpens the satire against uncritical orthodoxy and praises natural man in the essay "On Cannibals":

> I am not sory we note the barbarous horror of such an action, but grieved, that prying so narrowly into their faults, we are so blinded in ours. I think there is more barbarisme in eating men alive, then to feed vpon them being dead; to mangle by tortures and torments a body full of lively sense, to roast him in peeces, to make dogges and swine to gnawe and teare him in mammockes (as we have not only read, but seene very lately, yea and in our owne memorie, not amongst ancient enemies, but our neighbours and fellow-citizens; and which is worse, vnder pretense of piety and religion) then to roast and teare him after he is dead.
>
> (The Essayes, p. 104)

A tolerant interest in the religious practices of these foreign peoples often reinforced sympathetic study of ancient religious beliefs. The Jesuits, for example, became religious comparatists in their desire to smoothly introduce their conversion efforts into the culture of their new flock; the knowledge of foreign gods brought back by ex-

---

[56] Bacon, Works 5:370–73. I am grateful for the information supplied by the work in progress of Dr. Hal Cook, formerly graduate student in the Department of History, the University of Michigan, Ann Arbor, on early European views of indigenous Americans.

[57] The "Utopia" of Sir Thomas More, pp. 226–98; in particular:

But after they harde vs speake of the name of Christe, of his doctryne, lawes, myracles . . . yowe wyll not beleue with howe gladde myndes they agreed vnto the same; whether it were by the secrete inspiration of God, or els for that they thought it next vnto that opinion which amonge them is counted the chiefest.

(pp. 268–69)

plorers and settlers found its way into handbooks of classical mythology. The later editions of one of the most famous of these, Cartari's iconographic guide, *Le imagini de i Dei de gli Antichi*, contains appendices describing and illustrating the gods of the Americas
and the Far East.[58]

On the eve of the Protestant Reformation and the discovery of
the Americas, the Florentine neo-Platonists renovated and elaborated
a "historical" thesis about the rapprochement between Christian and
pagan cultures. It provided, for a time at least, a broader argumen-
tative framework within which religious differences between Christian and pagan, and also Christian and Christian, might be recon-
ciled.[59] They studied the Platonic texts through the haze of late
classical syncretism that saw Plato as himself the myth-making
transmitter of a much older tradition of religious revelation. Like
Augustine before them, they read Plato through the metaphysical
overlay of such neo-Platonists as Plotinus, Porphyry, and Iambli-
chus, and they were astonished to find a philosophical language that
closely paralleled, and in many cases even seemed to support, biblical revelation.

From whence did this seeming consanguinity spring? Augustine
provided a hint. Although he argued for the primacy of Hebrew
philosophy over any of the traditions of pagan wisdom, he alludes
to Acts 7:22 ("And Moses was learned in all the wisdom of the
Egyptians") and concedes:

> But it must be admitted that there was before Moses, not to
> be sure in Greece but among foreign nations, for example in
> Egypt, some learning which might be called the wisdom of
> these men; otherwise it would not have been written in the
> sacred Scriptures that Moses was learned in all the wisdom of
> the Egyptians.
>
> (*City of God* 18.37)

---

[58] See D. P. Walker, *The Ancient Theology*, pp. 194–230, and the 1647
Venetian edition of Cartari, now readily available in facsimile, ed. Walter Koschatzky.

[59] On the Renaissance rapprochement between pagan myth and Christian
revelation, see Wind, *Pagan Mysteries*, especially chap. 1; for the *prisca
theologia*, Frances Yates, *Giordano Bruno and the Hermetic Tradition*, especially chap. 1. I am much indebted to Yates's interpretation of the central
position of Egyptology in Renaissance religious thought.

Elsewhere in *The City of God* Augustine inveighs against the dae-monic beliefs of Hermes Trismegistus, the legendary Egyptian priest-philosopher; Hermes' mourning for the dying gods of Egypt signals the triumphant advance of Christianity. Still, Augustine is intrigued by the way in which the Hermetic pronouncements often seem to "shadow" biblical revelation:

> In fact he makes many statements about the one true God, the artificer of the universe, which closely resemble the asser-tions of Truth; and it is puzzling how by the "darkening of the mind" he falls so low as to require men always to be in subjection to gods who he admits are made by men, and so low as to bewail the future abolition of such things.
>
> (*City of God* 8.23)

The Church Father Lactantius, writing a century earlier in a more conciliatory vein, recorded that this Hermes "wrote books—many, indeed, pertaining to the knowledge of divine things—in which he vouches for the majesty of the supreme and single God and he calls Him by the same names which we use: Lord and Father." Lactan-tius, with unqualified enthusiasm, cites further striking resem-blances: the proper worship offered the one true God, man as the God-desiring *imago dei*, and the apocalyptic last day when the Son of God will come in glory. In his *De ira dei* he dates Hermes long before Plato and Pythagoras.[60]

The Florentine neo-Platonists believed they had recovered the works of this "thrice-great" Hermes in the so-called *Corpus Her-meticum*; Ficino even translated these texts before beginning work on Plato.[61] But they were not the work of an Egyptian contemporary of Moses, as Lactantius's chronology implies, rather a late classical syncretic blending of various strands of Hellenistic philosophy and the resurgent Eastern mystery religions. However, from the Church Fathers' statements and their own perceptions of the resemblances between the Hermetic texts and biblical teachings, Ficino and his followers constructed a genealogy of ancient wisdom that postulated an original divine revelation shared by Moses and the Egyptian

---

[60] See Lactantius, *The Divine Institutes*, 1.6, 6.25, 7.4, 9, 18; and see Yates, *Bruno*, p. 7.

[61] Yates, *Bruno*, p. 13.

Hermes. This shared revelation was assumed to have evolved as two separate strains: on the one hand, biblical revelation with its accompanying oral tradition, the Hebrew Cabbala; on the other, through Plato's contacts with an older tradition of sacred poetry and his reputed visits to Egypt, Graeco-Roman philosophical writing.[62]

To reunite this scattered body of ancient wisdom and thus persuade his contemporaries to an analogous liberal-minded contemplative endeavor—to cease sectarian wrangling and scholastic close-mindedness—Pico della Mirandola piously offered his disputation on 900 theses. In "The Oration on the Dignity of Man" he prefaces this seemingly eclectic collection with a creation myth that espouses man's absolute freedom as co-creator with God; this myth is a composite of the Genesis account, Plato's *Timaeus*, and the Hermetic *Asclepius*. This "prince of concord" placed what he believed to be the texts of the Egyptian religion near the source of the revelation of God working in man.

The hieroglyphs of Egyptian culture also contributed to the Renaissance conception of Egyptian religion as a pristine source of revelation. Despite Augustine's contempt for Egyptian totemism and divine statuary, their visually striking cult practices and hieroglyphic writing were often believed to be powerful attempts to bypass discursive reasoning for direct apprehension of God's working in the nature of things. Plotinus theorized that the hieroglyphs were Platonic ideas made visible:

> It seems to me that the Egyptian sages, either working by right reasoning or spontaneously, when they desired to represent things through wisdom, did not use letters descriptive of words and sentences, imitating the sounds and pronunciation of propositions, but drew pictures, and carved one picture for each thing in their temples, thus making manifest the description of that thing. Thus each picture was a kind of understanding and wisdom and substance and given all at once, and not discursive reasoning and deliberation.[63]

---

[62] Quasi-legendary reports of Plato's extensive travels, including voyages to Egypt, are offered by later classical writers, such as Cicero in *De Republica* and *De Finibus*, and the biographer Diogenes Laertius; later writers expand these into legends of visits to the Hebrews, the Babylonians, the Magi, etc. See *Dictionary of Greek and Roman Biography and Mythology* 3 : 393.

[63] Cited by George Boas, trans., *The Hieroglyphics of Horapollo*, p. 22.

Ficino seized on this passage and made it Christian:

> The Egyptian priests, when they wished to signify divine
> things, did not use letters, but whole figures of plants, trees,
> and animals; for God doubtless has a knowledge of things
> which is not complex discursive thought about its subject, but
> is, as it were, the simple and steadfast form of it.[64]

The visual image was at once immediate and complex, linking a particular manifestation with its divine creative and sustaining source.

This interpretation not only dignified the hieroglyphs but also
gave a significant impetus to the visual arts. They need no longer be
considered idolatrous or merely Platonic imitations of imitations,
but might elevate fallen nature toward its pristine source.[65] A vogue
ensued not only for such Egyptian, or actually pseudo-Egyptian,
sources as the *Hieroglyphica* of Horapollo but also for Renaissance
amplifications such as the *Hieroglyphica* of Piero Valeriano (1556).
Concurrently, enigmatical emblem literature and mythographical
and iconographic handbooks were produced to describe the significance of depictions of the gods and of complex allegorical figures.

Giordano Bruno's enthusiasm for the rich symbolic properties
of physical things was so great as to invert Augustine's concerns
about idolatry. Bruno thought the Egyptians grasped more profoundly than the image-prohibiting Jews and their timid Christian
successors the complex relationship between physical things and
divine forces, and he laments the loss of their gods. In his dialogue
Lo Spaccio de la bestia trionfante, Sophia defends the Egyptian religion for recognizing that it is Nature who communicates to us
the absolute God. She quotes the goddess Isis on the superiority of
the Egyptian religion:

> Senseless fools and true brutes (Isis continued) laugh at us
> gods for being worshiped in beasts and plants and stones and
> at my Egyptians, who in this manner used to recognize us.
> And they do not consider the fact that Divinity reveals herself

---

[64] Ibid., p. 28.

[65] E. H. Gombrich, "*Icones Symbolicae*: The Visual Image in Neo-Platonic
Thought," discusses the significance for the visual arts of Ficino's interpretation of Plotinus; but see also Wind, *Pagan Mysteries*, p. 127, for reservations
on Ficino's evaluation of the visual arts.

in all things, although by virtue of a universal and most excellent end, in great things and general principles, and by proximate ends, convenient and necessary to diverse acts of human life, she is found and is seen in things said to be most abject, although everything, from what is said, has Divinity latent within itself. For she enfolds and imparts herself even unto the smallest beings, and from the smallest beings, according to their capacity.

(Expulsion of the Triumphant Beast, p. 242)

Isis argues the efficacy of the Egyptian worship of emblematic beasts and vegetation, and even contends that Moses derived his capacity for divine revelation from the Egyptians, and that the Jews were at fault in abandoning the Egyptian cults. Thus Bruno turns the argument for philosophical and religious toleration, which created such interest in the myth of Egypt, to the end of a universal pantheism.

Shakespeare may have known the works of Augustine, Plotinus, Ficino, or Bruno.[66] However, the Egyptological sources most directly accessible to him embody the same range of interpretative possibility. Their authors are aware that people may rest idolatrously in the beautiful or fabulous properties of the images they describe; they urge them to look beyond this literal level to their wider philosophical and theological significance. In 1599 Cartari's oft-reprinted and translated mythographical handbook was partially translated into English by the gentleman poet Richard Linche. Linche's volume, *The Fovntaine of Ancient Fiction*, includes a translation of Cartari's introduction, which justifies the study of ancient images as signs of a universal religious impulse in man:

There haue liued verie few people, or rather none at all . . . which haue not among themselues embraced a certaine and peculiar sort of religious adoration. For the soule of man euen vpon her first entrance into this earth-framed and corrupted receptable of her celestiall essence, doth seeme to bring then with her a certaine kind of naturall religion, the diuinitie whereof procureth the discrepance betwixt men and beasts, which as they want the intellectual sence and feeling of any

---

[66] *Lo Spaccio de la bestia trionfante* was printed by John Charlewood in London in 1584 with a fictive Paris imprint; Yates and others argue the influence of Bruno as near to Shakespeare as the Sidney circle.

such motion, do therfore neither worship or reuerence any deitie: Onely man, whose bodie is framed erect, with his eies still looking on that perspicuous and thought-amazing composition of the heauens, is forcibly constrained to beleeue, that there hath been some one of eternall and infinit command, that hath had that vnspeakable wisdome, and inexcogitable care, as first to compose, then to gouerne and dispose this so rare and miraculous wonderment: and him they entearme by the name of GOD; as it were the giuer of al good things, who by his infinitenesse is eternal, incomprehensible, and inuisible.

(*Fovntaine*, Bi r–v)

Cartari cautions that these images are corrupt representations, often euhemeristic in origin. He admires the Jews for their tenacious adherence to a nonrepresentational worship of God. At the same time he indicates, citing the works of such pagan rationalists as Varro, that knowledgeable pagans did not intend the images to be taken literally, but to show

that the soule of man, which is imprisoned here in the fleshly dungeon of the bodie, resembles the diuine soules, which inhabite in the celestiall dwellings of the heauens: and for that the mind or soule cannot externally bee seene or proportioned, they did prefigure it, and make it apparent by the shape of a humane bodie.

(*Fovntaine*, Biii r)

Cartari's full exposition of the chief Egyptian goddess, Isis, is derived from a variety of classical sources; Linche's English abridgment, however, emphasizes the descriptions of Isis in the second-century picaresque romance, *The Golden Asse,* by the neo-Platonist Lucius Apuleius. There Lucius, seeking escape from his transformation into an ass, ecstatically envisions the Goddess, not as regional deity, but as the plenum of nature, comprehending all other divinities. This episode, Shakespeare's source for the thematically pivotal *discordia concors* of Bottom and Titania in *A Midsummer Night's Dream,* underlies his development of Cleopatra as Isis in *Antony and Cleopatra.*[67]

---

[67] The *discordia concors* of the literal-minded enthusiast Bottom and the subtle, angry, repressed Faerie Queene Titania, whose source is Lucius's mystery-initiate vision of Isis in Apuleius's *The Golden Asse,* resolves the

In "The Life of Marcus Antonius" Plutarch declares, "Now for Cleopatra, she did not onely weare at that time (but at all other times els when she came abroad) the apparell of the goddesse Isis, and so gave audience unto all her subjects, as a new Isis" (p. 291). When Shakespeare sought to explore the significance of this allusion, he turned to the essay "Of Isis and Osiris" in Philemon Holland's 1603 translation of Plutarch's *Moralia*. In his prefatory synopsis to "Of Isis and Osiris," Holland admires Plutarch's skill at discerning the allegorical readings of what would otherwise be "ridiculous & monstrous fables, in such sort, as we may cal this treatise a commentary of the Aegyptians Theologie and Philosophy" (p. 1286). Although Holland concludes with a cautious reflection on the idolatrous confusion of men deprived of revelation, he values Plutarch's efforts to reconstruct from the "fragments and peeces scattered heere and there" this central body of precious Egyptian lore, "the source and fountaine from whence have flowed into the world arts and liberall sciences, as a man may gather by the testimony of the first Poets and philosophers that ever were" (p. 1286).

Properly understood, then, these fables are a bulwark against atheism, for they show the universality of the religious impulse in man. As Plutarch reads them, "according to the mystical sense of the Isiake priests," they are not superstitious beast-worship or other species of vain imaginings, but poetic embodiments of truths of natural philosophy relevant to Egypt in particular and to natural proces-

---

imaginative crux of *A Midsummer Night's Dream*. It subliminally allows Titania to acknowledge tragic mortality, from which she has been withholding her dead votaress' little boy, even while it elevates Bottom to a comic synaesthetic vision patterned after St. Paul's rapture (*MND* 4.1.211–14; 1 Cor. 2:9). Literally, it leads to the happy resolution of all the crises in the play; metaphorically, it suggests the imaginative range between the grossly material and the supernatural that must underlie successful art and inspire our cooperation in its creation.

Fittingly, Shakespeare recurs to Apuleius's vision of the comprehensive goddess Isis, now dramatically enriched through the dynamic myth of Isis and Osiris from Plutarch's *Moralia*, for his characterization of Cleopatra, in a play that imaginatively recapitulates so much of his own work and the Renaissance myth of the re-creative artist. For critical commentary supporting my interpretation of *MND*, see Frank Kermode's neo-Platonic reading, "The Mature Comedies"; R. W. Dent, "Imagination in *A Midsummer Night's Dream*"; John A. Allen, "Bottom and Titania"; David P. Young, *Something of Great Constancy*, especially chap. 3.

ses in general. Through a neo-Platonic reading they may even be shadows of the divine. Plutarch's ascent from literal to natural philosophical to neo-Platonic readings of the myth of Isis and Osiris, in turn, can lead us through Shakespeare's dramatic development of Cleopatra, from her position as embodiment of the genius of her country, to her conception of her relationship to Antony, to her final attempt to transform their story beyond mutability and the sphere of tragedy into eternity.

The story of Isis and Osiris recounts the murder and dismemberment of the body of the great god Osiris by his half-brother Typhon, the reassembling, burial, and veneration of his body by his faithful wife-sister Isis, and the revenge on Typhon by their son Horus. Plutarch introduces Osiris, who is also known as Bacchus, as the civilizer of the Egyptians who "afterwards . . . travelled thorowout the world, reducing the whole earth to civility, by force of armes least of all, but winning and gaining the most nations by effectuall remonstrances & sweet perswasion couched in songs, and with all maner of Musicke" (p. 1292). He emphatically asserts the need for an allegorical reading of the tale:

> Now, that, if any there be who hold and affirme such fables as these touching the blessed and immortall nature, whereby especially we conceived in our minde the deity, to be true and that such things were really done or hapned so indeed,
>
> *We ought to spit upon their face*
> *And curse such mouthes with all disgrace.*
>
> as *Aeschylus* saith. . . . And yet you see verie well, that these be not narrations like unto old wives tales, or vaine and foolish fictions, which Poets or other idle writers devise out of their owne fingers ends. . . . And like as the Mathematicians say, that the rainbow is a representation of the Sunne, and the same distinguished by sundry colours, by the refraction of our eie-sight against a cloud: even so this fable, is an apparence of some doctrine or learning, which doeth reflect and send backe our understanding, to the consideration of some other trueth.
>
> (p. 1295)

Further, he rejects a euhemeristic interpretation, declaring that such ancient and universal myths are in fact a sign of man's natural religious disposition, rather than an elevation of human deeds.

While Plutarch notes in passing the analogy between this story and other fertility myths, he first gives his attention to a local interpretation:

> Let us (of those who are able to discourse somewhat Philosophically and with reason) consider first and formost such as deale most simply in this behalfe. And these be they that say, like as the Greeks allegorize that *Saturne* is time, *Juno* the aire, and the generation of *Vulcan*, is the transmutation of aire into fire; even so they give out that by *Osiris* the Aegyptians meane *Nilus*, which lieth and keepeth company with *Isis*, that is to say, the earth.
>
> (p. 1300)

In this reading the story embodies a natural philosophical explanation of the special geography and climate of Egypt, where the Nile's annual flood fertilizes the land: "they both hold and affirme, *Nilus* to be the effluence of *Osiris*; even so they are of opinion, that the body of *Isis* is the earth or land of *Aegypt*; and yet not all of it, but so much as *Nilus* overfloweth, and by commixtion maketh fertile and fruitfull" (p. 1302). Typhon may be either the sea—"into which *Nilus* falling loseth himselfe, and is dispatched heere and there, unlesse it be that portion thereof, which the earth receiveth and whereby it is made fertill" (p. 1300)—or the drought brought on by the burning winds from Ethiopia: "then *Typhon*, that is to say, drouth, is said to winne the better, and to burne up all; and so having gotten the mastery cleane of *Nilus*, who by reason of his weaknesse and feeblenesse, is driven in, and forced to retire a contrary way, he chafeth him, poore and low into the sea" (p. 1303).

Plutarch then moves from this particular Egyptian application to a more general allegory of the process of generation.

> But to returne to our matter: the priests as many as be of the wiser and more learned sort, understand by *Osiris*, not onely the river *Nilus*, and by *Typhon* the sea: but also by the former, they signifie in one word and simply, all vertue and power that produceth moisture and water, taking it to be the materiall cause of generation, and the nature generative of seed: and by *Typhon* they represent all desiccative vertue, all heat of fire & drinesse, as the very thing that is fully opposite and adverse to humidity.
>
> (p. 1300)

The union of Osiris and Isis signifies the union of moist semen and matter, which the excessive heat of Typhon can destroy. The phallus and its symbolic likeness, the "fig tree leafe, which . . . signifieth the imbibition and motion of all things" (p. 1301), are worshipped in Egypt. When Typhon dismembered the body of Osiris, his "male member" was eaten by fish, and Isis had to make and consecrate a new one.

However, the traditional identification of Isis as a moon goddess and the productive role of sun and heat in generation cause Plutarch to qualify this initial opposition between the fruitful moisture of Osiris and the destructive fire of Typhon. In a series of interpretative mutations he first considers that astronomical lore that would have Typhon be the solar and Osiris the lunar sphere:

> Inasmuch as the Moone hath a generative and vegetable light, multiplying that sweet and comfortable moisture which is so meet for the generation of living creatures, of trees and plants: but the Sunne having in it a pure firy flame indeed without any mixture or rebatement at all, heateth and drieth that which the earth bringeth forth, yea, and whatsoever is verdant and in the flower; insomuch, as by his inflamation he causeth the greater part of the earth to be wholly desert and [un]inhabitable, and many times subdueth the very Moone.
>
> (p. 1304)

The phases of the moon are linked to the fertilizing fluctuations of the Nile. This lunar world is next redefined as the scene of the creative interaction of Isis and Osiris:

> They solemnize a feast in the new Moone of the moneth Phamenoth, which they call The ingresse or entrance of *Osiris* to the Moone; and this is the beginning of the Spring season: and thus they put the power of *Osiris* in the Moone. They say also, that *Isis* (which is no other thing but generation) lieth with him; and so they name the Moone, Mother of the world; saying, that she is a double nature, male and female: female, in that she doth conceive and is replenished by the Sunne: and male, in this regard, that she sendeth forth and sprinkleth in the aire, the seeds and principles of generation.
>
> (p. 1304-5)

This hermaphroditic understanding of the moon allows Plutarch to cite those interpreters who regard the myth as an account of solar and lunar eclipses:

> For the Moone is ecclipsed, when she is at the full directly opposite to the Sunne, and commeth to fall upon the shadow of the earth: like as they say, *Orisis* was put into the chest or coffer abovesaid. On the other side, she seemeth to hide and darken the light of the Sunne, upon certaine thirtieth daies, but yet doth not wholly abolish the Sunne, no more than *Isis* doth kill *Typhon*.
>
> (p. 1305)

Osiris in the tomb represents the moon shadowed by earth; Isis victorious over Typhon represents the moon's eclipse of the sun.

The latent contradictions among these various interpretations of the myth (Osiris = moon; Isis = moon; Typhon = sun; Osiris = sun) are resolved as Plutarch dialectically rises to the height of neo-Platonic syncretism. Local Egyptian interpretations—the interaction of Typhon as the salt sea or desert heat, Osiris as inseminating moisture, and Isis as earth or matter—and cosmological interpretations, must be generalized philosophically. Typhon becomes the very principle of dryness and decay. Isis's restoration of the sexual potency of Osiris is a metaphor for creative movement back to original unity; for his lost phallus she substitutes an immortal re-creation:

> And therfore me thinks, it were not amisse to say, that in particular there is not any one of these expositions and interpretations perfect by it selfe and right, but all of them together cary some good construction: for it is neither drought alone, nor winde, nor sea, ne yet darknesse; but all that is noisome and hurtfull whatsoever, and which hath a speciall part to hurt and destroy, is called *Typhon*.
>
> (p. 1305)

> But generally throughout wheresoever the image of *Osiris* is exhibited in the forme of a man, they purtray him with the naturall member of generation stiffe and straight, prefiguring thereby the generative and nutritive vertue. The habiliment also, wherewith they clad his images is bright, shining like

fire: For they repute the Sunne to be a body representing the power of goodnesse, as being the visible matter of a spirituall and intellectuall substance. And therefore their opinion deserveth to be rejected who attribute unto *Typhon* the sphære of the Sunne, considering that unto him properly appertaineth nothing that is resplendent, healthfull and comfortable.

(p. 1308)

As moon goddess, Isis simultaneously governs the mortal world of change and looks toward the source of being, her immortal husband, Osiris, the sun. Her many-colored robes converge to his dazzling white light (p. 1318). She is not inert matter, but rather, as "the feminine part of nature," "the nurse and *Pandeches*," who has "an infinite number of names," she is the teleological realm of becoming:

There is imprinted in her naturally, a love of the first and principall essence, which is nothing else but the soveraigne good, and it she desireth, seeketh, and pursueth after. . . . enclined she is alwaies rather to the better, and applieth herselfe to engender the same, yea, and to disseminate and sowe the defluxions and similitudes thereof, wherein she taketh pleasure and rejoiceth, when she hath conceived and is great therewith, ready to be delivered. For this is a representation and description of the substance engendred in matter, and nothing else but an imitation of that which is.

(p. 1309)

Typhon's tragic action in murdering and dismembering her husband impels Isis to reassemble him on a metaphysical plane. "And thus much," concludes Plutarch, "may suffice for that sense and interpretation which is most beseeming the gods" (p. 1318).

From this polysemous myth Shakespeare derives his extraordinary portrait of Egyptian culture and its influence.[68] Egypt is a land of seeming contrarieties that in fact rounds them into a fertile cycle: "The higher Nilus swells, / The more it promises: as it ebbs, the seedsman / Upon the slime and ooze scatters his grain, / And shortly

---

[68] Michael Lloyd, "Cleopatra as Isis." Though I follow Lloyd's argument at many points, I disagree with his conclusion that Antony is not significantly drawn into the myth of Isis and Osiris, as my analysis will show.

comes to harvest" (2.7.20–23). The greatest harvest comes from seemingly greatest destruction; generation results from the warming action of sun on slime. The Egyptians rejoice in this natural *discordia concors*, and include in it the worship of an earthy sexuality. When Iras, extending her hand to the seer, declares "There's a palm presages chastity, if nothing else," Charmian ironically retorts "E'en as the o'erflowing Nilus presageth famine" (1.2.46–47). These women love "figs" and yearn after a promiscuous and fecund future.[69] Their curse of sexual frustration on Alexas—"O, let him marry a woman that cannot go, sweet Isis" (1.2.60–61)—playfully reverses Plutarch's punning tale of Isis's reanimating powers: "Over and besides, *Eudoxus* saith, that the Aegyptians devise of *Jupiter* this fiction, that both his legs being so growen together in one, that he could not goe at all, for very shame he kept in a desert wildernesse; but *Isis*, by cutting and dividing the same parts of his body, brought him to his sound and upright going againe" (p. 1312).

Cleopatra, identifying with Isis, is proud and unselfconscious about her sexuality, delighting in her multiple Roman conquests and indulging in erotic musings before her court. Her sexuality is sacred, expressive of the fertility of her country; the holy priests bless their riggish Queen (2.2.239–40). But her erotic energy, like the cycles of flood and harvest, has its terrifying side, as when, in a jealous rage, she wishes "infectious pestilence" on the messenger from Rome, and exclaims "Some innocents 'scape not the thunderbolt: / Melt Egypt into Nile! and kindly creatures / Turn all to serpents!" (2.5.77–79). Because fertility in Egypt is achieved through such destructive phases, not in denial of them, Cleopatra freely enacts such excesses as catharsis. She also welcomes the ambiguities of her identification with the wrinkled "serpent of old Nile" (1.5.25), those poisonous creatures spontaneously generated out of the mud. The Romans condemn her "poisonous" and "breeding" idleness, but she feeds herself "with most delicious poison" (1.5.27), delighting in her elemental power. The circularity of this image allies it with Antony's

---

[69] On *fig* as a sexual allusion, Eric Partridge, *Shakespeare's Bawdy*, s.v. "fig," cites "When Pistol lies, do this; and fig me, like the bragging Spaniard" (2H4 5.3.117–18) and explains: "A sexually allusive imprecation or adjuration—cf. *foutre*, on which it follows so closely. Cf. the It. *fico*, used expletively by several Jacobean dramatists." Charmian's phallic figs recall Plutarch's moist fig tree leaf.

tautological description of the crocodile: "It is shap'd, sir, like it-self, and it is as broad as it hath breadth: it is just so high as it is, and moves with its own organs. It lives by that which nourisheth it, and the elements once out of it, it transmigrates" (2.7.41–45). Antony's admiration of her whom "every thing becomes" and Eno-barbus's description of her Venereal "infinite variety" may be sub-sumed under Servius's oft-cited description of Isis as the "genius of Egypt" and Earth-Mother Nature, many-breasted and fructified by the warming sun.[70]

From the opening of the play Antony is obliquely associated with those elements of moisture and "vegetable" heat required to fer-tilize this "land"; Philo disapproves the Egyptian "overflow" of his glowing general. Antony, who in his Roman thoughts condemns the motion Cleopatra induces in him, at other moments vows her his "full heart" (1.3.43) and swears "By the fire / That quickens Nilus' slime, I go from hence / Thy soldier, servant, making peace or war, / As thou affects" (68–71). Cleopatra's characteristic teasing of Antony is a tactic deliberately designed to produce movement and heat, building to climax, flooding as procreative declarations of love. Antony, who knows so much of Egyptian natural science, leads the "Egyptian bacchanals" aboard Pompey's galley. The Soothsayer warns him "Hie you to Egypt again" and foresees his fate:

> Thy demon, that thy spirit which keeps thee, is
> Noble, courageous, high, unmatchable,
> Where Cæsar's is not. But near him, thy angel
> Becomes afeard; as being o'erpower'd, therefore
> Make space enough between you.
>
> (2.3.18–22)

Early in the play, Antony and Cleopatra's interaction is still largely directed at a very specific this-worldly end, the production

---

[70] 1.1.49; 2.2.235–36. Among citations of Servius, see, for example, Car-tari, *Imagini*, p. 118:

> Altri hanno detto, ch'ella è la terra, come riferisce il medesimo Seruio, e Macrobio ancora, ò veramente la Natura delle cose, che al Sole stà soggetta: e quindi viene, che faceuano il corpo di questa Dea tutto pieno, e carico di poppe, come, che l'vniuerso pigli nu-trimento dalla terra, ouero dalla virtù occulta della Natura; perche fù rappresentata etiandio la Natura con questa imagine da gli antichi.

of a dynasty, the continuation of a Hellenistic empire centered in Egypt. Cleopatra is politically astute and wins from Antony a promise to "piece / Her opulent throne with kingdoms" (1.5.45–46). This local Egyptian naturalistic interpretation culminates in their ritual coronation at Alexandria, where Cleopatra "In the habiliments of the goddess Isis" watches Antony proclaim her and their children rulers of the East (3.6.17). But this coronation of the earthly Isis and her Bacchic consort provokes full-scale Roman opposition. The Romans attempt to literalize the myth, to turn it into a merely human action that can be destroyed; their euhemerism elicits from Antony and Cleopatra a sense of the myth's daemonic, transcendent possibility. The middle scenes of the play chronicle a psychologically realistic tragic *sparagmos*, yet even in this dismemberment some Dionysiac wine "peep[s] through their scars" (3.13.191).

The couple's descent begins when Cleopatra declares they will fight by sea, and Antony, against all his countrymen's practical advice, agrees. The Romans' disapproval of her plan seems to reflect a difference in cultural assumptions: to the Romans to fight by sea is to trust "rotten planks," impressed peasants, and "chance and hazard"; but Cleopatra has confidence in the waters' fertile moisture and movement. However, the battle is fought not on the "o'erflowing Nilus," but rather on the "desiccative" salt sea, home of Typhon, and Cleopatra, literally out of her element, flees at Actium. The Roman Scarus's contemptuous description—"the breeze upon her, like a cow in June, / Hoists sails and flies" (3.10.14–15)—recalls Ovid's tale of Io, who was later equated with Isis.[71] Jupiter had disguised his beloved Io as a cow; a jealous Juno sent a gadfly (a "breese") to torment her. She fled throughout the world and found relief only at the river Nile. Lucian, in his *Dialogues of the Gods*, humorously has Zeus commission Hermes to compensate the poor persecuted girl by making her a local deity:

> ZEUS: You must fly down to Nemea—Argus is on his beat thereabouts—and kill him. Then take Io over the sea to Egypt, and make her into Isis. Hereafter let her be goddess of the folk there, raising the waters of the Nile, sending them their winds, and preserving seafarers from harm.
>
> (*Works* 7: 267–68)

---

[71] Robert G. Hunter, "Cleopatra and the 'Oestre Junonicque.' "

Lactantius uses the same story and the feast of the ship of Isis to illustrate polemically that pagan myths are a fictional embroidery of human deeds:

> In the same manner he [Jupiter] is related to have changed Io, daughter of Inachus, into a heifer. And so that she might escape the wrath of Juno, as she was then, "covered with hairs, for she was now a heifer," she is said to have swum across the sea and to have come into Egypt, and there, when her former appearance was recovered, she became the goddess who is now called Isis. By what argument, then, can it be proved that Europa did not sit on a bull and that Io was not changed into a heifer? The fact that a certain day is kept among the feasts on which the voyage of Isis is celebrated. This teaches that she did not swim across, but sailed.
>
> (*Divine Institutes* 1.11)

Thus the force of Scarus's imprecation is to reduce Cleopatra to a local totem, to confine her powers to the vicinity of Egypt. Antony, in despair at her apparent treacheries, will later recall the astronomical interpretation of a mutable Isis, "Alack, our terrene moon / Is now eclips'd, and it portends alone / The fall of Antony!" (3.13. 153–55).

Similarly the Romans seek to delimit Antony as the human descendent of Hercules. Through his illicit choice of Cleopatra he has doomed his heroic potential to a tragic end. The soldier who advises him against sea battle at Actium swears, "By Hercules, I think I am i' the right." Antony's general Canidius replies, "Soldier, thou art: but his whole action grows / Not in the power on't: so our leader's led, / And we are women's men" (3.7.67–70). The Soothsayer had claimed Antony would "play" well in Egypt, where his demon was strong; but for the Roman Canidius, Antony's emasculating attachment to Cleopatra only alienates his "action" from the true source of his power. Antony, defeated at Actium, at first espouses this tragic reading. combining bitter memories of his former martial heroism at Philippi with laments for his present unmanning: "for indeed I have lost command" (3.11.23). He then reproaches Cleopatra: "You did know / How much you were my conqueror, and that / My sword, made weak by my affection, would / Obey it on all cause" (65–68). And he dwells on the painful contrast between the victorious Caesar's untried youth and his own hoary impotence, his "siccity" recalling Plutarch's description of the drying action of Typhon on Osiris:

> They hold *Typhon* to be red of haire and of skin yellow. . . . Contrariwise they feigne *Osiris* to be of a blacke colour, because all water, causeth the earth, clothes and clowdes to appeare blacke with which it is mingled. Also the moisture that is in yong folke maketh their haire blacke; but grisled hoarinesse, which seemeth to be a pale yellow, commeth by reason of siccity unto those who be past their flower, and now in their declining age: also the Spring time is greene, fresh, pleasant, and generative: but the latter season of Autumne, for want of moisture, is an enemie to plants, and breedeth diseases in man & beast.

> (p. 1300)

The "boy" Caesar laughs at the bravado of a challenge "sword against sword / Ourselves alone" from Antony, this "old ruffian" (3.13.27–28; 4.1.4); the faithful Enobarbus despairs that "the full Cæsar will / Answer" the "emptiness" of this bombastic "sworder" (3.13.35–36, 31). As Antony readies himself to encounter Caesar's armies at Alexandria "the god Hercules whom Antony lov'd, / Now leaves him" (4.3.15–16); deprived of this deity's protection, and feeling he has been betrayed again by Cleopatra, he rages like that hero, wrapped in the poisonous cloak of the centaur Nessus. His mood as he prepares for his suicide is one of Stoic resignation, not heroic transcendence, and the Romans are careful to mourn him as a man, not celebrate him as a demigod.

However, the basic form of the myth of Isis and Osiris is tragicomic, be it local vegetation myth or neo-Platonic myth of emanation and return, its spirit not purely analytic, but dialectical. Even in the course of Antony's tragic *sparagmos*, his subliminal identification with Bacchus keeps comic possibility alive, if only as desire; as Plutarch reports, "the generative and nutritive Spirit is *Bacchus*; but that which striketh and divideth, is *Hercules*" (p. 1304). In the final scene of the play Cleopatra as Isis asserts that identification as transcendent fact, attempting to draw us, through her belief, to union with her husband, Bacchus-Osiris.

Antony's explicit identification with Hercules may contain

elements of transcendence as well as tragedy, if, as Cleopatra says, "this Herculean Roman does become / The carriage of his chafe" (1.3.84–85); "Be'st thou sad, or merry, / The violence of either thee becomes, / So does it no man else" (1.5.59–61). When the victorious Caesar orders "Observe how Antony becomes his flaw, / And what thou think'st his very action speaks / In every power that moves" (3.12.34–36), we may, ironically, be moved by his "heart" in defeat, and be reminded that Hercules' torment preceded his heroic suicide and deification. In Plutarch's "Life of Marcus Antonius" it is the god Bacchus, "whom Antonius bare singular devotion to counterfeate and resemble" who left Antony the night before his final defeat (p. 308). Shakespeare's substitution of Hercules for Bacchus, with the former's departure a superficial sign of Antony's decline, allows the possibility of a subsequent Bacchic regeneration myth.

Earlier in the play, the masterful thematic scene on Pompey's barge, like a breath of Egypt in the Roman world, has contrasted Octavius's analytic judgment with Antony's sensuous emotional engagement. Indifferent to Antony's descriptions of Egyptian wonders, Octavius resists as well the paradoxes induced by wine: "It's monstrous labour when I wash my brain / And it grows fouler" (2.7.97–98). When Antony urges "Be a child o' the time," Caesar coolly responds "Possess it, I'll make answer" (99–100). It is Caesar who calls an end to the revels, declaring "our graver business / Frowns at this levity. . . . the wild disguise hath almost / Antick'd us all" (118–19; 122–23). The Bacchic Antony, in contrast, enjoys this brief season of idleness and drink as ripening celebration. In the "Life of Marcus Antonius" Plutarch records of Antony and Cleopatra:

> In deede they did breake their first order they had set downe, which they called Amimetobion, (as much to say, no life comparable) and did set up an other which they called Synapothanumenon (signifying the order and agreement of those that will dye together) the which in exceeding sumptuousnes and cost was not inferior to the first.
>
> (p. 305)

In Shakespeare's play Antony's and Cleopatra's former scenes of revelry become rehearsals for their final attempts to create a life beyond death.

After defeat at Actium, one tear of Cleopatra's evokes Antony's forgiveness and a call for "some wine" (3.11.73). When he accuses her of treachery with Caesar's messenger, Thidias, her oath on her own and her country's fertility stirs Antony's memory of their former life together powerfully enough to satisfy him. Although Enobarbus regards it as emotional rant, Antony calls for "one other gaudy night" and declares "There's sap in't yet" (3.13.183, 192). His temporary heartening here and during his lover's night with Cleopatra leads to a brief repulse of Caesar's forces. In the erotic triumph of their reunion he discounts those dry gray hairs and wants to "drink carouses to the next day's fate" (4.8.34). Now, however, a note of fatalism haunts these celebrations: "The next time I do fight / I'll make death love me; for I will contend / Even with his pestilent scythe" (3.13.192–94); Antony bids his followers a tearful farewell, while Cleopatra has private misgivings, and Enobarbus deserts. But Enobarbus, previously skeptical of "loyalty well held to fools" (3.13.42) and of that "valour" which "preys on reason" (199), repents his betrayal; both Antony's magnanimity toward this "master-leaver" and Enobarbus's broken-hearted death offer moving examples of love beyond reason. Further, Enobarbus's tested faith prefigures Antony's changed motives for suicide. When he learns of Cleopatra's "death," the Bacchic Antony, robbed of his sword, willingly impales himself on the sword of Eros and "lightly" goes to her. He now embraces death as the means to an immortal life.

Once Cleopatra realizes that her role as earthly Isis is at an end, she devotes herself to declaring Antony's immortality and using it to evoke her own. At his death she begins to turn from "this dull world" (4.15.61), although her ambiguous self-possession, like that of the crocodile, allows her at least the appearance of earthly concern, even as she prepares for her "transmigration." With her maids she is never other than determined to die, but she plays shrewdly with the Romans while securing appropriate means. Betrayed by Proculeius, she moves Dolabella, through her transcendent description of Antony, to reveal Caesar's intentions. Her "scene" with Seleucus reads like bravura acting when we consider her contempt for the "dull Octavia" (5.2.55); rather than wanting her rival's mediation, she seems more likely to be seeking a relaxation of Caesar's guard. Knowing that Caesar means to lead her in *his* triumph, but having persuaded him that she is deceived, she exults to her maids and prepares to stage her own.

In the last scene, Cleopatra transforms "angling" for Antony (2.5.16) into elevating him, transforms sexuality into immortality, and transforms the barge at Cydnus into the celestial boat of the moon-goddess, now sailing away from the earth, which has fallen dark, to reflect her husband, the sun, directly.[72] Previously she had sought his traces on earth in the person of the heroic Antony; there, in his battle against the force that would dismember him, he had not always fulfilled his highest nature. He, looking at her, had been attracted, but had also seen in her variety a dangerous spell that threatened to wed him too strongly to transient things. But in the final scenes of the play it is as though they rise through phenomena, after a long period of human misapprehension, to see each other face to face. For Cleopatra after Antony's death, "there is nothing left remarkable / Beneath the visiting moon" (4.15.67–68); there are now no transcendent glimmers, and all is subject to Fortune and nourished on dung, "The beggar's nurse, and Cæsar's" (5.2.8). Caesar can "rule" that world. Cleopatra, fixing on death, ironically allows, " 'tis yours" (133). Preparing to suckle that serpent whose "biting is immortal" (245–46), she declares "I am fire, and air; my other elements / I give to baser life" (288–89).

Her decision to die is not a denial of her identification with Isis, but a transcendent redefinition: "My resolution's plac'd, and I have nothing / Of woman in me: now from head to foot / I am marble-constant: now the fleeting moon / No planet is of mine" (237–40). She is now that aspect of the moon that presents itself whole to the sun, rather than its "terrene" and "fleeting" side of monthly alteration. With the cry "Husband, I come" (286) she chastens the baroque suggestiveness of Enobarbus's description, turning from the many-colored robes of this world toward their single source.[73] Octavius, who will misinterpret these numinous

---

[72] Cf. Plutarch ["De Iside et Osiride"], pp. 1301, 1380ff.

[73] Cleopatra's "infinite variety" recalls Plutarch's and Apuleius's image of the many-colored robes of Isis, which represent the plenum of this sublunar world:

> Moreover the habilliments of *Isis* be of different tinctures and colours: for her whole power consisteth and is emploied in matter which receiveth all formes, and *becommeth all maner of things*,

mutations, is an "ass / Unpolicied!" (306–7), uninitiate, assuming that this story redounds to his credit, rather than to theirs.[74] But for Cleopatra, their very difficulties—Antony's divided personality, her variousness, their protracted defeat, misunderstandings, and separation, even in their death scenes—are overcome by creative love working through diversity to unity. The neo-Platonic reading of the myth of Isis and Osiris thus becomes the highest interpretation of the dramatic action they have performed.

Summary: From Verg Eoaic tnpli Shakespearean Tragicomedy

In the *Georgics* Vergil proposes, "modo vita supersit" ("if life but remain" 3.10), to write a poem placing Caesar Augustus in the midst, and himself in exultant celebration, of a triumphant theatrical scene:

in medio mihi Caesar erit templumque tenebit.
illi victor ego et Tyrio conspectus in ostro
centum quadriiugos agitabo ad flumina currus.
cuncta mihi, Alpheum linquens lucosque Molorchi,
cursibus et crudo decernet Graecia caestu.
ipse caput tonsae foliis ornatus olivae
dona feram. iam nunc sollemnis ducere pompas
ad delubra iuvat caesosque videre iuvencos,

---

to wit, light, darknesse, day, night, fire, water, life, death, beginning and end.

(Plutarch, p. 1318, emphasis mine)

In turning away from this world and its transient things, Cleopatra faces the sun-god Osiris, the masculine side of her androgynous nature; she is "marble-constant," or as Plutarch continues:

But the robes of *Osiris* have neither shade nor varietie, but are of one simple colour, even that which is lightsome and bright. For the first & primitive cause is simple; the principle or beginning, is without all mixture, as being spiritual and intelligible.

[74] A similar confusion is depicted by Geoffrey Whitney, *A Choice of Emblemes* (p. 8), when he adapts Alciati's famous emblem of the ass who carried an image of the goddess Isis and stupidly thought that the people bowed to him, not to it, a parodic inversion of Apuleius's initiation.

vel scaena ut versis discedat frontibus utque
purpurea intexti tollant aulaea Britanni.
in foribus pugnam ex auro solidoque elephanto
Gangaridum faciam victorisque arma Quirini,
atque hic undantem bello magnumque fluentem
Nilum ac navali surgentis aere columnas.

(3.16–29)[75]

(In the midst I will have Caesar, and he shall possess the
shrine. In his honour I, a victor resplendent in Tyrian purple,
will drive a hundred four-horse chariots beside the stream.
For me, all Greece, leaving Alpheus and the groves of Mol-
orchus, shall vie in races and with raw-hide gloves, and I,
with brows decked with shorn olive-leaves, will bring gifts.
Even now 'tis a joy to lead the solemn procession to the
sanctuary, and view the slaughter of the steers; or to watch
how the scene retreats with changing front, and how the in-
woven Britons raise the purple curtains. On the doors I will
fashion, in gold and solid ivory, the battle of the Ganges'
tribe, and the arms of conquering Quirinus; there, too, the
Nile, surging with war and flowing full; and columns soaring high with prows of bronze.)

Either vividly anticipating or symbolically recalling Octavius's
"triple triumph," held in 29 B.C. after the defeat of Antony and
Cleopatra, Vergil dislodges all other poetic subjects and vows Octavius possession of the shrine: "cetera quae vacuas *tenuissent*
carmine mentes, omnia iam volgata. . . . in medio mihi Caesar erit
templumque *tenebit*" ("Other themes, which else had *charmed* with
song some idle fancy, are now all trite. . . . In the midst I will have
Caesar, and he shall *possess* the shrine" 3.3–4, 16, emphasis mine).[76]
Although in a moment Vergil will descend to his agrarian theme, he
temporarily identifies his poetic vocation strongly with the conqueror; he will lead the Muses in triumph from Greece to Mantua
(11), as Octavius brings home the spoils of war. There he will embed

---

[75] All quotations and translations of the *Georgics* are from *Virgil in Two
Volumes*, trans. H. Rushton Fairclough.

[76] R. D. Williams, ed., *The Eclogues and Georgics*, p. 178, briefly reviews
whether Vergil composed these lines before or after Octavius's triple triumph
in 29 B.C. I am indebted to his textual notes throughout this discussion.

this splendor firmly in the native landscape of Italy: "templum de marmore ponam / propter aquam, tardis ingens ubi flexibus errat / Mincius et tenera praetexit harundine ripas" ("a temple in marble beside the water, where great Mincius wanders in slow windings and fringes his banks with slender reeds" 13–15).

One of the most striking features of this description of the temple and its inhabiting "god" is this rootedness and solidity, so appropriate to a poem more generally singing the Italian country-side. Octavius anchors the surrounding poetic movement, domesti-cating and sanctifying warfare as ritual game and sacrifice, and as celebratory art. In turn, the persona of the poet modulates from conqueror to charioteer, to president of the games, to priest, and to artisan as he gravitates around and inward. Even the verb tenses change as the stage setting "parts" ("scaena . . . discedat") and "turns" ("versis . . . frontibus") to reveal what lies within;[77] sud-denly we move from expectation to an intense, visionary, present: "iam nunc . . . iuvat" ("even now 'tis a joy"). The entire then-known world is organized around this center as Octavius's conquests are either anticipated (the far west of the "intexti . . . Britanni," the "in-woven Britons") or recalled (the far east of Antony's eastern troops, "pugnam Gangaridum," "the Ganges tribe").

The allusion to Octavius's victory at Actium (31 B.C.) marks this passage as one of the final additions to the Georgics (37 to 30 or 29 B.C.). By the time Vergil drafted the Aeneid, the poem these lines allegorically anticipate, the center is no longer Caesar but an ivory gate of "falsa . . . insomnia" ("false dreams" Aen. 6.896) that blurs the certainty of Anchises' prophetic vision of Roman fame. (The plains Aeneas and Anchises range are "aëris in campis latis," "broad," but also "misty" 6.887.) In the large structure of the poem, two scenes are equally balanced on either side of this skeptical center: the description of Aeneas's shield and the account of Dido's death, two scenes that are intimately related. As Vergil provided his poem with historical depth, developing it from a chronicle of recent events to a modernized Homeric epic, its domi-nant mode became tragedy rather than celebration. Octavius's tri-umph, now present only in prospect on the prophetic shield, is fur-

---

[77] Williams, Eclogues, p. 180, cites Servius for this explanation of the theatrical metaphors.

ther displaced and qualified by an ambivalent description, which stresses the pain of the defeated as much as the achievement of the victor.

In Book 8 the transition to the ekphrasis of the shield is a wonderful piece of mood music. Venus comes, bearing the Vulcan-wrought armor, to a somewhat weary and melancholy Aeneas, "natumque in valle reducta /ut procul egelido secretum flumine" ("apart in a secluded vale by the cool stream" 8.609–10). Unlike their other encounters, now she seeks her son's embrace, and he rejoices in it and in the gift; Aeneas is approaching his moment of triumph in Italy. But as is always the case in this poem, the gifts of the gods are ambiguous. The glowing armor ("arma . . . radiantia" 616) enflames the hero, until he resembles an upheaval in nature—a volcano, or a lowering thunderstorm—like that, incited by Juno, with which the poem began. He brings war to Latium, and the shield that he carries depicts war far more vividly and centrally than does the temple of *Georgics* Book 3.

Scholars have quarreled over the extent to which this shield can be accurately visualized.[78] If its major scenes are clear, their spatial relationships to one another are blurred by the shifting proportion and intensity of their treatment. The periphery is neatly diagramed: six tableaux. On the one side are Romulus and Remus, the Sabines and the Romans; on the other Mettus and Tarquin; at the top a triptych of Capitoline scenes, and balancing it below, the punishments and rewards of the underworld. However, "haec inter. . . . in medio" ("Amidst. . . . In the centre" 671,675) swells the unstable sea, and the blazing spectacle of Actium. Here the proud display of the *Georgics*—"atque hic undantem bello magnumque fluentem / Nilum ac navali surgentis aere columnas" ("there, too, the Nile, surging with war and flowing full; and columns soaring high with prows of bronze" 3.28–29)—is violently dislocated, and we are swept into the battle on lengthy, fluid description, and an insistent historical present. The scene expands beyond the ability of the *topoi* to contain it; we forget that a shield is being described, and immerse ourselves in events. The combatants are vividly characterized, and "in mediis" ("In the midst" 696) of this agitated center is Cleopatra with her "omnigenumque deum monstra" ("monstrous gods of

---

[78] R. D. Williams, "The Shield of Aeneas."

every form" 698) warring against the Olympians. At first bar-
barically proud, she is shadowed by death, and as the scene closes,
flees into the welcoming lap of the Nile. Inwardness here becomes
loss, the cost of history, as the defeated is folded away from our
sight.

Culturally, this is a far more noble and sympathetic treatment
of the defeated Antony and Cleopatra than that in the *Georgics*:
he is the victor over the exotic East; she, the representative of her
country and her religion. Their depiction is flooded by the full drama
of the first four books of the epic, which end with Dido, like Cleopatra, "pale at the coming of death" (4.644; 8.709). There Dido
suffers the tragedy of an antique, eastern, and Homeric past, while
Aeneas remembers it constructively. Having begun his poem with
the tragedy of Dido, Vergil achieves a historical depth that lends
shadowing to Octavius's triumph. On Aeneas's shield Caesar has
begun to assume his place; we shift abruptly from our last poignant
glimpse of Cleopatra to his entrance into Rome. But the narrator
dwells even there on the description of "victae longo ordine gentes, /
quam variae linguis, habitu tam vestis et armis" ("The conquered
peoples . . . in long array, as diverse in fashion of dress and arms as
in tongues" 722–23). Those diverse habits and voices are heard
again in the interpretative traditions that emanate from Vergil's
poem.

In the first chapter of this book I argued that Vergil's encounter
with radical historical change shapes his poem so as to make it fit
subject for imitations that are themselves self-conscious transvaluations of their source. The interpretative tradition of the disturbing
story of Dido forms the outstanding instance of this process. There
is a consistent direction to this literary change, despite many devi-
ations. It is simultaneously inward, toward the discovery of individual, personal life, and outward toward the confirmation of that
internal desire in an imagined otherworldly reality. The characterization of women, with their traditional ties to the irrational, becomes
a chief expressive vehicle for this change; they destabilize former
literary resolution, opening it to imaginative reformation. The process of literary transvaluation depends on an embrace of historical
change, and it can be figured forth in literature as the experience,
testing, and rectification of desire. Thus, in profound transvaluation of the *Aeneid*, Augustine moves from Carthage and Rome to

Mater Ecclesia, and Dante moves from courtly love lyric to "la vita nuova," while Spenser takes the further step of figuring the growth of imagination itself as the consciousness of a woman. Romantic epic becomes the comprehensive generic form from which tragicomedy descends, and virtually all the Renaissance dramas on the allied stories of Dido and Aeneas, and Antony and Cleopatra strain toward a new tragicomic resolution of their tragic plots.

The movement of Shakespeare's art is tragicomedic, and *Antony and Cleopatra* most clearly exemplifies its stages. The play begins with the memory of comedy, becomes a tragedy, and emerges triumphant. Philo's moralistic framing of the scene—a strumpet and her fool—only gradually restrains the initial playfulness, the role playing and sexual and cultural relativism, characteristic of romantic comedy.[79] But Philo's interpretation of the lovers' action is a noteworthy one, grounded in centuries of orthodox interpretation of the *Aeneid* and the virtues of Roman culture, in effect a literal, inanimate version of the great historical passages in the *Georgics* and the *Aeneid* discussed above. It culminates in Antony's tragic *sparagmos,* the dissolution of his character as he thinks he has discovered that Cleopatra "false-play'd my glory / Unto an enemy's triumph" (4.14.19–20).

This judgment is effectively reversed by Cleopatra's imaginative transformations as, through the divided catastrophe of the play, she turns Antony's suicide into her triumph. Anne Barton remarks of the "divided catastrophe" in general:

> A dramatist is likely to experiment with a divided catastrophe when he wants and needs, for some reason, to alter the way his audience has been responding to the experience of the play. Basically, it's a way of forcing reappraisal, a radical change of viewpoint just at that penultimate moment when our complacency is likely to be greatest: when we are tempted as an audience to feel superior or even dismissive because we think we understand everything.[80]

---

[79] Susan Snyder, *The Comic Matrix of Shakespeare's Tragedies,* is the most recent of many valuable studies of Shakespeare's flexible use of genre.

[80] " 'Nature's piece 'gainst fancy,' " p. 3. I read this essay as I was writing my conclusion; it corroborates at many points, from a slightly different structural perspective, my analysis.

Shakespeare, as late-Renaissance artist, wants to affirm, against skeptical objections, the transforming powers of poetry, and the ability of man as maker. In *Antony and Cleopatra* Cleopatra has to force reappraisal of the potent Roman historiographical tradition, the myth of the Roman mind. She does so not as transcendent *dea ex machina*, but as immanent enactor of fictions. The spiritual transformations of the last act of the play, the second half of this divided catastrophe, are latent in the play's earlier exercise of our imagination.[81] The verbal play, the play of the action, and the play of its myths—these poetic rhythms finally create assent, these generic transformations finally create ascent.

Nowhere is this clearer than in Cleopatra's remaking of Enobarbus's picture of her at Cydnus. In Enobarbus's speech Shakespeare transvalues the great shield of the *Aeneid* into an ekphrasis not of art, but of nature. Cleopatra lies in the midst of an adoring setting—not Vergil's dangerously latent, ambiguous Venus-within-a-Diana, but rather Lucretius's evocative *Venus genetrix*. But Shakespeare, whatever the predisposition of Renaissance literary theory, is not content merely to assert this marvel. He then dramatizes the potent Egyptian re-creative myth of Isis and Osiris, "collecting," in Pico's words, "all the parts like the limbs of Osiris into a unity." In the final act of this play he shows a very human, indulgent, scheming, and fearful woman gathering herself into ecstasy. We do not see Caesar's triumph, and we remember Cleopatra,

> That she did make defect perfection,
> And, breathless, power breathe forth.
>
> (2.2.231–32)

---

[81] Barton, " 'Nature's piece 'gainst fancy,' " p. 4:

> Both the *deus ex machina* and the divided catastrophe are ways in which dramatists can grapple with the immemorial problem of endings in fiction. Conclusions, as Frank Kermode has stated in his brilliant book *The Sense of an Ending*, are really satisfactory only when they "frankly transfigure the events in which they were immanent." . . . When used with skill, the divided catastrophe achieves a genuine transfiguration of the events in which it was immanent. It imposes a new angle of vision, an alteration of emphasis which, while it need not conflict with the previous development of the tragedy, will certainly modify our understanding of that development from a point beyond it in time.

Epilogue

In my analysis I have refrained from attributing ontologically privileged status to any of the interpretative levels within *Antony and Cleopatra*. Caesar's historical literalism, Antony's heroic strain, and Cleopatra's transmigrations are all perspectives developed through character, and they derive their substance from their detailed interplay. Nonetheless, the details of my analysis and its overall structure strongly imply a dramatic movement of ascent-assent, from which we may at any moment demur, that works to unify this multivalent play. That such was also the final direction of Shakespeare's art may be suggested by brief consideration of *The Tempest* and its deeply embedded, metaphorical transvaluation of the *Aeneid*.

The tempestuous opening of the play echoes the opening of the *Aeneid*, with certain important distinctions. Vergil first frames his action, his narrator's voice delineating the divine perspective and implying its historical and political consequences. Aeneas and his Trojans have set sail for Italy when, as a result of Juno's wrath, they are blown off course to Libya and Carthage. The remainder of the poem is devoted to reconciling Jove's overview with human experience. In contrast, Shakespeare plunges us into a death-dealing storm without any explanation or relation to human concepts of order: "What cares these roarers for the name of King?" (1.1.16–17). Only later do we discover that Alonso and his company are voyaging back to Italy from his daughter Claribell's wedding in Tunis, and that the storm, which shipwrecks them on a Mediterranean island, has in fact been caused by a human magician, Prospero, whose intentions are as yet unclear. The alteration of the moral geography of the *Aeneid*—Tunis, unlike Carthage, is not a deviation, but a potentially enriching alliance—parallels the alteration in the drama from what, in the epic, men may know and do. In place of the tragic confirmation of a difficult, preordained divine plan, we have the human evolution of a creative social order, which may also be a metaphor for a kinder transcendent providential order.

Prospero's island, like the bare Jacobean stage that figures it, is a blank, a theater for our imaginations. In act 2, scene 1 the main shipwrecked party exposes the opposite extremes of its interpretative possibility. To the kindly old councillor Gonzalo and his young

friend Adrian, it is "of subtle, tender and delicate temperance,"
sweet and green, the apt site for a primitive utopian commonwealth
in which harmony with nature would predispose harmony among
men. The cynical Machiavellians Sebastian and Antonio deride this
as subjective idealistic projection, "an eye of green" on a tawny
ground, and they undercut the others' vision with their snide asides
about the harsh "realities" of nature, sex, and politics. Each of
these interpretative attitudes is grounded in attitudes toward past
experience, story, and history. Gonzalo remembers the beautiful
ceremony of Claribell's marriage to the king of Tunis, and uses it
to support his vision of glorious new beginnings now; Sebastian
ironically calculates the poor "return." This memory prompts
Gonzalo to a conflation of his gracious queen of Tunis with "widow
Dido," queen of ancient Carthage; Sebastian and Antonio joke about
this facile revival and bowdlerizing of a passionate, tragic tale.
However, even in this literary quibble, both sides bear a truth: the
Elissa-Dido of earlier tradition, preserved in Trogus Pompeius's
universal history, was indeed a paradigm for chaste widowhood,
although Vergil then powerfully appropriated her dignity for his
passionate, Medea-like Queen.[82] Which of these versions of history
and experience shall we believe? Or how shall we make a concord of
this discord?

These interpretative issues all resolve in the mind and art of
Prospero. It was he who was exiled, and it is he who must decide on
the mode of his return. Two possibilities are outlined at the beginning and end of his first scene with Miranda: the benevolent "No
harm. / I have done nothing but in care of thee, / Of thee, my dear
one; thee, my daughter" and the ominous "bountiful Fortune, /
(Now my dear lady) hath mine enemies / Brought to this shore"
(1.2.15–17, 178–80). His long retrospective narrative structurally
echoes Aeneas's narration of the fall of Troy to Dido. But Aeneas's
narrative provided catharsis for its teller, enflamed Dido, and impelled his Roman epic mission at the expense of her tragedy and
the tragedy of the ancient world. In contrast, Prospero's narrative
is fraught with the ebb and flow of embittering anger and tender
and noble reconciliation; it resolves temporarily in the recollective
sleep of Miranda that prepares her for her first encounter with her
lover Ferdinand. Yet in Prospero's obsessive brooding on the past,

---

[82] D. C. Allen, "Marlowe's *Dido* and the Tradition."

his impatience with Miranda, and his occasionally disproportionate anger with Ariel, Caliban, and his potential successor-rival, Ferdinand, we are aware of a destructive power only narrowly held in check, of an impulse toward brutally authoritarian revenge tragedy. It was Prospero who began the tempest.

This impulse is held in check by the thought of his daughter. As she once prevented him from suicide, she now redirects his poisonous anger. In the *Aeneid* the tragedy of individuals caught in the flux of time is subsumed, if not justified, in the order of the lawful state and the realm of spirit. It entails severe renunciation of the world of matter, of human sexuality, of women. In *The Tempest* the noble but culpable tragedy of Prospero's life, brought on by a contemplative withdrawal from human affairs, can be contextualized by a careful alliance between his daughter and his enemy's son. The *Aeneid* can be rewritten on the pattern of Claribell's marriage to the king of Tunis: the chastity of Elissa combined productively with the sexuality of Dido to form a chaste dynastic marriage uniting former enemies. The central drama of *The Tempest* is Prospero's direction of all the elements of his "plot" toward this tragicomic-romantic resolution. This resolution, in turn, depends on the re-creative powers of his own personality.

The character of Prospero in many ways summarizes all of Shakespeare's authorial figures, from the megalomaniacal Richard III, to the shifty Duke Vincentio, to the aging Lear. Prospero is constantly tempted to slip into egocentrism or easy resolution. His first knotty exposition recaptures the temptation of the scholar: "I, thus neglecting worldly ends, all dedicated / To closeness and the bettering of my mind" (1.2.89–90). His anger sometimes seems to endanger the benevolent direction of his plot, as when he restrains Ariel's desire for freedom with heated threats. He leans toward identifying totally with his staging of an inhospitable banquet of the Harpies, so warmly does he congratulate Ariel, so completely does he relish his control:

> Bravely the figure of this Harpy hast thou
> Perform'd, my Ariel; a grace it had devouring:
> · · · · · · · · · · · · · · · · · · ·
>   My high charms work,
> And these mine enemies are all knit up
> In their distractions: they now are in my power.
>   (3.3.83–84, 88–90)

Prospero is recalled from uncritical involvement with revenge by his romantic plot, but the complementary marriage masque he then stages to temper the ardor of the young lovers only partially reassures us of the developing creative sublety of his art. The masque of the Harpies does provoke moral consciousness in Alonso, though it is insufficient to reform Antonio and Sebastian; the marriage masque impresses its ideal vision on Ferdinand and Miranda. Yet these plays are simplistic dichotomies of Prospero's own experience. Within the marriage masque it is possible to present an uncomplicated vision of chaste married love. The two great opponent goddesses of the *Aeneid* are simplified and separated: wanton Venus is dismissed while majestic Juno blesses the union. However, this idealistic projection of Prospero's "fancies," this "vanity of my art," distracts him from the unreformed appetites of "that foul conspiracy / Of the beast Caliban and his confederates / Against my life" (4.1.139–41). All of Prospero's own passion comes flooding back and breaks the masque.

From this reflux, this tempest in his mind, comes that speech which can be alternately read as a statement of most profound skepticism or implied hope:

> You do look, my son, in a mov'd sort,
> As if you were dismay'd: be cheerful, sir.
> Our revels now are ended. These our actors,
> As I foretold you, were all spirits, and
> Are melted into air, into thin air:
> And, like the baseless fabric of this vision,
> The cloud-capp'd towers, the gorgeous palaces,
> The solemn temples, the great globe itself,
> Yea, all which it inherit, shall dissolve,
> And, like this insubstantial pageant faded,
> Leave not a rack behind. We are such stuff
> As dreams are made on; and our little life
> Is rounded with a sleep.
>
> (5.1.146–58)

From the recognition of his own creative limitations, his own mortality, Prospero hypothesizes either despair—his happy vision is but a dream—or cheer—those ideal visions that are in mortal life but a dream, are "rounded" in eternal life into a reality.

He decides finally the tragicomic direction of his plot: "the rarer action is / In virtue than in vengeance" (5.1.27–28). But this decision is weighted with the full melancholy of his tragic past, and he now retains that active power to curb "this thing of darkness I/ Acknowledge mine" (275–76). Prompted by his humanity, Prospero surrenders his potentially terrifying manipulative art—"my so potent Art. . . . this rough magic" (50)—for the harmonious arts of music and society. He entrusts part of his play's resolution to the reformed Alonso and the educated lovers. Finally, he offers it all to us.

The halting rhymed tetrameter lines of the play's epilogue allow us to see through his fiction even as they entreat us to reenact it. They appeal to us, as gods of the stage, to resolve the tempest into a gentle breath that will return Prospero to Italy, into applause that will allow the actor a graceful exit from the stage. They remind us that this fiction of benevolent order is all that we assuredly have, but that to preserve our frailty it is well worth sustaining. Shakespeare makes human the skeptical quest of the *Aeneid*.

Bibliography

Sources

Appian. *An Avncient Historie and exquisite Chronicle of the Romanes warres, both Ciuile and Foren. . . .* Translated by W. B[arker?]. London: Raufe Newbery and Henrie Bynniman, 1578.

Appian. *Shakespeare's Appian: A Selection from the Tudor Translation of Appian's Civil Wars.* Edited by Ernest Schanzer. Liverpool: Liverpool University Press, 1956.

Apuleius. *The XI Bookes of the Golden Asse, Conteininge the Metamorphosie of Lucius Apuleius.* Translated by William Adlington. London: Henry Wykes, 1566.

Aristotle. *Poetics.* Translated by S. H. Butcher. New York: Hill and Wang, 1961.

Augustine. *The City of God Against the Pagans.* Translated by George E. McCracken, et al. 7 vols. London: William Heinemann; Cambridge, Mass.: Harvard University Press, 1957–1972.

Augustine. *Confessions.* Translated by William Watts. 2 vols. London: William Heinemann; Cambridge, Mass.: Harvard University Press, 1912.

Augustine. *On Christian Doctrine.* Translated by D. W. Robertson, Jr. Indianapolis: Bobbs-Merrill, 1958.

Bacon, Francis. *Works.* Edited by James Spedding, et al. 15 vols. New York: Hurd and Houghton, 1869.

Bernardus Silvestris. *The Commentary on the First Six Books of the "Aeneid" of Vergil Commonly Attributed to Bernardus Silvestris.* Edited by Julian Ward Jones and Elizabeth Frances Jones. Lincoln: University of Nebraska Press, 1977.

Boccaccio, Giovanni. *Boccaccio on Poetry, Being the Preface and Fourteenth and Fifteenth Books of Boccaccio's Genealogia Deorum Gen-*

tilium. Translated by Charles G. Osgood. Princeton: Princeton University Press, 1930.

Bruno, Giordano. *The Expulsion of the Triumphant Beast.* Translated by Arthur D. Imerti. New Brunswick, N.J.: Rutgers University Press, 1964.

Cartari, Vincenzo. *The Fovntaine of Ancient Fiction, Wherein is liuely depictured the Images and Statues of the gods of the Ancients, with their proper and perticular expositions.* Translated by Richard Linche. London: Adam Islip, 1599.

Cartari, Vincenzo. *Le imagini de i Dei de gli Antichi nelle qvali si contengono gl'Idoli, Riti, ceremonie, & altre cose appartenenti alla Religione de gli Antichi.* Venice: Francesco Ziletti, 1580.

Cartari, Vincenzo. *Imagini delli dei de gl'Antichi.* . . . [1647]. Introduction by Walter Koschatzky. Facsimile reprint. Graz, Austria: Akademische Druck, 1963.

Cesari, Cesare de'. *Cleopatra.* Venice: Giovanni Grifio, 1552.

Cesari, Cesare de'. *Romilda.* Venice: Francesco Bindoni, 1551.

Cesari, Cesare de'. *Scilla.* Venice: Giovanni Grifio, 1552.

Chaucer, Geoffrey. *The Works of Geoffrey Chaucer.* Edited by F. N. Robinson. 2d ed. Boston: Houghton Mifflin, 1957.

Conti, Natale. *Natalis Comitis Mythologiae, Sive Explicationis Fabvlarvm, Libri decem.* Frankfurt: Andrea Wechelus, 1587.

Daniel, Samuel. *The Tragedie of Cleopatra.* In *Narrative and Dramatic Sources of Shakespeare,* vol. 5, edited by Geoffrey Bullough. London: Routledge and Kegan Paul; New York: Columbia University Press, 1964.

Dante, Alighieri. *De Monarchia.* Translated by Herbert W. Schneider. Indianapolis: Bobbs-Merrill, 1957.

Dante, Alighieri. *Il Convivio.* Edited by Maria Simonelli. Bologna: Ricardo Pàtron, 1966.

Dante, Alighieri. *The Divine Comedy.* Translated by John D. Sinclair. 3 vols. New York: Oxford University Press, 1939.

Dio Cassius Coccenanius. *Dio's Roman History.* Translated by Earnest Cary. 9 vols. London: William Heinemann; New York: Macmillan, 1914–1927.

Dolce, Lodovico. *Didone.* Venice: Aldus, 1547.

Du Bellay, Joachim. *La Défense et Illustration de la Langue Française.* Paris: Librarie Garnier Frères, 1930.

Du Bellay, Joachim. *Le quatriesme livre de l'Énéide de Vergile, traduict en vers Françoys. La Complaincte de Didon à Énée, prinse d'Ovide.* . . . Paris: Vincent Certenas, 1552.

Erasmus, Desiderius. *The Praise of Folly and Letter to Martin Dorp.* Translated by Betty Radice. Harmondsworth, England: Penguin Books, 1971.

Eutropius. *A briefe Chronicle, where in are described shortlye the Originall, and the successive estate of the Romaine weale publique.* . . . Translated by Nicholas Haward. London: Thomas Marshe, 1564.

Florus, Lucius Anneaus. *The Roman Histories of Lucius Iulius Florus from the foundation of Rome, till Caesar Augustus, for aboue DCC. years, & from thence to Traian near CC. years, divided by Florus into IV ages.* Translated by E[dward] M[aria] B[olton]. London: Thomas Dewe, [1618?].

Fulgentius. *Fulgentius the Mythographer.* Translated by Leslie George Whitbread. Columbus: Ohio State University Press, 1971.

Garnier, Robert. *Marc Antoine, Hippolyte.* Edited by Raymond Lebègue. Paris: Société des Belles Lettres, 1974.

Gioannini da Capugnano, Jeronimo. *Hecatommithi, ouero Cento Novelle di M. Giovanbattista Giraldi Cinthio Nobile Ferrarese . . . Et aggivntavi la vita dell'avttore, Scritta de Ieronimo Gioannini da Capugnano Bolognese.* Venice: Dominico Imberti, 1593.

Giovius, Paulus. *Le Iscrittione Poste Sotto le vere Imagini de gli Huomini Famosi.* . . . Translated by Hippolito Orio. Florence: Lorenzo Torrentino, 1552.

Giraldi Cinthio, Giovambattista. *Discorsi . . . intorno al comporre de i Romanzi, delle Comedie, e delle Tragedie, e di altre maniere di Poesie.* Venice: Gabriel Giolito, 1554.

Giraldi Cinthio, Giovambattista. *Hecatommithi, ouero, Cento Novelle di M. Giovanbattista Giraldi Cinthio Nobile Ferrarese.* . . . Venice: Domenico Imberti, 1593.

Giraldi Cinthio, Giovambattista. *Le Tragedie di M. Gio. Battista Giraldi Cinthio.* Venice: Guilio Cagnacini, 1583.

Henslowe, Philip. *Henslowe's Diary.* Edited by R. A. Foakes and R. T. Rickert. Cambridge: Cambridge University Press, 1961.

Homer. *Homer's Odysses.* Translated by George Chapman. London: Richard Field for Nathaniell Butler, [1614?].

Horace. *The Odes and Epodes.* Translated by C. E. Bennett. London: William Heinemann; Cambridge, Mass.: Harvard University Press, 1964.

Horapollo. *The Hieroglyphics of Horapollo*. Translated by George Boas. New York: Pantheon Books. 1950.

Jodelle, Étienne. *Œuvres complètes*. Edited by Enea Balmas. 2 vols. Paris: Gallimard, 1965–1968.

Jodelle, Étienne. *Œuvres et meslanges poëtiques d' Éstienne Jodelle sieur du Lymodin*. Edited by Charles de la Mothe. Paris: Nicholas Chesneau and Mamert Patison, 1574.

Jodelle, Étienne. *Le Recueil des Inscriptions, Figures, Devises, et Masquarades*. . . . Paris: A. Wechel, 1558.

Justin. *Justin, Cornelius Nepos, and Eutropius*. Translated by John Selby Watson. London: Henry G. Bohn, 1853.

Lactantius. *The Divine Institutes Books I–VII*. Translated by Sister Mary Francis McDonald. Washington, D.C.: The Catholic University of America Press, 1964.

Livius, Titus. *The Romane Historie Written by T. Livivs of Padva*. . . . Translated by Philemon Holland, London: Adam Islip, 1600.

Lucian. *The Works*. Translated by A. M. Harmon, et al. 8 vols. London: William Heinemann; Cambridge, Mass.: Harvard University Press, 1953.

Lucretius. *De Rerum Natura*. Translated by W. H. D. Rouse, revised by Martin F. Smith. Rev. ed. Cambridge, Mass.: Harvard University Press, 1975.

Machiavelli, Niccolò. *The Prince*. Translated by Luigi Ricci. New York: New American Library, 1952.

Macrobius. *The Saturnalia*. Translated by Percival Vaughan Davies. New York: Columbia University Press, 1969.

Maier, Michael. *Michael Maier's Atalanta Fugiens: Sources of an Alchemical Book of Emblems*. Ed. H. M. E. de Jong. Leiden: E. J. Brill, 1969.

Marlowe, Christopher. *The Complete Works of Christopher Marlowe*. 2 vols. Edited by Fredson Bowers. Cambridge: Cambridge University Press, 1973.

Marlowe, Christopher. *Dido, Queene of Carthage and the Massacre at Paris*. Edited by H. J. Oliver. London: Methuen, 1968.

Montaigne, Michel de. *The Essayes or Morall, Politike, and Millitarie Discourses of Lo: Michaell de Montaigne, Knight*. Translated by John Florio. London: Val Sims, 1603.

More, Thomas. *The "Utopia" of Sir Thomas More, in Latin from the Edition of March 1518, and in English from the First Edition of*

Ralph Robynson's Translation in 1551. Edited by J. H. Lupton. Oxford: Clarendon Press, 1895.

Ovid. *Heroides and Amores.* Translated by Grant Showerman. London: William Heinemann; New York: G. P. Putnam's Sons, 1925.

Pasquier, Estienne. *Recherches de la France.* Amsterdam, 1723.

Pazzi, Alessandro de' Medici. *Le Tragedie Metriche.* Edited by Angelo Solerti. Bologna: Romagnoli dall'Acqua, 1887.

Peacham, Henry. *The Garden of Eloquence.* London: H. Jackson, 1577.

Pico, Giovanni della Mirandola. "Oration on the Dignity of Man." Translated by Elizabeth Livermore Forbes. In *The Renaissance Philosophy of Man,* edited by Ernst Cassirer, Paul Oskar Kristeller, and John Herman Randall, Jr. Chicago: University of Chicago Press, 1948.

Pistorelli, Celso. *Marc'Antonio e Cleopatra.* Verona: Sebastian dalle Donne, & Giovanni fratelli, 1576.

Plato. *The Dialogues of Plato.* Translated by Benjamin Jowett. 4th ed. 4 vols. Oxford: Clarendon Press, 1953.

Pliny. *The Historie of the World, Commonly Called the Natvrall Historie of C. Plinivs Secvndvs.* Translated by Philemon Holland. London: Adam Islip, 1601.

Plutarch. *The Lives of the Noble Grecians and Romanes, Compared.* Translated by Sir Thomas North. London: Thomas Vautroullier, 1579.

Plutarch. *The Philosophie commonlie called, The Morals written by the learned Philosopher Plutarch of Chæronea.* Translated by Philemon Holland. London: Arnold Hatfield, 1603.

Puttenham, George. *The Arte of English Poesie.* London: Richard Field, 1589.

Quintilian. *Institutio Oratoria.* Translated by H. E. Butler. 4 vols. London: William Heinemann; New York: G. P. Putnam's Sons, 1920–1922.

Rabelais, François. *The Histories of Gargantua and Pantagruel.* Translated by J. M. Cohen. Harmondsworth, England: Penguin Books, 1955.

Seneca, Lucius Annaeus. *Ad Lucilium Epistulae Morales.* Translated by Richard M. Gummere. 3 vols. London: William Heinemann; New York: G. P. Putnam's Sons, 1917–1925.

Servius. *Servii grammatici: qvi ferontvr in Vergilii carmina commentarii.* Edited by George Thilo and Hermann Hagen. 2 vols. Leipzig: Teubner, 1881–1884.

Sidney, Mary. *The Countess of Pembroke's Antonie*. Edited by Alice Luce. Weimar: Emil Felber, 1897.

Sidney, Philip. *An Apology for Poetry*. Edited by Geoffrey Shepherd. London: Thomas Nelson and Sons, 1965.

Spenser, Edmund. *Spenser: Poetical Works*. Edited by J. C. Smith and E. de Selincourt. London: Oxford University Press, 1912.

Suetonius, Caius Tranquillus. *The historie of tvvelve Caesars, emperovrs of Rome.* . . . Translated by Philemon Holland. London: M. Lownes, 1606.

Suetonius. *The Lives of Illustrious Men*. Translated by J. C. Rolfe. 2 vols. London: William Heinemann; Cambridge, Mass.: Harvard University Press, 1914.

Tasso, Torquato. *Discorsi.* . . . *Dell' Arte Poetica; Et In particolare del Poema Heroico.* . . . Venice: Giulio Vassalini, 1587.

Tasso, Torquato. *Discorsi del poema heroico.* . . . Naples: P. Venturini, 1594.

Valeriano, Piero. *Hieroglyphica*. Basel: Michael Isengrin, 1556.

Valla, Lorenzo. *"De Vero Falsoque Bono": Critical Edition*. Edited by Maristella de Panizza-Lorch. Bari: Adriatica, 1970.

Varchi, Benedetto. *Lezzioni di M. Benedetto Varchi Accademico Fiorentino, Lette da lui publicamente nell' Accademia Fiorentina, sopra diuerse Materia Poetiche, e Filosofiche*. Florence: Filippo Guinti, 1590.

Vegius, Maphaeus. *Maphaeus Vegius and His Thirteenth Book of the "Aeneid": A Chapter on Vergil in the Renaissance*. Edited and introduced by Anna Cox Brinton. Stanford: Stanford University Press, 1930.

Vida, Marco Girolamo. *The De arte poetica of Marco Girolamo Vida*. Translated by Ralph G. Williams. New York: Columbia University Press, 1976.

Virgil. *The Eclogues and Georgics*. Edited by R. D. Williams. New York: St. Martin's Press, 1979.

Virgil, Publius Maro. *Virgil in Two Volumes*. Translated by H. Rushton Fairclough. Rev. ed. London: William Heinemann; Cambridge, Mass.: Harvard University Press, 1935.

Whitney, Geoffrey. *A Choice of Emblemes*. Edited by Henry Green. New York: Benjamin Blom, 1967.

Xenophon. *Memorabilia and Oeconomicus*. Translated by E. C. Marchant. London: William Heinemann; New York: G. P. Putnam's Sons, 1923.

Studies

Adelman, Janet. *The Common Liar: An Essay on "Antony and Cleopatra."* New Haven: Yale University Press, 1973.

Allen, D. C. "Marlowe's *Dido* and the Tradition." In *Essays on Shakespeare and Elizabethan Drama in Honor of Hardin Craig,* edited by Richard Hosley. Columbia: University of Missouri Press, 1962.

Allen, D. C. "The Rehabilitation of Epicurus and His Theory of Pleasure in the Early Renaissance." *Studies in Philology* 41 (1944): 1–15.

Allen, John A. "Bottom and Titania." *Shakespeare Quarterly* 18 (1967): 107–17.

Alpers, Paul. *The Poetry of "The Faerie Queene."* Princeton: Princeton University Press, 1967.

Auerbach, Erich. *Mimesis: The Representation of Reality in Western Literature.* Translated by Willard Trask. Princeton: Princeton University Press, 1953.

Auerbach, Erich. *Scenes from the Drama of European Literature: Six Essays.* New York: Meridian Books, 1959.

Austin, R. G. *P. Vergili Maronis Aeneidos: Liber Qvartvs.* Oxford: Clarendon Press, 1955.

Bakeless, John. *The Tragicall History of Christopher Marlowe.* 2 vols. Cambridge, Mass.: Harvard University Press, 1942.

Balmas, Enea. *Un Poeta de Rinascimento Francese, Étienne Jodelle: La sua vita, il suo tempo.* Florence: Olschki, 1962.

Barber, C. L. *Shakespeare's Festive Comedy: A Study of Dramatic Form and Its Relation to Social Custom.* Princeton: Princeton University Press, 1959.

Baron, Hans. *The Crisis of the Early Italian Renaissance: Civic Humanism and Republican Liberty in an Age of Classicism and Tyranny.* Rev. ed. Princeton: Princeton University Press, 1966.

Barroll, J. Leeds. "Antony and Pleasure." *Journal of English and Germanic Philology* 57 (1958): 708–20.

Barroll, J. Leeds. "Enobarbus' Description of Cleopatra." *Texas Studies in English* 37 (1958): 61–78.

Barton, Anne. " 'Nature's piece 'gainst fancy': The Divided Catastrophe in *Antony and Cleopatra.*" Inaugural lecture at Bedford College, The University of London, May 1973.

Battenhouse, Roy. *Marlowe's "Tamburlaine": A Study in Renaissance Moral Philosophy.* Nashville: Vanderbilt University Press, 1941.

Bennett, Josephine Waters. *The Evolution of "The Faerie Queene."* Chicago: University of Chicago Press, 1942.

Berger, Harry, Jr. *The Allegorical Temper: Vision and Reality in Book II of Spenser's "Faerie Queene."* New Haven: Yale University Press, 1957.

Berthé de Besaucèle, Louis. *J.-B. Giraldi, 1504–1573: Étude sur l'évolution des théories littéraires en Italie au XVIᵉ siècle.* Paris: Auguste Picard, 1920.

Bevington, David. *From Mankind to Marlowe: Growth of Structure in the Popular Drama of Tudor England.* Cambridge, Mass.: Harvard University Press, 1962.

Bloch, Herbert. "The Pagan Revival in the West at the End of the Fourth Century." In *The Conflict Between Paganism and Christianity in the Fourth Century,* edited by Arnaldo Momigliano. Oxford: Clarendon Press, 1963.

Bloom, Harold. *The Anxiety of Influence: A Theory of Poetry.* New York: Oxford University Press, 1973.

Bouwsma, William J. "The Two Faces of Humanism: Stoicism and Augustinianism in Renaissance Thought." In *Itinerarium Italicum: The Profile of the Italian Renaissance in the Mirror of its European Transformations,* edited by Heiko A. Oberman. Leiden: E. J. Brill, 1975.

Bowra, C. M. *From Virgil to Milton.* London: Macmillan, 1948.

Broch, Hermann. *The Death of Virgil.* Translated by Jean Starr Untermeyer. New York: Grosset & Dunlap, 1965.

Brodwin, Leonora Leet. *Elizabethan Love Tragedy, 1587–1625.* New York: New York University Press; The University of London Press, 1971.

Brooks, Robert A. "Discolor Aura: Reflections on the Golden Bough." *American Journal of Philology* 74 (1953): 260–80.

Brower, Reuben. *Hero and Saint: Shakespeare and the Graeco-Roman Heroic Tradition.* New York: Oxford University Press, 1971.

Brown, Horatio. *The Venetian Printing Press: An Historical Study.* London: J. C. Nimmo, 1891.

Brown, Peter. *Augustine of Hippo: A Biography.* Berkeley and Los Angeles: University of California Press, 1967.

Brown, Peter. *The Making of Late Antiquity.* Cambridge, Mass., and London: Harvard University Press, 1978.

Bullough, Geoffrey. *Narrative and Dramatic Sources of Shakespeare.* Vol. 5, *The Roman Plays: Julius Caesar, Antony and Cleopatra, Coriolanus.* London: Routledge and Kegan Paul; New York: Columbia University Press, 1964.

Cain, Thomas H. *Praise in "The Faerie Queene."* Lincoln: University of Nebraska Press, 1978.

Calderwood, James. *Metadrama in Shakespeare's Henriad: Richard II to Henry V.* Berkeley and Los Angeles: University of California Press, 1979.

Calderwood, James. *Shakespearean Metadrama.* Minneapolis: University of Minnesota Press, 1971.

The Cambridge Ancient History. Vol. 10, *The Augustan Empire, 44 B.C.–A.D. 70.* Edited by S. A. Cook, et al. Cambridge: Cambridge University Press, 1934.

Camps, W. A. *An Introduction to Virgil's "Aeneid."* London: Oxford University Press, 1969.

Chambers, E. K. *The Elizabethan Stage.* 4 vols. Oxford: Clarendon Press, 1923.

Chenu, Marie-Dominique. *Nature, Man, and Society in the Twelfth Century: Essays on New Theological Perspectives in the Latin West.* Translated by Jerome Taylor and Lester K. Little. Chicago: University of Chicago Press, 1968.

Cicogna, Emmanuele Antonio. "Memoria intorno la vita e gli scritti di Messer Lodovico Dolce, Letterato Veneziano del Secolo XVI." In *Memorie dell' I.R. Instituto Veneto di Scienze, Lettere ed Arti,* vol. 2. Venice: Palazzo Ducale, 1862.

Coffin, H. C. "Allegorical Interpretation of Vergil with Special Reference to Fulgentius." *Classical Weekly* 15 (1921): 33–35.

Cole, Douglas. *Suffering and Evil in the Plays of Christopher Marlowe.* Princeton: Princeton University Press, 1962.

Colie, Rosalie. *Shakespeare's Living Art.* Princeton: Princeton University Press, 1974.

Commager, Steele. *The Odes of Horace: A Critical Study.* New Haven: Yale University Press, 1962.

Comparetti, Domenico. *Vergil in the Middle Ages.* Translated by E. F. M. Benecke. London: Swan Sonnenschein; New York: Macmillan, 1895.

Cope, Jackson. "Marlowe's *Dido* and the Titillating Children." *English Literary Renaissance* 4 (1974): 315–25.

Cormier, Raymond J. *One Heart, One Mind: The Rebirth of Virgil's*

Hero in Medieval French Romance. University, Miss.: Romance Monographs, 1973.

Courcelle, Pierre. "Interprétations neo-platonisantes du livre VI de l'Énéide." In *Fondation Hardt pour l'étude de l'antiquité classique.* Vol. 3, *Recherches sur la tradition platoncienne.* Verona: Stamperia Valdonega, 1957.

Cutts, John. "Dido, Queen of Carthage." *Notes and Queries* 203 (1958): 371–74.

Cutts, John. *The Left Hand of God: A Critical Interpretation of the Plays of Christopher Marlowe.* Haddonfield, N.J.: Haddonfield House, 1973.

Dannenfeldt, Karl H. "Egypt and Egyptian Antiquities in the Renaissance." *Studies in the Renaissance* 6 (1959): 7–27.

Dent, R. W. "Imagination in *A Midsummer Night's Dream*." *Shakespeare Quarterly* 15 (1964), 115–29.

Dessen, Alan C. "The Intemperate Knight and the Politic Prince: Late Morality Structure in *1 Henry IV*." *Shakespeare Studies* 7 (1974): 147–71.

Di Cesare, Mario A. *The Altar and the City: A Reading of Vergil's "Aeneid."* New York: Columbia University Press, 1974.

Di Cesare, Mario A. *Vida's Christiad and Vergilian Epic.* New York: Columbia University Press, 1964.

Dickey, F. M. *Not Wisely but Too Well: Shakespeare's Love Tragedies.* San Marino: The Huntington Library, 1957.

Dictionary of Greek and Roman Biography and Mythology. Edited by William Smith. 3 vols. Boston: Charles C. Little and James Brown, 1849.

Dronke, Peter. *The Medieval Lyric.* London: Hutchinson, 1968.

Else, Gerald F. *Aristotle's Poetics: The Argument.* Cambridge, Mass.: Harvard University Press, 1957.

Elton, William R. *King Lear and the Gods.* San Marino: The Huntington Library, 1966.

Febvre, Lucien, and Henri-Jean Martin. *L'apparition du livre.* 2d ed. rev. Paris: A. Michel, 1971.

Febvre, Lucien. *Le Problème de l'incroyance au seizième siècle: La Religion de Rabelais.* Paris: A. Michel, 1947.

Festugière, A. J. *Epicurus and His Gods.* Translated by C. W. Chilton. Oxford: Basil Blackwell, 1955.

Fichter, Andrew. "*Antony and Cleopatra*: 'The Time of Universal Peace.'" *Shakespeare Survey* 33 (1980): 99–111.

Fisch, Harold. "*Antony and Cleopatra*: The Limits of Mythology." *Shakespeare Survey* 23 (1970): 59–67.

Fitch, Robert E. "'No Greater Crack?'" *Shakespeare Quarterly* 19 (1968): 3–17.

Fraisse, Simone. *L'Influence de Lucrèce en France au seizième siècle: Une Conquête du rationalisme*. Paris: A. G. Nizet, 1962.

Frame, Donald. *Montaigne's Discovery of Man: The Humanization of a Humanist*. New York: Columbia University Press, 1955.

Frank, Robert Worth, Jr. *Chaucer and "The Legend of Good Women."* Cambridge, Mass.: Harvard University Press, 1972.

Fraser, Russell. "On Christopher Marlowe." *Michigan Quarterly Review* 12 (1973): 136–59.

Fyler, John M. *Chaucer and Ovid*. New Haven: Yale University Press, 1979.

Giamatti, A. Bartlett. *The Earthly Paradise and the Renaissance Epic*. Princeton: Princeton University Press, 1966.

Gibbons, Brian. "Unstable Proteus: Marlowe's *The Tragedy of Dido, Queen of Carthage*." In *Christopher Marlowe*, edited by Brian Morris. New York: Hill and Wang, 1968.

Girard, René. *"To double business bound": Essays on Literature, Mimesis, and Anthropology*. Baltimore: Johns Hopkins Press, 1978.

Godenne, René. "Étienne Jodelle, traducteur de Virgile." *Bibliothèque d'Humanisme et Renaissance* 31 (1969): 195–204.

Gohlke, Madelon. "'I wooed thee with my sword': Shakespeare's Tragic Paradigms." In *The Woman's Part*, edited by Carolyn Ruth Swift Lenz, Gayle Greene, and Carol Thomas Neely. Urbana: University of Illinois Press, 1980.

Goldin, Frederick. *The Mirror of Narcissus in the Courtly Love Lyric*. Ithaca: Cornell University Press, 1967.

Gombrich, E. H. "*Icones Symbolicae*: The Visual Image in Neo-Platonic Thought." *Journal of the Warburg and Courtauld Institutes* 11 (1948): 163–92.

Graves, T. S. "A Tragedy of Dido and Aeneas Acted in 1607." *Modern Language Review* 9 (1914): 525–26.

Gray, H. D. "Did Shakespeare Write a Tragedy of Dido?" *Modern Language Review* 15 (1920): 217–22.

Greene, Gayle. " 'Excellent Dumb Discourse': Silence and Grace in Shakespeare's *Tempest.*" *Studia Neophilologica* 50 (1978): 193–205.

Greene, Thomas M. *The Descent from Heaven: A Study in Epic Continuity.* New Haven: Yale University Press, 1963.

Greene, Thomas M. "Petrarch and the Humanist Hermeneutic." In *Italian Literature, Roots and Branches: Essays in Honor of Thomas Goddard Bergin,* edited by Giose Rimanelli and Kenneth John Atchity. New Haven: Yale University Press, 1976.

Greene, Thomas M. *The Light in Troy: Imitation and Discovery in Renaissance Poetry.* New Haven: Yale University Press, 1982.

Greenlaw, Edwin. "Spenser and Lucretius." *Studies in Philology* 17 (1920): 439–64.

Grendler, Paul F. *The Roman Inquisition and the Venetian Press, 1540–1605.* Princeton: Princeton University Press, 1977.

Hadzsits, George Depue. *Lucretius and His Influence.* New York: Cooper Square Publishers, 1963.

Harbage, Alfred. *Shakespeare and the Rival Traditions.* New York: Macmillan, 1952.

Hardison, O. B., Jr. *The Enduring Monument: A Study of the Idea of Praise in Renaissance Literary Theory and Practice.* Chapel Hill: University of North Carolina Press, 1962.

Harper's Dictionary of Classical Literature and Antiquities. Edited by Harry Thurston Peck. 2nd ed. 1897. Reprint. New York: Cooper Square Publishers, 1965.

Harrison, Thomas P. "Shakespeare and Marlowe's *Dido, Queen of Carthage.*" *University of Texas Studies in English* 35 (1956): 57–63.

Hathaway, Baxter. *The Age of Criticism: The Late Renaissance in Italy.* Ithaca: Cornell University Press, 1962.

Hathaway, Baxter. *Marvels and Commonplaces: Renaissance Literary Criticism.* New York: Random House, 1968.

Herrick, Marvin. "The Fusion of Horatian and Aristotelian Literary Criticism, 1531–1555." *Illinois Studies in Language and Literature* 32 (1946): 1–117.

Herrick, Marvin. *Italian Tragedy in the Renaissance.* Urbana: University of Illinois Press, 1965.

Horne, P. R. "Reformation and Counter-Reformation at Ferrara: Antonio Musa Brasavola and Giambattista Cinthio Giraldi." *Italian Studies* 13 (1958): 62–82.

Horne, P. R. *The Tragedies of Giambattista Cinthio Giraldi*. London: Oxford University Press, 1962.

Hughes, Merritt Y. "Virgil and Spenser." *University of California Publications in English* 2 (1929): 263–418.

Hulubei, Alice. "Virgile en France au XVIe siècle: Éditions, traductions, imitations." *Revue du XVIe Siècle* 18 (1931): 1–77.

Hunter, Robert G. "Cleopatra and the 'Oestre Junonicque.'" *Shakespeare Studies* 5 (1969): 236–39.

Ide, Richard. *Possessed with Greatness: The Heroic Tragedies of Chapman and Shakespeare*. Chapel Hill: University of North Carolina Press, 1980.

Iversen, Eric. *The Myth of Egypt and Its Hieroglyphs in European Tradition*. Copenhagen: Gad, 1961.

Jacobson, Howard. *Ovid's "Heroides."* Princeton: Princeton University Press, 1974.

Johnson, W. R. *Darkness Visible: A Study of Vergil's "Aeneid."* Berkeley and Los Angeles: University of California Press, 1976.

Jondorf, Gillian. *Robert Garnier and the Themes of Political Tragedy in the Sixteenth Century*. London: Cambridge University Press, 1969.

Jones, J. W., Jr. "Allegorical Interpretation in Servius." *Classical Journal* 56 (1961): 217–26.

Jones, J. W. "Vergil as Magister in Fulgentius." In *Classical Medieval and Renaissance Studies in Honor of Berthold Louis Ullmann*, vol. 1, edited by Charles Henderson, Jr. Rome: Edizioni di Storia e Letteratura Azienda Beneventana Tipografica Editoriale, 1964.

Kaiser, Walter. *Praisers of Folly: Erasmus, Rabelais, Shakespeare*. Cambridge, Mass.: Harvard University Press, 1963.

Kermode, Frank. "The Mature Comedies." *Early Shakespeare*. Stratford-Upon-Avon Studies, no. 3 (1961): 211–27.

Knight, J. Wilson. *The Crown of Life: Essays in Interpretation of Shakespeare's Final Plays*. London: Oxford University Press, 1947.

Knowles, Richard. "Unquiet and the Double Plot of 2 Henry IV." *Shakespeare Studies* 2 (1966): 133–40.

Knox, Bernard. "The Serpent and the Flame: The Imagery of the Second Book of the *Aeneid*." *American Journal of Philology* 71 (1950): 379–400.

Krier, Theresa. "The Lineaments of Desire: Love and Art in *The Shepheardes Calender*." Unpublished paper.

Kuhl, E. P. "Contemporary Politics in Elizabethan Drama: Fulke Gre-
ville." *Philological Quarterly* 7 (1928): 299–302.

Leavenworth, Russell E. *Daniel's Cleopatra: A Critical Study.* Salzburg:
Institut für Englische Sprache und Literatur, 1974.

Leech, Clifford. "Marlowe's Humor." In *Essays on Shakespeare and the
Elizabethan Drama in Honor of Hardin Craig,* edited by Richard
Hosley. Columbia: University of Missouri Press, 1962.

Lees, F. N. "*Dido, Queen of Carthage* and *The Tempest.*" *Notes and
Queries* 209 (1964): 147–49.

Leube, Eberhard. *Fortuna in Karthago: die Aeneas-Dido–Mythe Ver-
gils in den romanischen Literaturen vom 14. bis zum 16. Jahr-
hundert.* Heidelberg: Carl Winter, 1969.

Levin, Harry. *The Overreacher: A Study of Christopher Marlowe.*
Cambridge, Mass.: Harvard University Press, 1952.

Lewis, C. S. *The Allegory of Love: A Study in Medieval Tradition.*
London: Oxford University Press, 1936.

Lloyd, Michael. "Cleopatra as Isis." *Shakespeare Survey* 12 (1959):
88–94.

Logan, Oliver. *Culture and Society in Venice, 1470–1790: The Renaissance and Its Heritage.* London: B. T. Batsford, 1972.

MacCaffrey, Isabel. *Spenser's Allegory: The Anatomy of Imagination.*
Princeton: Princeton University Press, 1976.

Mack, Maynard. *King Lear in Our Time.* Berkeley and Los Angeles:
University of California Press, 1965.

McLane, Paul E. *Spenser's "Shepheardes Calender": A Study in Elizabethan Allegory.* Notre Dame: University of Notre Dame Press,
1961.

Major, John M. "Desdemona and Dido." *Shakespeare Quarterly* 10
(1959): 123–25.

Mayo, Thomas Franklin. *Epicurus in England: 1650–1725.* N.p.: South-
west Press, 1934.

Michel, Laurence, and Cecil Seronsy. "Shakespeare's History Plays and
Daniel: An Assessment." *Studies in Philology* 52 (1955): 549–77.

Mouflard, Marie-Madeleine. *Robert Garnier, 1545–1590: La Vie,
l'oeuvre, les sources.* 3 vols. La Roche-sur-Yon: Imprimerie Cen-
trale de L'Ouest, 1961–1964.

Murrin, Michael. *The Allegorical Epic: Essays in Its Rise and Decline.*
Chicago: University of Chicago Press, 1980.

Murrin, Michael. *The Veil of Allegory: Some Notes Toward a Theory* of *Allegorical Rhetoric in the English Renaissance.* Chicago: University of Chicago Press, 1969.

Neri, Ferdinando. "La prima tragedia di Étienne Jodelle." *Giornale Storico della Letteratura Italiana* 74 (1919): 50–63.

Neri, Ferdinando. *La Tragedia Italiana del Cinquecento.* Florence: Galletti e Cocci, 1904.

de Nolhac, Pierre. "Virgile chez Pétrarque." In *Vergilio nel medio evo,* edited by Vincenzo Ussani. *Studi Medievali* n.s. 5 (1932): 217–25.

Norman, A. M. Z. "Daniel's *The Tragedie of Cleopatra* and *Antony and Cleopatra.*" *Shakespeare Quarterly* 9 (1958): 11–18.

Norman, A. M. Z. "*The Tragedie of Cleopatra* and the Date of *Antony and Cleopatra.*" *Modern Language Review* 54 (1959): 1–9.

O'Donnell, J. R. "The Sources and Meaning of Bernard Silvester's Commentary on the *Aeneid.*" *Mediaeval Studies* 24 (1962): 233–49.

Ornstein, Robert. *A Kingdom for a Stage: The Achievement of Shakespeare's History Plays.* Cambridge, Mass.: Harvard University Press, 1972.

Otis, Brooks. "The Originality of the *Aeneid.*" In *Virgil,* edited by D[onald] R. Dudley. London: Routledge & Kegan Paul, 1969.

Otis, Brooks. *Ovid As an Epic Poet.* 2nd ed. Cambridge: Cambridge University Press, 1970.

Otis, Brooks. *Virgil: A Study in Civilized Poetry.* Oxford: Clarendon Press, 1963.

Panizza Lorch, Maristella de. " '*Voluptas, molle quoddam et non invidiosum nomen*': Lorenzo Valla's Defense of *voluptas* in the Preface to His *De voluptate.*" In *Philosophy and Humanism: Renaissance Essays in Honor of Paul Oskar Kristeller,* edited by Edward P. Mahoney. New York: Columbia University Press, 1976.

Panofsky, Erwin. *Hercules am Scheidewege.* Leipzig: B. G. Teubner, 1930.

Panofsky, Erwin. *Meaning in the Visual Arts.* Garden City, N.Y.: Doubleday, 1955.

Panofsky, Erwin. *Studies in Iconology: Humanistic Themes in the Art of the Renaissance.* Oxford: Oxford University Press, 1939. Reprint. New York: Harper & Row, 1962.

Parry, Adam. "The Two Voices of Virgil's *Aeneid.*" *Arion* 2 (1963): 66–80.

Partridge, Eric. *Shakespeare's Bawdy: A Literary and Psychological Essay and a Comprehensive Glossary.* New York: E. P. Dutton, 1969.

Pearce, T. M. "Evidence for Dating Marlowe's *Tragedy of Dido*." In *Studies in the English Renaissance Drama: In Memory of Karl Julius Holzknecht*, edited by Josephine Waters Bennett, et al. New York: New York University Press, 1959.

Pigman, G. W. "Versions of Imitation in the Renaissance." *Renaissance Quarterly* 33 (1980): 1–32.

Poggioli, Renato. "Tragedy or Romance? A Reading of the Paolo and Francesca Episode in Dante's *Inferno*." *PMLA* 72 (1957): 313–58.

Popkin, Richard. *The History of Scepticism from Erasmus to Descartes*. Rev. ed. New York: Harper & Row, 1968.

Porter, Joseph A. *The Drama of Speech Acts: Shakespeare's Lancastrian Tetralogy*. Berkeley and Los Angeles: University of California Press, 1979.

Pöschl, Victor. *The Art of Vergil: Image and Symbol in the "Aeneid."* Translated by Gerda Seligson. Ann Arbor: University of Michigan Press, 1962.

Prior, Moody. *The Drama of Power: Studies in Shakespeare's History Plays*. Evanston, Ill.: Northwestern University Press, 1973.

Rand, E. K. "Is Donatus' Commentary on Vergil Lost?" *Classical Quarterly* 10 (1916): 158–64.

Read, John. *Through Alchemy to Chemistry: A Procession of Ideas and Personalities*. London: Bell, 1957.

Rees, Joan. "An Elizabethan Eyewitness of *Antony and Cleopatra*?" *Shakespeare Survey* 6 (1953): 91–93.

Rees, Joan. "Shakespeare's Use of Daniel." *Modern Language Review* 55 (1960): 79–82.

Roche, Thomas. *The Kindly Flame: A Study of the Third and Fourth Books of Spenser's "Faerie Queene."* Princeton: Princeton University Press, 1964.

Rose, Mark. *Heroic Love: Studies in Sidney and Spenser*. Cambridge, Mass.: Harvard University Press, 1968.

Roskill, Mark. *Dolce's "Aretino" and Venetian Art Theory of the Cinquecento*. New York: New York University Press, 1968.

Saccio, Peter. *The Court Comedies of John Lyly: A Study in Allegorical Dramaturgy*. Princeton: Princeton University Press, 1969.

Schanzer, Ernest. "Daniel's Revision of His *Cleopatra*." *Review of English Studies* n.s. 8 (1957): 375–81.

Schanzer, Ernest. *The Problem Plays of Shakespeare: A Study of Julius*

Caesar, Measure for Measure, Antony and Cleopatra. London: Routledge & Kegan Paul, 1963.

Seaton, Ethel. *"Antony and Cleopatra and the Book of Revelation." Review of English Studies* 22 (1946): 219–24.

Seronsy, Cecil. "The Doctrine of Cyclical Recurrence and Some Related Ideas in the Works of Samuel Daniel." *Studies in Philology* 54 (1957): 387–407.

Seronsy, Cecil. *Samuel Daniel*. New York: Twayne Publishers, 1967.

Simmons, Joseph. *Shakespeare's Pagan World: The Roman Tragedies*. Charlottesville: University Press of Virginia, 1973.

Solerti, Angelo, and Domenico Lanza. "Il teatro ferrarese nella seconda metà del secolo XVI." *Giornale storico della letteratura italiana* 18 (1891): 148–85.

Snyder, Susan. *The Comic Matrix of Shakespeare's Tragedies: Romeo and Juliet, Hamlet, Othello, and King Lear*. Princeton: Princeton University Press, 1979.

Spencer, T. J. B. "Shakespeare and the Elizabethan Romans." *Shakespeare Survey* 10 (1957): 27–38.

Spillebout, G. "Jodelle l'hétérodoxe." In *Aspects du libertinisme au XVIe siècle. Acts du Colloque International de Sommières, De Pétrarque à Descartes*, no. 30. Paris: J. Vrin, 1974.

Steadman, John. *Epic and Tragic Structure in "Paradise Lost."* Chicago: University of Chicago Press, 1976.

Steane, J. B. *Marlowe: A Critical Study*. Cambridge: Cambridge University Press, 1954.

Surtz, Edward. *The Praise of Pleasure: Philosophy, Education, and Communism in More's Utopia*. Cambridge, Mass.: Harvard University Press, 1947.

Tarn, W. W. "The Battle of Actium." *The Journal of Roman Studies* 21 (1931): 173–99.

Taylor, Beverly. "The Medieval Cleopatra: The Classical and Medieval Tradition of Chaucer's *Legend of Cleopatra*." *The Journal of Medieval and Renaissance Studies* 7 (1977): 249–69.

Travis, Albert H. "Donatus and the Scholia Danielis: A Stylistic Comparison." *Harvard Studies in Classical Philology* 53 (1942): 157–69.

Tillyard, E. M. W. *Shakespeare's History Plays*. New York: Macmillan, 1946.

Turner, Robert. *Didon dans la tragédie de la renaissance italienne et française*. Paris: Fouillot, 1926.

Tuve, Rosemund. *Allegorical Imagery: Some Mediaeval Books and Their Posterity*. Princeton: Princeton University Press, 1966.

Waddington, Raymond. *"Antony and Cleopatra:* 'What Venus did with Mars.'" *Shakespeare Studies* 2 (1966): 210–27.

Waddington, Raymond. "The Iconography of Silence and Chapman's Hercules." *Journal of the Warburg and Courtauld Institutes* 33 (1970): 248–63.

Waith, Eugene. *The Herculean Hero in Marlowe, Chapman, Shakespeare, and Dryden*. New York: Columbia University Press; London: Chatto & Windus, 1962.

Walker, Daniel Pickering. *The Ancient Theology: Studies in Christian Platonism from the Fifteenth to the Eighteenth Century*. Ithaca: Cornell University Press, 1972.

Wardman, Alan. *Plutarch's Lives*. London: Paul Elek, 1974.

Weinberg, Bernard. *A History of Literary Criticism in the Italian Renaissance*. 2 vols. Chicago: University of Chicago Press, 1961.

Whitfield, J. H. *Dante and Virgil*. Oxford: Basil Blackwood, 1949.

Williams, R. D. "The Shield of Aeneas." *Vergilius* 27 (1981): 8–11.

Wind, Edgar. *Pagan Mysteries in the Renaissance*. Rev. and enl. ed. New York: W. W. Norton, 1968.

Witherspoon, A. M. *The Influence of Robert Garnier on Elizabethan Drama*. New Haven: Yale University Press, 1924.

Yates, Frances. *Astraea: The Imperial Theme in the Sixteenth Century*. London: Routledge & Kegan Paul, 1975.

Yates, Frances. *The French Academies of the Sixteenth Century*. London: Warburg Institute, University of London, 1947.

Yates, Frances. *Giordano Bruno and the Hermetic Tradition*. Chicago: University of Chicago Press, 1964.

Young, David P. *Something of Great Constancy: The Art of "A Midsummer Night's Dream."* New Haven: Yale University Press, 1966.

Index

Achates: in Giraldi's *Didone*, 93–
96; in Jodelle's *Didon*, 108–9,
111, 112, 115; in Vergil's *Aeneid*,
13
Actium, battle of, 38, 83; in
Shakespeare's *Antony and Cleopatra*, 207; in Vergil's *Aeneid*,
216–17; in Vergil's *Georgics 3*,
214–15
Adelman, Janet, 150n.13
Aeneas: in Dolce's *Didone*, 89;
in Giraldi's *Didone*, 92–97;
in Jodelle's *Didon*, 107–16; in
Marlowe's *Dido*, 129–37; in
Ovid's *Heroides*, Letter 7, 42;
in Pazzi's *Dido*, 88; in Shakespeare's *Antony and Cleopatra*,
5, 187; in Spenser's *Faerie
Queene*, 78; in Vergil's *Aeneid*,
2, 7, 10–39, 59, 71, 76–77, 220,
221, 216–17
Aeneas and Dido, story of: relationship to history of Antony
and Cleopatra, in Renaissance
vernacular drama, 82, 83, 87,
88, 90, 103, 218; relationship
to history of Antony and Cleopatra in Vergil's *Aeneid*, 3,
83, 85–87
Agrippa: in Garnier's *Marc Antoine*, 118; in Giraldi's *Cleopatra*, 99–100; in Jodelle's
Cléopatre, 104, 105, 107; in

Shakespeare's *Antony and
Cleopatra*, 161, 169–70, 173
Ajax: in Homer's *Odyssey*, com-
pared with Vergil's Dido, 26n
Alain de Lille, *De planctu natura*,
114n, 173. *See also* Natural-
ism; *Venus genetrix*
Alexas: in Shakespeare's *Antony
and Cleopatra*, 205
Allen, D. C.: "Marlowe's *Dido*,"
67n, 128–29n.41, 134n.46,
221n; "Rehabilitation of Epi-
curus," 174n.37
Allen, John A., 199n
Alonso: in Shakespeare's *Tem-
pest*, 220, 223, 224
Alpers, Paul, 64n.31
Amoret: in Spenser's *Faerie
Queene*, 74–75, 78, 79, 177,
179, 182
Anchises: in Vergil's *Aeneid*, 10,
18, 18n, 31–32, 33, 39, 65n,
215
Anna: in Giraldi's *Didone*, 93–
94; in Vergil's *Aeneid*, 21, 76
Antillo: in Pistorelli's *Marc'An-
tonio*, 90n
Antonio: in Shakespeare's
Tempest, 221, 223
Antony: in Daniel's *Cleopatra*,
122–23, 125; in Garnier's *Marc
Antoine*, 4, 116–21; in Giraldi's
Cleopatra, 97–102; in Jodelle's

Cléopatre, 104, 106; in Pistorelli's *Marc'Antonio*, 90n; in Plutarch's *Life*, 152–53, 155–59; in Plutarch's *Life*, as Bacchus, 158, 159, 172, 209–11; in Plutarch's *Life*, as Herculean hero, 155–57; in Plutarch's *Life*, as Stoic, 159; in Shakespeare's *Antony and Cleopatra*, 5, 150, 167–73, 183–90, 200, 205–13, 218, 220; in Shakespeare's *Antony and Cleopatra*, as Bacchus, 158, 159, 172, 207, 209–11; in Shakespeare's *Antony and Cleopatra*, as Herculean hero, 159–67, 209–11; in Shakespeare's *Antony and and Cleopatra*, as Stoic, 160, 165, 165n.29, 186, 209; in Shakespeare's *Julius Caesar*, 145

Antony and Cleopatra, history of: relationship to story of Aeneas and Dido, in Renaissance vernacular drama, 82, 83, 87, 88, 90, 103, 218; relationship to story of Aeneas and Dido, in Vergil's *Aeneid*, 3, 83, 85–87

Apelles, painting of *Aphrodite Anadyomene*, 180–81. *See also* Venus

Apollo: in Vergil's *Aeneid*, Aeneas compared to, 27–28

Apollonius Rhodius, *Argonautica*: influence on Pazzi's *Dido*, 88; influence on Vergil's *Aeneid*, 2, 26n, 67, 88. *See also* Medea

Apuleius, *The Golden Asse*, 191, 198, 212n.73; influence on Shakespeare's *Antony and Cleopatra*, 114, 198; influence on Shakespeare's *Midsummer Night's Dream*, 198, 198–99n. 67. *See also* Isis

Ariel: in Shakespeare's *Tempest*, 222

Aristotle: *Poetics*, and Giraldi's

Discorsi, 91; *Poetics*, on relationship of epic to tragedy, 83–84, 84n; *Poetics*, translated by Pazzi, 88, 88n.9; *Politics*, 39n

Arius: in Daniel's *Cleopatra*, 123

Arthegall: in Spenser's *Faerie Queene*, 75–79, 81

Artist, Renaissance ideal of, 3, 5, 81, 140–51; in Pico's "Oration," 140–41, 150–51; in Shakespeare, 4–5, 140–51, 219; in Sidney's "Apology," 140–41, 150

Ascanius (Iülus): in Jodelle's *Didon*, 109; in Marlowe's *Dido*, 129, 131; in Vergil's *Aeneid*, 18, 28n.18, 29, 31–32, 33

Asiatic oratory: in Plutarch's Antony, 156; in Shakespeare's Antony, 163

Asiatic style, in Vergil's *Aeneid*, 28, 86

Auerbach, Erich: *Mimesis*, 8n, 10, 40, 51, 51n.16; *Scenes*, 51, 51n.16

Augustine, 45–50

—*On Christian Doctrine*, 80, 80n

—*City of God, The*, 46–48, 193–94, 195; genre of, 46–48, 46–47n.13; influenced by Vergil's *Aeneid*, 2, 45–48, 79–80, 81. *See also* Egypt, wisdom of; Hermes Trismegistus; *Mater Ecclesia*

—*Confessions*, 45–50; genre of, 50; imagery in, 46; influence on Dante's *Divine Comedy*, 2, 50, 50n; influenced by Vergil's *Aeneid*, 2, 45–50, 79–80, 81, 217–18. PASSAGES CITED: 1.13, 45–46, 46n.10, 47; 1.17, 45–46, 46n.10; 3.1, 46n.12, 49n; 5.8, 46n.12; 7.20–21, 48–49, 60; 8.12, 49; 9.10, 50. *See also* Bible; Dido; Heroism, Monica; Neo-Platonism; Rome; *Sortes Vergilianae*

Ausonius, poem on Dido by, 107n. 24

Austin, R. G., 25n, 36n.25

Bacchus (Osiris): in Plutarch's "Of Isis and Osiris," 200; in Shakespeare's *Antony and Cleopatra*, Marc Antony as, 158, 159, 172, 207, 209–11

Bacon, Francis, *The New Atlantis*, 191–92. *See also* Virtuous heathen

Balmas, Enea, 107n.23, 111n, 112n

Baron, Hans, 89n.11

Barroll, J. Leeds, 162n.26

Barton, Anne, 218, 218n.80, 219n

Beatrice: in Dante's *Divine Comedy*, 45, 58n, 58–61, 70

Belphoebe: in Spenser's *Faerie Queene*, 16n, 63, 67, 70–75, 182

Bennett, Josephine Waters, 61n

Berger, Harry, Jr., 64n.31, 71n, 181n.50

Bernard, and allegorization of Vergil's *Aeneid*, 43–44, 44n, 51

Bernardus Sylvestris, *De mundi universitate*, 114n, 173. *See also* Naturalism

Bevington, David, 135n

Bible: compared with Vergil's *Aeneid*, 40; dramatizations of, 85. *See also* Shakespeare, *Antony and Cleopatra*, Biblical allusion in

—Acts 7:22, and wisdom of the Egyptians, 193

—Epistles, in Augustine's *Confessions*, 49

—Genesis: in Augustine's *Confessions*, 50; influence on Pico's "Oration," 195

—Isaiah 2:4, and Shakespeare's *Antony and Cleopatra*, 170

—Matthew 21:9, in Dante's *Divine Comedy*, 58

—Psalms, in Augustine's *Confessions*, 47

Bloch, Herbert, 46n.11

Boas, George, 195n.63

Boccaccio, Giovanni, *Genealogia Deorum Gentilium*, 182; and allegorization of Vergil's *Aeneid*, 44

Botticelli, Sandro, "Primavera" and "The Birth of Venus," 166. *See also* Neo-Platonism; Venus

Bottom: in Shakespeare's *Midsummer Night's Dream*, 198, 198–99n.67

Bouwsma, William, 174n.38

Bowra, C. M., 8n

Braggadocchio: in Spenser's *Faerie Queene*, 71–72

Brinton, Ann Cox, 44n.8

Britomart: in Spenser's *Faerie Queene*, 3, 45, 63, 65, 72, 74n.43, 75–79, 81, 138, 182

Britomartis: in pseudo-Vergilian *Ciris*, 76

Brooks, Robert A., 36n.26

Brower, Reuben, 8n, 146n

Brown, Peter: *Augustine of Hippo*, 45n, 46n.11, 46–47n.13, 50, 80n; *Late Antiquity*, 39n

Bruno, Giordano, *Lo Spaccio de la bestia trionfante*, 196–97; and Sidney circle, 197n.66. *See also* Egypt, wisdom of; Isis; Moses

Brute: in Spenser's *Faerie Queene*, 78

Brutus: in Shakespeare's *Julius Caesar*, 145

Bullough, Geoffrey, 89n.12, 144n

Busyrane: in Spenser's *Faerie Queene*, 78n.52, 78–79

Cabbala, and Hermes Trismegistus, 195

Cain, Thomas, 70n.38, 71n, 79n

Calderwood, James, 142n.1

Caliban: in Shakespeare's *Tempest*, 222, 223

Calidore: in Spenser's *Faerie Queene*, 69

Camoëns, Luiz de, and neo-Vergilian epic, 51

Canidius: in Shakespeare's *Antony and Cleopatra*, 164n, 208

Cartari, Vincenzo, *Imagini de i Dei de gli Antichi*, 154, 176, 176n.45, 193, 197–98; translated by Linche, 197–98. *See also* Egypt, myth of; Isis; *Venus genetrix*

Carthage: in Augustine's *Confessions*, 46, 217; in Jodelle's *Didon*, 108–9, 112, 115; in Marlowe's *Dido* (Temple of Juno), 132; in Vergil's *Aeneid*, 12, 17, 28n.19, 29, 33, 37, 40, 220; in Vergil's *Aeneid* (Temple of Juno), 13, 15, 20, 22, 26, 33, 71–72, 132. *See also* Tunis

Cassius: in Shakespeare's *Julius Caesar*, 145

Cesari, Cesare de', *Cleopatra*, 87, 89; influenced by other works, 89n.12; modeled after Sophocles' *Antigone*, 89. *See also* Cleopatra; Greek tragedy; Octavius; Senecanism

Cesarione: in Pistorelli's *Marc'Antonio*, 90n

Chapman, George, as translator of Homer's *Odyssey*, 168. *See also* Venus, "What Venus did with Mars"

Charles V (Holy Roman Emperor), and Jodelle's *Cléopatre*, 103–4, 108

Charmian: in Shakespeare's *Antony and Cleopatra*, 205

Chaucer, Geoffrey, *Legend of Good Women*, 42; influenced by Ovid's *Heroides*, 42. *See also* Cleopatra; Dido; Mercury; Troy, fall of

Chenu, Marie-Dominique, 173n

Chrysogonee: in Spenser's *Faerie Queene*, 74

Cicero: and Marc Antony, 157, 158; on Plato's travels, 195n.62. *See also* Epicureanism

Cicogna, Emmanuele Antonio, 88n.10

Claribell: in Shakespeare's *Tempest*, 220, 221, 222

Claudian, 114n. *See also* Naturalism

Cleopatra: in Cesari's *Cleopatra*, 89, 137; in Chaucer's *Legend of Good Women*, 42; in Daniel's *Cleopatra*, 122–27; in Garnier's *Marc Antoine*, 116–21; in Giraldi's *Cleopatra*, 97–102; historians' view of, 86–87; in Horace's ode, 87n; in Jodelle's *Cléopatre*, 104–6; as Ovidian martyr, 86, 89; in Pistorelli's *Marc'Antonio*, 90; in Plutarch's *Life of Antony*, 153, 155–59; in Shakespeare's *Antony and Cleopatra*, 5, 115, 117, 121, 126–27, 137, 150, 151, 160–62, 167–73, 180–90, 200, 205–13, 218–19, 220; in Shakespeare's *Antony and Cleopatra*, and interpretation of Herculean Antony, 162–67; in Shakespeare's *Antony and Cleopatra*, as Isis, 114, 150, 198, 198–99n.67, 204n, 205–13, 219; in Shakespeare's *Antony and Cleopatra*, as Venus, 116–73, 183–90, 219; in Vergil's *Aeneid*, 2, 85–86, 216–17

Clown: in Shakespeare's *Antony and Cleopatra*, 190

Colie, Rosalie, 160n.24

Colin: in Spenser's *Faerie Queene*, 69–70; in Spenser's *Shepheardes Calender*, 64–69

Commager, Steele, 87n

Comparetti, Domenico, 43n.6, 52n.18

Conti, Natale, *Mythologiae*, 154, 176, 176n.45. *See also* Venus genetrix

Cook, Hal, 192n.56

Cope, Jackson, 128–29n.41, 131, 131n
Cormier, Raymond J., 42n.3
Courcelle, Pierre, 44n
Creüsa: in Vergil's *Aeneid*, 18, 18n, 31–32, 33n.23, 65n
Cupid: in Dolce's *Didone*, 89; in Jodelle's *Didon*, 113; in Marlowe's *Dido*, 129, 131, 133; in Vergil's *Aeneid*, 18
Cutts, John, 134n.47

Daniel, Samuel, 4, 121–27
—*Cleopatra*, 121–27; as influence on Shakespeare's *Antony and Cleopatra*, 3, 121, 125–27, 138; influenced by Machiavelli, 121, 124; influenced by Ovid's *Heroides*, 125; influenced by Plutarch's *Life of Antony*, 122, 123, 125; influenced by Shakespeare's *Antony and Cleopatra*, 121; and Mary Sidney, 121; and Philip Sidney, 121. PASSAGES CITED: *408*, 123; *409*, 123; *413–14*, 123; *414*, 124; *420–21*, 123–24; *427*, 123; *435*, 125; *444*, 125, *446*, 125–26; *448*, 127; *449*, 127. See also Antony; Arius; Cleopatra; *Discordia concors*; Dolabella; Egypt; Isis; Octavius; Rome; Stoicism
Dannenfeldt, Karl, 191n.54
Dante, as character in Dante's *Divine Comedy*, 52–55, 57, 58–61, 70
Dante Aligheri, 51–61. See also Holy Roman Empire
—*Convivo*, and Fulgentian allegory of Vergil's *Aeneid*, 51n.17, 52, 52n.19. See also Dido
—*De Monarchia*, 51–52n.18. See also Rome
—*Divine Comedy*: genre of, 50, 53–55, 54–55n, 57–61; influenced

by Augustine's *Confessions*, 2, 50, 50n; influenced by Vergil's *Aeneid*, 3, 45, 51–61, 79, 80–81, 218; influenced by Vergil's *4th Eclogue*, 51. PASSAGES CITED: *Inf.* 1.25–27, 57; *Inf.* 1.85, 53; *Inf.* 1.91, 57n; *Inf.* 1.112–29, 57; *Inf.* 4, 191n.55; *Inf.* 4.44, 80; *Inf.* 5.37–39, 52; *Inf.* 5.56, 54; *Inf.* 5.61–62, 53; *Inf.* 5.71, 54; *Inf.* 5.82–87, 53n; *Inf.* 5.100–106, 54; *Inf.* 5.112–13, 54; *Inf.* 5.113, 61; *Inf.* 26.21–22, 57n; *Inf.* 26.90–99, 56; *Inf.* 26.125, 57; *Inf.* 26.138, 56; *Par.* 20.94–99, 80; *Par.* 29–30, 191n.55; *Purg.* 1–2, 191n.55; *Purg.* 7.1–39, 58; *Purg.* 9.127–28, 81; *Purg.* 17.103–5, 55; *Purg.* 19.7–15, 56; *Purg.* 19.19, 59; *Purg.* 19.22–24, 56n; *Purg.* 19.26–33, 56; *Purg.* 21.104–36, 58; *Purg.* 27–30, 191n.55; *Purg.* 28.136, 58; *Purg.* 30.48, 3, 58; *Purg.* 30.50–51, 58–59; *Purg.* 30.55–57, 59–60; *Purg.* 30.57, 80; *Purg.* 30.62–64, 60; *Purg.* 30.71–75, 60; *Purg.* 31.43–46, 60; *Purg.* 31.47–63, 69; *Purg.* 31.70–75, 59. See also Beatrice; Dante; Dido; Francesca da Rimini; Heroism; Homeric epic; Rome; Siren; Statius; Ulysses; Vergil; Virtuous heathen
—*La vita nuova*, 55, 60
Decembrio, Pier Candido, as author of thirteenth book of Vergil's *Aeneid*, 44
Deianira, 156
Dent, R. W., 199n
Dessen, Alan, 143n.3
Diana: in Spenser's *Faerie Queene*, 70–71, 73; in Vergil's *Aeneid*, Dido compared to, 16, 27–28, 28n.18. See also Venus; *Venus virgo*
Di Cesare, Mario: *Altar and City*,

12nn.4–5, 19n, 22n, 28n.18, 37n;
Vida's Christiad, 85
Dickey, F. M., 87n, 162n.26
Dido (Elissa): in Augustine's
Confessions, 2, 46nn.10,12,
46–47, 59, 79, 81; in Ausonius,
108n.24; in Chaucer's *Legend of
Good Women*, 42; in Dante's
Convivio, 52, 52n.19; in Dante's
Divine Comedy, 3, 52–54, 58–59,
60; in Dolce's *Didone*, 88, 137;
in Giraldi's *Didone*, 92–97; in
Jodelle's *Didon*, 4, 107–16; in
Marlowe's *Dido*, 129–137; in
Ovid's *Heriodes*, Letter 7, 42–
43; as Ovidian martyr, 86; in
Pazzi's *Dido*, 88; in Ronsard,
113, 113n.28; in Shakespeare's
Antony and Cleopatra, 5, 187;
in Shakespeare's *Tempest*, 221;
in Spenser's *Shepheardes Cal-
ender*, "November," 67–69; in
Trogus Pompeius's *Universal
History*, 67, 67n, 221, 221n;
in Vergil's *Aeneid*, 7, 11, 13–29,
33–38, 45, 58, 67, 71, 76, 120,
217, 221
Dio Cassius, *Roman History*, influence of: on Cesari's *Cleopatra*,
89n.12; on Giraldi's *Cleopatra*,
97, 99–100; on Jodelle's *Cléopatre*, 105; on Pistorelli's
Marc'Antonio, 90n
Diogenes Laertius, 114n, 173; on
Plato's travels, 195n.62
Diomedes: in Shakespeare's
Antony and Cleopatra, 186, 187–
88
Discordia concors: in Daniel's
Cleopatra, 121, 122; in Marlowe's *Dido*, 129; in Shakespeare's *Antony and Cleopatra*,
4–5, 150, 205
Dolabella: in Daniel's *Cleopatra*,
125; in Shakespeare's *Antony
and Cleopatra*, 189, 211
Dolce, Lodovico, *Didone*, 87, 88–

89, 88–89n.10, 128, 137; in-
fluenced by Ovid and by Vergil's
Aeneid, 88–89, 137. *See also*
Senecanism
Donatus, Aelius, and allegorization
of Vergil's *Aeneid*, 43n.6
Dronke, Peter, 51n.16
Du Bellay, Joachim, as translator
of Dido materials, 42–43, 107,
107n.24, 110

Edgar: in Shakespeare's *Lear*, 148,
182
Egypt. *See also* Isis and Osiris,
myth of
—in Daniel's *Cleopatra*, 122–24,
127
—myth of: in Cartari's *Imagini*,
197–98; hieroglyphs, 195–97
—in Shakespeare's *Antony and
Cleopatra*, 29, 117, 150, 158,
184, 204–13
—wisdom of: in Augustine's *City
of God*, 193–94, 195; in the
Bible, 193; in Bruno's *Lo Spaccio*,
196–97; in Ficino, 194–96; in
Lactantius, 194, 194n.60; and
Moses, 193–94; in Pico's
"Oration," 195; and Plato, 195,
195n.62
Egyptology, Renaissance, 191–
204
Eirenicism, 174–76; in Jodelle's
Didon, 108, 112, 112n; in
Montaigne, 112, 175, 192; in
Rabelais, 112; in Shakespeare's
Antony and Cleopatra, 151
Elissa. *See* Dido
Eliza: in Spenser's *Shepheardes
Calender*, 64–67
Elizabeth I (queen of England),
and Spenser's *Faerie Queene*,
63–65, 69–75
Ellmann, Marie-Pierre, 168n.35
Else, Gerald, 84n.1
Elton, William, 114n, 148n.8

Enobarbus: in Shakespeare's *Antony and Cleopatra*, 162, 189, 190, 206, 209, 211, 212; description of Cleopatra by, 169–73, 180–83, 219

Epicureanism, 166; in Cicero, 114n; in Diogenes Laertius, 173; in Erasmus, 114n, 174; in Montaigne, 114n, 150, 150n, 175; in More's *Utopia*, 114n, 174; in Rabelais, 114n; Renaissance revival of, 112n, 114n, 173–75; in Shakespeare, 114n; in Shakespeare's *Antony and Cleopatra*, 166–90; in Valla's *De Vero Falsoque Bono*, 114n, 173–74. *See also* Lucretius

Erasmus, 114n, 174

Ercole II (duke of Ferrara), 90

Eros: in Shakespeare's *Antony and Cleopatra*, 187, 211

Euripides: *Heracles*, 153; influence on Spenser's *Faerie Queene*, 76; influence on Vergil's *Aeneid*, 20, 22n, 24, 28n.18, 37, 67, 76. *See also* Greek tragedy; Medea; Megara

Evander: in Vergil's *Aeneid*, 28n. 19, 32n.154

Falstaff: in Shakespeare's second tetralogy, 143–44

Febvre, Lucien, 112n, 114n

Ferdinand: in Shakespeare's *Tempest*, 221–22, 223, 224

Festugière, A. J., 174n.40

Fichter, Andrew, 190n

Ficino, 194–96

Fisch, Harold, 190n

Fitch, Robert, 162n.26

Florentine Academy, 173, 193–96. *See also* Neo-Platonism

Fraisse, Simone, 112n, 114n, 175n.41

Frame, Donald, 150n.12

Francesca da Rimini: in Dante's *Divine Comedy*, 52–55, 61

Frank, Robert Worth, Jr., 21n.4

Fraser, Russell, 128n.40

French religious wars, 174–75; influence on Garnier, 116; influence on Jodelle's *Didon*, 107

Fulgentius, and allegorization of Vergil's *Aeneid*, 43, 43n, 51, 51n.17, 52, 52n.19, 85, 96, 133–34, 134n.46, 137

Fulvia: in Plutarch's *Life of Antony*, 157; in Shakespeare's *Antony and Cleopatra*, 163, 184

Fyler, John M., 42n.4

Ganymede: in Marlowe's *Dido*, 129, 130, 131, 132, 134n.46, 136

Garnier, Robert, 4, 116–21

—*Marc Antoine*, 4, 116–21, 138; as influence on Shakespeare's *Antony and Cleopatra*, 4, 116–17, 119–21, 138; influenced by French religious wars, 116; influenced by Plutarch's *Life of Antony*, 4, 116–21, 138; influenced by Vergil's *Aeneid*, 116–17; translated by Mary Sidney, 116. PASSAGES CITED: *18*, 117; *19*, 117; *19*, 119; *63*, 119; *64–65*, 119–20; *70*, 118; *97*, 120. *See also* Agrippa; Antony; Cleopatra; Hercules, myth of; Octavia; Octavius; Venus, "What Venus did with Mars"

Genre: epic and heroic drama, 3, 83–139; romance, and assimilation of classical epic, 3, 41–82; romance, and tragicomedy, 4, 82, 137–39, 149–50, 149n.11, 218; tragedy and tragicomedy, 4–5, 82, 90–102, 137–39, 149–51, 186–90, 209–13; tragicomedy, defined, 149n; Vergilian epic and autobiography, 40, 50,

58. *See also under individual works*

Gibbons, Brian, 128–29n.41

Giraldi, Celso, and allegorization of Giovambattista Giraldi's *Didone*, 92–94

Giraldi, Giovambattista Cinthio, 3, 90–102, 137; and genre, tragicomedy, 90–91, 91nn.14–15; and genre, tragicomedy and tragedy, 90–102, 137; influenced by Counter-Reformation, 93, 93n; providentialism in, 3, 93, 95–97, 107, 137

—*Cleopatra*, 97–102, 137; influenced by Dio's *Roman History*, 97, 99–100; influenced by Plutarch's *Life*, 97, 98–99, 100, 101; influenced by Seneca's *Octavia*, 99n.21, 99–100. PASSAGES CITED: *Prologue*, 97–98; *1.1*, 98; *1 Chorus*, 97, 99; *2.1*, 99; *2 Chorus*, 97, 100–101; *3 Chorus*, 97; *5.2*, 101–2; *5 Chorus*, 97. *See also* Agrippa; Antony; Cleopatra; Maecenas; Octavius.

—*Didone*, 91–97, 128, 137; influenced by allegorizations of Vergil's *Aeneid*, 91–94, 96, 137; influenced by Pico's "Oration," 93n, 95–96; influenced by Sophocles' *Antigone*, 93n; influenced by Vergil's *Aeneid*, 3, 91–97, 137. PASSAGES CITED: *Prologue*, 92; *1.2*, 94; *1.4*, 94; *1.5*, 94–95; *1 Chorus*, 95; *2.2*, 92n.17, 93, 95; *3.3*, 92n.17; *3 Chorus*, 92n.17, 95–96. *See also* Achates; Aeneas; Anna; Dido; Juno; Jupiter; Mercury; Neo-Platonism; Stoicism; Venus

—*Discorsi*: and Aristotle's *Poetics*, 91; critical theories in, 84n.3, 90–91, 91nn.14–15, 97

Girard, René, 55n

Glauce: in Spenser's *Faerie Queene*, 76

Gloriana: in Spenser's *Faerie Queene*, 69, 70

Gloucester: in Shakespeare's *Lear*, 148

Godenne, René, 107n.24

Gohlke, Madelon, 148n.9

Goldin, Frederick, 51n.16, 76n.45

Gombrich, E. H., 196n.65

Gonzalo: in Shakespeare's *Tempest*, 220, 221

Greek tragedy, influence of: on Renaissance drama, 87, 88, 89, 93n; on Spenser's *Faerie Queene*, 76; on Vergil's *Aeneid*, 2, 20, 22n, 24, 26n, 28n.18, 37, 67, 76. *See also* Euripides; Sophocles

Greene, Gayle, 149n.10

Greene, Thomas M.: *Descent from Heaven*, 8n, 44n.8, 52n.18, 77n.49; *Light in Troy*, 1n

Greenlaw, Edwin, 177n

Guyon: in Spenser's *Faerie Queene*, 64n.31, 181

Hadzsits, George Depue, 175n.41

Hal: in Shakespeare's second tetralogy, 137, 142–44, 181

Hamlet: in Shakespeare's *Hamlet*, 146–47, 182

Hardison, O. B., Jr., 84n.3

Harpies: in Shakespeare's *Tempest*, 222–23

Hathaway, Baxter, 84nn.2–3

Hector: in Vergil's *Aeneid*, 17n, 21, 31, 33n.23

Henry II (king of France), and Jodelle's *Cléopâtre*, 103–4, 106, 108

Hercules, myth of, 153–55; in Euripides' *Heracles*, 153, 154–55; in Garnier's *Marc Antoine*, 4, 116, 119; in Plutarch's *Life*, 4, 5, 153, 155–59; in Prodicus, 154, 154n.20, 155; in Salutati's *De Laboribus Herculis*, 154; in Seneca's *Hercules Furens*, 153,

154–55; in Seneca's *Hercules Oetaeus*, 166–67; in Shakespeare's *Antony and Cleopatra*, 5, 150, 159–67; in Sophocles' *Trachinian Women*, 153; in Spenser's *Faerie Queene*, 62–63; in Vergil's *Aeneid*, 154

Hermes Trismegistus: and *Asclepius*, 195; in Augustine's *City of God*, 194; influence of, on Pico's "Oration," 195; in Lactantius, 194, 194n.60; and Plato, 195

Hermione: in Shakespeare's *Winter's Tale*, 149

Heroism: in Augustine's *Confessions*, 50; in Dante's *Divine Comedy*, 50, 56–61, 80; in Homer, 2, 20, 30–34, 56–57, 57n, 80; in Vergil's *Aeneid*, 2, 30–34, 56–61, 57n, 80

Herrick, Marvin: "Fusion," 84n.3; *Italian Tragedy*, 88n.9, 99n.21

Hieroglyphs, 195–97

Holland, Philemon, as translator of Plutarch's "Of Isis and Osiris," 199

Holy Roman Empire, 44, 44n.8, 51, 80, 81; in Dante, 80; in Jodelle, 103–4, 108, 137

Homer, *Odyssey*, 19, 32n, 36n.27, 146. *See also* Ajax; Heroism; Homeric epic; Odysseus; Penelope; Siren; Telemachus; Venus, "What Venus did with Mars"

Homeric epic, influence of: on Dante's *Divine Comedy*, 56–57, 57n, 60; on Pistorelli's *Marc'Antonio*, 90, 90n; on Vergil's *Aeneid*, 2, 8n, 8–9, 12, 19–26, 29–40, 45, 53, 97, 143–44, 215, 217

Horace, ode on Cleopatra, 87n

Horapollo, *Hieroglypica*, 196. *See also* Egypt, myth of; Hieroglyphs

Horatio: in Shakespeare's *Hamlet*, 146

Horne, P. R.: "Reformation," 93n; *Tragedies*, 91n.14, 99n.20

Hughes, Merritt Y., 61n

Hulubei, Alice, 43n.5

Hunter, Robert G., 207n

Hyperbole: in Marlowe's *Dido*, 4, 122, 129n.41, 130, 134, 136, 138; in Shakespeare's *Antony and Cleopatra*, 4–5, 129n.41, 136–37, 138, 163

Ide, Richard, 150n.13

Io (Isis): in Lactantius's *Divine Institutes*, 208; in Lucian's *Dialogues of the Gods*, 207; in Ovid's *Metamorphoses*, 207; in Shakespeare's *Antony and Cleopatra*, 207. *See also* Isis

Iras: in Shakespeare's *Antony and Cleopatra*, 205

Isis: in Apuleius's *Golden Asse*, 191, 198, 212n.73; in Bruno's *Lo Spaccio*, 196–97; in Cartari's *Imagini*, 198; in Daniel's *Cleopatra*, 123; in Jodelle's *Cléopatre*, 105; in Plutarch's "Of Isis and Osiris," 200–204, 212–13n.73; in Servius, 206, 206n; in Shakespeare's *Antony and Cleopatra*, 114, 190, 205, 207; in Spenser's *Faerie Queene*, 182

Isis and Osiris, myth of, 199–204, 209

—in Pico's "Oration," 140, 150–51, 219

—in Plutarch's "Of Isis and Osiris," 199–204; cosmological interpretation, 202–3; euhemeristic interpretation, 200; natural philosophical interpretation, 201–2; neo-Platonic interpretation, 200, 203–4

—in Shakespeare's *Antony and*

Cleopatra, 5, 150–51, 190, 204–13, 219
—in Spenser's *Faerie Queene*, 78, 81
Isocrates, and the Gallic Hercules, 154
Iülus. *See* Ascanius
Iverson, Eric, 191n.54

Jacobson, Howard, 42n.2
Jean de Meun, *Roman de la Rose*, 114n. *See also* Naturalism
Jesuits, conversion efforts of, 192
Jodelle, Étienne, 3–4, 103–16, 137–38; and French Holy Roman Empire, 3, 103, 108, 137–38; and Vergil's *Aeneid*, 3–4. *See also* Holy Roman Empire; Pléiade
—*Cléopatre captive*, 103–7, 137–38; influenced by Dio's *Roman History*, 105; influenced by Ovid's *Heroides*, 106; influenced by Plutarch's *Life*, 104; influenced by Seneca's *Agamemnon*, 104; influenced by Seneca's *Thyestes*, 104. PASSAGES CITED: *Prologue*, 94, 106; *93*, 103; *94*, 104; *114*, 105; *118*, 105; *132*, 104; *135–36*, 106; *139*, 106. *See also* Agrippa; Antony; Charles V; Cleopatra; Henry II; Isis; Octavius; Proculeius; Seleucus; Senecanism
—*Didon se sacrifiant*, 103, 107–16, 128, 138; influenced by Du Bellay's translations of Dido materials, 107, 107n.24, 110; influenced by French religious wars, 107; influenced by Lucretius's *De Rerum Natura*, 108, 110, 113–15, 138, 175; influenced by Ovid's *Heroides*, Letter 7, 107, 108, 109–110, 112–114, 138; influenced by Vergil's *Aeneid*, 107–116, 138. PASSAGES

CITED: *151*, 108–9; *153*, 109; *154*, 109; *159–60*, 110; *162–63*, 115; *163*, 113; *166*, 115; *181*, 116; *186*, 113–114, *186–88*, 113n.29; *191*, 111; *206*, 115, 210–11, 111–12.
John of Salisbury, and allegorization of Vergil's *Aeneid*, 44, 51
Johnson, W. R., 8n, 9–10, 13n, 28n.18, 30n, 40, 40n, 86n.6
Jondorf, Gillian, 116n
Julius Caesar: in Shakespeare's *Julius Caesar*, 144–45
Juno: in Giraldi's *Didone*, 94; in Jodelle's *Didon*, 109; in Shakespeare's *Tempest*, 223; in Vergil's *Aeneid*, 12, 19, 22–25, 29, 46, 216, 220
Jupiter: in Giraldi's *Didone*, 92–93; in Marlowe's *Dido*, 129, 130, 131, 132, 136; in Vergil's *Aeneid*, 14, 15, 16, 19, 23, 23n, 35, 136, 220

Kaiser, Walter, 114, 150n.12, 166n, 174n.39
Kermode, Frank, 199n
Knight, G. Wilson, 149, 149n.10
Knowles, Richard, 143n.3
Knox, Bernard, 19n, 29n
Krier, Theresa, 68n

Lactantius: *De ira dei*, 194; *Divine Institutes, The*, 194, 194n.60, 208. *See also* Egypt, wisdom of; Hermes Trismegistus; Io
Landi, Giulio, *Life of Cleopatra*, influence on Cesari's *Cleopatra*, 89n.12
Landino, Christoforo, and allegorization of Vergil's *Aeneid*, 44, 85
Lavinia: in Vergil's *Aeneid*, 44
Lear: in Shakespeare's *Lear*, 147–48

Leavenworth, Russell, 121n.34, 124n
Leda and the swan, myth of: in Spenser's Faerie Queene, 74, 74n.43
Leech, Clifford, 128–129n.41
Leontes: in Shakespeare's Winter's Tale, 148–49
Lepidus: in Shakespeare's Antony and Cleopatra, 151–52, 155, 169
Leube, Eberhard, 42n.3
Lewis, C. S., 61n
Lichas, 155; in Shakespeare's Antony and Cleopatra, 161
Linche, Richard, as translator of Cartari's Imagini, 197–98
Lloyd, Michael, 204n
Lord, Albert, 8n
Lucian: Dialogues of the Gods, 207; and the Gallic Hercules, 154
Lucretius, De Rerum Natura, 112n; influence on Jodelle's Didon, 108, 110, 113–15, 138, 175; influence on Montaigne, 175, 175n.42; influence on the Pléiade, 114n, 175, 175n.41; influence on Shakespeare's Antony and Cleopatra, 173–83, 188; influence on Spenser's Faerie Queene, 176–82; interpretation of, 173–83. See also Epicureanism; Venus genetrix

MacCaffrey, Isabel, 64n.31, 70n.37
Machiavelli, influence of, on Daniel's Cleopatra, 121, 124
Mack, Maynard, 147n
McLane, Paul, 67n
Macrobius, Saturnalia, and allegorization of Vergil's Aeneid, 43n.6, 45–46, 46n.10, 85
Maecenas: in Giraldi's Cleopatra, 99–100; in Shakespeare's Antony and Cleopatra, 161, 169
Maier, Michael, 190n
Marcellus: in Dante's Divine

Comedy, 58n; in Vergil's Aeneid, 10, 58n
Mardian: in Shakespeare's Antony and Cleopatra, 168, 183, 185–86
Marlowe, Christopher, 4, 127–37; compared with Ovid, 136
—Dido, Queene of Carthage, 4, 127–37; and children's theater, 127–37; and Fulgentian allegory of Vergil's Aeneid, 133–34, 134n. 46; influence on Shakespeare's Antony and Cleopatra, 4, 129n. 41, 130; influenced by Vergil's Aeneid, 4, 127–37; irony in, 127–28, 135. PASSAGES CITED: 1.1.29–31, 136; 1.1.49, 132; 1.1.124, 131; 1.1.155–56, 131; 2.1.281, 135; 2.1.305, 134; 3.1.82–88, 131; 3.1.116–27, 131–32; 4.4.123, 136; 4.5.25–28, 129; 4.5.26, 136; 4.5.30,34, 129; 5.1.228, 135; 5.1.243–61, 135. See also Aeneas; Ascanius; Carthage; Cupid; Dido; Discordia concors; Ganymede; Hyperbole; Jupiter; Neo-Platonism; Nurse; Priam; Skepticism; Troy, fall of; Venus
—Dr. Faustus, 135
Mars, myth of. See Venus
Mater Ecclesia, in Augustine, 46n.12, 50, 81, 218
Mayo, Thomas Franklin, 175n.42
Medea, 88; in Apollonius Rhodius's Argonautica, 2, 26n, 67, 88; in Euripides' Medea, 67
Megara: in Euripides' Heracles, 154–55; in Seneca's Hercules Furens, 154–55
Mercury: in Chaucer's Legend of Good Women, 42; in Giraldi's Didone, 93, 95; in Jodelle's Didon, 109; in Vergil's Aeneid, 28n.19, 33
Merlin: in Spenser's Faerie Queene, 76–78
Milton, John, Paradise Lost, 5

Miranda: in Shakespeare's *Tempest*, 221, 223, 224

Monica: in Augustine's *Confessions*, 46, 49–50, 80

Montaigne, Michel de: influence on Shakespeare, 150, 150n.12, 176; influenced by Lucretius's *De Rerum Natura*, 175, 175n.42. *See also* Eirenicism; Epicureanism; Naturalism; Stoicism; Virtuous heathen

More, Thomas, *Utopia*, 114n, 174, 192. *See also* Epicureanism; Virtuous heathen

Moses: in Bruno's *Lo Spaccio*, 197; and the wisdom of the Egyptians, 193–94

Mouflard, Marie-Madeleine, 117n

Murrin, Michael, 10n.3, 44n.8

Naturalism: in Alain's *De planctu natura*, 114n, 173; in Bernardus's *De mundi universitate*, 114n, 173; in Claudian, 114n; in Jean de Meun's *Roman de la Rose*, 114n; in Montaigne, 175, 178, 192; in Ovid, 114n; in Rabelais, 114n

Neo-Platonism: and allegorizations of Vergil's *Aeneid*, 40, 43–45; in Augustine's *Confessions*, 48–49, 79; in Botticelli, 166; and distinctions in love, 69–79, 75n, 85–87; effect of, on Aristotelian concept of imitation, 84–85; of the Florentine Academy, 173, 193–96; in Giraldi's *Didone*, 95–96, 137; in Marlowe's *Dido*, 131, 134n.46, 136; in Plutarch's "Of Isis and Osiris," 5, 200, 203–4; in Shakespeare's *Antony and Cleopatra*, 5, 29, 150–51, 166–67, 173, 181, 190, 213; in Spenser's *Faerie Queene*, 3, 70, 77, 177–82; in Titian, 166

Neoptolemus. *See* Pyrrhus

Neri, Ferdinando, 88n.9, 88–89n.10

Nessus, 155; in Shakespeare's *Antony and Cleopatra*, 209

New Academy, skepticism in, 10n.3

Nile: in Plutarch's "Of Isis and Osiris," 201–4; in Shakespeare's *Antony and Cleopatra*, 204–7; in Vergil's *Aeneid*, 217

Nolhac, Pierre de, 44n.8

Nurse: in Marlowe's *Dido*, 129, 130, 134

Octavia: in Garnier's *Marc Antoine*, 117; in Shakespeare's *Antony and Cleopatra*, 160, 161–62, 165, 166, 183, 211

Octavius, 38, 40, 43; in Cesari's *Cleopatra*, 89, 137; in Daniel's *Cleopatra*, 124–25; in Garnier's *Marc Antoine*, 117–18; in Giraldi's *Cleopatra*, 97–102; in Jodelle's *Cléopatre*, 103–6, 108; in Pistorelli's *Marc'Antonio*, 90; in Shakespeare's *Antony and Cleopatra*, 153, 160, 161–62, 164–65, 169, 184, 185, 188, 189, 209–12, 219, 220; in Shakespeare's *Julius Caesar*, 145; in Vergil's *Aeneid*, 10, 83, 85–86, 215, 217; in Vergil's *Georgics 3*, 213–15

Odysseus: in Homer's *Odyssey*, 19, 26n, 32n, 36n.27. *See also* Ulysses

Oliver, H. J., 128n.39, 132n.45

Omphale, and unmanning of Hercules, 155, 160

Ornstein, Robert, 142n.1

Osiris (Bacchus): in Plutarch's "Of Isis and Osiris," 200–204, 209, 213n.73. *See also* Isis

Otis, Brooks: "Originality," 8n, 8–10, 15n, 22n, 26n, 29n; *Ovid as Epic Poet*, 28n.19, 42n.1; *Virgil*, 8n, 8–10, 28n.19, 154n.19

Ovid: compared with Marlowe, 128, 136; influence on Dolce's *Didone*, 88–89, 137. *See also* Naturalism
—*Heroides*, 42–43; influence on Chaucer's *Legend of Good Women*, 42; influence on Daniel's *Cleopatra*, 125; influence on Jodelle's *Cléopatre*, 106; influence on Renaissance drama, 43, 86, 88, 89; Letter 7, 42–43; Letter 7, influence on Jodelle's *Didon*, 7, 107, 108, 109–10, 112–14, 138. PASSAGES CITED: *7.31–36*, 110; *7.56–60*, 110; *7.58*, 113. *See also* Aeneas; Dido; Venus
—*Metamorphoses*, influenced by Vergil's *Aeneid*, 41–42. *See also* Io

Palinurus: in Jodelle's *Didon*, 109
Panizza Lorch, Maristella de, 174n.38
Panofsky, Erwin: *Meaning*, 66n; *Studies*, 75n, 134n.46
Paridell: in Spenser's *Faerie Queene*, 74n.43, 78, 78n.51
Parry, Adam, 18, 18n.11, 39n, 85–86
Parry, Milman, 8n
Partridge, Eric, 205n
Pazzi, Alessandro de' Medici: *Dido in Carthagine*, 87, 88, 88n.9, 129; influenced by Apollonius Rhodius's *Argonautica*, 88; on tragedy, 84, 84n.2; as translator of Aristotle's *Poetics*, 88, 88n.9. *See also* Aeneas; Dido; Senecanism; Sychaeus
Penelope: in Homer's *Odyssey*, 36n.27
Penthesilia: in Spenser's *Faerie Queene*, 71; in Vergil's *Aeneid*, 22, 71–72

Perdita: in Shakespeare's *Winter's Tale*, 149
Petrarch, Francesco: and allegorization of Vergil's *Aeneid*, 44; and neo-Vergilian epic, 51
Phidias, 178–79
Philo: in Shakespeare's *Antony and Cleopatra*, 161, 164n, 168–69, 170, 180, 185, 187, 206, 218
Pico della Mirandola, "Oration on the Dignity of Man," 140; as influence on Giraldi's *Didone*, 93n, 95–96 influenced by Genesis, 195; influenced by Hermetic *Asclepius*, 195; influenced by Plato's *Timaeus*, 195. *See also* Artist, Renaissance ideal of; Egypt, wisdom of; Isis and Osiris, myth of
Pistorelli, Celso, *Marc'Antonio e Cleopatra*, 87, 88, 89–90, 137; influenced by Dio's *Roman History*, 90n; influenced by Homeric epic, 90, 90n. *See also* Antillo; Antony; Cesarione; Cleopatra; Octavius; Senecanism
Plato: and the Florentine neo-Platonists, 193–194; and Hermes Trismegistus, 195; *Sophist*, as influence on Sidney's *Apology for Poetry*, 77n.47; in Spenser's *Faerie Queene*, 62–63; *Timaeus*, as influence on Pico's "Oration," 195; and the wisdom of Egypt, 195, 195n.62
Pléiade: and Étienne Jodelle, 103; influenced by Lucretius, 114n, 175, 175n.41
Pliny, *Natural History*, influence of: on Cesari's *Cleopatra*, 89n. 12; on Shakespeare's *Antony and Cleopatra*, 180–81; on Spenser's *Faerie Queene*, 178–79
Plotinus: and the Florentine neo-Platonists, 193, 195. *See also* Egypt, myth of; Hieroglyphs

Plutarch, 4–5, 152–59, 199–204
—"Of Isis and Osiris," 4–5, 199–
204; influence on Shakespeare's
Antony and Cleopatra, 4–5, 150–
51, 204–13; translated by
Philemon Holland, 199. PASSAGES
CITED: 1286, 199; 1292, 200;
1295, 200; 1300, 201, 209;
1301, 202, 212n.72; 1302, 201;
1303, 201; 1304, 202, 209;
1304–5, 202; 1305, 203; 1308,
203–4; 1309, 204; 1312, 205;
1318, 204, 212–13n.72; 1380,
212n.72. See also Bacchus; Isis;
Isis and Osiris, myth of; Neo-
Platonism; Nile; Osiris; Typhon
—Life of Marc Antony, 4, 5, 87n,
152–59; influence on Cesari's
Cleopatra, 89n.12; influence on
Daniel's Cleopatra, 122, 123,
125; influence on Garnier's
Marc Antoine, 4, 116–21, 138;
influence on Giraldi's Cleopatra,
97, 98–99, 100, 101; influence
on Jodelle's Cléopatre, 104; influence on Shakespeare's Antony
and Cleopatra, 5, 151–67, 170–
73, 199. PASSAGES CITED: 254,
156; 255, 156–57; 257, 155–56;
261, 158; 262, 157; 271, 158;
272, 159–60; 274, 70–72, 159;
275, 158–59; 276, 167; 286–87,
156; 291, 199; 305, 159, 210;
308, 210; 310, 159; 318, 152.
See also Antony; Cleopatra;
Fulvia; Hercules, myth of
—Lives, 83, 151–52
Poggioli, Renato, 54–55n
Pompey: in Shakespeare's Antony
and Cleopatra, 161, 169, 206, 210
Pope, Alexander, The Essay on
Man, 5
Popkin, Richard, 112n
Porter, Joseph, 142n.1
Pöschl, Viktor, 8n
Praxiteles, 179
Priam: in Marlowe's Dido, 133,
135; in Shakespeare's Hamlet,
146; in Vergil's Aeneid, 17n,
31, 36, 146
Prior, Moody, 142n.1
Proculeius: in Jodelle's Cléopatre,
105; in Shakespeare's Antony
and Cleopatra, 189
Prodicus, and story of Hercules,
154, 154n.20, 155, 161. See also
Hercules, myth of
Prospero: in Shakespeare's Tem-
pest, 120–24, 148–49
Pygmalion: in Vergil's Aeneid, 17n
Pyrrhus (Neoptolemus): in Shake-
speare's Hamlet, 146; in
Vergil's Aeneid, 17n, 22, 31

Quintilian, 43n.6

Rabelais, François, 112, 114n.
See also Eirenicism; Epicureanism; Naturalism
Radigund: in Spenser's Faerie
Queene, 78–79, 78n.52, 79n
Read, John, 190n
Renaissance vernacular drama:
influenced by Ovid, 43, 86, 88,
89; influenced by Seneca, 87,
137; and relationship of story
of Aeneas and Dido to history
of Antony and Cleopatra, 82,
83, 87, 88, 90, 103, 218. See also
individual playwrights
Ridley, M. R., 186n
Ripheus: in Dante's Divine Comedy, 80
Roche, Thomas, 64n.31, 74nn.42,
43, 76n.46, 78n.51
Roman Empire, as tyrannical, 4,
89–90, 104–5, 106–8, 111–12,
137, 138
Rome: in Augustine's City of God,
46–48, 51–52n.18; in Augustine's Confessions, 45–46, 217;
in Daniel's Cleopatra, 124, 127;

in Dante's *De Monarchia*, 51–
52n.18; in Dante's *Divine Comedy*, 51, 51–52n.18; in Shakespeare's *Antony and Cleopatra*,
4–5, 150, 153, 161–62, 164–66,
168–70, 189–90, 208–9; in
Vergil's *Aeneid*, 2, 10, 12, 28n.
19, 29, 37–40, 86
Ronsard, Pierre de: on Dido, 113,
113n.28; and neo-Vergilian epic,
51. *See also* Dido
Rosalind: in Spenser's *Shepheardes
Calender*, 65–69
Rose, Mark, 74n.41, 76n.46, 78n.
52, 79n
Rumor: in Shakespeare's *2 Henry
IV*, 143; in Vergil's *Aeneid*, 143

Saccio, Peter, 132n.45
Salutati, Coluccio, *De Laboribus
Herculis*, 154. *See also* Hercules,
myth of
Scarrus: in Shakespeare's *Antony
and Cleopatra*, 161, 207, 208
Schanzer, Ernest: "Daniel's Re-
vision," 121n.34; *Problem Plays*,
144n
Scudamor: in Spenser's *Faerie
Queene*, 177, 179
Scylla: in pseudo-Vergilian *Ciris*,
76
Seaton, Ethel, 190n
Sebastian: in Shakespeare's *Tempest*, 221, 223
Seleucus: in Jodelle's *Cléopatre*,
105; in Shakespeare's *Antony
and Cleopatra*, 211
Seneca: *Agamemnon*, influence
on Jodelle's *Cléopatre*, 104;
Hercules Furens, 153, 154–55
(*see also* Megara); *Hercules
Oetaeus*, 166–67; *Octavia*, influence on Giraldi's *Cleopatra*,
99–100, 99n.21; *Thyestes*, influence on Jodelle's *Cléopatre*,
104

Senecanism: in Cesari's *Cleopatra*,
89; in Dolce's *Didone*, 88–89,
137; in Jodelle's *Cléopatre*, 104,
106; in Pazzi's *Dido*, 88; in Pistorelli's *Marc'Antonio*, 89, 137;
in Renaissance drama, 87, 137;
in Shakespeare's *Antony and
Cleopatra*, 186, 186n
Seronsy, Cecil, 122n.35
Serpents: in Shakespeare's *Antony
and Cleopatra*, 190, 190n, 205,
212
Servius, and allegorization of
Vergil's *Aeneid*, 43n.6, 85, 215n.
See also Isis
Shakespeare, William, 4–5, 140–
213, 218–24; influence of Vergil's *Aeneid* on, 2, 4–5, 8n, 138–
39, 141–51, 162, 187; romances
and romantic comedies by, 4;
tragedies by, 4. *See also* Artist,
Renaissance ideal of; Epicureanism; Skepticism
—*Antony and Cleopatra*: Biblical
allusions in, 170, 190, 190n;
genre of, 4–5, 82, 150, 151–67,
165n.3, 183–90, 218–20; influence on Daniel's *Cleopatra*, 121;
influenced by Apuleius's *Golden
Asse*, 114, 198; influenced by
Daniel's *Cleopatra*, 4, 121, 125–
27, 138; influenced by Garnier's
Marc Antoine, 4, 116–17, 119–
21, 138; influenced by Lucretius's *De Rerum Natura*, 173–83,
188; influenced by Marlowe's
Dido, 4, 129n.41, 130; influenced
by Montaigne, 150, 150n.12,
176; influenced by Pliny's *Natural History*, 180–81; influenced
by Plutarch's "Of Isis and Osiris," 4–5, 150–51, 204–13; influenced by Plutarch's *Life*,
5, 151–67, 170–73, 199; influenced by Spenser's *Faerie
Queene*, 176–80; influenced by
Vergil's *Aeneid*, 1, 3, 4–5, 45,

87, 138–39, 142, 150–51, 162,
187, 213–19. PASSAGES CITED:
1.1.1–13, 164n, 168–69; *1.1.1–*
62, 166; *1.1.10*, 161, 161–62n.25;
1.1.13, 161, 161–62n.25, *1.1.14–*
17, 163; *1.1.21*, 159–60n.23;
1.1.40–43, 163; *1.1.43–47*, 167;
1.1.52–54, 165; *1.2.46–47*, 205;
1.2.60–61, 205; *1.2.80*, 165n.29;
1.2.101–15, 164; *1.2.102–6*, 166;
1.2.113–14, 160; *1.2.126–27*,
161; 161–62n.26; *1.2.134–37*,
183; *1.2.137–42*, 183; *1.2.141*,
188; *1.2.144–49*, 183; *1.2.190–*
92, 161, 161–62n.26; *1.3.35–37*,
163; *1.3.37–39*, 184; *1.3.43*, 206;
1.3.62–65, 163; *1.3.68–71*, 206;
1.3.78–80, 184; *1.3.78–85*, 163;
1.3.84–85, 210; *1.3.99*, 159–
60n.23; *1.4.5–6*, 164n; *1.4.9–10*,
153; *1.4.10–15*, 151; *1.4.16–25*,
164–65; *1.4.56*, 169; *1.4.61–63*,
160; *1.5.9–10*, 186; *1.5.15–18*,
168; *1.5.25*, 205; *1.5.27*, 205;
1.5.45–46, 207; *1.5.53–61*,
165n.29; *1.5.59–61*, 210; *2.1.20–*
27, 161–62n.25; *2.1.21*, 164;
2.2.114–53, 161, 161–62n.26;
2.2.179–80, 161; *2.2.191–226*,
229–33, 235–40, 170–72; *2.2.226–*
28, 161–62n.25, 169; *2.2.231–*
32, 219; *2.2.239–40*, 205; *2.2.*
241–43, 161, 161–62n.25; *2.3.6–*
7, 161, 161–62n.25; *2.3.18–22*,
206; *2.3.38–39*, 160; *2.5*, 165;
2.5.8–9, 186; *2.5.10–18*, 164;
2.5.12, 188; *2.5.16*, 212; *2.5.18–*
23, 160, 164; *2.5.23*, 159–60n.23;
2.5.77–79, 205; *2.5.116–18*,
167; *2.6.120,123*, 160; *2.7.17–23*,
180; *2.7.20–23*, 205; *2.7.26–27*,
169; *2.7.41–45*, 206; *2.7.97–98*,
210; *2.7.97–125*, 169; *2.7.99–100*,
210; *2.7.118–19*, 210; *2.7.122–*
23, 210; *3.2.23–33*, 161, 161–
62n.26; *3.3*, 165; *3.4.161*, 161–
62n.26; *3.6.17*, 207; *3.6.67*, 161,

161–62n.25; *3.6.95*, 161, 161–
62n.25; *3.7.1–19*, 165n.29;
3.7.67–70, 208; *3.7.69–70*, 164n;
3.10.10, 161, 161–62n.25;
3.10.14–15, 207; *3.11.23*, 208;
3.11.65–68, 164n, 208; *3.11.67*,
159–60n.23; *3.11.73*, 211; *3.12.*
15, 162; *3.12.34–36*, 210; *3.13*,
185; *3.13.27–28*, 209; *3.13.31*,
209; *3.13.35–36*, 209; *3.13.42*,
211; *3.13.89*, 161, 161–62n.26;
3.13.105–9, 161, 161–62n.25;
3.13.107–8, 166; *3.13.110*, 161,
161–62n.26; *3.13.117*, 161, 161–
62n.26; *3.13.153–55*, 208;
3.13.167–94, 165n.29; *3.13.173–*
74, 160; *3.13.175*, 159–60n.23;
3.13.183, 211; *3.13.191*, 207;
3.13.192, 211; *3.13.192–93*, 211;
3.13.192–94, 185; *3.13.199*, 211;
4.1.4, 209; *4.2*, 160; *4.3.15–16*,
209; *4.4.7*, 185; *4.4.20–21*, 185;
4.4.35–38, 165n.29; *4.6.5–7*,
162; *4.6.9–11*, 162; *4.8.14–16*,
185; *4.8.16–18*, 185; *4.8.34*,
211; *4.12.10*, 161, 161–62n.
26; *4.12.13*, 161, 161–62n.26;
4.12.25, 161, 161–62n.26;
4.12.28, 161, 161–62n.26;
4.12.30, 161, 161–62n.26;
4.12.43–47, 160–61; *4.14.10–11*,
126, 161; *4.14.13–14*, 160;
4.14.19–20, 218; *4.14.22*, 186;
4.14.22–23, 159–60n.23; *4.14.23–*
24, 164; *4.14.37–43*, 187; *4.14.*
50–54, 116–17, 150, 187; *4.14.78*,
187; *4.14.99–101*, 187; *4.14.119–*
27, 188; *4.15.23*, 189; *4.15.32–*
40, 164, 188; *4.15.47–48*, 189;
4.15.61, 211; *4.15.67–68*, 212;
4.15.80–91, 165n.29; *5.1.14–15*,
162; *5.1.36*, 162; *5.2.1–8*, 165n.
29; *5.2.8*, 212; *5.2.55*, 211;
5.2.95–99, 189; *5.2.138*, 212;
5.2.207–21, 166; *5.2.213–20*,
189–90; *5.2.227–28*, 190; *5.2.*
235–36, 190; *5.2.236–40*, 165n.

29; *5.2.237–40*, 212; *5.2.245–46*,
212; *5.2.280*, 126, 190; *5.2.286*,
212; *5.2.288–89*, 212; *5.2.302–4*,
126n; *5.2.306–7*, 213; *5.2.310–11*,
190; *5.2.315–16*, 126. See also
Discordia concors; Eirenicism;
Epicureanism; Hercules, myth
of; Hyperbole; Isis; Isis and
Osiris, myth of; Neo-Platonism;
Senecanism; Serpents; Stoicism;
Venus; Venus, "What Venus did
with Mars"; *Venus genetrix; and
names of individual characters
and places*
—*As You Like It*, 147, 165
—*Hamlet*, 146–47, 148; influenced
by Vergil's *Aeneid*, 146. PAS-
SAGES CITED: *1.5.174–75*, 146;
2.2.448–49, 146; *3.1.64–68*, 147;
3.2.239, 146; *5.2.215–20*, 146.
See also Hamlet; Horatio;
Priam; Pyrrhus; Skepticism
—*1 Henry IV*, 142. PASSAGES
CITED: *1.2.86–95*, 143n.4; *1.2.
190–212*, 142n.2; *1.2.190–
202*, 142n.2; *1.2.203–12*,
143n.4; *2.4.8–14*, 143n.4; *2.4.
475*, 142n.2, 143; *5.4.102–3*,
144. See also Falstaff; Hal
—*2 Henry IV*, 143–44. PASSAGES
CITED: *2.2.6*, 143; *2.2.32–65*,
143; *2.2.45*, 143; *4.1.1*, 143n.3;
4.5.88–137, 143; *5.5.47–48*, 143.
See also Rumor
—*Henry V*, 144. PASSAGES CITED:
2.1.88, 143; *4.1*, 143
—*Julius Caesar*, 144–45. PASSAGES
CITED: *1.2.212–84*, 145; *3.1.111–
13*, 116–18, 145. See also Antony; Brutus; Cassius; Julius
Caesar; Octavius; Skepticism
—*King Lear*, 147–49. PASSAGES
CITED: *2.4.266–69*, 147; *3.2.70–
71*, 147; *4.1.36–37*, 148; *4.6.126–
27*, 148; *5.3.323–24*, 148. See
also Edgar; Gloucester; Lear;
Skepticism

—*Midsummer Night's Dream, A*,
74, 137, 165n.30; influenced
by Apuleius's *Golden Asse*, 198,
198–99n.67. See also Bottom;
Titania
—*Much Ado About Nothing*, 147
—*Othello*, 147
—*Richard II*, 4
—*Richard III*, 142
—second tetralogy, influenced by
Vergil's *Aeneid*, 4, 138, 141–43.
See also Falstaff; Hal
—*Tempest, The*, 5, 147–49, 220–
24; influenced by Vergil's
Aeneid, 5, 220–24. PASSAGES
CITED: *1.1.16–17*, 220; *1.2.15–17*,
221; *1.2.89–90*, 222; *1.2.178–
80*, 221; *3.3.83–84*, 222; *3.3.
88–90*, 222; *4.1.139–41*, 223;
5.1.27–28, 224; *5.1.50*, 224;
5.1.146–58, 223; *5.1.275–76*,
224. See also *names of individual characters and places*
—*Twelfth Night*, 147
—*Winter's Tale, The*, 148–49.
PASSAGES CITED: *4.4.89–97*, 149.
See also Hermione; Leontes;
Perdita
Sibyl: in Vergil's *Aeneid*, 18, 77
Sidney, Mary: and Daniel's *Cleopatra*, 121; as translator of Garnier's *Marc Antoine*, 116
Sidney, Philip: *Apology for Poetry*,
140–41; *Apology for Poetry*,
influenced by Plato's *Sophist*,
77n.47; *Apology for Poetry*,
and Spenser's *Faerie Queene*,
70, 77, 77n.47, 179, 179n.48;
circle of, and Giordano Bruno,
197n.66; and Daniel's *Cleo-
patra*, 121. See also Artist,
Renaissance ideal of
Simmons, Joseph, 144–45n
Sinon: in Vergil's *Aeneid*, 22
Siren: in Dante's *Divine Comedy*,
55–56, 59–60; in Homer's
Odyssey, 56

Skepticism: in Jodelle's *Didon*, 110–12, 112n; in the New Academy, 10n.3; in Marlowe's *Dido*, 128; in Shakespeare, 4, 140; in Shakespeare's *Hamlet*, 146; in Shakespeare's *Julius Caesar*, 144–45; in Shakespeare's *Lear*, 148n.8; in Vergil's *Aeneid*, 10n.3, 10–11, 215, 224

Snyder, Susan, 218n.79

Soothsayer: in Shakespeare's *Antony and Cleopatra*, 160, 206, 208

Sophocles: *Antigone*, influence on Cesari's *Cleopatra*, 89; *Antigone*, influence on Giraldi's *Didone*, 93n; *Trachinian Women*, Hercules in, 153. *See also* Hercules, myth of

Sortes Vergilianae: in Augustine's *Confessions*, 49; in Vergil's *Aeneid*, 43, 43n.6

Spenser, Edmund, 2–3, 61–79, 81–82, 176–82, 218; genre, Vergilian progress from eclogues to epic, 63, 63n.30, 65–70; and neo-Vergilian epic, 51

—*Faerie Queene, The*, 3, 5, 16n, 45, 61–79, 81, 113, 117–82; genre of, 61–64, 79, 81; influence on Shakespeare's *Antony and Cleopatra*, 176–80; influenced by Euripides, 76; influenced by Lucretius's *De Rerum Natura*, 176–82; influenced by Pliny's *Natural History*, 178–79; influenced by pseudo-Vergilian *Ciris*, 76, 76n.46; influenced by Vergil's *Aeneid*, 3, 61–64, 70–79, 81–82, 138, 218; and Sidney's *Apology*, 70, 77, 77n.47, 179, 179n.48; Tudor myth in, 77, 77n.48, 81. PASSAGES CITED: 1.1.37, 77n.50; 2.3.22–30, 72; 2.3.31, 71; 2.8.1–2, 77n.49; 3 Proem 5, 70; 3.1.34–38, 181;

3.2.17, 76; 3.2.19, 76, 78; 3.2.23, 75; 3.2.29, 39, 76; 3.2.30–35, 77n.47; 3.2.49–52, 76; 3.3.8, 77; 3.3.22, 77; 3.5.27, 73n; 3.5.28, 73; 3.5.30, 73; 3.5.35, 73n; 3.6.29–52, 181–82; 3.9.46, 78; 3.12.46, 179; 4 Proem 1–5, 62–63; 4 Proem 5, 75; 4.6.21–22, 79; 4.10.23, 120; 4.10.39, 178; 4.10.39–47, 113n.29; 4.10.40, 178, 4.10.40–41, 178; 4.10.42, 178; 4.10–44.47, 177–78; 5.6.3–15, 78; 5.6.25, 27, 78; 5.7.9–10, 78; 5.7.12–17, 78; 5.7.12–27, 182; 6 Proem, 76; 6.10.1–3, 69; 7.7.57, 181; 7.8.1–2, 182. *See also* Hercules, myth of; Isis; Isis and Osiris, myth of; Neo-Platonism; Stoicism; Tree, symbolic in epic; Venus; *Venus armata*; *Venus genetrix*; *Venus virgo*; *and names of individual characters and places*

—*Shepheardes Calender, The*, 64–69; influenced by Vergil's *Aeneid*, 64–69; "Aprill," 16n, 64–67; "November," 67–69. PASSAGES CITED: "Aprill," 13–16, 65; "Aprill," 57, 67; "Aprill," 127–35, 67–68; "October," 47, 65; "October," 88–102, 66; "November," 38, 68; "November," 58, 68; "November," 158–62, 68; "November," 162–63, 68–69; "December," 149–50, 66. *See also* Colin; Dido; Eliza; Rosalind; *Venus virgo*

Spillebout, G., 112n

Statius: as character in Dante's *Divine Comedy*, 51, 58

Steane, J. B., 132n.44

Stoicism: in Daniel's *Cleopatra*, 125; in Giraldi's *Didone*, 95; in Jodelle's *Didon*, 110; in Montaigne, 150, 150n; in Shakespeare's *Antony and Cleopatra*,

5, 150, 160, 165–66, 186; in
Spenser's *Faerie Queene*, 62–63,
69
Suetonius: *History of Twelve
Caesars*, influence of, on Cesari's
Cleopatra, 89n.12; *Lives of Il-
lustrious Men, The*, 43n.6
Surtz, Edward, 114n, 166n
Sychaeus: in Pazzi's *Dido*, 88; in
Vergil's *Aeneid*, 17n, 19, 19n,
22, 23
Symmachus, Quintus Aurelius,
46, 46n.11

Talus: in Spenser's *Faerie Queene*,
78
Tarn, W. W., 86n.7
Tasso, Torquato, and heroic poetry,
84n.2
Taylor, Beverly, 87n
Telemachus: in Homer's *Odyssey*,
146
Thidias: in Shakespeare's *Antony
and Cleopatra*, 184, 211
Tillyard, E. M. W., 142n.1
Timias: in Spenser's *Faerie Queene*,
72–74
Titania: in Shakespeare's *Mid-
summer Night's Dream*, 74, 198,
198–99n.67
Titian, "Sacred and Profane Love,"
166. *See also* Neo-Platonism
Transvaluation, 1; defined, 1;
distinguished from imitation in
general, 3, 4, 83, 103; Vergil's
Aeneid as ground for, 2, 8,
38–40, 41–45, 85, 217
Tree, symbolic in epic: in Dante's
Divine Comedy, 59, 59n; in
Spenser's *Faerie Queene*, 77; in
Vergil's *Aeneid*, 31, 35–36, 59
Trogus Pompeius, *Universal His-
tory*, Dido (Elissa) in, 67, 67n,
221, 221n
Troy, fall of: in Chaucer's *Legend

of Good Women*, 42; in Jodelle's
Didon, 110; in Marlowe's *Dido*,
132–33, 135; in Spenser's *Faerie
Queene*, 74n.43, 78, 81; in Ver-
gil's *Aeneid*, 2, 11–13, 18, 20–22,
29–33, 37, 38, 40, 110, 221;
in Vergil's *Aeneid*, paralleled
with Dido's trials, 17n, 19, 37
Troynovant: in Spenser's *Faerie
Queene*, 78
Tunis: in Shakespeare's *Tempest*,
5, 220–21, 222
Turner, Robert, 88n.9, 88–89n.10
Typhon: in Plutarch's "Of Isis and
Osiris," 200–204, 209

Ulysses: in Dante's *Divine Comedy*,
56–57, 57n, 60

Valeriano, Piero, *Hieroglyphica*,
196
Valla, Lorenzo, *De Vero Falsoque
Bono*, 114n, 173–74. *See also*
Epicureanism
Vegius, Maphaeus, as author of
thirteenth book of Vergil's
Aeneid, 44, 174
Venice: in Dolce's *Didone*, 88,
88–89n.10, 89, 137
Venus: in Apelles' painting, 180–
81; in Botticelli's "Primavera"
and "The Birth of Venus," 166;
in Giraldi's *Didone*, 94; in Jo-
delle's *Didon*, 110, 112–15; in
Marlowe's *Dido*, 129, 132–33; in
Ovid's *Heroides*, Letter 7, 42; in
Spenser's *Faerie Queene*, 63, 75,
75n, 113, 176–82; in Shake-
speare's *Tempest*, 223; in Titian's
"Sacred and Profane Love," 166;
in Vergil's *Aeneid*, 15, 16, 18–20,
19n, 32, 216
Venus, "What Venus did with

Mars," 166–90; in Garnier's *Marc Antoine*, 118–19; in Homer's *Odyssey*, 168; in Shakespeare's *Antony and Cleopatra*, 5, 166–90; in Shakespeare's *Antony and Cleopatra*, Egyptian interpretation of, 168, 183–90; in Shakespeare's *Antony and Cleopatra*, Roman interpretation of, 168–73

Venus armata: in Spenser's *Faerie Queene*, 79

Venus genetrix: in Alain's *De planctu natura*, 114n, 173; in Cartari's *Imagini*, 176, 176n.45; in Conti's *Mythologiae*, 176, 176.n.45; in Lucretius's *De Rerum Natura*, 175–76; in Lucretius's *De Rerum Natura*, influence on Shakespeare's *Antony and Cleopatra*, 175–90, 219; in Lucretius's *De Rerum Natura*, influence on Spenser's *Faerie Queene*, 176–82; tradition of, 173–83

Venus virgo: in Spenser's *Faerie Queene*, 16n, 76, 79, 81; in Spenser's *Shepheardes Calender*, 16n, 64–65, 64n.32, 70–75; in Vergil's *Aeneid*, 16n, 16–18, 28, 64–65, 64n.32, 67, 71, 219

Vergil: as character in Dante's *Divine Comedy*, 3, 45, 51, 53, 56–61, 80

Vergil
—*Aeneid*: allegorizations of, 40, 43–45, 51–52, 85; allegorizations of, influence on Dante's *Divine Comedy*, 51–52; allegorizations of, influence on Giraldi's *Didone*, 91–94, 96, 137; allegorizations of, influence on Marlowe's *Dido*, 133–34, 134n.46 (*see also* Bernard; Boccaccio; Donatus; Fulgentius; John of Salisbury; Landino; Macrobius; Petrarch; Servius); Book 1, first meeting

of Aeneas and Dido, 14–18; Book 2, fall of Troy, 29–33; Book 4, hunt scene, 14, 26–29; Book 4, passion of Dido, 20–26, 215; Book 4, translated by Du Bellay, 42; Book 6, ivory gate, 115; Book 8, shield of Aeneas, 85–86, 215–17, 218; and chthonic gods, 22n, 24–25, 28n.18; compared with Bible, 40; as encyclopedic authority, 43, 85; genre of, 2, 7, 14, 19–26, 26n, 29–40, 45; genre of, and relationship of tragedy to epic, 2, 7–40, 45, 215–17; and grammarians, 43, 85; and Hellenistic world, 2, 8, 8n, 28n.19; and Homeric epic, 2, 8n, 8–9, 12, 19–26, 29–40, 45, 53, 97, 143–44; imagery in, 8, 8n, 19n, 20, 28, 31, 35–36, 39, 59; influenced by Apollonius Rhodius's *Argonautica*, 2, 26n, 67, 88; influenced by Euripides, 20, 22n, 24, 28n.18, 37, 67, 76; influenced by Greek tragedy, 2, 20, 22n, 24, 26n, 28n, 37, 67, 76; as Latin literary classic, 2, 5, 39, 43–46, 85, 218; narrative technique in, 8n, 8–40; relationship of story of Aeneas and Dido to history of Antony and Cleopatra, 3, 83, 85–87; thirteenth books of, 44; unity of, 7–11. PASSAGES CITED: 1.7, 12; 1.11, 12; 1.37–49, 46; 1.50, 12; 1.50–64, 12; 1.92–101, 29; 1.147–56, 12; 1.157, 13; 1.184–93, 28; 1.198–207, 13, 133; 1.202–7, 13–14; 1.209, 14; 1.218, 14; 1.223, 14; 1.257–58, 16; 1.274–75, 17n; 1.278–79, 48; 1.299, 19, 25; 1.303–4, 10; 1.304, 19; 1.314–417, 28, 64; 1.316–50, 17n; 1.325, 17; 1.353–55, 17n; 1.364, 19; 1.405–10, 17; 1.437, 17, 58; 1.441ff., 132; 1.446–93, 30; 1.462, 35, 45; 1.464, 13; 1.488,

20; 1.491–93, 22, 72; 1.498–502, 71; 1.498–504, 16; 1.498–506, 27, 28; 1.512–14, 36; 1.558–59, 36; 1.561, 15; 1.582, 15; 1.588–89, 20; 1.595–610, 35; 1.597, 15; 1.626–29, 36; 1.628–29, 17n; 1.629–30, 15; 1.630, 25; 1.631–34, 28n.19; 1.657–58, 19n; 1.659–60, 20; 1.673–75, 19n; 1.685–88, 19n; 1.688, 20; 1.712, 26; 1.713, 20; 1.717–22, 19n; 1.718, 26; 1.749, 26; 2.2, 29; 2.3, 13; 2.268–97, 33n. 23; 2.316–17, 30; 2.370–401, 30; 2.445–49, 30–31; 2.463–65, 22; 2.499–505, 17n; 2.503, 31; 2.547–53, 17n; 2.556–58, 31; 2.559–63, 31–32; 2.588–633, 32; 2.626–31, 31; 2.728–29, 22; 2.729, 33; 2.771–89, 33n.23; 2.792–93, 18n; 2.792–94, 65n; 2.804, 15; 3.94–98, 33n.23; 3.154–71, 32n.23; 3.247–57, 33n.23; 3.374–462, 33n.23; 3.718, 15; 4.1–2, 20; 4.2, 15; 4.9–23, 21; 4.15–30, 19n; 4.22, 133; 4.23, 3, 20, 58; 4.54–59, 19n; 4.56–59, 23n; 4.59, 23; 4.65–69, 20; 4.68, 26; 4.68–69, 24; 4.68–73, 28; 4.74–76, 23; 4.76–79, 20–21; 4.84–85, 18–19; 4.90–128, 94; 4.133, 28; 4.136–50, 27; 4.160–72, 19n, 28; 4.166, 23n; 4.166–72, 23; 4.173–97, 143; 4.259–67, 28n.19; 4.296ff., 46n.12, 110; 4.300, 20; 4.300–303, 24; 4.305, 26; 4.314–19, 35; 4.316, 23; 4.316–24, 19n; 4.321–23, 19n; 4.327–29, 35; 4.331–36, 18; 4.333–37, 34; 4.337–39, 19n, 23; 4.338–39, 24n; 4.340–50, 33–34, 4.340–61, 18; 4.351–61, 33; 4.360, 20; 4.364, 20; 4.366, 26; 4.386, 26; 4.393, 26; 4.424, 26; 4.431, 23; 4.431–34, 19n; 4.437–49, 35–36; 4.449, 36n.25, 144; 4.450,

26; 4.460–61, 19n; 4.469–73, 24; 4.474–521, 25n; 4.478–521, 76; 4.510–11, 24; 4.550–52, 19n; 4.607–10, 24–25; 4.638, 25; 4.644, 217; 4.653–58, 25; 4.669–71, 20, 37; 4.693, 25; 4.697, 20, 26; 6.129, 18; 6.440–86, 187; 6.475, 26; 6.700–702, 18; 6.721, 39; 6.743, 25; 6.770–72, 65n; 6.847–53, 28n.19; 6.851–53, 37; 6.883, 58n; 6.887, 215; 6.896, 10, 215; 7.1–4, 11; 7.59–67, 36; 8.362–65, 28n.19; 8.609–10, 216; 8.616, 216; 8.671, 216; 8.675, 216; 8.675–728, 86n.5, 187; 8.696, 216; 8.698, 216–17; 8.709, 217; 8.722–23, 217; 9.614–16, 28n.19. See also Asiatic style; Hercules, myth of; Heroism; Neo-Platonism; Skepticism; Sortes Vergilianae; Transvaluation; Tree, symbolic in epic; Troy, fall of; Venus; Venus virgo; and names of individual characters and places

—Aeneid, influence of: on Augustine, 2, 45–50; on Augustine's City of God, 2, 45–48, 79–80, 81; on Augustine's Confessions, 2, 45–50, 79–80, 81, 217–18; on Dante's Divine Comedy, 3, 45, 51–61, 79, 80–81, 218; on Dolce's Didone, 88–89, 137; on Garnier's Marc Antoine, 116–17; on Giraldi's Didone, 3, 91–97, 137; on Jodelle's Cléopatre, 104–5, 107; on Jodelle's Didon, 3–4, 107–16, 138; on Marlowe's Dido, 4, 127–37; on narrative, 2–3, 41–82; on Ovid's Metamorphoses, 41–45; on Renaissance vernacular drama, 3–4, 83–139; on Roman historiography, 10, 85, 86; on Shakespeare's Antony and Cleopatra, 1, 3, 4–5, 45, 87, 138–39, 142, 150–51, 162, 187, 213–19;

on Shakespeare's *Hamlet*, 146;
on Shakespeare's second tetralogy, 4, 138, 141–43; on Shakespeare's *Tempest*, 5, 220–24; on
Spenser's *Faerie Queene*, 3,
61–64, 70–79, 81–82, 138, 218;
on Spenser's *Shepheardes Calender*, 64–69
—*Ciris* (pseudo-Vergilian), influ-
ence on Spenser's *Faerie Queene*,
76, 76n.46
—*Eclogues, 4th*, influence on
Dante's *Divine Comedy*, 51
—*Georgics*, 3, 39, 86, 213–17, 218.
PASSAGES CITED: *3.3–4*, 214;
3.10, 213; *3.11*, 214; *3.13–15*,
215; *3.16*, 214; *3.16–29*, 213–14;
3.16–39, 86n.5; *3.28–29*, 216.
See also Actium; Octavius
Vida, Marco Girolamo, and
Christianization of Vergilian
epic, 85n
Virtuous heathen: in Bacon's *New
Atlantis*, 191–92; in Dante's
Divine Comedy, 58, 191; among
Jesuits, 191; in Montaigne's "On
Cannibals," 192; in More's
Utopia, 192

Waddington, Raymond, 154n.20,
168n.23

Waith, Eugene, 153, 153n, 154,
154nn.18,21, 155, 155n, 167n
Walker, D. P., 81n, 193n.58
Wardman, Alan, 152n.15
Weinberg, Bernard, 84n.2, 88, 88n,
91n.14
Whitfield, J. H., 52n.18
Whitney, Geoffrey, 213n.74
Williams, R. D., 214n.76, 215n,
216n
Williams, Ralph, 56n
Wind, Edgar, 16n, 64n.32, 74n.43,
75n, 166, 166n, 173–74, 174n.37,
176n.44, 181n.49, 193n.59,
196n.65
Witherspoon, A. M., 121n.33
Wordsworth, William, *The Pre-
lude*, 5

Xenophon, *Memorabilia*, and
Prodicus's story of Hercules,
154n.20

Yates, Frances: *Astraea*, 44n.8,
52n.18, 77n.48, 108n; *French
Academies*, 108n, 112n, 113n,
114n, 175n.41; *Giordano Bruno*,
81n, 193n.59, 194nn.60–61
Young, David P., 199n

Designer: Rick Chafian
Compositor: Heritage Printers, Inc.
Printer: Heritage Printers, Inc.
Binder: The Delmar Company
Text: 10/12 Palatino
Display: Palatino